Joe Joyce is a freelance journalist. He was born in Ballinasloe, County Galway, in 1947 and lives in Dublin. He is a former reporter with the *Irish Times* and *Hibernia* and is now correspondent in Dublin for the *Guardian*. During 1982, he reported extensively on political developments in Ireland and Fianna Fáil's internal difficulties. He is married and has two children.

Peter Murtagh is security correspondent of the *Irish Times*. He was born in Dublin in 1953 and lives in County Wicklow. He dabbled in journalism as a student but had a variety of jobs before becoming a full-time reporter with *Southside* newspaper and later, the *Irish Times*. In 1982, he revealed details of the political interference with the gardaí, including the official tapping of journalists' telephones.

THE BOSS

CHARLES J. HAUGHEY
IN GOVERNMENT

JOE JOYCE &
PETER MURTAGH

poolbeg press

First published 1983 by
Poolbeg Press Ltd.,
Knocksedan House,
Swords, Co. Dublin, Ireland

© Joe Joyce and Peter Murtagh, 1983

ISBN 0 905169 69 7

Cover design by Steven Hope
With a photograph by Derek Speirs
Typeset by O'Brien Promotions Ltd.,
Barrow Street, Dublin 4
and Printed in the Republic of Ireland

To all those who tell reporters what is really going on

Acknowledgements

Writing about such recent history poses several problems, not the least of which is the fact that many of those concerned are still actively involved in public affairs. In spite of that, scores of people helped us enormously in our research for this book. Charles J. Haughey did not co-operate with us and instructed the current front bench of Fianna Fáil to follow his example. All of our interviews were conducted on the basis that we would not name our sources. Indeed, those whom we need to thank most would thank us least for identifying them here. Our sincere thanks to all of them.

Our thanks also to the staff of the *Irish Times* library for allowing us to rifle their files and to Ann Kennedy, Cormac Ó Cuilleanáin and Hilary O'Donoghue for bringing it all together.

Joe Joyce and Peter Murtagh
4 Clare Street, Dublin 2
October 1983

Abbreviations

AGSI — Association of Garda Sergeants and Inspectors
GRA — Garda Representative Association
ISB — Intelligence and Security Branch of the Garda Síochána
PABX — Private Automatic Branch Exchange

List of Illustrations

Prologue

It was 2.20 in the morning, and there was a suspicious number of cars parked outside Keaney's pub. The two guards on routine night patrol pulled off the Boyle to Ballyfarnan Road and stopped. Garda Tim Griffin, the older of the two, took the front door. Garda Jim Mooney went around the back. Griffin's knock on the front door was answered almost immediately by Michael Keaney. Inside, there were eleven customers.

The guards had them cold.

One man made a half-hearted attempt to escape, dodging around the bar and into the kitchen. He ran into Garda Mooney and was ushered back into the bar. The gardaí produced their notebooks, began writing down names and asking for explanations. Several of the customers said that they had been at a Fianna Fáil meeting: one added that he had been canvassing for Seán Doherty earlier that night. It was February 6th, 1982. The surprise general election campaign, caused by the downfall of Garret FitzGerald's coalition government on January 27th, was nearing its half-way point.

Michael Keaney was convinced that the garda raid and the election were connected. Earlier that night, the local Fianna Fáil TD, Seán Doherty, had arrived at his pub after a party meeting in nearby Ballinafad. Keaney believed that someone from Ballinafad had phoned the gardaí to tip them off about the after-hours drinking, and that the caller's motives were political. But there had been some misunderstanding: Doherty and the party activists with him had come to Keaney's in the belief that a second campaign meeting was to be held there. Doherty left around closing time when it became clear that there was no meeting. Some of his group stayed on, however, and they were still there when the gardaí arrived.

Keaney's belief that the raid had been sparked off by political opponents reflected his general view of local events. He was a returned emigrant who had given vent to his nationalist feelings by joining Fianna Fáil and becoming secretary of his local cumann, after years in England and Belfast. It was apparent to any casual visitor to his pub where his party, and his personal, allegiances lay. The pendulum on a wall clock was covered with an election sticker showing Doherty's picture against a tricolour.

The pub itself was a typical Irish hybrid. The two-storey building had living accommodation upstairs, a small shop at one end of the ground floor, the bar in the centre, and a "singing lounge" tacked onto the other end. In the car park in front there was a lone petrol pump. Business was not great, however. It was five miles from Boyle in north Roscommon, an area of low hills and lakes with damp beauty and sparse population. It was near to the picturesque Lough Key but on the wrong side of the lake to benefit greatly from the holiday centre and forest park on the southern shore.

Keaney had to keep his year-round customers happy, and to him that meant allowing some after-hours drinking. But that policy had landed him in regular trouble. In his first year the pub was raided by the gardaí on three occasions. He got away with a warning the first time: the second and third raids led to court hearings and two endorsements on his publican's licence.

Just after Christmas, 1980, he was raided for the fourth time. It was the Sunday night between Christmas and the New Year and the guards arrived about 11.30, only an hour and a half after the official closing time. Keaney was outraged: it was the holiday season and it was not really the middle of the night. He was so upset he phoned Seán Doherty, then the junior Minister for Justice in Charles Haughey's first Government, at his home in Cootehall, just four miles away. Doherty agreed to see what he could do about it.

Doherty did not waste much time. He phoned the garda station in Boyle looking for the policeman who had carried out the raid. The garda was not there at the time but he returned the Minister's call shortly after 3 a.m. Nothing more was heard of the raid.

Keaney had not had any other encounters with the law since that incident. Now, in February 1982 and in the midst of the general election campaign, eleven people had been caught drinking in his bar more than three hours after closing time. He decided to use his political contacts again, to ask Doherty to do something about his fifth raid.

Nobody could have foreseen the consequences.

Chapter One

Say Yes!
Charles Haughey, February 1982

Charles J. Haughey, leader of Fianna Fáil, was given a new lease of political life by the unexpected collapse of Garret FitzGerald's coalition government on its first full budget in January 1982.

Six months in opposition had shown Haughey to be weak, indecisive and apparently unable to come to terms with his new role. He always maintained that he had not really "lost" his first general election in June 1981: a quirk of the electoral system and the hunger strikes by Republican prisoners in Northern Ireland had robbed him of victory, he insisted. But by the start of 1982, he had a problem. He had still not appointed an opposition front bench, and one of his backbenchers was testing his strength.

Charles McCreevy, the 32-year-old Kildare TD who had once been among Haughey's most enthusiastic backers, was severely critical of his party leader in an interview with the *Sunday Tribune*. Haughey was forced to face down McCreevy by seeking his expulsion from the parliamentary party. McCreevy, left to his fate by nervous opponents of Haughey, resigned just ahead of being expelled.

Within a week, however, all was suddenly forgiven. On January 27th, Garret FitzGerald's Fine Gael and Labour Party coalition produced its first full budget. Two seats short of a Dáil majority, the coalition relied on two Independents, Noel Browne and Jim Kemmy, who had backed FitzGerald as Taoiseach. The savage budget turned out to be utterly unacceptable to Kemmy, a long-time socialist from Limerick and in his first Dáil. The cabinet had not taken seriously his advance warnings.

There was little enough excitement when the division bells summoned deputies to the first of the normal series of votes on budget measures. As they gathered in the lobbies, however, it became clear that all was not well. FitzGerald knelt by Kemmy's seat, giving him some new figures and trying to persuade him to allow the Government time to amend the budget. Kemmy shook his head. He went into the "níl" lobby, rejecting the budget along with the 78 Fianna Fáil members, the one Workers' Party man and two other Independents. Browne stayed with the coalition. There was an uneasy calm while the votes were counted. Ministers looked glum: Fianna Fáil deputies looked happy and kept counting and re-counting the number of Independents on their side of the lobby. A cheer went up from the opposition with the first proof of victory: the Fianna Fáil chief whip, Ray Burke, carried the result down to the Ceann Comhairle, in accordance with the practice that the winner presents the outcome to the chair. The government was beaten by a single vote: 82 votes to 81. Haughey sat in the opposition leader's seat, his face flushed as party members pumped his hand. He had been right. Almost alone among politicians, he had predicted and firmly believed that the coalition would not last long. The injustice of the 1981 election result would be put right.

Within ten minutes of the Dáil vote, Haughey announced publicly that he was available "for consultation by the President should he so wish". He tried to talk by telephone to President Patrick Hillery to suggest that he would form a government. At the same time, Haughey had chats with several Independents, including Neil Blaney and McCreevy, now formally an Independent, to make sure of their support should he be able to put together a new administration.

Whether he seriously expected an opportunity to form a government without an election is not clear. But as many as five attempts were made by Haughey and leading members of Fianna Fáil to get through to Hillery.

They never succeeded in talking to the President.

Meanwhile, FitzGerald went off to Árus an Uachtaráin to

15

seek the Dáil's dissolution. Key Fine Gael workers were already gathering in the party rooms. The party's press office was packed: nobody said anything, they just watched the reporting of events unfold on RTE television. One of their publicists tried to put a brave face on it. It was, he said, all a matter of responsibility, of running the country properly. It was, he went on, a question of live now and pay later or the other way around. Even as he said it, the problem of fighting an election on the basis of paying now and living later clearly depressed him.

FitzGerald himself was, surprisingly, in top form, telling a hastily arranged press conference that he would fight the election on the budget. Already two budget proposals were seen as central to the government defeat and to the election campaign. These were the reduction of state subsidies on food and the extension of Value Added Tax to clothes and footwear. Children's shoes could not have been exempted, FitzGerald explained, because that exemption would also benefit women with small feet. In spite of his buoyant mood, it was obvious that Fine Gael was in trouble. It had to fight an election on an unpopular budget with all its harshness exposed to an electorate that had hitherto been treated to carefully sanitised election packages.

Charles Haughey, by contrast, did not appear very buoyant next day as he held his first campaign press conference. Flanked by the Fianna Fáil general secretary Frank Wall, and front bench colleague Albert Reynolds, he appeared blasé and dismissive. His demeanour suggested that he was at the end of something rather than the beginning — that the election was more or less over. He was totally opposed to the budget, he said. He wondered why people seemed to be hypnotised by government overspending, borrowing and all the financial sins that so preoccupied the coalition.

The coalition government had, during its brief term in office, managed to switch public attention to the question of state spending and borrowing. Earlier in January, RTE's *Late Late Show* had given over a programme to the subject, during which the editor of *Magill,* Vincent Browne, had carried into the electronic medium his monthly efforts to make politicians accountable for the amounts of taxpayer's money, both past and future, that they were spending. McCreevy's criticisms of Haughey, and of politics in general, were along the same lines. Practically all economists and most commentators agreed that the state's spending and borrowing had become critically important.

Haughey, however, had always been a believer in big spending, in the theory that investment generates more money and jobs. In a much-quoted television address in January 1980, a month after he became leader of Fianna Fáil and Taoiseach, he had said the country was living beyond its means. Action would have to be taken to reduce the government's deficit, he indicated. His subsequent actions failed to live up to his predictions: the spending deficit widened considerably under his rule and borrowing shot up between 1979 and mid-1981. It was clear from his first campaign press conference that he did not believe there was a crisis in public spending and that he thought such suggestions were damaging to the country.

But his rejection of conventional economic and political wisdom prompted an immediate reaction within his own party and the first U-turn of the campaign, forced on Haughey by Martin O'Donoghue.

Stung by McCreevy's criticisms, Haughey had finally appointed a shadow cabinet just before the collapse of the coalition. The main surprise was the selection of Martin O'Donoghue, a 49-year-old economics professor, as the party spokesman on finance. O'Donoghue had had a meteoric rise and fall within Fianna Fáil. He had been an adviser to the previous party leader, Jack Lynch, until his election to the Dáil in 1977 when a new Ministry of Economic Planning and Development was created for him. His profession had left him with a tendency to rationalise everything and to try and put order on the eccentricities of practical politics. But his earnestness and his ready answers for every problem left many of his party colleagues uneasy about what they saw as his academic qualities. He had been one of the architects of the 1977 Fianna Fáil election manifesto which abolished domestic rates and car tax in a vote-winning ploy that, in theory, would be matched later by wage restraint from a contented workforce. The voters took the handouts and ignored the payment.

O'Donoghue was dropped peremptorily by Haughey when

he took over the party leadership in December 1979 and his Department of Economic Planning and Development was dissolved. The loss of his cabinet position in such circumstances had been a harsh experience for O'Donoghue who was not as accustomed as more seasoned colleagues to the sudden falls of politics. But he had kept his disappointment private and some pressure had developed to have him brought back into the centre of things. However, neither Haughey nor O'Donoghue had any great respect for each other's economic approach. If Haughey had implicitly blamed O'Donoghue for the economic failures of the Lynch government, O'Donoghue had been equally unimpressed by Haughey's handling of the economy as Taoiseach.

O'Donoghue was determined that Haughey's negative approach to opposition would not continue. Two days before the coalition budget, the newly formed opposition front bench had discussed its likely response. O'Donoghue had won agreement for his view that the party should not necessarily reject everything proposed. In particular, he persuaded his colleagues to accept one of the central figures of the budget, the projected deficit and day-to-day spending for the year ahead. Fianna Fáil, therefore, would accept the central thesis of the budget but argue about the details. Yet, the day after the budget, Haughey launched the party campaign at a press conference that O'Donoghue did not even know was taking place. And Haughey had dismissed the coalition budget out of hand. The first O'Donoghue knew of it and of what Haughey had been saying was when several reporters told him in the Leinster House restaurant. He was visibly angered.

Next morning, the party's front bench met to draw up its election policies. Haughey was left in no doubt that O'Donoghue would not accept his return to what he perceived as financial profligacy. No explicit threats were made but it was hinted that if Haughey were to continue as he had begun, three senior members of the party — O'Donoghue, George Colley, the deputy leader, and Desmond O'Malley, the spokesman on industry and commerce — would simply have nothing to do with the election campaign. Haughey suggested at first that O'Donoghue make a speech, if he wanted, but after some discussion he gave in to O'Donoghue's view that he, Haughey, must make a public statement. O'Donoghue went out of the room to dictate the speech to a secretary. The draft was discussed and some minor changes agreed. Haughey delivered the speech that night in Skerries, Co. Dublin, making public his return to the policy approach that had been agreed at the party's front bench before the budget.

Fianna Fáil was now committed to accepting the aim of the coalition's budget, that the planned deficit for the year should be held to £715 million. That effectively took the steam out of the central economic debate. The argument over the budget would rest for the remainder of the campaign on points of detail. The opposition party also bound itself to come up with an alternative budget which would explain where it planned to raise the £119 million that the coalition intended to gather from VAT on clothes and shoes, and from cuts in food subsidies.

Some of that same £119 million was exercising the minds of the coalition cabinet as well. FitzGerald decided that electoral realities were more important than consistency, and announced that clothes and shoes for children under ten would be exempted from VAT. The gap in the budget calculations was to be made up by an extra 2p on cigarettes and alcohol and an increase in the proposed tax on charter holidays abroad of £10 per seat. There was no more mention of women with small feet.

Fianna Fáil eventually came up with its own plans after accepting an unusual offer from the government allowing the opposition to use the civil service to cost its proposals. By the last full week of the campaign, Fianna Fáil had come around to fighting the election on the coalition's terms: financial responsibility, as defined by FitzGerald's administration, was the springboard for everything else. In the event, the Fianna Fáil alternative was a slick piece of footwork, choreographed mainly by O'Donoghue, which provided a relatively painless way of ditching the more unpleasant elements of the coalition budget. The centrepiece of the plan was the collection of V.A.T. on imports as they arrived in the country, an earlier collection of company taxes and levies on banks and insurance companies. Few people doubted that the cost of such measures would eventually fall on voters but it would not be as immediate or as apparent as the coalition proposals. FitzGerald's Finance Minister, John Bruton, retorted that it was "funny money".

The charge was a calculated part of Fine Gael's strategy to damage Fianna Fáil by direct and indirect attacks on Haughey himself. Leaks of Department of Finance documents drawn up after the 1981 budget showed how Haughey, in government, had prepared spending estimates which were unrealistic, in an apparent attempt to put a better face on the projected deficit for the year. Civil servants in the Department were reported to have considered resigning over the affair. Publication of the documents and of the charges during the election campaign highlighted this aspect of Haughey's previous term in office. But there was no doubt among Fianna Fáil's opponents that Haughey was the party's Achilles' heel.

Always a colourful and controversial figure, Haughey himself had become one of the main issues in Irish politics by the time of the February 1982 election. His fitness to be Taoiseach had been challenged directly by FitzGerald in December 1979 when the Dáil was asked to vote Haughey in as leader of the government after he had won the Fianna Fáil leadership contest. FitzGerald's unexplained reference to a "flawed pedigree" had rebounded to some extent on the Fine Gael leader: his excuse that he could not say precisely what he meant was particularly feeble as he was speaking with parliamentary privilege.

Throughout his political career Haughey always excited adulation or hatred: as Taoiseach these reactions had been heightened. Those who loved him loved him more; those who hated and distrusted him believed their views were confirmed by his actions. One of the more obvious causes of distrust was the legacy of the 1970 arms crisis when he had been arrested and tried on suspicion of conspiring to smuggle arms into the country. That affair had split Fianna Fáil in two, revealing the cracks in the party's philosophy that had been papered over during the previous decade as it became identified with big business and boasted of its pragmatism.

It was no accident that Haughey should find himself torn apart politically by the affair. He had appeared to be one of the new breed of ministers of the 1960s: confident, brash and determined to see themselves as the generation for whose benefit independence had been won. He had also appeared to be the model of this new generation and new style of Fianna Fáil leader: self-made, rich and a long way in attitudes and approach to life from the bulk of the party's founders. By the time the North interposed the reality of street violence on top of the rhetoric of Fianna Fáil's republicanism, Haughey had been a cabinet minister for seven consecutive years. All the unresolved conflicts of political identity within the party and within Haughey culminated in his arrest, trial and acquittal.

It was a bruising experience for both the individual and the party. For the party, it set in motion a conflict over policy and over its very ethos which was reflected by and expressed in personality differences. But the main complaint about Haughey, within Fianna Fáil and even more so outside the party, was the lengths to which he was believed to be prepared to go to achieve his ambition. Noel Browne, the long-time socialist TD, was much more explicit than FitzGerald in his objections to Haughey in the debate on his appointment as Taoiseach by the Dáil. Describing him as a mixture of former US President Richard Nixon and the Portuguese dictator Dr. Antonio Salazar, he wondered if Haughey would hand over power if defeated in a subsequent election.

Haughey, of course, did hand over power: there was no evidence whatever that he was less than a democrat. Nevertheless, the suspicion of his motives was so strong in Browne that he voted for FitzGerald's budget against all his other principles and instincts, simply to try and avoid an election which might return Haughey to power.

Fine Gael tried in numerous ways and with considerable success to capitalise on Haughey's personality, believing that many voters shared its suspicions and doubts about Haughey. FitzGerald was constantly promoted: full-page newspaper advertisements stressed that a vote for Fine Gael was a vote for Garret FitzGerald. The clear implication was that a vote for Fianna Fáil was a vote for Charles Haughey. In the opening days of the campaign, FitzGerald challenged Haughey to a television debate, an unusual move by an incumbent Taoiseach. Fine Gael was trying to turn the tables, to focus the spotlight on Haughey. Normally, the Taoiseach seeking re-election was the focal point of the campaign: FitzGerald and his party could only win by putting pressures on Fianna Fáil through Haughey and thereby deflecting attention from their own budgetary plans.

From Fine Gael's viewpoint, it was an extremely successful campaign. By most political yardsticks, the party should not have had a chance from the moment the election was declared. But the first opinion polls, a week after the coalition collapsed, actually showed the two sides running neck-to-neck. One of the final polls, carried out for the *Irish Times* by Irish Marketing Surveys during the last days of the campaign and after the Fianna Fáil alternative budget, gave the opposition party a five per cent lead.

Haughey's personal standing, according to the polls, showed a totally different pattern. Going into the June 1981 general election, he and FitzGerald had been on a par in popularity. Asked for their preference as Taoiseach, 43% chose Haughey and 44% opted for FitzGerald. By December 1981, five months after FitzGerald had become Taoiseach, there was a significant gap between them. FitzGerald was still the choice of 44% of those questioned by Irish Marketing Surveys: Haughey was now chosen by 36%. With the collapse of the coalition administration, FitzGerald's stock increased dramatically. After a week's campaigning, 51% said they would prefer him as Taoiseach: by the end of the campaign 56% favoured him. At the comparable times, Haughey was the choice of 31% and 33% respectively. In terms of satisfaction with party leaders, FitzGerald increased his lead to end the campaign with a commanding advantage of 23 points: 59% were satisfied with him against 36% who said they were satisfied with Haughey.

Fianna Fáil's problems with its leader were considerable. Midway through the campaign, his picture was quietly dropped from much of the party's literature. The emphasis in its newspaper advertisements was on Fianna Fáil's "know-how", its experience and its concern about employment. Bad weather and dark evenings did not encourage presidential style campaigns by the party leaders throughout the country, as had been done in 1981, but FitzGerald was more frequently on display than Haughey.

Fianna Fáil tried to counter criticism of its leader with accusations of a personal smear campaign against Haughey. One of the more extraordinary charges of the campaign was the claim by Albert Reynolds that Fine Gael had orchestrated a "whispering campaign" against Haughey in pubs. FitzGerald, he said, had launched a personal, vindictive attack on Haughey from the day of his election as Taoiseach. Could any journalist, he asked rhetorically at a press conference, point to a single fault in Haughey's handling of a single issue?

The party's own nervousness over its leader was regularly visible at its press conferences. Time and again, Haughey looked on nervously as other front bench members were asked questions. At most press conferences he hoarded the only microphone, doling it out briefly to his colleagues only when it would have been embarrassing not to do so. His apprehension was justified as well. With the divisions between himself, O'Donoghue and O'Malley well known to reporters, it was inevitable that the awkward questions should be asked. In spite of Haughey's apparent conversion to "fiscal rectitude" (as it had become known), many people were not convinced that he had really changed his attitude. The whole question of state spending and political responsibility was encapsulated in some specific issues, notably the plan to build an international airport to serve the Marian shrine at Knock, Co. Mayo. Reporters wanted to know what other Fianna Fáil leaders thought of the plan.

Haughey said that the party would resume work on the Connacht regional airport and that, he added, was party policy. O'Malley admitted that he might never have started it but he maintained that it would be wasteful not to complete it once it had been started. O'Donoghue was asked did he support the project. Haughey leaned towards him and said in a whisper that carried through to the microphones before them: "say yes!". O'Donoghue replied to the questioner: "no!". After a brief pause he added: "I don't think government commitments should be dropped".

Fianna Fáil's divisions, however, were more than matched on the coalition side of the fence by the Labour Party, which was split quite openly, and irreconcilably.

Labour's administrative council, led by chairman Michael D. Higgins, insisted that it was campaigning on its own policies and had nothing to do with the government. Its leader, Michael O'Leary, who was also the Tánaiste, said it was seeking support on the basis of the government's policies. The occasional attempts by O'Leary to explain how his party could be called united did nothing but confuse the issue even more. Labour campaigned as if it were two separate parties, each opposed to the other and with nothing binding them together.

Compared to Labour, Fianna Fáil could maintain some pretence at unity. On the other hand, some people within the party suspected that Haughey was merely using people like O'Donoghue to help him win the election. Anti-Haughey members faced a difficult dilemma: they had to do everything possible to win the election in the full knowledge that they might be helping to make Haughey a Taoiseach once again. To do otherwise, however, would be to leave themselves vulnerable to accusations that they did not have the best interests of the party at heart. The middle of an election campaign was no time to start debating such difficulties. Nevertheless, there were occasional suggestions that Haughey could be ousted during the campaign and the election won even after changing leaders in mid-stream. This was not a realistic prospect, however, merely wishful thinking by some of Haughey's internal opponents.

Their suspicions that Haughey's conversion to financial orthodoxy was merely expediency were confirmed by his attitude once released from Dublin. In spite of a tight rein on promises, Fianna Fáil managed to spend, in theory at least, hundreds of millions of pounds in providing new facilities around the country. Haughey himself promised £15 million for a new extension to Castlebar Hospital during a visit to the town. Two days later and in another town he was covering his tracks: Castlebar would wait its turn, he said. Whitegate oil refinery and Clondalkin Paper Mills, threatened with permanent closure, were to be nationalised, and the Tuam sugar factory was to receive more state aid.

Haughey's penchant for promising state assistance to practically every deserving cause had been a major feature of his first term in government and, arguably, one of the reasons why the state finances had got into such a mess. But he was justified in complaining, occasionally with some bitterness, that he was being singled out for his electoral promises. In 1981, he maintained, he had stood on his government's record and promised little: in 1981, Fine Gael had promised plenty and insisted, for instance, that they would not put VAT on clothes and shoes.

The perception of the rivals for the Taoiseach's office was otherwise. Haughey was clearly the underdog by the time he and FitzGerald faced each other across an RTE television studio for their first direct confrontation. Expectations had been built up to a fine pitch: the difficulties of arranging the debate had been a persistent story throughout the campaign. In addition, a crucial part of the campaign had been the regular, almost nightly, debates between individual ministers and their Fianna Fáil shadows on the main RTE current affairs television programme, *"Today Tonight"*.

Thirty-six hours before the polls opened, Haughey emerged the victor from the climax of the television coverage of the campaign. In the debate he appeared more confident, less weary, than FitzGerald and dealt in generalities rather than in specifics. FitzGerald made a botched attempt to claim that Haughey had got his government into such financial straits that the Central Bank had earlier refused to lend it £350 million a year. Questioned about his claims at a final press conference on the following day, FitzGerald cited official documents but refused to quote from them or release them. Haughey opined that this was extraordinary behaviour and complained of a breach of official confidentiality. The issue never took off. The television debate, however, had dragged on too long and had probably lost all but the most dedicated viewers long before it ended. After all that had been written, said and implied about him, Haughey probably appeared like an agreeable surprise, an ordinary, undramatic politician rather than a strange ogre.

Polling day, February 18th, was as dull as polling days ever are. Most commentators declared, with the aid of opinion polls, that the results were too close to call. The parties all agreed that the number of people who had voted was less than in the previous general election. The only thing out of the ordinary was an accusation that Haughey's election agent, Patrick O'Connor, and some members of his family had voted twice in the constituency of Dublin North.

Chapter Two

You never do the obvious thing in politics.
Martin O'Donoghue, February 1982

In a television interview as the votes were being counted, Jim Gibbons opened up the possibility of an assault on Haughey's leadership. Gibbons remarked, almost casually, that he expected Fianna Fáil's new parliamentary party would meet "for the purposes of putting forward a candidate for the leadership". But the remark was far from casual. Gibbons was flying a kite for the one political ambition which superseded all others: he wanted to see the political demise of Charles J. Haughey.

Gibbons, a morose-looking 57-year-old farmer from Kilkenny, had been a bitter enemy of Haughey since the 1970 arms trial in which Gibbons was chief prosecution witness against his former colleague in government. There had been a direct conflict of evidence between Gibbons and Haughey which had never been resolved even though Gibbons claimed ten years later that Haughey promised subsequently to clear his name. After the trial, Gibbons kept his senior ministerial position while Haughey was relegated to the political wilderness, but when Haughey finally took over as party leader and Taoiseach in 1979, he dropped Gibbons from his cabinet. In the June 1981 election, Gibbons failed to be elected. The February 1982 contest saw him back again to haunt Haughey.

During the election campaign a few TDs had privately wanted the party to dump Haughey before polling day, but prior to Gibbons's public remark, there had never been any doubt, implied or otherwise, that Haughey would automatically continue to lead the party and therefore would be the Fianna Fáil nominee for Taoiseach. Normally the new parliamentary party would meet for the first time just before the sitting of the new Dáil. But this time it was different. Other senior party members failed to discount Gibbons's suggestion when interviewed on the same programme and before the counting of votes was over, Haughey knew that he had another battle on his hands.

As the counting proceeded on Friday, 19th February, it became clear that nobody had won an overall majority. Against all the odds, Fine Gael had increased its percentage share of the poll but the quirks of the electoral system had redressed the balance on this occasion in favour of Fianna Fáil. The number of Fine Gael seats dropped by two to 63 but Fianna Fáil's representation rose from 78 seats to 81 — two short of an overall majority. The Labour party held its representation at fifteen seats, but the Workers' Party made a breakthrough with its lone TD being joined by two others. These three along with four Independents — John O'Connell, Jim Kemmy, Neil Blaney and Tony Gregory — held the balance of power. Garret FitzGerald refused to concede defeat but Haughey declared himself confident that Fianna Fáil would form a government and remain in power for a full term.

Despite Haughey's public display of confidence, every Fianna Fáil TD knew that the party had a problem with its leader. For the second time he had failed to win an overall majority, but this time it was in an election in which his opponents should have been hopelessly wrongfooted. Instead of being able to capitalise on the government's budget fiasco, Fianna Fáil candidates and election workers, especially in areas of Dublin, had been forced to defend Haughey when they canvassed voters. Constituency organisations were split down the middle between pro- and anti-Haughey factions. In some well-publicised cases, Fianna Fáil candidates seemed to put more energy into fighting each other rather than their coalition government opponents. Anti-Haughey candidates happily reported the depth of feeling against their leader and pro-Haughey candidates stopped, in some instances, stressing their loyalty to him.

The anti-Haughey candidates did well. The return of Jim

Gibbons in Carlow-Kilkenny at the expense of Tom Nolan, an out-going pro-Haughey TD, was just one example. Similarly in Cork South-West, anti-Haughey candidate Joe Walsh regained his seat at the expense of Flor Crowley, a dyed-in-the-wool Haughey man. In Galway West, Mark Killilea ran a tough campaign stressing his support for Haughey but was swamped by Bobby Molloy who, as Haughey once put it delicately, had not been dropped from the new cabinet in 1979 but had simply not been included in it. Molloy topped the poll and Killilea was ousted by anti-Haughey colleagues. In Dublin South, Síle de Valera, her support for Haughey somewhat muted, failed again to win a seat. But in the same constituency, Séamus Brennan, widely identified as an anti-Haughey man, headed the list of Fianna Fáil candidates, more than 3,000 votes ahead of his nearest party rival. In Wicklow, Paudge Brennan lost his seat to Gemma Hussey of Fine Gael. Brennan had resigned as parliamentary secretary to the Minister for Local Government in protest at the dismissal of Haughey by Lynch during the arms crisis and contested the 1973 election as an Independent. The only Fianna Fáil candidate to be elected in the Wicklow constituency was Ciaran Murphy, an anti-Haughey man.

The most remarkable result was the success in Kildare of Charles McCreevy. His first preference vote shot up from a respectable 7,053 in the June 1981 election to an astonishing 11,497 at the top of the poll, the third highest vote of all Fianna Fáil candidates. The only explanation for McCreevy's performance was the massive publicity he had received six weeks previously following his interview in the *Sunday Tribune* in which he had criticised the direction of the party. McCreevy said there were people who were less than satisfied with the direction of the party in opposition. When asked if he was disillusioned with Haughey, McCreevy gave a "no comment" reply. Haughey's response, demanding that McCreevy be expelled from the parliamentary party, may have reflected his fear that the backbenchers who had helped to bring him to power in 1979 were now turning against him and using the same tactics they had employed to undermine the leadership of Jack Lynch.

Haughey had no way of knowing whether or not

McCreevy's remarks in the *Sunday Tribune* were part of a larger push against him, but he tried to stamp out any challenge by having McCreevy expelled. He sent his state car to McCreevy's home in Sallins with a message asking McCreevy to get in touch with him. Not to be outdone, McCreevy had a Mercedes and driver carry his reply to Haughey's home at Kinsealy in north Dublin. Síle de Valera was hauled in as an intermediary at one stage but McCreevy remained unrepentant. The ripples caused by McCreevy's remarks travelled far and fast. Motions of no confidence in Haughey were passed by cumainn in Cork and Galway and it appeared possible that the party's spring Árd Fheis would be faced with calls for Haughey's removal.

McCreevy also caused much soul-searching among Haughey's better-known opponents: they agreed with what he said but were they now to condone the sort of sniping that had undermined Lynch and to which they had objected so strongly? In the event McCreevy let everyone off the hook by resigning from the parliamentary party just as Haughey was about to call for the vote on his expulsion.

McCreevy's career as an Independent was probably the shortest on record. Seven days after resigning, the election had been called and he was back as a Fianna Fáil candidate with no objection from Haughey. By the time people cast their votes, McCreevy was one of the best-known politicians in the country and the issue which had made him famous had been raised by many voters during the campaign.

Nobody in Fianna Fáil was in any doubt after the election as to what people thought of Charles J. Haughey, and Haughey himself knew that Gibbons's remark might be the start of something big. He moved quickly and decisively to ensure that the rumbling discontent did not grow to pose a real threat to his position as leader.

On the morning of Saturday, 20th February, Haughey and a number of senior party members were in Fianna Fáil headquarters in Mount Street in Dublin examining the final results and assessing their overall position after the election. Party officials were getting reports from around the country and among them came word that Haughey was going to be challenged. Brian Lenihan immediately set about checking if this was true. He telephoned some of his contacts and it became clear that moves were afoot to depose Haughey. Ray Burke, the party whip, was also in Mount Street and Haughey instructed him to contact every one of the party's TDs to tell them that the parliamentary party meeting to which Gibbons had referred on television the previous night was being brought forward to the following Thursday. Haughey had decided that if he was going to be challenged, he would meet it head-on.

Next, he attempted to neutralise the two people who, more than any others, could be expected to conspire against him: Charlie McCreevy and George Colley. On Saturday night, he contacted McCreevy and arranged for him to call to Kinsealy on Sunday afternoon. Haughey also arranged to meet Colley in Mount Street in the morning.

Colley and Haughey had been rivals for more than twenty years. They had gone to school together, but Haughey's first election to the Dáil at the expense of Colley's father did little to foster friendships. The rivalry between the two grew to enmity after Jack Lynch became leader of the party in 1966, and by the time Lynch retired their differences were irreconcilable. But when Haughey took over as leader and Taoiseach, Colley was too powerful within the party to be dropped from the cabinet. Haughey let him stay on as Tánaiste and Minister for Energy — a demotion from his position under Lynch as Tánaiste and Minister for Finance plus Minister for the Public Service. Although Colley remained Haughey's biggest threat his public image was somewhat grey, dull and lacklustre. Television did not project George Colley very well.

When Haughey met him that Sunday morning, he offered him the position of Tánaiste in the government he said he would form. Colley told Haughey there would be a problem over his leadership. Notwithstanding this, Colley did not want to serve a second term in government with Haughey as Taoiseach. He did not say so at the time because he had yet to find the right excuse to refuse a cabinet post under Haughey.

If Haughey had any lingering doubt about a challenge to his position, he had only to read that morning's edition of the *Sunday Tribune*. The paper's lead story confidently predicted that an assault on Haughey was underway. At lunchtime an interview with Haughey was broadcast on RTE's "This Week" radio programme in which he said that if he worked for the

Tribune, "I would be inclined to look after my own position very carefully". The *Tribune* report was written by the paper's political correspondent, Geraldine Kennedy.

Later in the afternoon Haughey met McCreevy for about an hour and a half. He told McCreevy that he had a great future in the party. He said he had brought forward the meeting of the parliamentary party and that it would be asked to endorse him as candidate for Taoiseach. Haughey said there must be no hiccups at the meeting.

Haughey's repeated assertion that he would form a government was his most potent weapon against those who would attempt to unseat him. But as well as actually wanting to form a government, he had to be seen to be working to this end in order to undermine any threats to his leadership. Everyone knew that the balance of power in the new Dáil would be held by four Independents and the three Workers' Party TDs. It was crucial to Haughey's strategy for survival as leader that he be seen to be negotiating with these people. If Haughey succeeded, Fianna Fáil would be back in power and up to thirty ministerial posts would be in the offing.

Haughey needed the support of two Independents. While most of them were already national figures, few people had heard of Tony Gregory. Over the weekend, Haughey contacted Noel Mulcahy, a long-standing party activist whom he had known in the Sixties. Mulcahy had drawn up a number of plans over the years for Dublin's inner-city area, and Haughey pumped him for information about Gregory, the new inner-city TD. The word spread quickly throughout the party that Haughey was preparing for negotiations with the Independents and the Workers' Party. Ray Burke and Brian Lenihan spent most of Sunday telephoning Fianna Fáil TDs to tell them of the parliamentary party meeting the following Thursday. TDs all over the country were also calling each other and discussing the results and the doubt which had arisen about Haughey being the party's nominee for Taoiseach when the Dáil met.

On Monday morning, a special post-election edition of *Magill* magazine published an article entitled "The Dump Haughey Campaign". The article included a list of TDs, 30 of whom were claimed to be anti-Haughey, 17 pro-Haughey and 34 whose preference was unknown. Throughout Monday morning and early afternoon, a number of anti-Haughey TDs discussed the chances of a successful challenge and how it should be mounted. Charlie McCreevy met Jim Gibbons in Naas and later went to Dublin where he met Séamus Brennan in the Dáil restaurant. Later still, he had lunch with Martin O'Donoghue who produced the *Magill* list and proceeded to mark in his own alterations. Bobby Molloy also went to Dublin and had separate meetings with O'Donoghue, George Colley and Desmond O'Malley in each of their homes. Brennan did much the same, but the challenge to Haughey did not begin to take concrete form until a later afternoon meeting in O'Donoghue's home. The backbenchers had made it clear that O'Donoghue, Colley and O'Malley were to decide amongst themselves what strategy should be used, and who should go forward against Haughey. If they decided this, the others would work to ensure victory.

O'Donoghue's and Colley's opposition to Haughey was well known, and it was hardly surprising that they should have plotted once the notion of a challenge had been raised. But while there had never been any doubt about Desmond O'Malley's views on Haughey, he had never engaged in a conspiracy to depose him and was not popularly seen as Haughey's main opponent.

O'Malley was a 43-year-old TD from Limerick who had been elected first to the Dáil in the 1968 by-election caused by the death of his uncle, Donogh O'Malley. Jack Lynch had made him his parliamentary secretary and secretary to the Minister for Defence plus government whip. He was Minister for Justice from 1970 to 1973 in the turbulent aftermath of the arms crisis. With IRA violence at its height in Northern Ireland, O'Malley's period in Justice was an extremely rough time for a young and inexperienced politician. It gained him a reputation for being hard-line and abrasive, as he piloted through amendments to the Offences Against The State Act, set up the non-jury Special Criminal Court, and enacted the Forcible Entry Act which was designed to stop the occupation of buildings as part of street protests. Within the party, he had not built up a great following because of his curt manner and obvious impatience with the back-slapping aspect of politics.

O'Malley survived relatively unscathed when Haughey took over from Lynch. He retained his Industry and Commerce portfolio but he found Haughey extremely difficult to work with. Haughey began to take decisions outside cabinet and failed to consult his ministers.

The Talbot deal was a case in point. Just before the June 1981 election, Haughey privately conducted a deal with Talbot car assembly workers, many of whom lived in his constituency, which guaranteed them state salaries for life when the factory closed. As Minister for Industry and Commerce, O'Malley knew nothing of the deal and felt it had been wrong. One of O'Malley's few close personal friends in the party was Séamus Brennan and as the challenge to Haughey developed, Brennan advised O'Malley.

The meeting in O'Donoghue's south Dublin home began at around 4 p.m. There was agreement that Haughey should go but there were differences about how his departure should be effected. Colley argued that there should be two votes at the parliamentary party meeting: one to get rid of Haughey, the other to select his successor. Despite his protestations that he neither wanted to be party leader nor Taoiseach, this procedure would have left the way open for Colley to put himself forward once Haughey had gone. O'Malley favoured a single vote to decide the party's nominee for Taoiseach and in effect, to select its leader. O'Donoghue favoured no vote at all. He wanted to speak to other senior party members to see if a meeting could decide Haughey's departure plus an agreed replacement. A delegation would then go to Haughey and present him with a *fait accompli*. The others felt that O'Donoghue saw himself as the agreed replacement but allowed him to proceed with his plan; they felt it had no chance of success. It was agreed meanwhile that Colley and O'Malley would contact TDs to find out if there really was widespread support for removing Haughey and if either of them was preferred as his replacement.

Just before the meeting ended, the three conspirators were given an eerie reminder that Haughey was still very much in command. The O'Donoghues' telephone rang and was answered by one of the family. A head appeared around the door of the room and announced that Haughey's office was looking for O'Donoghue. O'Donoghue said he would call back later.

After Colley and O'Malley left, O'Donoghue returned Haughey's call. Haughey asked him to drop into his office the following day, Tuesday, as he wanted to discuss the government he was about to form.

O'Donoghue kept the appointment and went to see Haughey in his office on the fifth floor of Leinster House. Haughey spoke of the problems which his new government would have to tackle. They would have to produce a budget quickly and new policies would also have to be drawn up. The clear impression was that O'Donoghue had a place in the government.

As O'Donoghue left the room, Haughey said: "By the way, I hope you are not involved in any of these stories I hear".

"What stories?" quipped O'Donoghue as he continued his exit.

Haughey called a number of other TDs to his office that Tuesday. Among them were Mary Harney, Hugh Byrne, Clem Coughlan and Ciaran Murphy. They were all young and relatively new TDs, and they were told they had bright futures ahead of them. Meanwhile, pro-Haughey people were contacting constituency officers around the country, urging them in turn to call their TDs to tell them to support Haughey at Thursday's meeting. If necessary, they were to threaten the TDs with motions of no confidence from the constituency organisation.

Colley and O'Malley contacted as many TDs as possible and sounded out their views on Haughey and who should replace him if he were to go. The anti-Haughey feeling was strong and O'Malley emerged as the more popular choice to succeed him. Many TDs thought that a Colley-Haughey fight would be a re-run of their 1979 contest to succeed Jack Lynch, with possibly the same result. O'Malley, on the other hand, held out the promise of a clean break with the past. He might also be the man to revitalise the party and bring back some order to its internal affairs. Colley accepted the verdict by the time the three met again in O'Donoghue's home.

Earlier in the day Séamus and Ann Brennan had attended the christening of their new baby, Síne. Jack and Maureen Lynch were godparents and the ceremony provided Séamus with the opportunity to give Jack a progress report on the move against Haughey. In 1977 Lynch had joked that if Fianna Fáil won 3 seats in Limerick East in the election, he would hand over the party leadership to O'Malley. By now, Lynch was hoping that O'Malley would go forward against Haughey and would win.

O'Donoghue continued to plough his own furrow, and told the others he had arranged to meet Albert Reynolds. The meeting took place that night in Reynolds's Ballsbridge apartment. O'Donoghue told him that a substantial number of TDs wanted Haughey to go. He suggested that senior people meet, agree a replacement and then go to Haughey. Reynolds said there was no chance of success. He told O'Donoghue that Ray MacSharry, Haughey's closest confidant in the party, would be back in Dublin in the morning and he would talk to him. O'Donoghue left saying he would contact Reynolds again to arrange the meeting of senior people.

At about the same time that Tuesday night when O'Donoghue was talking to Reynolds, Haughey was holding his first meeting with Tony Gregory. Before he met Gregory, Haughey instructed Ray Burke and Brian Lenihan to go to O'Malley and find out definitely if a challenge was going to take place. Burke and Lenihan met O'Malley in an unoccupied house in Clonskeagh which he had been able to borrow. The meeting lasted for about an hour but their efforts were fruitless. O'Malley said he was determined to stand against Haughey. He disagreed strongly with Haughey's style of leadership and he pointed to the election result as evidence enough that he had failed the party. Burke and Lenihan knew that despite all efforts to fend off the challenge, it was going to go ahead and they had a fight on their hands.

Things began to go seriously wrong for the conspirators on Wednesday.

The *Irish Independent's* political columnist, Bruce Arnold, reported across the top of the front page that 46 of Fianna Fáil's 81 TDs were backing O'Malley compared to 20 for Haughey. The views of the remaining 15 were unknown. The report named 36 of those supporting O'Malley and 15 who were backing Haughey. At the time of publication, the list was believed by the conspirators to be accurate, but instead of creating a bandwagon effect behind O'Malley it exposed many of his would-be-supporters who had wished to remain secret. Haughey now had a list of those TDs who needed persuading. Indeed, as soon as the list was published, several needed no persuading at all — they fell over themselves to declare their support for Haughey. He got party headquarters to rouse key activists in the constituencies to put pressure on TDs to support him. Throughout the day he called TDs to his office in Leinster House for private talks.

Meanwhile, influential Haughey supporters ran a parallel campaign. Burke and Lenihan, Seán Doherty, Pádraig Flynn and Ray MacSharry contacted TDs with whom they had personal or long-standing relationships, and extracted commitments in support of Haughey. A commitment given to one of them was checked and double-checked by the others to ensure that nobody was lying when they gave an initial promise to support Haughey. This technique of double-checking enabled Haughey's supporters to build up a fairly accurate picture of what TDs were thinking. Most emphasis was placed on the so-called middle-ground TDs, those whom it was felt had no strong convictions either for or against Haughey.

MacSharry was interviewed for the RTE mid-morning programme, "Day By Day", and gave a chilling warning to any TDs whose support for Haughey might be wavering. He said the party would not easily forgive anyone who jeopardised Fianna Fáil's prospects of forming a government.

On the fifth floor of Leinster House, Noel Mulcahy was working in an office next door to Haughey's. Mulcahy was using his knowledge of the problems of central Dublin to compile proposals for the inner city which Haughey wanted to bring to Tony Gregory following their first meeting. The radio was on as he worked. Haughey, Doherty, Albert Reynolds and Martin Mansergh (another Haughey adviser) piled into Mulcahy's room when they heard MacSharry's voice on the radio. They listened attentively and cheered his tough support for the Boss. When the interview ended, Haughey returned to his room to resume his meetings with individual TDs.

Des O'Malley's office was in room 340 in Setanta House,

a harsh red-brick office block opposite Leinster House in Molesworth Street. From early morning his supporters began to assemble for the campaign to ensure he would beat Haughey when the parliamentary party met the next day.

Among the first to arrive were Charlie McCreevy and Liam Lawlor, a 37-year-old TD who had just regained his seat in Dublin West. Years earlier, Lawlor and Haughey had been close. They had travelled the country together as Haughey built a new power base after the arms crisis and Lawlor sought election to the party's national executive.

Lawlor and McCreevy had met at a party function earlier in the week and arranged to rendezvous in the Green Isle Hotel on Wednesday and go together to O'Malley's office. Instead, Lawlor and a friend drove to McCreevy's home, collected him and then drove back to Dublin to O'Malley's office. When they arrived, Lawlor began phoning TDs as part of the campaign. During the morning and afternoon, various helpers came and went. They included Mary Harney, Bobby Molloy, Séamus Brennan and George Colley. The impact of the Arnold list was apparent as TDs were contacted. Some backed off their support for O'Malley and expressed annoyance that they had been exposed. More significant, as far as the O'Malley campaigners were concerned, was the disappearance of a number of TDs on whose support they were counting. Suddenly, it seemed, there were people who did not want to know them. Lawlor left O'Malley's office around midday to see Haughey.

O'Malley's supporters were concerned that the effect of MacSharry's mid-morning radio interview should somehow be countered. The 1.30 p.m. radio news programme wanted an O'Malley supporter for interview and McCreevy was persuaded to go on. As no public challenge had yet been made, McCreevy found himself in the awkward position of trying to encourage support for O'Malley, or at least not dissuade people, even though O'Malley had not confirmed he was going forward against Haughey. The uncertainty in McCreevy's voice and his fudging of answers were in sharp contrast to the strength of purpose evident in the MacSharry interview. McCreevy's efforts did little to encourage reluctant O'Malley supporters. The O'Malley camp was further demoralised when Lawlor returned from his meeting with Haughey and was noticeably less enthusiastic about the challenge.

The tension between the two camps was evident when P.J. Mara, a long-time associate and close confidant of Haughey's, was discovered by McCreevy lurking in the vicinity of Setanta House. He was shooed away, while protesting limply that he was waiting for his wife, who had gone to buy a fur coat. Séamus Brennan's suspicions had earlier been aroused by the arrival opposite his south Dublin home of some men who set up what appeared to be a Post Office workman's hut. Brennan was satisfied that the men were pro-Haughey spies. While driving past them he rolled down his car window and asked them casually: "Find what you're looking for, lads?". He thought they looked a little shifty and embarrassed.

Martin O'Donoghue continued throughout Wednesday to pursue the strategy of seeking a meeting of senior party members to get agreement that Haughey should go, and at the same time a replacement leader should be chosen. Working from Leinster House, he also managed to have discussions with a number of people in the Labour Party, including Barry Desmond and party leader Michael O'Leary. O'Donoghue suggested to them that it was not in Labour's interest to always limit its partnership options to Fine Gael. He was told that Labour did not rule out a relationship with Fianna Fáil — so long as Haughey was not leader. Around tea-time O'Donoghue finally tracked down MacSharry. What was happening, asked MacSharry, was there going to be a meeting or what? O'Donoghue said he had not yet managed to get in touch with everyone, but he would contact MacSharry later that evening. He left MacSharry convinced that the O'Malley camp was becoming desperate. O'Donoghue then tried to call O'Malley's office in Setanta House, but there was no reply, so he went home for tea.

O'Malley's supporters had slipped away from Setanta House via the basement car park in order to avoid an RTE camera crew waiting by the main entrance. Many wanted also to stay away from their homes because some were besieged by reporters trying to find out what was happening. The problem of finding a headquarters for the evening was solved with the offer of a room and telephone in number 99, St Stephen's Green. The building was owned by a friend of Brennan's, Eoin

O'Brien, who ran the English Language Institute and lived on the top floor. Most of the key O'Malley people had gathered in O'Brien's quarters by the time "Today Tonight" came on the air after RTE television's main evening news. They watched reporter Forbes MacFall broadcast live from outside Setanta House where, he said, a meeting was taking place. He named several of those present and included Martin O'Donoghue, who at this stage had not been seen by O'Malley's supporters for several hours, much to their disturbance. The remainder of the programme was taken up with interviews with Lenihan and McCreevy. Once again, McCreevy found himself talking in circles around the challenge to Haughey because, still, nothing had been admitted publicly. Lenihan, popular with the media because of his willingness to be interviewed at awkward moments when everyone else played shy, backed Haughey to the hilt. The real shock of the programme came at the end when it was announced that RTE had received a message from O'Donoghue denying that he had been attending any meetings. O'Malley, Brennan and the others were amazed when they heard the announcement. Just before, they had received a disturbing phone call from Liam Lawlor. Lawlor told O'Malley that he was at home and that there were several Fianna Fáil constituency officers standing by him as he spoke. He asked O'Malley whether he was sure he was doing the right thing. O'Malley said he was, but the conversation had done little to bolster his confidence. The message was clear: Lawlor was on the other side. On top of this it now appeared to them that O'Donoghue was making an effort to dissociate himself as well.

Martin O'Donoghue had been at home watching the television programme when he heard the erroneous report that he was attending a meeting. His first concern was that Reynolds, MacSharry and the others might think he had double-crossed them. They would think, he feared, that he was conspiring with O'Malley while at the same time trying to put them off on the wrong trail with his proposal for a meeting of senior TDs. He immediately telephoned RTE and asked them to announce that he was at home watching the programme and was not attending a meeting. The emphasis of his message when broadcast was a blunt denial that he was meeting anyone, and O'Donoghue realised that it would not clear the air with either camp. In desperation, he tried to telephone everyone. He was unable to get either Reynolds or MacSharry but got through to O'Malley's home and was given the number of the St Stephen's Green headquarters. It was constantly engaged, however, and he went into town to try to explain the mess.

Meanwhile Charlie McCreevy was leaving the RTE television studios in Donnybrook after his "Today Tonight" interview, only to realise that his car was where he left it that morning when Lawlor picked him up — at home in County Kildare. Eventually, someone from RTE was prevailed upon to drive him home.

By the time O'Donoghue arrived in St Stephen's Green and explained the mix-up over his statement to RTE, O'Malley's supporters were arguing over a different matter. About thirty people were there when O'Donoghue arrived. Besides O'Malley and Brennan, they included Gerry O'Mahony, Jack Lynch's former press officer in Cork; George Colley; Joe Walsh, the Cork TD; David Andrews, the Dun Laoghaire TD who was a junior minister under Lynch but dropped by Haughey; Mary Harney and Bobby Molloy. There were also a number of friends, party activists and members of the Fianna Fáil National Executive. They argued over whether or not a statement should be issued declaring publicly that O'Malley would challenge Haughey. Brennan, who at this stage had become O'Malley's campaign manager, wanted a brief statement sent out in time for the late night newspaper deadlines. But at the back of his mind there were nagging doubts about the consequences for O'Malley should the challenge fail; O'Malley was more than a party colleague, he was also a friend. Harney supported Brennan's argument for a short statement. Eventually one was drafted saying that O'Malley had decided to let his name go forward "in response to demands from many people within the Fianna Fáil organisation".

Brennan was charged with distributing the announcement to the newspapers and RTE, but he delayed. He wanted to know who would propose O'Malley at the parliamentary party meeting in the morning. Everyone ran for cover. Colley ruled himself out because of his record of challenging Haughey. O'Donoghue said with annoyance that he would not propose

him, because the process of consultations with Haughey supporters, which he believed they had agreed as a strategy, had
not been played out. He stressed that he would support
O'Malley — but others noticed that O'Donoghue no longer
referred to the conspirators as "we" but rather as "you".

He continued to urge a meeting of senior people and
reminded the others that he was committed to contacting
Reynolds to arrange it. The others told O'Donoghue that he
was pursuing the wrong tactic at the wrong time. "You never
do the obvious thing in politics," he retorted.

O'Donoghue was abruptly told that time had run out, and
that he could tell Reynolds what he liked. He was also overruled when he argued that no statement at all should be issued.
He telephoned Reynolds and told him that O'Malley was about
to confirm publicly that he would challenge Haughey. Brennan
continued his search for a proposer for O'Malley, but was
forced to accept that he would have to do it himself. The
statement announcing the challenge was eventually telephoned
to the newspapers and RTE by Gerry O'Mahony. Brennan
went home ill at ease.

Reynolds telephoned MacSharry at his Dublin home in
Harold's Cross once O'Donoghue had told him that O'Malley
was definitely going ahead, and that the newspapers were being
alerted. They had been expecting such an announcement before
9 o'clock that evening, in time for RTE's main television bulletin. It was now around midnight and Reynolds, a former
provincial newspaper owner, realised that the newspapers
would be desperate for comment once they had O'Malley's
statement. He called the *Irish Independent* but they had not
received the statement. Reynolds filled them in, and gave them
plenty of comment as well. Later he went to Jury's Hotel, a
short distance from his Anglesea Road apartment, where he
met Seán Doherty and Tom Meaney, a Cork TD and strong
Haughey supporter. From the hotel Reynolds telephoned the
Cork Examiner to tell them of the impending O'Malley statement. He also called the *Irish Times* and the *Irish Press.* From
midnight until the small hours, a number of pro-Haughey TDs
made telephone calls checking up that minds had not been
changed and that support for Haughey was firm.

The opposing factions sat at different tables and at different ends of the Dáil restaurant on Thursday morning as the 11.30 am deadline for the meeting drew closer. Near the door sat Reynolds, MacSharry and Padráig Flynn, Jim Tunney, Leas-Cheann Comhairle in the old Dáil, and Gerry Brady, the new TD for Kildare. O'Donoghue entered and was met by a stare from Reynolds. He paused and had a word with them. They suggested he tell O'Malley to "have sense" and that he didn't stand a chance.

O'Donoghue walked down the restaurant to where O'Malley and his lieutenants were having coffee. He told O'Malley he should withdraw the challenge to avoid splitting the party. O'Malley said he was going ahead.

Several conversations were taking place simultaneously at the table. Bobby Molloy was also questioning the wisdom of going ahead and Seamus Brennan was beginning to wonder how O'Malley could back down without losing face. But O'Malley insisted he would push things to a show-down even if he only got one vote. Molloy argued that there had been too many defections during the night but George Colley said that the situation had not changed much since midnight. He too felt that O'Malley should go ahead. He believed that it was as important to establish openly that a section of the party was unhappy with Haughey as much as it was to beat him. If they succeeded in making that point but lost the battle, it would still have been worth it, he believed. O'Donoghue left the table to make a personal phone call.

Molloy and Brennan went out of the restaurant together, still debating what O'Malley should do. Brennan conceded that a second plan of action might be needed to extract O'Malley from the challenge if there was a groundswell against him at the meeting. Molloy believed that this plan indicated that O'Malley would withdraw. He went to the Fianna Fáil room on the fifth floor where the meeting was to be held, waited outside the door for O'Donoghue, and told him that O'Malley would withdraw.

O'Malley arrived for the meeting still determined to go ahead. On his way into the room, he met MacSharry who told him he was "very foolish". O'Malley and Brennan sat beside each other, O'Malley apparently unaware of the confusion among his supporters. As the room filled with TDs there was no great rush to sit beside them; Brennan and he were alone in the crowd. The already tense atmosphere was heightened by the presence of television lights, cameras and newspaper photographers. Haughey, Burke and Lenihan had decided to stage-manage Haughey's entrance. Nobody was sitting at the table at the top of the room in front of the gathering TDs. A cardboard ballot box, deliberately made shoddy and held together with bits of sellotape, was beside the top table which had been left bare.

Suddenly, the door beside the table swung open. Ray Burke strode in, clapping his hands as he went and declaring: "Deputies and Senators, I give you our party leader and the next Taoiseach, Charles J. Haughey". Everyone leapt to their feet clapping. It was all over, bar the talking. Haughey had won an enormous psychological victory but some ritual talking still had to be observed.

The key speaker was Pádraig Faulkner, the Louth TD and former Ceann Comhairle who had backed Colley in the 1979 leadership contest with Haughey. He urged both sides to get together in the interests of the party. There should be no contest; instead, O'Malley and Haughey should be discussing together the formation of the government. As O'Donoghue listened to Faulkner, it dawned on him that not all O'Malley's supporters might realise, as he did because Molloy had told him, that O'Malley was going to withdraw. He stepped in to support Faulkner's line and urged O'Malley to withdraw. O'Donoghue's speech startled O'Malley and Brennan. Colley still wanted O'Malley to go ahead and push it to a vote. He even tried to catch O'Malley's eye to signal encouragement but it was too late. O'Malley rose to his feet and said he would withdraw. Haughey spoke and said there was nobody he would like more to talk about forming a government with than O'Malley. It was over in less than an hour, and Haughey's supporters rushed from the meeting to spread the good news to the waiting reporters.

There were recriminations and accusations among the conspirators in the disarray which followed. O'Donoghue was charged publicly with being a Judas, a slur he bitterly resented. But in the main he was the scapegoat. Molloy and Brennan fell out for a while in a dispute over who said what to whom — the confusion which had led to O'Donoghue's unexpected speech. O'Malley and O'Donoghue did not speak to each other for seven months. Jack Lynch made one of his rare public comments since his retirement. He said O'Malley had been right to challenge Haughey and he was confident that O'Malley would one day lead the party and be Taoiseach. He said O'Malley was right because Fianna Fáil had failed to win an overall majority in the election. More than anything else that had been said, Lynch's statement infuriated Haughey.

At an impromptu press conference, flanked by MacSharry and Reynolds, Charles J. Haughey declared: "We are a totally united party . . . we are going to give this country stable government for the next five years".

It was midday on Thursday, February 25th, 1982.

Chapter Three

You know what I want: what do you want?
Charles Haughey, February 1982

The telephone at Tony Gregory's house rang almost continuously all morning on Saturday, February 20th. Even before the final seats in the new Dáil were allocated, it had become clear that Independents and smaller parties were going to hold the balance of power. Among these crucially important deputies, Tony Gregory, the newly-elected TD for Dublin Central, was the least known to the establishments within Fianna Fáil and Fine Gael.

A prominent local politician and member of Dublin City Council, some of his contacts with government ministers had not come about through the normal channels of communication. Around Christmas 1980, he had been among a group of people who had occupied the ministerial office of Michael Woods, the Fianna Fáil man then in charge of the Department of Health. They were protesting at cuts in the Combat Poverty programme which had been one of the benefactors of the North City Centre Community Action Project, a community group founded by Gregory and two associates which ran courses and helped local people battle with bureaucracy. The occupation was successful: Woods saw to it that the funding of the centre was continued by his department.

So, when Fianna Fáil wanted someone to talk to Gregory in the immediate aftermath of the election, Woods was obviously the man. He was among the telephone callers that Saturday morning, telling Gregory that Fianna Fáil wanted to talk to him. Gregory, not yet acclimatised to his new position, put him off until after the weekend.

Elsewhere around the country, the Fianna Fáil machine lost no time switching its attention from the election campaign to the new circumstances. There was still a battle to be fought to get into power and the party began to fight it.

Members of the Workers' Party, which now held three Dáil seats, were approached by Fianna Fáil activists in their localities, enquiring about the party's intentions. They stressed a common bond through republicanism and a mutual antipathy towards the "blueshirts" of Fine Gael. In many cases, a misplaced emphasis on a common approach towards "the national question" illustrated the ignorance within Fianna Fáil of the Workers' Party policy on the North.

How orchestrated the Fianna Fáil approaches were is a matter for conjecture, but there was no doubting the party's determination to find out where everybody stood and to persuade the crucial TDs to back Haughey for Taoiseach. The new Workers' Party TD for Dublin North West, Proinsias de Rossa, was approached by a neighbour who said that Haughey wanted to find out what would be required to win the party's support in the Dáil. Haughey was willing and anxious to talk, de Rossa was told.

The North was not an issue on which Fianna Fáil and the Workers' Party would agree. In fact, the only one of the Independents for whom it was of crucial importance was Neil Blaney, the Independent Fianna Fáil TD who had continued to represent Donegal North East after his expulsion from Fianna Fáil in 1971 over the party's policy on Northern Ireland. Blaney had always maintained that the party had left him, not he the party, by abandoning its traditional nationalist stance on the Six Counties. But Blaney had never opposed Fianna Fáil in the Dáil, and most members of the party thought his backing could be taken for granted.

The fourth element in the formation of the Government was John O'Connell, the outgoing Ceann Comhairle, who had been returned automatically. A medical doctor, businessman and self-made millionaire, O'Connell made no secret of his admiration for Haughey. The coalition government had made O'Connell Ceann Comhairle in July 1981, and everyone would be content for him to remain in the chair when the new Dáil met on March 9th.

The other independent TD was Jim Kemmy, who had voted against FitzGerald's budget. But nobody believed he would ever support Haughey for Taoiseach.

Haughey's task as he faced the new Dáil with Fianna Fáil two votes short of an overall majority was to persuade at least two more people to back him. Provided O'Connell took the chair and Blaney was true to previous form, he needed Gregory or the Workers' Party to give him a majority. Either would do; together they would give him a virtual landslide. For a variety of reasons, Gregory looked the best bet.

Over the weekend, while Haughey was facing the first stirrings of the internal Fianna Fáil revolt against his leadership, Gregory was making sure that he was not going to be isolated from his supporters and friends by his new role. He met his advisers to decide their approach to the new Dáil. Gregory knew that he would have to vote for either Haughey or FitzGerald, that he would have to choose between them. His own instincts and attitudes gave him a preference for Haughey.

Gregory was 34, a teacher of history through Irish at Coláiste Eoin, a secondary school in Stillorgan, Co. Dublin. He had come to community politics through militant republicanism. In the early 1970s he had been a member of Official Sinn Féin, the precursor of the Workers' Party. He left the Officials shortly before the split which saw the birth of the Irish Republican Socialist Party, headed by Séamus Costello. Despite his admiration for Costello, Gregory chose not to pursue his political career in the IRSP but immersed himself in local politics in the North inner city area of Dublin. He was elected onto Dublin City Council in 1979 on a community platform but failed in his first attempt to win a Dáil seat in 1981. He believed that FitzGerald was a "collaborator" with the British on the North, as well as being the leader of the South's most reactionary party. Haughey, he felt, was more sympathetic towards his anti-imperialist stance.

His nationalist views were balanced, when it came to deciding who to support for Taoiseach, by the attitudes of two of his closest associates, Mick Rafferty and Fergus McCabe. Both subscribed to the "two nations" theory which held that the border separating North from South actually partitioned two distinctly different peoples from each other. The theory was totally at odds with traditional nationalist views which saw Ireland as one nation divided by a British created border. Rafferty and McCabe leant towards FitzGerald in any contest between him and Haughey.

But the North was not to be a factor in Tony Gregory's decisions. He and his advisers agreed that Gregory would be accompanied by some of them at all meetings. There would be no private sessions. They also drew up a list of issues of concern to them and to the inner city area in which they lived and worked. Arrangements for the first meeting with Haughey were made eventually by Ned Brennan, who was the Fianna Fáil leader on Dublin City Council and also a newly-elected TD in Michael Woods's constituency of Dublin North East. Gregory suggested that Haughey meet him at number 20, Summerhill Parade, the offices of the North City Centre Community Action Project on Tuesday February 23rd. Rafferty and McCabe were to be present as well.

An interesting sidelight on Haughey's tactics emerged on the eve of that meeting. Gregory was approached by John Stafford, Fianna Fáil's director of elections in Dublin Central and a family friend of Haughey. Stafford said he knew about the arrangements for the meeting but, he asked, would Gregory like to go and visit Haughey privately at Kinsealy beforehand? Gregory said no.

Charles Haughey climbed the stairs and entered the grubby room in 20 Summerhill Parade. He was alone. "You know what I want", he said to Gregory. "What do you want?".

Gregory produced two typed pages which listed his priorities under five headings: employment, housing, education, health and general. It contained an apparently haphazard collection of items which ranged from specific local issues to the lead content of petrol and preschool education. The first item on the list concerned a 27-acre site owned by Dublin Port and Docks Board at Custom House Quay, bounded by Connolly railway station and Sheriff Street. The Board planned to sell it off piecemeal after receiving planning permission for a huge development of offices, shops and luxury apartments covering the entire site. Gregory wanted the development to concentrate more on housing and on industries appropriate to the local workforce. The site presented, in his view, an opportunity to do something about the high unemployment rate in the area and to stem the drift of people from the city centre out to the suburbs.

Haughey went through the list, accepting most of the proposals and rejecting a few. Those he rejected included the implementation of the Kenny Report, a report compiled for the state which proposed curbs on land speculation. The recommendations had not been put into practice because, it was claimed, they would interfere with the constitutional rights of private property. Haughey said there would be problems with the report but he told Gregory he would produce some alternatives which would have the same effect.

Gregory, McCabe and Rafferty were impressed with Haughey. He had clearly been well briefed, had a strong grasp of local issues and was decisive and businesslike. Besides, he was agreeing to most of their proposals. "You're pushing an open door," he kept saying. Before he left he promised to draw up a detailed response to the problems which they had isolated. He had the advantage of having access to much of the background knowledge and experience of the inner city that he needed. Apart from Haughey's own personal knowledge of the area (it had formed part of his first constituency), he could seek the advice of people like Noel Mulcahy, a member of Fianna Fáil's general election committee, and relatives like his brother, Seán Haughey, an assistant manager with Dublin Corporation.

Mulcahy, a consultant and lecturer with the Irish Management Institute, had put a lot of political work into the area to build himself an electoral base there. His involvement had resulted in the formation of an inter-departmental inner city committee in 1978. The civil service group had continued to meet, but its activities had made little impact on the ground. In 1979 Mulcahy had produced his own plan for the Port and Dock Board's 27 acres, proposing that the two unused docks on the site be turned into a fishing harbour by opening them up to trawlers. That was to be the focal point for a village-style development on the rest of the site. Mulcahy's own political ambitions were stymied, partly by the decision of George Colley to move into the area after constituency re-alignments, and partly by the emergence of Gregory as a political force. He and Gregory knew each other well as political rivals and, in 1979, Gregory had beaten Mulcahy to a seat on Dublin City Council. After a brief spell as a Senator under Jack Lynch, Mulcahy's electoral ambitions had waned but he had continued to work for Fianna Fáil as a backroom volunteer, a role he had played since the late 1960s. He had also maintained an interest in the inner city and in developments there.

Martin Mansergh, a former civil servant in the Department of Foreign Affairs and now a fulltime adviser to Haughey and Fianna Fáil, had the task of co-ordinating Fianna Fáil's response to Gregory. Information was gathered from various sources. Former Fianna Fáil ministers whose portfolios had covered relevant issues were called upon to make a contribution to the material being collected and collated. Mulcahy wrote a lengthy and sympathetic account of what needed to be done in the inner city, covering jobs, houses, community development and the reasons for decay. He proposed specifically that the inter-departmental committee on the inner city be replaced with a new body which would have stronger powers and greater freedom of action, an Inner City Authority. Fianna Fáil should also appoint a Junior Minister at the Department of the Environment who would have responsibility for urban affairs. New taxes were suggested for office blocks in the area and concessions proposed for new industries which were suitable to the area. The 27 acre site was to be used to create "a new economically and socially viable neighbourhood and community which will bring new life and opportunity to this part of the inner city". Proposals on housing were very specific: 1,600 new local authority houses were to be built in Dublin in 1982 and 2,000 in 1983. Funds for maintenance were to be restored after cuts by the coalition government, and a scheme to provide showers in centre-city flats was to be started in 1983.

Other proposals drawn up by Mansergh suggested a tax of between 3% and 5% on derelict property and a 45% capital gains tax on land which had been given planning permission for a use which made it more valuable. Local authorities were to be given power to buy houses in a poor state of repair, refurbish them and sell them on the commercial market. This, it was suggested, would provide £500,000 for Dublin Corporation,

£100,000 for Cork and a further £400,000 to be spread among other centres. On the plan for a controversial eastern by-pass of the city centre, Fianna Fáil promised that it would not support a proposal which failed to secure "a reasonable level of support from the local communities which would be affected by it". All of the proposals were brought together in a 42-page document that was spiral-bound and finished off with a stiff blue cover: it was entitled "The Inner City Problem" and was stamped "private and confidential" in silver lettering. The final page said that the proposals would represent a concerted attack on the most pressing social problems in Ireland. The same commitment must be brought to solving the problems of the inner city as had been brought, a generation earlier, to the successful elimination of slum tenements and tuberculosis, it declared. Armed with this document as well as maps, the investment plan for 1981 under his last government, and a speech he had made as Minister for Health, Haughey was ready to return to Gregory for a second meeting.

Meanwhile, Haughey's first meeting with the Workers' Party had been scheduled for Thursday, February 25th, the day of the Fianna Fáil parliamentary party meeting and Des O'Malley's abortive challenge. The meeting was postponed until the following day because of the uncertainty that preceded the Fianna Fáil session. Both parties met in Leinster House in the Fianna Fáil rooms. Haughey was accompanied by a number of his front bench members. Tomás MacGiolla, leader of the Workers' Party, headed a delegation that included the party's three new Dáil deputies, Proinsias de Rossa, Joe Sherlock and Paddy Gallagher. The atmosphere and path followed in the talks were significantly different from those in the contacts between Haughey and Gregory. Haughey had apparently decided to adopt a formal approach to the discussions with the Workers' Party, as if they were leaders of two separate nations conferring with each other. He dominated the Fianna Fáil side of the table, proferring statements in reply to the statements of the Workers' Party men.

Haughey referred to MacGiolla repeatedly as "Mr President" in an unusually formal recognition of his title as president of the Workers' Party. The effect was undermined, however, by the tendency of Haughey's front bench colleagues to refer to Haughey as "Boss". Their contribution to the talks was to endorse Haughey's comments or expand upon them occasionally. But their interjections were sprinkled with phrases such as "Yes, Boss" or "Right, Boss". Interestingly, the party's front-bench members had cleaned up their act for the second meeting with the Workers' Party. On that occasion, they referred to Haughey as "President", his title within the Fianna Fáil organisation. Haughey continued to call MacGiolla "Mr President".

During their meetings, the Workers' Party raised issues like housing, social welfare, divorce and the North. The problem of Northern Ireland was one of the most difficult issues for the party if it was to support Haughey. Over the previous two decades, it had moved away from the traditional nationalist belief that ending partition was the primary goal, and had adopted instead a distinctly Marxist philosophy. The building of socialism in both parts of the island was now a more immediate objective than the removal of the border which separated the two.

Progress towards this policy had been marked by severe internal traumas within the republican movement. The disputes over the new approach were inevitably accentuated by the turn of events in the North after the initial civil rights marches in 1968. The pressures caused by the eruption of violence led to the formation of Provisional Sinn Féin and the Provisional IRA. Sinn Féin, now known as Official Sinn Féin to distinguish it from the breakaway group, was adamant at that time that Fianna Fáil members had encouraged the formation of the Provisionals in return for undertakings that they would confine their military operations to the North and would not upset the ideological status quo in the South. While the Provisionals emerged in the North as the main practitioners of physical force to achieve unity, the Official IRA eventually scaled down its military activities, and Official Sinn Féin concentrated on Marxist politics. The Officials fragmented further in the mid 1970s when the more militant elements who had remained after the Provisional breakaway finally left to form the Irish Republican Socialist Party and the Irish National Liberation Army.

The political development of the Officials was reflected by

changes in the group's name. To Sinn Féin they appended The Workers' Party, to give themselves the most unwieldy title in politics for several years. The metamorphosis was completed in 1982 when the annual Árd Fheis took the decision to drop Sinn Féin from the party's title. The party's recent history made it inevitable, however, that some members, particularly those in the North, should have felt uneasy at any prospect of their Dáil deputies supporting Haughey, because they saw him as a representative of that wing within Fianna Fáil which, they believed, had helped to split Sinn Féin.

In their talks with Haughey, the Workers' Party asked him specifically to tone down his strident opposition to the British government's plans to hold elections and set up an assembly in the North. The detailed proposals had not yet been published, but Britain's intentions were clear and Haughey was adamant that the idea was disastrous. He repeated to the Workers' Party the basis for his approach to the North, his assertion that the area had failed as a political entity. Therefore, any attempt that was aimed at making it work politically was doomed to fail. The Workers' Party argued that the assembly plan might not be perfect but it represented a political initiative which deserved to be supported. By the end of their discussions, the Workers' Party had gained the impression that Haughey would not actively oppose the assembly plan.

Haughey was more sympathetic towards their arguments that state-owned companies should be properly financed and allowed to compete with private enterprise in profitable areas. On housing, he shared the Workers' Party opposition to the coalition government's plan to claw back to central government all the proceeds from the sale of local authority houses. The plan removed one of the few remaining sources of revenue that had been left to the discretion of local authorities, and the loss of money threatened to undercut the maintenance programmes of many councils.

The Workers' Party also sought a commitment to a referendum to remove the constitutional ban on divorce. Haughey had previously opposed any piecemeal changes in the constitution, but had altered his position in 1981 when he and Garret FitzGerald were persuaded to make commitments to add a "pro-life" amendment to the constitution. FitzGerald had tried later to have the anti-abortion measure included in a wider review of the constitution, but Haughey had stood by the simple promise to hold a single-issue referendum. On divorce, Haughey said that he was personally against the lifting of the ban, although there were others in the party who did not agree with his views. He thought it would be difficult to get a majority within Fianna Fáil to support divorce. As the discussion broke up, one Fianna Fáil man went over to MacGiolla and whispered: "I'm one of the pro-divorce people".

Behind all the formalities, however, there was another level to the discussions between the Workers' Party and Fianna Fáil. A secret meeting had been arranged by people with contacts in both parties and was held in the Gresham Hotel in Dublin between Brian Lenihan and the general secretary of the Workers' Party, Seán Garland. The most unusual aspect of the meeting was that those who arranged it had a common interest in Iraq. Several Fianna Fáil members, notably Haughey himself as Minister for Health, had developed contacts with the middle eastern country; party supporters were among the businessmen who exploited new export opportunities there. The Workers' Party had an ideological affinity with Iraq, a socialist country that adopted a non-aligned but distinctly left-wing approach to international affairs. This tenuous connection was seen by Haughey's friends as yet another avenue that should be explored in the search for Dáil votes. Garland was non-committal about the Workers' Party plans, but he dropped some hints that it was unlikely to vote for Garret FitzGerald.

Meanwhile, Neil Blaney was preparing as well for formal talks with Haughey. The assumption among many Fianna Fáil people and among commentators that Blaney would automatically support Haughey had irked some Blaney supporters in his constituency in Donegal North East. Blaney, a Dáil deputy since 1948, was not a person to pass up an opportunity like that presented to him by the latest general election result. With his support, members of his organisation decided to send a six-man delegation to Dublin to see Haughey formally, and to discuss their TD's vote. He and his deputation put two demands to Haughey. They wanted him to adopt a tough line on the North and to do so in public and, secondly, they wanted him to encourage employment by promoting the construction industry. Blaney had been Minister for Local Government for eight years until 1966 and he was a firm advocate of using the construction industry, especially in time of recession, to generate jobs and economic activity. On the North, Blaney did not want any more private assurances that Haughey agreed with his attitude towards the problem. He wanted Haughey to articulate those views in public. Blaney and his supporters were determined that they would not support Haughey unless they got assurances on both counts. He was unlikely to vote for anyone else as Taoiseach, but his abstention could have been crucial. At their first meeting they got firm undertakings verbally from Haughey on both issues.

· Blaney and his supporters also made clear their opposition to some of the Republic's measures for dealing with the IRA and subversion. They objected to the government ban on broadcasting interviews with IRA spokesmen, the laws used against subversive groups, and some of the special Garda squads which pursued them.

Blaney subsequently struck an agreement with Haughey over the Senate. He pointed out to Haughey that Fianna Fáil, even with the Taoiseach's power to appoint eleven senators, was unlikely to have more than thirty of the sixty seats in the upper house. Haughey would therefore face the prospect of having his government's measures delayed or disrupted by being in a minority in the Senate. Blaney proposed to him that his supporters would back Fianna Fáil candidates on all Senate panels and, in return, Haughey would appoint a Blaney man to the Senate as one of the Taoiseach's nominees. The proposal, Blaney made clear, did not affect the agreement on which he would support Haughey as Taoiseach. Haughey agreed. Blaney believed he could command some twenty-eight votes in the Senate election through county councillors who supported him and he pitched them behind Fianna Fáil. The tactic apparently worked: Fianna Fáil won an extra seat and Haughey, after he became Taoiseach, appointed one of Blaney's people, James Larkin, a senator.

The fact that all the people with the power to make or break a government were, apart from Blaney, left-wingers, inevitably gave rise to attempts to form an alliance of the left in the new

Dáil. Jim Kemmy was the main proponent of an agreement between himself, Gregory and the Workers' Party. But it was clear from an early stage that the prospects of even a loose arrangement among them were slender. Kemmy proposed that they all agree to support a government for a year or eighteen months on the basis of an agreed policy covering as many as eighteen points. His desire, however, that the government to be supported should be led by Garret FitzGerald made the other participants uneasy. The Workers' Party said it was prepared to go along with an agreed left-wing programme but it must be independent of any particular government. Gregory supported the idea of them all sticking together and getting action on their joint demands. Thus, they all favoured different tactics which divided them as well as the ideological differences that existed among their brands of socialism. The five of them held two meetings but the formation of an alliance was not the prime consideration for any of them and the idea never got off the ground. Kemmy's desire to support the outgoing coalition was an unacceptable precondition to the others. Both Kemmy and Gregory believed that the Workers' Party did not really want agreement and that it was primarily concerned with consolidating its own position and maintaining its identity. The Workers' Party believed that Kemmy was pro-coalition and Gregory was pro-Haughey. None of them wanted to be seen to scupper the possibility of an alliance, so their discussions dragged on. But they were never anything more than a sideshow to the attempts by the two main political parties, Fianna Fáil and Fine Gael, to get their nominees for Taoiseach each elected.

Garret FitzGerald was in the market for an agreement as well as Charles Haughey. His Fine Gael and Labour coalition could command, if it stuck together, 78 seats in the Dáil, five votes short of an overall majority. Labour adherence to coalition was uncertain but, in any event, FitzGerald needed as well to win the backing of the Workers' Party, Gregory and Kemmy in order to stay in power. He waited a week after the election count before he began to seek meetings with the Independents and the Workers' Party, by sending his official car down to Gregory's Summerhill offices on Friday, February 26th, with a note asking Gregory to phone him at the Taoiseach's office during the following week. FitzGerald also set up a meeting with the Workers' Party.

FitzGerald had two meetings with Gregory and his colleagues. In Gregory's office in Summerhill Parade, Fitz-Gerald produced a 49-page document in a student's ring folder. The first 24-page section covered the coalition's plans to set up educational task forces for deprived areas. It went into minute detail about the staffing and operation of preschool playgroups but some specific commitments were added for the inner city on Dublin, including a community college, special youth groups and home management centres for parents. The extra cost, excluding the community college, was put at £350,000. The section concluded with details of a plan by a multi-national company to set up educational and training centres in Ireland which would operate by means of computer terminals linked into a computer bank in London. The centres would offer a variety of courses through the central computer and would, according to FitzGerald's document, be well suited to an inner-city location because of the demand for education in such areas and the jobs the centres would provide. Each centre would cost less than £1 million to equip.

On jobs, FitzGerald promised £500,000 to implement a proposal by the Inter-Departmental Inner City Committee for an incentive scheme for employers who took school leavers or long term unemployed people from the inner city. The number of people employed by Dublin Corporation on environmental works would be doubled to 300, thanks to an extra allocation of £1.9 million. But he made a point of stressing that such assistance would also be extended to other inner-city areas as well. On housing, he undertook that Dublin Corporation would be given all the funds necessary to achieve a target of 2,000 house completions annually by 1984. The Port and Docks Board's 27 acres was to be taken over by a consortium of Dublin Corporation, An Bord Telecom, the Industrial Development Authority and private interests; half the area would be used for local authority accommodation. Some 400 dwellings were envisaged but the precise number depended on the height of apartment blocks. In addition a two-acre leisure centre was to include a pop concert hall and conference facilities. There would be a 5% tax on derelict sites.

FitzGerald spent almost two hours discussing the document

with Gregory, but concentrated most of his attention on the educational section. The proposal for computer-based courses in the inner city helped to convince Gregory and his colleagues that FitzGerald was totally out of touch with their concerns. To make matters worse, FitzGerald said he had to leave for another appointment by the time he got around to the details of his plan for the Port and Docks Board site and the other issues central to Gregory's decisions. Gregory and his friends were not impressed with FitzGerald: he struck them as sincere and concerned about the state of the national economy, but he had no feel for their area and, they felt, no real grasp of the problems that concerned them.

FitzGerald's pitch to the Workers' Party was along the lines that it and Fine Gael were closer on the North and that Fine Gael was more progressive socially than Fianna Fáil. The Workers' Party pointed out that its three deputies would not support the same budget which the party had opposed at the cost of precipitating an election on January 27th. The day before the new Dáil met, FitzGerald arrived in the Workers' Party room in Leinster House just as Gregory, Kemmy and the party members were discussing a left-wing alliance. He stepped inside the door for a moment to tell them all that his cabinet had decided to drop its plan to impose VAT on clothes and shoes and to cut subsidies on food. The electorate had rejected those proposals, he explained.

Michael O'Leary, the Labour Party leader and Tánaiste, had meetings separately with Gregory and the Workers' Party. He and Gregory shared a constituency but could not agree where to meet. O'Leary refused to go to Gregory's office in Summerhill and rented a room in Wynne's Hotel for their discussions instead. They drank coffee and chewed biscuits. O'Leary was pessimistic and the discussions got nowhere. The talks between Labour and the Workers' Party were equally unproductive: O'Leary declared that any socialists who voted for Fianna Fáil would be dead politically. Meanwhile, Labour's administrative council was preparing to meet on March 8th, the eve of the new Dáil session, to decide if it was going to continue in coalition with Fine Gael.

By that stage, Gregory had made considerable progress with Haughey. The Fianna Fáil leader's document on "the inner city problem" had been given a cool reception by Gregory and his friends initially. They pointed out to Haughey that it lacked specifics and they wanted specific details rather than general commitments. They drew up a detailed and written response to the document which accepted the outline of many of Fianna Fáil's proposals but raised the stakes. They suggested that Gregory be chairman of the Inner City Authority and have power to nominate five members and that the Authority be given a budget of double the amount suggested by Fianna Fáil, £2 million rather than £1 million. The Authority was to have power to approve a plan for the Port and Docks Board site which was to be acquired by May 9th, two months after the government taking office. Ten acres was to be devoted to housing, eight to industry, six to offices and three to leisure. Dublin Corporation, which Gregory had consulted, could take on 500 more men on environmental works for £4 million a year, he pointed out in his response. He wanted a commitment that 1,500 of the 1,655 housing unit sites in the north city be developed over three years: that would require an annual £25 million. Dublin Corporation would need an extra £20 million to maintain services and another £1 million to employ the hundred craftsmen needed to upgrade the maintenance department. The tax on derelict sites should be 5% and the eastern by-pass should be scrapped.

Gregory got most of what he asked for. There were some modifications. The deadline for the acquisition of the Port and Docks Board site would be the end of June. Gregory would not be chairman of the Inner City Authority, but would have power to nominate the chairman who would then be able to appoint five members.

As March 9th approached, pressure increased on all the participants to decide who they would support as Taoiseach and to declare their preferences. The numerous permutations that were possible meant that, in theory at least, anything could happen. It was possible, for instance, that both Haughey and FitzGerald could be defeated when they were each proposed as Taoiseach. The uncertainty was playing upon both the individuals concerned as well. On Sunday, March 7th, after a meeting Haughey asked Gregory what way he intended to vote. He needed to know, Haughey explained, so that he could arrange to have his wife and children in the public gallery of the Dáil if he was going to be elected Taoiseach. Gregory was non-committal.

On Monday, March 8th, there was a flurry of last-minute meetings. The Workers' Party Árd-Chomhairle met in Dublin that night to decide its strategy. Its twenty members had been lobbied extensively by Fianna Fáil acquaintances and neighbours, and this was their second meeting to discuss the matter. Seán Garland gave a report on the party's discussions with other groups and Independents. They opted for Haughey, on the basis that he had the best chance of forming a government and providing some political stability. The decision was almost unanimous but no announcement was made in public that night.

The Labour Party met the same evening to try and resolve its internal contradictions over coalition. The joint session of the administrative council and the parliamentary party went on until the early hours of Tuesday morning. Half-way through, members were told that the Workers' Party had decided to back Haughey for Taoiseach. The administrative council members voted to back FitzGerald for Taoiseach but they decided that Labour deputies would not join FitzGerald's cabinet if he were re-elected to government. The decision was made easier by the knowledge that the coalition administration faced certain defeat, but it was a last blow by the administrative council against the parliamentary party in the internal battle that had been waged since the January budget.

The coalition cabinet also met on Monday and decided to alter the budget proposals which had caused the general election and upon which it had fought the campaign. It declared that it was now clear that the electorate had rejected those aspects of the budget. FitzGerald was also due to have a meeting with Gregory and his advisers in Government Buildings that day.

As they waited in the ante-room to the Taoiseach's office, Gregory and his associates were discussing what the new TD was going to do. By that stage there was no doubt in their minds that he would back Haughey. They decided there and then to phone Haughey and ask him to call on their Summerhill offices at 8.30 that evening. They made the call from the phone outside

FitzGerald's office. They also contacted Michael Mullen, the general secretary of the Irish Transport and General Workers' Union, who had offered to act as an independent witness to any agreements that were made. He, too, was invited along to Summerhill at 8.30. Back in their own office Gregory, whose right arm and wrist were in plaster after he fell while putting up election posters, dictated the agreement to his brother, Noel. It was typed by Pauline Kane, the administrator at the centre, from Noel Gregory's handwriting. Several pages from Haughey's document "The Inner City Problem" were photocopied and inserted unchanged into the new document.

When Haughey arrived, he had to wait until the typing of the thirty page document headed "Agreements reached by Charlie Haughey TD and Tony Gregory TD" was finished. Mullen read it all out to him: Haughey nodded his agreement and sometimes commented that he had agreed to those items. There were no last minute negotiations. But the document made no mention of several important understandings that had been reached between Haughey and Gregory.

During their discussions, Haughey had assured Gregory that he was only interested in his vote for Taoiseach. He gave Gregory to understand that once he, Haughey, had been elected Taoiseach, Gregory was free to vote whatever way he liked. It seemed to Gregory and his advisers that Haughey had failed to realise that they were deeply interested in many issues that were not related specifically to the problems of the inner city. They were also sceptical of his assertion that he would be able to survive in the Dáil once he had been elected Taoiseach without Gregory's continuing support. Gregory explained that there were some issues on which he would vote against Fianna Fáil. He told Haughey he would definitely vote against any Criminal Justice Bill which attempted to remove the right of people to remain silent when arrested by the gardaí — one of the main demands made by the gardaí. Both Fianna Fáil and Fine Gael had committed themselves during the election campaign to giving the gardaí greater powers of arrest, detention and interrogation. Gregory told Haughey that he would not support right-wing law and order measures. Haughey said there would be no problem in this regard. Gregory also raised the issue of capital punishment, but Haughey gave an instant and categoric assurance that his government would never allow a death sentence to be carried out.

The absence of these commitments from the document was not sinister. Under extreme pressure from all sides, Gregory had overlooked a number of disparate issues on which he had reached agreement with Haughey. They had, for instance, agreed that VAT should be taken off books and that CIE fares should not increase for the remainder of that year. By this stage, word had travelled that Gregory was in a position to make things happen. He received a stream of representations from people he knew working in Eason's, the booksellers, about the detrimental effects of VAT on books. A number of lawyers had contacted him to make sure that draconian powers were not given to the gardaí.

Indeed, other members of the new Dáil had also come to realise as quickly as outsiders that the handful of people who could decide who was to be Taoiseach were in an unusually powerful position. Proinsias de Rossa, the Workers' Party TD, was at a meeting about vandalism and other local problems in Finglas in his own constituency during that period. His Fianna Fáil constituency rival, Jim Tunney, was there as well. He turned to de Rossa and said to him privately: "One million pounds would do a lot for Finglas."

The proof of Gregory's influence lay in the fact that Haughey was prepared to sign the document he had drawn up as a result of their discussions. He and Gregory signed on page 30 on a line each alongside their typed names. Mullen witnessed the signatures and added the date.

Haughey prepared to leave after the signing. "As Al Capone said", he remarked, "I like doing business with you".

Chapter Four

What about the rest of the country?
Eddie Collins, March 1982

Everyone was watching the four Independent and three Workers' Party TDs as the Dail chamber and public gallery, packed and overflowing, waited anxiously for the election of the next Taoiseach. Garret FitzGerald still refused to concede publicly that he had lost the general election and while Charles Haughey insisted confidently that he would form a government, nobody knew for sure exactly what the Independents and the Workers' Party would do when the moment came to vote in the new Taoiseach. The clerk of the Dáil, Michael Healy, began the formal proceedings just after 3 pm by reading the traditional prayer and the proclamation by President Hillery dissolving the old Dáil. He then read the long, tedious list of returning officers in the election and the names of all the candidates elected in the country's 41 constituencies. Finally, he came to the business of the election of the Ceann Comhairle, the chairman of the Dáil. All eyes shifted to the Independents, sitting together in the back row of the centre section of the semi-circular chamber, when Healy called for nominations. People in the public gallery strained forward to peer down into the chamber and see who would make the first move.

Neil Blaney stood up. "I wish to move", he announced, "that Deputy John O'Connell be elected as Ceann Comhairle". O'Connell had been Ceann Comhairle during the brief life of the last government. He was indecisive, and so easily intimidated by bullying TDs that business frequently came to a standstill amid bickering. But then as now, Fianna Fáil, Fine

Gael and Labour were content to give the job to O'Connell, thereby reducing the number of Independents and the possibility of defeat. In a tied vote, the Ceann Comhairle traditionally supported the government with his casting vote and preserved the status quo.

Blaney spoke in fulsome praise of O'Connell. His proposal was seconded by FitzGerald and endorsed by Haughey. There were no dissenting voices. O'Connell was elected without a division and took his place on the dais. He thanked his fellow TDs, was congratulated by Oliver J. Flanagan, but moved quickly on to the business everyone was waiting for: the election of the Taoiseach.

Brian Lenihan proposed Charles Haughey. He was seconded by Ray MacSharry but neither of them made any speech. Michael O'Leary, outgoing Tánaiste and leader of the Labour Party, immediately proposed Garret FitzGerald who, he said, offered the country wise and courageous leadership. He was seconded by Peter Barry, Fine Gael deputy leader. Nobody said anything else but all heads again turned towards the Independent and Workers' Party TDs. It was their move next. Joe Sherlock jumped up first and began speaking.

"On behalf of my party, Sinn Féin the Workers' Party, I wish to say that my party decided to support the nomination of deputy Charles J. Haughey". There was an immediate burst of applause from the public gallery. The waiting was over. Haughey had made it. But those who had decided to support him felt they had to explain themselves. Sherlock said that he and his colleagues in the Workers' Party, Paddy Gallagher and Proinsias de Rossa, were supporting Haughey because the electorate had indicated a preference for a Fianna Fáil government. He added that the economic and industrial policies of Fianna Fáil seemed to be what the country needed. He emphasised that no deal or pact had been concluded with Fianna Fáil, and that his party would judge each issue on its merits and vote accordingly.

Blaney rose next and surprised no-one when he confirmed that he would vote for Haughey. Jim Kemmy, the Independent TD from Limerick, spoke after that. Like Blaney's preference for Haughey, Kemmy's preference for FitzGerald surprised nobody.

Then it was the turn of Tony Gregory. He stated that since the general election, he and his advisers had had extensive talks with Haughey, FitzGerald and O'Leary. In deciding whom he should support for Taoiseach, Gregory said he was guided by a desire to do something for the people he now represented, and to stimulate the development of class politics. But his decision was based specifically on a clear difference between the responses given by Haughey and FitzGerald. Haughey had given a commitment, witnessed and signed by Mickey Mullen, general secretary of the Irish Transport and General Workers' Union, which Gregory said had left him no alternative. Everyone waited in complete silence for details of the commitment.

Gregory announced a promise of £91 million for housing in 1982, and 2,000 houses to be built in Dublin by 1984. Construction on 400 of the houses would start during the year in Dublin's north city area, he added. There was consternation among Fine Gael and Labour TDs. "What about the rest of the country?" shouted Eddie Collins, Fine Gael TD for Waterford. O'Connell appealed for silence, pointing out that this was Gregory's maiden speech, traditionally granted immunity from heckling. Gregory proceeded. Deputy Haughey had promised £20 million for Dublin Corporation to stop a breakdown in its services, said Gregory. The Corporation's Environmental Works scheme was to get a boost of £4 million, for the employment of 500 workers. The repairs and maintenance section was to get £1,500,000 to pay for 150 extra jobs. Clondalkin Paper Mills were to be nationalised, saving 500 jobs there. No motorway would be built through Dublin. The 27-acre Port and Docks Board site would be nationalised. Pre-school education facilities in the city centre would get a £3 million boost. Special taxes would be imposed on derelict sites, office blocks and financial institutions. A national community development agency would be set up with funds of £2 million. Gregory said the items detailed were just some of a very comprehensive list of policies agreed between himself and Haughey. He said that FitzGerald had been sincere and genuine during their talks, but "did not approximate remotely to the commitments given by Fianna Fáil". There was uproar from Fine Gael benches but Haughey remained motionless and expressionless. Gregory spoke through the heckling and finished his speech by saying he would support Fianna Fáil in government so long as the agreement with Haughey was implemented, and other policies pursued by the government were acceptable to him.

Gregory sat down. John O'Connell called the vote "that Deputy Charles J. Haughey be nominated Taoiseach". *"Tá"*, came the cry from one side of the chamber. *"Níl"*, shouted TDs on the other side. A roll-call vote was demanded and O'Connell ordered that the division bells be sounded. The bells rang throughout the Leinster House complex and grounds, warning TDs that in three minutes the doors into the chamber would be locked and the vote taken.

On occasions such as the election of the Taoiseach it was hardly necessary to call TDs to the chamber to vote — they were already there to witness and participate in the event. But during the passage of legislation, many TDs carried on working in their offices while a few colleagues debated in the chamber. They relied on the division bells to warn them that a vote had been called and their presence was needed.

Haughey's political friends left their seats and went over to congratulate him on his impending election as Taoiseach. TDs on all sides of the chamber began chatting to each other. Fine Gael and Labour TDs, and some Fianna Fáil TDs, were astonished by Gregory's speech and talked of the problems his deal with Haughey would create for them. TDs outside Dublin in particular knew they were in for a rough time in the weeks ahead. The air of stiff formality which had pervaded the debate on Haughey's nomination dissolved as more and more TDs began talking to each other and some left their seats to walk about the chamber.

The three Workers' Party men left their places too. Paddy Gallagher desperately wanted a cigarette, and Joe Sherlock wanted to go to the toilet. Accompanied by Proinsias de Rossa, they walked out the main door of the chamber, in plenty of time to return before the division bells stopped and O'Connell called for the voting to begin.

The area just outside the main door was crammed with people. Hundreds of day-passes to Leinster House had been issued to TDs, families, friends and party workers. It was one of those special days on which anyone who had anything to do with politics wanted to be in Leinster House. The stairs up to the public gallery were completely blocked. The stairs down to the entrance hall were also crowded with people and barely passable. Sherlock slowly managed to push and edge his way down the stairs to the toilet. Gallagher waited just outside the door and lit his cigarette. De Rossa stood beside him. Neither he nor Gallagher had any idea of the rules of the House or how Dáil business was conducted. They stood there, cramped and squashed, Gallagher nervously smoking his cigarette and both of them surrounded by Fianna Fáil supporters congratulating them for deciding to vote for Haughey. Time passed.

Suddenly they noticed Sherlock struggling to get back up the stairs, pushing and heaving against the tide of people. There was panic on his face and he gesticulated instructions to them but they didn't understand. Eventually he reached them — too late. The bells had stopped and the doors into the chamber had been locked from the inside. The Taoiseach was about to be elected and they were going to be unable to vote. De Rossa wondered how they would explain themselves.

"This way, lads!" came a voice from the crowd. It was Mark Killilea, the defeated Fianna Fáil TD from Galway. He directed them to a side door which led to the press gallery. Sherlock, Gallagher and de Rossa frantically forged their way through the crowd and plunged through the door into a group of reporters crammed into the narrow press gallery corridor. Pushing and shoving, they managed to reach the door into the gallery itself. From there they jumped into the Distinguished Visitors box (occupied at the time by Haughey's wife, Maureen, and a number of diplomats). and down into the chamber proper. They were just in time.

O'Connell formally called on the TDs to vote their preference on whether or not Haughey should be nominated Taoiseach. Tellers were appointed, TDs began walking up the steps at the back of the chamber and were ready to vote. At the top of the steps, they had to turn right or left and pass through a gate where a teller would tick their name off a list of all members of the House. Those who turned left supported Haughey, while those who went right were against him. All the Fianna Fáil TDs turned left, and so did Sherlock, Gallagher and de Rossa, Blaney and Gregory. Through the right-hand lobby went all the Fine Gael and Labour TDs plus Jim Kemmy.

It was a landslide for Haughey: 86 for him, 79 against. O'Connell announced the result amid cheers from the public gallery. Haughey announced that he was going to President Hillery to be appointed Taoiseach. FitzGerald congratulated him. O'Connell suspended business until 7 p.m.

As Charles Haughey left the chamber and made his way through crowds of cheering supporters to the state car and escort which would take him to Áras an Uachtaráin, his colleagues in Fianna Fáil wondered who among them would be included in the Cabinet to be announced later that evening.

George Colley had already ruled himself out. Shortly after the abortive leadership challenge by Desmond O'Malley, Haughey had spoken to Colley about the formation of the government. He told Colley that there would be no question of him being Tánaiste again, because of his role in the challenge. Haughey's attitude had changed. When the challenge to his leadership was gathering momentum prior to the crucial meeting of the parliamentary party, Haughey had publicly proclaimed that he could not contemplate a government without Colley. If he had said otherwise at the time, he would have run the risk of alienating potential supporters in the party. But once the challenge had collapsed and Haughey was the undisputed leader, all that changed. When Haughey told Colley he could not be Tánaiste he offered him the job of Education Minister. Colley refused unless he could be Tánaiste as well.

In Haughey's first government from 1979 to 1981 Colley had made certain demands to which Haughey had acceded. The most important, as far as Colley was concerned, had been a veto he exercised over the appointment of the Ministers for Justice and Defence. Colley sought the veto to ensure that the security policy pursued by Lynch would be continued under Haughey. He also feared that certain specific security operations, unknown to Haughey, would be discontinued if Haughey or his subordinates discovered them. These involved the undercover methods by which gardaí got information on subversive activities including surveillance and sources close to and within paramilitary groups. In the decade since the Northern troubles erupted, the south's security forces had developed an intelligence network which Colley feared would be placed at risk if some of Haughey's associates were to learn details of its operations.

When he became Taoiseach in 1979, Haughey told Colley that Gerry Collins would remain as Justice Minister but that Paddy Power would be made Minister for Defence. Although he had been TD for Kildare since 1969, Power had made little impact as a national politician and was not seen as one of the bright sparks in Fianna Fáil. He had, however, supported Haughey in the leadership contest with Colley. When Colley was told he was being made Defence Minister, he exercised his veto. He believed that Power was too extreme in his republican views, and too hot-headed. Colley feared that if put in charge of the Army, Paddy Power might do something rash. Haughey accepted the veto and put Power in charge of Fisheries and Forestry. Pádraig Faulkner, TD for Louth and an anti-Haughey man, was demoted from being Minister for Posts and Telegraphs and put into Defence.

But in March 1982, Colley was in no position to make demands of Haughey. When Haughey withdrew the offer of Tánaiste, Colley had the excuse he wanted not to serve in any capacity in government with Haughey.

Martin O'Donoghue had taken a weekend break in London with his wife after the abortive leadership challenge. When he returned, he had a brief and not particularly friendly meeting with Haughey. Haughey let fly at him, demanding to know why he had been involved in O'Malley's challenge, but he ended the meeting by telling O'Donoghue that he was forming a government and would be in touch. Later the same week Haughey met Desmond O'Malley and offered him the job of Education. O'Malley refused but settled for Trade, Commerce and Tourism — a downgrading from his former position as Minister for Industry and Commerce. Haughey finally filled the Education post by offering it to O'Donoghue on the afternoon that the Dáil met.

O'Malley in Trade, Commerce and Tourism and O'Donoghue in Education were the only Cabinet concessions Haughey offered his opponents in the party. When choosing the members of his government, Haughey paid scant regard to the spirit of Faulkner's appeal for co-operation between both factions of the party — the appeal which had helped persuade O'Malley to withdraw his challenge. All the important economic ministries were allocated primarily on the basis of loyalty to Haughey. Haughey was also free to appoint whoever he wanted to Justice and Defence.

He was in his Leinster House office before the Dáil resumed. TDs were being called to see him to be told they were being offered positions in the government. Haughey had spent some time during the day trying to get Michael O'Kennedy to take the job of Attorney General.

O'Kennedy, a 46-year-old TD from Tipperary North, had been Ireland's EEC Commissioner from 1981 to 1982 in succession to Dick Burke. He had had an undistinguished career in Brussels and, although he had considerable cabinet experience as Minister for Foreign Affairs, Minister for Finance and Minister for Transport and Power, he was not seen as one of the party's great innovators. He had surprised Lynch and Colley by supporting Haughey in the 1979 leadership contest. Now, he refused Haughey's offer of the Attorney General's position, because he wanted to be a minister and able to remain a full member of the Cabinet. A number of people tried to persuade him to become AG so that he would retain at least a toe-hold in government. But O'Kennedy would settle for nothing less than a ministry, so Haughey left him out of the administration altogether.

He decided instead to appoint a senior counsel, who had been a member of his defence team during the arms trial: an experienced barrister named Patrick Connolly.

Seámus Brennan was summoned to Haughey's office. Brennan, somewhat surprised, went along. On his way, he passed a number of his colleagues. "Congratulations", whispered Ray Burke as Brennan went in.

Once inside the office, however, it was a different story. Haughey told Brennan in blunt terms that he was not getting a job in the government. The charade of calling Brennan to his office had been a calculated exercise to humiliate him.

The top job — Tánaiste and Minister for Finance — went to Ray MacSharry. It was ironic that MacSharry, a 43-year-old TD from Sligo-Leitrim, should have got George Colley's job. MacSharry's first ministerial experience had been as junior minister to Colley in the Department of Finance, from 1977 to 1979. MacSharry appeared to take something of a gamble and openly allied himself with Haughey during the 1979 leadership contest, proposing him as party leader. When Haughey won, he rewarded MacSharry by making him Minister for Agriculture.

He earned the reputation of being a competent and hard-working minister. MacSharry had jet black hair, deep-set eyes and appeared to be always enveloped in a cloud of cigarette smoke. One commentator described him as being endowed with Transylvanian good looks.

There was some surprise in the party that MacSharry should have been made Tánaiste. Indeed MacSharry himself appeared to be extremely surprised. When Haughey called him to his office and told him he was going to be Tánaiste and Minister for Finance, MacSharry replied: "I will in my fuck!" The two of them argued for a while, until Haughey simply stood up and walked out of the room.

It had been expected that Brian Lenihan would get the job of Tánaiste. Lenihan, a 51-year-old TD from Dublin West, was the only member of the new Cabinet to have served in government with Haughey in the 60s. He was a gregarious and well-liked character. But when, after marching into the Dáil chamber with his new team behind him, Haughey announced that Lenihan was to be Minister for Agriculture, there were howls of laughter from the Fine Gael and Labour TDs. They were apparently unable to contain themselves at the prospect of Lenihan trying to cope with the endless stream of figures, statistics, tables and projections that fly about during negotiations in Brussels. Lenihan had been Foreign Affairs Minister in Haughey's first government and had held that brief as party spokesman in opposition, while also being put in charge of party policy and planning.

Apart from MacSharry in Finance, the two other main economic ministries also went to Haughey supporters: Gene Fitzgerald in Labour and the Public Service and Albert Reynolds in Industry and Energy.

Fitzgerald, from Cork South Central, was well-known for his distinctive rasping voice, and was given to heckling in the Dáil. He had been made Labour Minister by Lynch, and supported Colley in the leadership contest with Haughey. Once

Haughey had won, however, Fitzgerald quickly changed sides and managed to survive. He was made Finance Minister in December 1980 when O'Kennedy became EEC Commissioner, and was notably weak in that position, allowing Haughey to push him around and usurp much of his role.

Reynolds, a 46-year-old businessman from Longford-Westmeath, had made money in dance-halls and pet foods before entering politics. He was a strong supporter of Haughey and had been rewarded with the ministry of Posts, Telegraphs, Transport and Power in Haughey's first government. Between them, Fitzgerald and Reynolds were to be responsible for industrial relations and job creation in the new administration. Foreign Affairs went to Gerry Collins, a 43-year-old TD from Limerick West. Collins had supported Colley in 1979 but since then had managed to remain aloof from the leadership squabbles. He had experience in government in the Departments of Justice and Posts and Telegraphs. John Wilson, from Cavan-Monaghan, was made Minister for Posts and Telegraphs. The oldest member of the cabinet at 58, Wilson was a classicist, teacher and lecturer — an academic more than a politician. He became politically active late in life, only joining Fianna Fáil in the early 70s and becoming a TD in 1973. He had been spokesman on Arts and Education when Lynch made him Education Minister in 1977. He survived the Haughey takeover, although he had supported Colley. During the O'Malley challenge, he supported Haughey.

Ray Burke, a 38-year-old former auctioneer from Dublin North, was given Environment, a post he had held from October 1980 to July 1981 in Haughey's first administration. When Haughey reshuffled his front bench in January 1982, Burke was demoted and made party chief whip. In 1979 he had supported Colley, but his active involvement in fending off the O'Malley challenge as chief whip restored his fortunes. Michael Woods was made Minister for Health and Social Welfare, a job Haughey had previously given him in 1979. Woods, a doctor of agricultural sciences, had supported Colley in 1979. In the summer of that year, he was made junior minister in the Taoiseach's Department and also government chief whip. He feared that his political rise was over when Haughey won but he was in fact promoted and developed a curious relationship with the new leader. Haughey appeared to have little respect for Woods and frequently abused him verbally in front of his colleagues. Woods did whatever Haughey told him to do; during his first term as Health Minister he was largely ineffective and initiated nothing without Haughey's approval.

Three men with no previous experience in Cabinet were also appointed, to the surprise of some in the party. Brendan Daly (42), also a strong Haughey supporter from Clare, was given Fisheries and Forestry. He had been a junior minister in Haughey's first government. His elevation to the Cabinet was caused partly by the absence of Colley and O'Kennedy but was also designed to do down his constituency colleague, Sylvester Barrett. Another surprise was Pádraig Flynn, a 42-year-old former national school teacher and publican from Mayo West, who was made Minister for the Gaeltacht. Like Daly, Flynn's main claim to fame was his support for Haughey — but Flynn had always been more open about his loyalty to the Boss. Previously Haughey had made Flynn a junior minister in Transport and Power and he had been expected to get another junior ministry this time.

Haughey finally got his way and was able to appoint Paddy Power Minister for Defence. But the biggest surprise, even among some Haughey supporters, was the last post announced: Seán Doherty, Minister for Justice. Doherty, a 37-year-old TD from Roscommon, was one of Haughey's most strident supporters in the parliamentary party and was a junior Justice Minister from 1979 to 1981.

This appointment surprised O'Malley and shocked Colley. A number of Haughey supporters were also disturbed. Doherty was a former member of the Garda Siochána. He joined the force in 1965 and served in Sligo. In 1971 he moved to Dublin, first to the suburban station at Donnybrook, and subsequently to the Special Branch, based in Dublin Castle. He resigned from the guards in 1973 to be co-opted to Roscommon county council on the death of his father. Before leaving the gardaí, Doherty registered for law courses in University College, Dublin and the King's Inns, but he graduated from neither. He was elected to the Dáil in 1977, and was one of the back-benchers who worked to ensure that Haughey succeeded Lynch. When Doherty was junior Justice Minister under Gerry

Collins, the two did not get on particularly well. Doherty was given responsibility for law reform but did little or no work in that area — he longed for the power of being a full minister. Despite the fact that Haughey had made Doherty the spokesman on justice when the party was in opposition, not everyone believed he would give him the job in government. This was because of his background as a Garda, and particularly because of the unusual position Doherty would be in as an ex-Garda dealing with the Garda Commissioner, Patrick McLaughlin.

O'Malley and Colley had not imagined that Haughey would appoint Seán Doherty Justice Minister in the new government. They had briefly discussed the likely composition of the cabinet, but were not especially worried about the security ministries, Justice and Defence, because, to their knowledge, nothing unusual had happened in either area during Haughey's first government. O'Malley and Colley both believed that Doherty would be totally unsuitable for Justice — they saw him as power-hungry, ruthless and ill-equipped to handle some of the routinely sensitive functions of the ministry. Colley toyed with the idea of voting against approval of the government if Haughey put Doherty into Justice. But they decided that Haughey, as a former occupant of the office, was too aware of the potential danger of having Doherty in Justice and would appoint someone else.

They were wrong.

When Haughey announced his Cabinet to the Dáil, he said he would be appointing junior ministers at a later date. He defended the deal with Tony Gregory and said the effort to revive the inner city of Dublin would be made in the interests of the whole nation. Reflecting worry that people outside the capital might not think much of the deal, Haughey said that success in Dublin would be followed by similar efforts in every part of the country. Economic problems would be dealt with by the government with courage, determination, imagination and vision. But the Northern Ireland problem would be the first political priority of the government, he proclaimed. "No opportunity can be lost which offers any prospect of finding a lasting solution". He went on to state his hope that the initiative begun in December 1980 by himself and Margaret

Thatcher, the British Prime Minister, would be resumed. But it was clear that the lasting solution to which Haughey referred had only one meaning, as far as he was concerned. He said his government would actively seek "the final withdrawal of the British military and political presence".

Neil Blaney, sitting on the back benches to Haughey's left, was pleased. The Taoiseach was living up to his first commitment to the Donegal TD — he was saying publicly and in clear terms what Blaney knew he believed (and said) in private. James Prior, the Northern Ireland Secretary, was not so well pleased. He was in the middle of trying to get the political parties in Northern Ireland to agree to join the Northern Ireland Assembly: a partial internal solution to the North's problem which Haughey had, by implication, written off before it had even started. Haughey also told the Dáil that he would go to Washington for a St Patrick's Day luncheon in the White House with President Ronald Reagan. Blaney hoped Haughey would use the occasion to underline further his attitude to Northern Ireland.

Garret FitzGerald and Michael O'Leary both spoke against the new government announced by Haughey but the remainder of the debate was marked more by a speech from Oliver J. Flanagan, the 61-year-old Fine Gael TD from Laois-Offaly. Flanagan, a right-wing politician, aggressively conservative on moral and social issues, made a lengthy and somewhat bizarre address in which he attacked the media, praised Haughey, offered advice to ministers in the new government, approved the Gregory deal and attacked FitzGerald, his party leader, by implication throughout the entire address. Tom Fitzpatrick, the Fine Gael TD for Cavan-Monaghan, irritated Haughey by highlighting the absence of George Colley from the Cabinet and wondering out loud how Brian Lenihan would handle his new ministry. But Haughey remained calm — he knew he had won the day and nothing could stop him forming the government of his choice. The division was called and the new government was approved by a majority of seven votes.

George Colley stole some of the limelight from Haughey by issuing a statement just after the government was approved explaining why he was not a member of it. Colley acknowledged that Haughey refused to make him Tánaiste because of his "recent activity in the party" but he maintained the underlying cause was Haughey's determination to reduce Colley's influence on government policy.

But while Haughey had cause for celebration on his election as Taoiseach and the successful formation of his government, he was acutely aware that his was a minority administration. Things would have been so much easier if Fianna Fáil had just won more seats — it was a problem which had first exercised his mind some weeks ago, on February 20th in fact, the day the counting of votes in the general election finished. On that day, Haughey met a number of his close associates both in his home at Kinsealy and in Fianna Fáil's headquarters in Mount Street. It was apparent that even with the assured support in the Dáil of Neil Blaney, the party was still one short of an overall majority. Some of Haughey's associates suggested that informal approaches be made to Oliver J. Flanagan to see if he was willing to be Ceann Comhairle. Others suggested that the same proposal should be put to Seán Treacy, the 58-year-old Labour TD from Tipperary South who was Ceann Comhairle during the Cosgrave coalition government. Had either accepted, John O'Connell would have remained free to vote for Fianna Fáil —an option which would have appealed to him, given his declared admiration for Haughey.

But there was another option open to Haughey. Because Michael O'Kennedy had resigned his post in Brussels, the government would have to appoint a new EEC Commissioner — a plum job carrying a salary of around £70,000 plus a lot of prestige. Haughey could give the job to a Fine Gael TD, who would have to resign his Dáil seat, thereby causing a by-election which Fianna Fáil would fight and, with any luck, would win. It was an idea so politically outrageous, so daring — almost swashbuckling — that even Fine Gael people spoke of it as a joke in the immediate aftermath of the election. They thought it so preposterous that not even Haughey would try it. But as the election results became clear, this was exactly what Haughey *was* considering.

MacSharry advised Haughey to give the job to Ted Nealon, the Fine Gael TD in MacSharry's constituency, Sligo-Leitrim. MacSharry believed that Nealon was disenchanted with Fitz-Gerald's leadership of Fine Gael, and disappointed he had been made only a junior minister in FitzGerald's government. He also believed that the prospect of a spell in opposition did not appeal to Nealon and that he could be tempted to take the Brussels job. Another suggestion was that the job be offered to Dick Burke, one of Fine Gael's three TDs in Dublin West. Burke, a 49-year-old former Education Minister and Fine Gael chief whip, had been the EEC Commissioner from 1977 to 1981 in succession to Patrick Hillery. He returned to domestic politics by being re-elected for Dublin West in June 1981, and again in February 1982. Burke was reputed to be at odds with Fitz-Gerald and resentful of not being given a job in his government.

The first moves to get a Fine Gael TD to take the EEC job were made by Ray MacSharry. On Tuesday, February 23rd — five days after the general election, and two days before the parliamentary party meeting at which Desmond O'Malley was expected to challenge Haughey's leadership — MacSharry offered the job to Nealon. Both men were in Sligo for the funeral in Ballyrush of Garda Patrick Reynolds, who had been murdered a few days before while on duty in Tallaght, Dublin. MacSharry approached Nealon and said that Fianna Fáil was going to form a government in which he would have a position of great influence. Jobs were up for grabs. There was the job in Brussels. Fianna Fáil had three out of four of the seats in Sligo-Leitrim: they wanted the fourth. Was Nealon interested? Nealon told MacSharry that if Fianna Fáil wanted his seat, they would have to beat him for it in a general election. MacSharry knew that in a by-election, Fianna Fáil would almost certainly win. They had won over 53% of the vote in the general election just contested, compared to Fine Gael's $37\frac{1}{2}\%$.

As MacSharry was tempting Nealon in Sligo, a similar feeler was put out to Dick Burke in Dublin. On his way into Leinster House, he met Albert Reynolds. The two engaged in small talk about the election and Burke agreed that it seemed as though Fianna Fáil would be forming a government; the odds were in their favour. Reynolds mentioned that jobs would have to be allocated. The government would have to fill the Brussels post . . . certainly they would have to get someone to stay longer than Michael O'Kennedy. "You went the full term in your time, Dick", Reynolds mused, "don't suppose you would be interested in going back?" Burke didn't say no. But the conversation was overheard by someone who tipped off the *Evening Herald.* The following day, the newspaper headline "FF Offer Top Euro Job To Burke" led to much speculation. A Fianna Fáil statement denied the report, claiming that no representations of any kind had been made to Burke on behalf of Fianna Fáil. Nonetheless, the seed had been planted, and it continued to grow.

Burke refused to deny completely that he had been unofficially offered the job, but the affair disappeared from the headlines when the newspapers were swamped by O'Malley's abortive challenge to Haughey. Behind the scenes, however, Burke was considering the proposal. Shortly after the *Herald* report appeared, he spoke briefly with Liam Hourican and Michael Lillis. Hourican, formerly RTE's diplomatic correspondent and press officer in Burke's first *cabinet*, was government press secretary at the time and was about to be out of a job if, as seemed likely, FitzGerald lost power. Lillis was a career diplomat in the Department of Foreign Affairs. He had worked in the Irish Embassy in Washington until mid-1979, when he went to Brussels to work for Burke. He later returned to Foreign Affairs but then FitzGerald brought him into his office as advisor to the Taoiseach on diplomacy. The chances of Burke being offered the job still seemed a little remote at this stage.

One man who was able to tell Haughey quite a lot about Burke was Pádraig Ó hAnnracháin, who was in Haughey's home immediately after the election.

Pádraig Ó hAnnracháin was a career civil servant who once worked in Bord na Móna. He was private secretary to Éamon de Valera in the 50s, and he also worked with Dev when Fianna Fáil was in opposition. He was head of the Government Information Service under Dev, Seán Lemass and Jack Lynch. In 1973 when Fianna Fáil went into opposition for the first time in 16 years, Ó hAnnracháin transferred to the Department of Education as an assistant secretary. Burke was Minister at the time and he and Ó hAnnracháin got on extremely well. By the time Burke left the Department in 1977 when Fianna Fáil swept back to power, Ó hAnnracháin was a trusted confidant.

On the first day that Haughey was Taoiseach in December

1979, Ó hAnnracháin was back in Government Buildings, once more at the centre of power. He was, in effect, Chief of Staff in Haughey's office, although such a post did not exist. When Haughey arrived in his office every morning he would ask for Ó hAnnracháin to discuss the day's work. Ó hAnnracháin would often then delegate tasks to others or perhaps spend some time contacting newspaper editors to ensure they understood what the government and Haughey were doing. Haughey consulted Ó hAnnracháin on almost everything: Ó hAnnracháin had been close to de Valera but he was even closer to Haughey. He proved an immediate asset to Haughey by acting as go-between when Haughey was trying to get Burke to accept the EEC job. A number of meetings took place between the two men in their respective homes — Ó hAnnracháin's in Sutton, Burke's in Donnybrook. The Dáil was due to re-assemble on March 23rd. A few days before, after Haughey returned from his St. Patrick's Day visit to the United States, Burke was formally offered the job.

Burke began to put together a team to go with him to Brussels. On Monday evening, March 22nd, he contacted Hourican and offered him a place in his *cabinet*. Hourican accepted but said he wanted FitzGerald to approve. Burke had not contacted FitzGerald to tell him what was going on, but the following day he spoke to Lillis and asked him to go and talk with FitzGerald. Lillis told FitzGerald that Haughey had offered the job to Burke, and that Burke wanted to accept it with his blessing. FitzGerald was dismayed, but admitted that he had not treated Burke well. Twice he had made him run in a constituency where he was ill-at-ease. Burke, whose public image was that of a patrician, rather pompous man with right-wing views, was like a fish out of water among the new working-class housing estates of Dublin West. Burke believed that Fine Gael could win the by-election in Dublin West, and he wanted FitzGerald to make a speech in the Dáil welcoming the appointment after it was announced by Haughey. FitzGerald did not commit himself during the conversation with Lillis.

The Fine Gael parliamentary party was to hold its weekly meeting the following day, Wednesday March 24th. Haughey had told his Cabinet that he had offered the job to Burke. It was the first time the matter had come up for discussion, despite all the rumours. When Haughey made the announcement, Gene FitzGerald looked at him and remarked: "A master stroke, Taoiseach, 'tis only yourself could think of it". Not everyone around the table agreed with his assessment; Fine Gael had the edge on Fianna Fáil in Dublin West and if the percentage support for both parties remained the same, Fine Gael would hold the seat in a by-election. But Haughey had already informed Gaston Thorn, President of the EEC Commission, that Ireland's new Commissioner was to be Dick Burke. Thorn in turn informed his fellow Commissioners at about 10.15 that morning — 9.15 Irish time. The word spread fast in Brussels, and RTE radio reported the news as Fine Gael TDs were driving to Leinster House for their meeting.

They savaged Burke. During the meeting he sat at the back of the room and listened to his colleagues as they castigated him. They forced him to reject Haughey's offer and withdraw his earlier acceptance of it. Few TDs took Burke's side — Oliver J. Flanagan and John Bruton were among them, while John Kelly said it was unfair to pressurise Burke either way —and many were against. Particularly scathing in his comments was Jim Mitchell, the party's senior TD in Dublin West, who had played a major role in securing Burke's election there.

In the middle of the meeting, FitzGerald and Burke went for a stroll in the Leinster House garden, to allow the party to discuss Fine Gael's leadership in the light of the general election results. Burke agreed to withdraw his acceptance of the offer. He later issued a statement saying he was grateful for the honour of being offered the job, but was declining. Haughey commented tersely that he and Burke had shaken hands on the deal, but he added that the offer was still open.

After the Fine Gael parliamentary party meeting, Burke went home to bed, exhausted and drained, not a little shaken by the ferocity of the opposition within his own party to him taking the job. The following day in the Dáil, Burke caused a minor flurry during the budget debate when he left his seat in the opposition benches and crossed the floor to have a talk with his Fianna Fáil namesake, Ray Burke. Dick said he wanted to talk about the offer, but Ray said that the Dáil chamber was not the most appropriate place to have such a conversation. So both men left the chamber and went to Ray's office. They discussed the offer of the job at length, and it was clear that Dick wanted to accept it. When the meeting ended, Dick slipped quietly away; Ray re-emerged outside the Dáil chamber and was surrounded by reporters. "We were talking about roads and local government", he declared. Meanwhile Haughey, clearly desperate to cause a by-election, saw to it that Ted Nealon was again approached and offered the job. Nealon again refused. But Haughey need not have worried: early on Friday Richard Burke was in Brussels, talking about coming back.

Burke met Gaston Thorn. Thorn had not got on well with Michael O'Kennedy, and was ready to accept Burke back into the Commission. At the same time, however, he was not in a position to haggle there and then over what responsibilities might be given to Burke if he returned. Burke also met Christopher Tugendhat, Britain's Commissioner, who had clashed with O'Kennedy when the Irishman tried to take over some of his portfolio. He had lunch with Frederika Wegwitz, his former secretary, who he hoped would come and work for him again.

By the end of the day, Burke had definitely made up his—mind — he was going to accept the offer, irrespective of what Fine Gael might say. The attractions of a commissioner's life in Brussels finally smothered his loyalty to Fine Gael. By going to Brussels and talking with Thorn and the others, Burke convinced himself that Europe needed him more than Fine Gael.

That Sunday, Charles Haughey flew to Brussels for the following day's celebrations to mark the 25th anniversary of the Treaty of Rome and founding of the EEC. Haughey was booked into the same hotel as Burke, the Hyatt Regency. The city was awash with top politicians and men long retired from the political scene, including former Taoisigh Jack Lynch, Garret FitzGerald, and Liam Cosgrave, and former Foreign Affairs Ministers Jim Dooge and Michael O'Kennedy. Haughey and Burke both ate lunch on Monday at the Royal Palace, where they spoke briefly. Burke was in his element —surrounded by enough important people to reassure him of his own importance. That night he flew back to Dublin.

The following morning, Tuesday, Hourican and Lillis met

Burke in his home, but he told them that he could not decide which of them he should appoint *chef de cabinet.* He decided they should toss a coin: Hourican won; at £45,000 a year, he was £10,000 better off than Lillis, who settled for deputy *chef de cabinet.* That evening, Hourican flew out to Brussels, and was followed by Burke.

Haughey announced that he had nominated Burke for the EEC job because he was the only person available with the necessary qualifications. FitzGerald replied that it was a case of simple political opportunism. But many of Haughey's supporters did not like seeing a top job go to a Fine Gael man, and Haughey's opponents in the party were also most unhappy. They disliked the "stroke-pulling" image, and were highly displeased with Haughey's recent selection of junior ministers, announced in the middle of the Burke controversy.

Two junior posts had gone to TDs who had promised to support Haughey during the O'Malley challenge: Ber Cowan from Laois-Offaly and Terry Leyden from Roscommon. Desmond O'Malley had been to Haughey to plead for posts for Seamus Brennan and Mary Harney. If Haughey was unable to bring himself to draw from all sides of the party to make up the cabinet, perhaps he could at least do it with the junior ministries. O'Malley was to be disappointed: Haughey flatly refused to appoint Brennan. He summoned Harney to his office, where he told her she had become very petty and had been acting like a schoolgirl. Harney snapped back that it was he who had become petty. Haughey demanded examples. Harney said he had struck certain TDs' names off his Christmas card list. Haughey denied ever having done any such thing; in front of Harney he rang O'Malley and asked if he had got his Christmas card. O'Malley said he hadn't, and Haughey hung up. Later that day there was a row in the Dáil about the Burke affair, but Haughey still found time to call Harney back to his office. *Look,* he said, *there's my Christmas card list and everybody's on it.* Harney examined the list. There were little ticks beside all the names indicating that cards had been sent. How could anybody suggest that he would not send them a Christmas card?

Haughey was like that. He paid attention to the little things.

Chapter Five

I don't intend to be a prisoner of my past.
Charles Haughey, October 1982

Several days after he had become leader of Fianna Fáil in December 1979, Charles Haughey was having lunch in the restaurant in Leinster House. Among the company at his table was Martin O'Donoghue. The menu was passed around and O'Donoghue ordered duck for his main course. The waitress told him the duck was off: O'Donoghue selected something else. Haughey remarked that he had some of the finest duck in Ireland on his lands at Kinsealy. There were polite expressions of interest and the conversation moved on to other topics. Several weeks later, Haughey's garda driver called to O'Donoghue's house in Dartry in south Dublin. O'Donoghue was not at home but the driver left a package with his wife Evelyn. Inside, she found a dead duck and a card from Haughey. The card read: "Shot on Saturday".

The incident encapsulated one of the central features of the new Taoiseach. His actions gave rise to wildly diverging interpretations while his own motives remained enigmatic. Haughey's friends said that the gift of the duck was a gesture of reconciliation to O'Donoghue, who had been dropped peremptorily from Haughey's first cabinet. Haughey's enemies within Fianna Fáil saw it as a Mafia-style message, rubbing home the fact that O'Donoghue's ministerial career was as dead as the duck. Both interpretations may be unjust to Haughey. But his studied mannerisms and his instinct for the telling gesture suggested that most of his actions were calculated. In any event, after the most controversial career in modern Irish politics, few people were prepared to grant Haughey the benefit of innocence.

By March 1982, however, most people were prepared to acknowledge that Haughey had the political abilities to keep his new minority administration in power. He had failed to win an overall majority in the Dáil but he had put together the parliamentary votes which had brought Fianna Fáil back into government. The cost of those votes had opened up a new seam of criticism, but nobody in Leinster House doubted that Haughey was the person most likely to keep such a precariously balanced government in power. In spite of his poor showing in the public opinion polls, and the best efforts of his internal Fianna Fáil enemies to dump him, Haughey was Taoiseach in his own right. He was no longer reliant on the Dáil majority bequeathed him by his predecessor.

Outside his own constituency, where he enjoyed massive personal support, Haughey had never been a popular politician. In the mid 1970s, he and Conor Cruise O'Brien, the former Labour Party minister who made a political career out of debunking nationalism and dogging Haughey's heels, vied with each other for the distinction of being, according to opinion polls, the least popular political figures in the country. The polls showed after 1979 that Haughey never matched the popularity of Jack Lynch, even at Lynch's lowest ebb during his last months as Taoiseach. Yet Haughey came to dominate politics and, by 1982, had become an election issue in himself. The February general election was fought to an unusually high degree around his political record, his potential and his personal ambitions. Although he was never particularly well liked, he excited more public interest than any other politician, aroused the strongest political passions, and fascinated his enemies as much as he delighted his friends.

Friends and enemies alike had been mesmerised by his relentless pursuit of power. He was living proof of the usefulness of the dictum that, in politics, one should never resign. He wore his ambition on his sleeve in a totally un-Irish manner, the antithesis of the Lynch type of "reluctant politician" who had to be persuaded into every office. Haughey *wanted* to be Taoiseach, and few people seemed to have doubted that from his first steps into electoral politics, in 1951, the year in which he married Maureen Lemass, daughter of Fianna Fáil founding member and future Taoiseach, Seán Lemass. His progress towards his goal was interrupted by events which appeared, literally and figuratively, to have almost killed him. But he pursued the job with a degree of determination that demanded to be noticed and that set him apart from his colleagues. He got things done, often by doing nothing himself but merely by being there. That, at the end of the day, was how he became Taoiseach in 1979.

Haughey was introduced to Fianna Fáil at secondary school by George Colley and Harry Boland, two classmates from Fianna Fáil families at St. Joseph's Christian Brothers school in Fairview on the north side of Dublin. It took him six years and three elections to get into the Dáil, but within his first term which began in 1957, he stepped up the first rung of the ministerial ladder. In spite of later suggestions that his father-in-law, then Taoiseach, slowed down Haughey's advancement to avoid accusations of nepotism, Seán Lemass appointed him parlimentary secretary (junior minister) to the Minister for Justice. The following year, 1961, and after a general election, Lemass promoted him to the cabinet as Minister for Justice.

For the remainder of the 1960s Haughey was a cabinet minister, occasionally controversial and always the embodiment of the spirit of the age, when something akin to the American dream hit Ireland. From Justice, he went to Agriculture, as part of a sudden Lemass reshuffle to limit the damage caused by the resignation of the incumbent in that department, Paddy Smith. In spite of tough battles with farmers over food prices, he retained the portfolio after the 1965 general election. Haughey had come far enough by then to be among the contenders to succeed Lemass when he retired in 1966. But he was not particularly popular with party backbenchers, who found him inaccessible as a minister, arrogant and inconsiderate of their needs. When he went looking for support for the leadership, he found little enough. His school friend, George Colley, was the choice of the party's old guard and was seen as the standard bearer for Fianna Fáil's traditions and republicanism. Neil Blaney was also in the running, but Lemass decided to seek a compromise and avoid a contest. He persuaded Jack Lynch to stand and the others, except Colley, stood down. Colley was beaten by 52 votes to 19.

Haughey's power and influence continued to grow under Lynch, initially a weak leader who exercised little control over the younger elements in the Cabinet. He appointed Haughey to Finance, the most powerful ministry outside the Taoiseach's department, where Haughey's standing was increased by the boom in the economy as the dismantling of protectionist trade policies was completed to make way for a rawer brand of capitalism.

By the end of the 1960s, the main political problem was not the economy but the North, where marches in support of civil rights for the Catholic minority had begun. The temperature and the counter-violence escalated until a new and more vicious phase of street battles and sectarian attacks on Catholic areas developed in August 1969 after the annual Apprentice Boys' parade in Derry. As the first deaths were recorded and streets of houses burned out in Belfast, thousands of refugees travelled to the South from Belfast's threatened Catholic areas. Their representatives followed them to Dublin for meetings with ministers and officials, seeking help in the form of financial aid and of arms. Public opinion in the South was inflamed by events in the North: Fianna Fáil's own rhetoric had caught up with it. The party, in government, had to do something.

Jack Lynch declared that Dublin could not stand by, and sent his Foreign Minister, Patrick Hillery, off to New York to seek United Nations involvement. At home, Lynch announced that mobile military hospitals would be set up in border areas, to treat nationalist victims of violence. Haughey, as Minister for Finance, announced that the government was making funds available "for the relief of victims of the disturbances in the Six Counties" and that the money would be channelled through the Irish Red Cross. The cabinet decided, but did not announce, that the Army was to prepare contingency plans; it also decided to make available whatever money was needed for it to re-equip. A cabinet committee was set up to develop contacts with people in the North. This committee was composed of Charles Haughey, Neil Blaney, Padraig Faulkner and Jim Gibbons.

In that highly charged atmosphere of autumn 1969, an elaborate plan was developed to import arms into the South for use in the North, to defend nationalist areas. Captain James

Kelly, an Army intelligence officer who had been operating in the North, acted as a go-between for the intended recipients of the weapons and certain members of the southern government, and as the arms purchaser. During the following months and into the early summer of 1970, he met Haughey and other members of the cabinet committee on a number of occasions. Meanwhile, the state had paid out almost £100,000 for the "relief of distress" in the North, as the object of the fund was termed when it was retrospectively sanctioned by the Dáil in April 1970. Some was paid to help people who found themselves homeless in Belfast and to aid other victims of the troubles. Most of the money was paid to the Irish Red Cross which was used, by arrangement, as a conduit for laundering the money through to a committee of respectable Northerners. The Irish branch of the Red Cross could not, under its own rules, become involved, in the North. Much of the money ended up in two bank accounts, held under fictitious names, in Dublin and Clones, Co. Monaghan. Captain Kelly drew money from the Dublin account to make a down payment to a West German arms dealer for a consignment that was to include 500 pistols and 180,000 rounds of ammunition. The consignment was due to arrive by ship at Dublin port in March 1970 but was not dispatched, apparently because of customs problems in Belgium. Only a load of bullet-proof vests got through. The bulk of the shipment was then due to arrive by air at Dublin Airport during a weekend in mid-April 1970. But by then, something had gone seriously awry.

Precisely what had happened is still a matter of dispute. The Garda Special Branch had learned of the shipment and was waiting to seize it when it arrived. Lynch was told about it on Monday, April 20th, by the Secretary of the Department of Justice, Peter Berry. Two days later, as Haughey was due to present his budget to the Dáil, he ended up in hospital seriously ill with a fractured skull. He had fallen, it was announced, from a horse at his stables in Kinsealy. Lynch saw him in hospital in the middle of the following week and asked for an explanation about the arms shipment; Haughey requested time to consider his position. In early May, however, the opposition leader, Liam Cosgrave, received an anonymous note implying that several ministers were involved in arms imports. He went to

Lynch and forced his hand. On May 5th, Lynch demanded the resignations of Haughey and Blaney after they had refused to offer them. At 2.50 a.m. the following morning, Lynch announced the dismissals, on the grounds that the two ministers "did not subscribe fully to government policy on the North". A third minister, Kevin Boland, resigned in sympathy with the two men, as did Paudge Brennan, the junior minister in Boland's Department of Local Government. Haughey denied in a public statement that he had played any part in any illegal or attempted illegal importation of arms. He added that he accepted fully the Taoiseach's decision "as I believe that the unity of the Fianna Fáil party is of greater importance to the welfare of the nation than my political career".

Haughey, Blaney and three others, Captain Kelly, John Kelly (a militant republican from Belfast), and Albert Lukyx (a Belgian businessman living in Ireland) were charged with trying to import arms illegally. The district court dismissed the case against Blaney, but the other four were sent for trial to the Central Criminal Court, now accused of conspiring with each other and with persons unknown to import firearms and ammunition illegally. The trial opened finally on October 6th and ended just over two weeks later on October 23rd, with the jury finding the four accused men not guilty. It took the jurors two hours and twelve minutes to decide their verdict.

Amid the welter of detailed and often sensational evidence, the prosecution case centred around a series of conversations which Haughey was alleged to have had with three others —Jim Gibbons, the Defence Minister, Peter Berry, the Secretary of the Department of Justice, and Anthony Fagan, a civil servant who had acted as Haughey's private secretary and press officer. Berry told the court that Haughey had phoned him at home on Saturday, April 18th; Haughey asked him if the cargo due at Dublin Airport the next day would be allowed through if a guarantee was given that the goods would go directly to the North. Berry said it would not, and repeated that it would be seized by the gardaí.

The following day, Fagan got a phone call from Captain Kelly who was in Vienna asking for instructions from "the boss man". Fagan told Haughey about the call next morning, April 20th; Haughey said he had discussed the matter with Gibbons and they had agreed that the whole thing should be called off. Fagan phoned Kelly to tell him before midday, the deadline given him by Kelly during his first call. Gibbons said he did not talk to Haughey until later on Monday, April 20th. Haughey said he would stop the consignment for a month but Gibbons urged him to stop it altogether.

That was the prosecution's account of events. But in his evidence, Haughey told a different story. He had phoned Berry, he said, because he had been told the Special Branch wanted a minister to sanction the cargo due to arrive at the airport. He had asked Berry questions. When Berry told him the consignment would be seized by the Special Branch, Haughey had replied: "it had best be called off so, whatever it is". He denied that he had given Fagan instructions to telephone Captain Kelly in Vienna. As for the conversation which Gibbons had described, Haughey said, on oath: "That did not happen". The trial judge, Mr. Justice Séamus Henchy, declared in his summing up that it was not possible to reconcile the differences in evidence between Haughey and Gibbons and between Haughey and Berry. "I would like to be able to suggest some way you can avoid holding there is perjury in this case," he added.

Haughey maintained that he did not know the details of Captain Kelly's operation, but believed that they were part of the Army's compliance with the government directive that it should prepare for all contingencies. Haughey said he had a free hand in the distribution of the "aid fund", but he did not know the details once he had taken the broad decisions. He denied under cross-examination that he knew from Captain Kelly, or from any other source, that an attempt was underway to import arms. Asked if he had contemplated that the "aid fund" be used to buy arms he replied: "No". He arranged customs clearance for the arms because he thought that the request had come from Army Intelligence. He believed the confusion about the consignment at Dublin Airport was due to disputes between the Special Branch and Army Intelligence.

The verdict of Not Guilty sparked off jubilant scenes around the Four Courts where the trial had taken place. Amid renditions of "A Nation Once Again" and shouts of "We're the real Republicans", Haughey addressed his co-defendants as "fellow patriots" and gave an impromptu press conference at which he called upon those who were responsible for the débâcle to "take the honourable course that is open to them". If, as everyone assumed, he meant that Lynch should resign, he was disappointed. Lynch returned from a visit to the United States three days later, to be met at Dublin Airport by a clear majority of his Dáil deputies and, symbolically, by President Éamon de Valera's secretary.

Unlike Blaney, Boland and Brennan, who all left Fianna Fáil over the arms crisis, Haughey decided to stay on. It was a difficult decision to implement, but Haughey stuck with it. It required him to humiliate himself by voting confidence in Jim Gibbons in the Dáil when everyone in the Chamber knew exactly what he thought of Gibbons. It also required him to back Lynch repeatedly, although it was well known that he despised his party leader. But he used his time productively, touring the country to address meetings of party cumainn, making himself accessible to party members inside the Dáil as well as outside and keeping his political image alive with the occasional soft speech or attendance at some event, preferably cultural.

In 1975, during Liam Cosgrave's coalition government, Lynch was forced to bring Haughey back onto his front bench, as the party was suffering from low morale in the mid-point of its first term in opposition since 1957. Jim Gibbons subsequently insisted that Haughey had promised to clear his (Gibbons's) name prior to assuming his front bench post as shadow health minister. Gibbons wanted a public statement from Haughey to the effect that Gibbons had told the truth during the arms trial: this invited Haughey to admit, by implication at least, that he had committed perjury. He did not take up that invitation.

With Fianna Fáil's landslide victory in 1977, Haughey was back at the cabinet table, with responsibility for Health and Social Welfare. The portfolio was an ideal one to further his career: it was remote from the economic ministries, which found themselves in trouble within two years, and it brought Haughey into close contact with backbenchers through their incessant representations on behalf of constituents to the Department of Social Welfare. Haughey made no secret of his contempt for some of his cabinet colleagues; they reciprocated by treating him with extreme suspicion. One illustration of this mutual suspicion developed during the lengthy post office strike during the first half of 1979. The ministers concerned most directly with the dispute felt that it was of crucial importance to hold the line against an excessive pay rise which would then snowball through the public service. As pressure to settle the strike increased with public frustration and the political requirements of local and European Parliament elections, Haughey told his colleagues that he was having private talks with a leader of the post office union with whom he was friendly. Other ministers were content to have Haughey do this for a time, but then they became suspicious that he was trying to prolong the strike in anticipation of the damage it would cause to Lynch's leadership. Thereafter, Haughey was excluded from all discussion of the progress of the strike, which took place outside the cabinet or in committees of which he was not a member.

Lynch and his colleagues were right to fear the consequences of the strike on the two sets of elections. Fianna Fáil did exceptionally badly in the European elections, winning only five of the fifteen seats with 35% of the votes cast, the lowest vote Fianna Fáil had ever achieved in a national election. Lynch's troubles multiplied after that. The party's back benchers, left out of the centre of things more than ever because of the government's twenty-seat majority, were restive and apprehensive about the next election.

A caucus meeting during the autumn of 1979 attracted 21 dissatisfied deputies. When challenged by Lynch at a full party meeting only one person, Pádraig Flynn, admitted being there. The chairman of the ad hoc group was Jackie Fahey, a 52-year-old deputy from Waterford who had been in the Dáil since 1965, and its secretary was Charles McCreevy. The declared aim was to discuss the direction of the party, but the intention was to weaken Lynch and to promote Haughey's candidature for the leadership.

Their efforts were helped considerably by a controversy over the granting of permission to British aircraft to overfly border areas. The more Lynch tried to explain that there was nothing very new in the procedure, the more difficulty he found himself in with his back benchers. Eventually Bill Loughnane, a hard-line nationalist from Clare, declared publicly that Lynch had lied about the affair. Lynch was in the US at the time, and in his absence, Colley oversaw a move to expel Loughnane from the parliamentary party. The attempt to discipline Loughnane failed, serving to undermine further the authority of the party leadership. Síle de Valera had also dealt Lynch a serious blow with a speech which questioned his policy on the North; she maintained that it was out of tune with the attitude of the party founded by her grandfather, Éamon de Valera. The impact of her criticism was all the greater because she had rejected attempts by Lynch to dissuade her from delivering the speech at a commemoration for Liam Lynch, the leader of the anti-treaty IRA in 1922.

Lynch's fate was sealed when Fianna Fáil lost two by-elections in Cork on November 7th, 1979; the party won only 36% of the votes cast. By the end of November, Fahey, McCreevy, Seán Doherty and Tom McEllistrim, a Kerry TD who also supported Haughey, were trying to arrange a petition to Lynch urging him to resign.

Their method of operation led one of them to call the enterprise "The Sting", after a film about an elaborate confidence trick. They had two sheets of paper with a single line typed at the top saying that the undersigned requested Lynch to resign. One sheet was to contain the signatures: the second was blank but for the sentence on top and was to be shown to likely dissidents. The conspirators set about getting a majority of the party to sign but, contrary to their expectations, they found it a difficult task.

Deputies wanted to know how many others had signed.

"A lot", they were told, but nobody could see the list of signatories until they themselves had signed.

Some of those who committed themselves and signed their names on the discreetly folded sheet were taken aback when the page was opened out for their inspection. There were not a lot of names on it. But those who *had* signed now found it was in their interest to help to create the impression that Lynch was to be pushed. Some of them became enthusiastic workers for the cause, in the hope of expanding the list. After six days of effort, the list had 18 signatures, and the organisers were finding it extremely difficult to get any more. But the enterprise had the desired effect: the party was alive with rumours that a majority of the 82 deputies had signed the petition. Lynch heard the rumours and decided to bring forward his retirement plans.

On December 5th, as the conspirators were about to admit the defeat of their ploy, Lynch announced his resignation as party leader.

The election of his successor took place two days later. Haughey's moment had arrived, and he threw himself into the contest against George Colley with enthusiasm. In spite of claims to the contrary, Haughey had not been directly behind the challenge to Lynch on his Northern policy in earlier months. He had not had any part in Síle de Valera's attack on Lynch's nationalism, nor had he done anything to save Bill Loughnane from expulsion. But he had been waiting on the sidelines as the alternative leader, and the party's dissidents had gravitated to his camp, often for very different reasons. With the party under Lynch's leadership now able to command only 36% of the popular vote, many feared that their future in politics would be cut short at the next election. Colley, identified as the heir apparent and the candidate of the party establishment, did not appear likely to improve the situation. Besides, he ran a bad campaign that assumed the support of many deputies while publicly declaring his confidence of victory. Haughey personally asked almost everyone to vote for him.

On the day before the vote, he and his supporters held a lengthy meeting to decide who should propose him. Ray MacSharry, who was present, was chosen because he was the only minister, senior or junior, who could be relied upon to back Haughey publicly.

Michael O'Kennedy, the Foreign Minister, had stayed determinedly on the fence for the first day of the campaign, apparently in the hope that there might be a last-minute move to avert a Haughey/Colley clash. But he decided that night to back Haughey. Early next morning, Haughey phoned influential members of the party from his home. "O'Kennedy is backing me; spread the word", he said and hung up. The news shattered the Colley camp, which had assumed O'Kennedy to be among its numbers.

Haughey won the leadership by six votes: 44 to 38.

Left alone in the party rooms after the vote, Jack Lynch commented to a fellow Cork TD, Pearse Wyse: "I'll be blamed for this".

In the aftermath, the claims by the pro-Haughey conspirators within the party that they had orchestrated the putsch against Lynch led Colley and his supporters to give them greater credit than they deserved. Colley made it clear that he believed the tradition of loyalty to the party leader had been tossed out by their actions. He denied pointedly Haughey's public claim that he had pledged loyalty and support to the new leader: he offered Haughey "conscientious and diligent support" for his efforts as Taoiseach, but said nothing about his position as Fianna Fáil's leader. He merely insisted that the rules had been changed.

Haughey, however, was the man in the spotlight. There appeared to have been a certain inevitability about his arrival at the head of government. Yet he was, in many respects, an unknown quantity. His ambition had been well documented; his administrative abilities as a minister had reached near-legendary proportions; his interest in the arts and culture was regularly praised; his style of living, talking and acting won him the accolade of being the politician who most interested the man in the street. But many people remained unsure of what to expect from him as Taoiseach. In the nine years and eight months since he had been fired from the Cabinet by Lynch, he had made numerous speeches and given occasional interviews. But he had never been very clear about what he wanted to do when he achieved his ambition. He wanted power, he told friends, for what he could do with it. He never spelled out precisely what it was he wanted to do with power.

Fine Gael was also unsure of what to expect. Its general secretary, Peter Prendergast, commissioned a personnel consultant to draw up a psychological assessment of Haughey. The report, a one-page document, concluded that Haughey would be indecisive and weak on major issues but would show flair and imagination on minor matters. The assessment was contrary to most people's expectations of the new Taoiseach. The report said nothing more, and Fine Gael kept its findings secret.

The so-called arms crisis was a pivotal event in Haughey's career. The experience of being fired, arrested, charged and acquitted left him deeply embittered towards those whom he held responsible. But it also raised many questions about Haughey's style of political leadership, his judgement and his actions. The trial revealed an unexpectedly close involvement by government ministers in covert attempts to import arms into the country. Even if the importation was in line with government policy, it appeared unusual that ministers should be so involved in the activities of military intelligence. Haughey, as Minister for Finance, had been responsible for the spending of public money on arms purchases, when he admitted that he had not approved of its use in that manner. Although he disclaimed knowledge of the details, he was still accountable politically under the conventions of the parliamentary system. The unease and uncertainty that hovered around Haughey's political reputation after the trial was concentrated into the implications of the affair for his general policy towards the North.

Prior to 1969 Haughey had not been considered to be on Fianna Fáil's nationalist wing. He had epitomised the new image of the party, allied to business and setting more store by pragmatism than by any ideology. He was seen to be in the Lemass mould, a practical Dubliner who was not welcomed by the party's old guard, which had also been suspicious of Lemass. In August 1969, Haughey had taken a strong line on the North in cabinet discussions, but contemporary accounts of his dismissal in May 1970 reflected surprise that he should be involved in a row over Northern policy. Haughey had not come from a traditional Fianna Fáil family, opposing the Anglo-Irish treaty and fighting against those who had accepted it in the civil war in 1922. Quite the contrary. His father, Seán Haughey and his mother, Sarah McWilliams, were both involved in the IRA in their native area around Swatragh in Co. Derry. Seán Haughey was the local IRA commander, but he moved South and joined the Free State Army after the treaty. He was serving as an Army commandant in Castlebar, Co. Mayo when Charles was born in 1925. The young Charles later spent many holidays with his parents' relatives in Co. Derry where he developed a feeling for the position of nationalists in the North. Later, while a student at University College, Dublin, he achieved some notoriety when he and a colleague prompted a minor riot outside Dublin's other university, Trinity College, on the day the Second World War ended in Europe in 1945. Trinity flew the Union Jack to mark the occasion but Haughey and his colleague, Séamus Sorahan, showed their displeasure by burning the British flag in front of the college.

In government, however, Haughey applied the normal Fianna Fáil policy of tough action against militant republicans. His first experience of government in the Department of Justice had coincided with the latter stages of the IRA's five year campaign along the border. It was already waning when he became junior minister at the Department in 1960: internment, for instance, had been ended in the South in March 1959; but the government continued to take tough action against the IRA. As part of that, Haughey secretly met the Northern Ireland Home Affairs Minister, Brian Faulkner, in London to co-ordinate the campaign against the IRA. Just after the general election in October 1961, when Haughey became Minister for Justice, the IRA ambushed a group of RUC men at a road block in Co. Armagh. One of the RUC men was shot dead and three other policemen were wounded. In response, Haughey re-introduced military tribunals, courts made up of Army officers and without juries to try IRA suspects and hand down severe sentences. The government's tough stance was a major factor in persuading the IRA to call off its campaign formally three months later. Haughey as Taoiseach 20 years later also adopted a hard line on security. Co-operation between the Gardaí and the RUC against the Provisional IRA was improved through closer communications and a greater pooling of information. Nevertheless, the search for a solution to the Northern problem was the dominant concern of his first term as Taoiseach and the one area of policy in which he was able to claim considerable success.

Haughey's political reputation had been based on his record as an administrator of government departments where he had excelled in making things happen, in cutting through red tape and in taking small but inspired decisions. He came out of the Department of Justice with a reputation as an able and liberal adminstrator. He abolished hanging for all but a few categories of murder: he reformed the law to guarantee widows a third of their husband's property: and he provided the first prison for young offenders to take them out of the adult prisons. But it was as Minister for Finance that he refined his political instincts to introduce a series of measures, none major in itself but all of considerable benefit to those who received them. They suggested a commitment to social reform and a concern for the poor and elderly, but they avoided any fundamental re-distribution of wealth. While the poor waited for the rising economic tide to lift all boats — as the current political maxim promised — Haughey gave old age pensioners free electricity and free transport in his first budget in 1967. The following year, old age pensioners got free television and radio licences: disabled motorists got free petrol in 1969: deserted wives were given an allowance in his last budget in 1970. His most imaginative gesture, and the one which won him more favourable comment than any other single action in his political career, did not benefit the poor but the arts. His income tax exemption for creative writers and artists underscored his patronage of the arts and earned him enormous goodwill in subsequent years.

As Health Minister after 1979, he made maximum publicity use of anti-smoking drives, campaigns of physical fitness and the distribution of free toothbrushes to schoolchildren. He occasionally managed to combine such gestures with a neat sideswipe at some of his colleagues. At one Fianna Fáil Árd-Fheis, he banned smoking on the platform in the interests of giving good example to the nation. The move forced Lynch, a constant pipe smoker and Desmond O'Malley, a heavy cigarette smoker, to skulk behind the scenes like schoolboys whenever they wanted a smoke. On one of the more contentious issues, he legalised contraception but took his direction from the Catholic Church with an attempt to restrict birth control to married couples. His instinct for the brilliant political gesture turned out to be of less value to him as head of government than it was to him when he was a minister making the best of his limited lot.

As Taoiseach, Haughey lost his direction. He had fulfilled his ambition but he did not have any clear idea of what he wanted to do with the task. Instead, he set about consolidating his control over the government. More power was concentrated into the Taoiseach's department, especially over economic matters: the number of Cabinet meetings almost doubled and Haughey took a close interest in details of policy in other departments. Although it became the norm rather than the exception to hold two cabinet meetings a week, it did not necessarily follow that Ministers were better informed about government policy. On several occasions, cabinet members learned of government decisions through the newspapers. The most noteworthy of those decisions, and the one that rankled most with Haughey's critics, was the decision to build the Connacht Regional Airport near Knock in Co. Mayo. It was never sanctioned by the cabinet. The increased frequency of cabinet meetings did not mean, either, that there were fuller discussions of government business. Instead, Haughey used meetings as a way of involving himself in the details of departmental business in which he was interested. He had his revenge from being excluded from cabinet talks on the post office strike by excluding many members of his own cabinet from the discussions about the final settlement of that dispute. But his method of operating occasionally bordered on the bizarre. He once asked one of his ministers to put forward the name of a certain person for appointment to a state board at a cabinet meeting. The minister did so and Haughey argued against the appointment. Then, after discussion, Haughey appeared to relent and declared that the minister's choice was the correct one. The person whom Haughey had secretly suggested for the job was appointed although most of his cabinet colleagues thought the Taoiseach had been persuaded to accept the minister's proposal.

Haughey put as much energy into Fianna Fáil party matters as he did into controlling the government. He took control personally of preparations for the party's first Ard Fheis under his leadership, setting up a committee which operated from the Taoiseach's Department and included two civil servants, Padraig O hAnnracháin and Brendan O'Donnell, whom Haughey had moved into his office. Very little was left to chance or to spontaneity. Several new publicity-winning features were introduced, such as a recital by the Irish Transport and General Workers' Union band as delegates arrived for the opening session. Behind the scenes, Haughey was angry when

George Colley was allowed to address the delegates twice.

In government, Haughey had no time for the long term, preferring to run his administration on a series of crises. Sometimes the crisis was real and sometimes it was exaggerated but Haughey operated best in that type of atmosphere. He did not believe in too much planning ahead or in committing himself to unalterable courses of action. Long-term policy, he reckoned, could always be sorted out later: the main problem was the immediate crisis. Asked once about drawing up a party manifesto for the next election Haughey ostentatiously picked up a copy of the famous 1977 party document and fed it into the paper shredder in the Taoiseach's office. "That's what I think of that and don't mention it again", he said. Governments should run for re-election on their record, he believed: oppositions should run on the basis of attacking the government. This short-term approach to politics suited his talents totally. He was a master tactician at the day-to-day business of party politics, wrong-footing opponents and pulling off small but neatly conceived victories.

Haughey loved power for the most basic reason, the fact that it gave him the ability to make things happen. Most of his energies were devoted to making small things happen: to granting favours to friends and occasionally causing problems for enemies. His response to difficulties was to "fix" them rather than to resolve them. His policy goals tended to be on a grand scale: he wanted to re-unite the country and to make its citizens happy. The first goal of unity, however, required considerable patience and diplomatic dexterity if any progress was to be made. He showed himself capable of exercising the political skills necessary by persuading the British Government in 1980 to take a hard and serious look at the future of the North. But he did not have the patience to follow through on his success. He wanted credit instantly: he oversold the significance of the breakthrough and thereby helped to ensure that it failed. His second goal of wanting to make his citizens happy was based on his desire for popularity. That led him to shirk decisions that might cause unpopularity and to cave in when presented with a more determined force.

His attitude to the exercising of power and popularity led him into a King Canute stance. He believed that a Taoiseach could make things happen simply by declaring them to be so. This approach was accentuated by his belief that Garret Fitz-Gerald had severely damaged the country by concentrating on its economic problems in public. Haughey, the politician of the boom 1960s, seemed to think that all things were possible with a little positive thought. Thus, within his first year as Taoiseach, he declared that the recession was over. He went on to behave as if it was over, spending money in response to wage demands and for capital investment, keeping interest groups sweet and pretending all was well economically. He pursued his new vision relentlessly, taking over control from his Finance Minster, Gene Fitzgerald, for many of the preparations for the 1981 budget. That budget ended up with glaring inconsistencies: the expectations of government spending were clearly unrealistic in some areas. But the figures all added up to put an optimistic gloss on the economic situation. Civil servants were uneasy about the practice, and at least one senior official in the Department of Finance contemplated resignation. The world recession took no notice of his declaration that it had ended.

In power, Haughey behaved like an actor, savouring the role that had been given to him. The main point about power was that it thrust Haughey into the limelight, all day for every day that he kept it. He loved the trappings of power, the reaction of people to the Taoiseach, the ability to have his whims gratified. He played the role for all it was worth, occasionally hamming it up by replacing comment with imperious waves of the hand. He never wore a watch, relying on some aide to have him wherever he should be on time. He adopted a statesman-like walk which, like his method of delivering speeches or comments, was slow and measured. But the inflexibility of his act sometimes served him badly: while he was sharp, witty and entertaining in private conversation, his public persona frequently presented an expressionless face that spoke only in clichés and boring declarations. He was always conscious of his performance, however, thanking the "wonderful audience" in the Dáil's public gallery on the night of his re-election as Taoiseach on March 9th. A week later, with the applause of luncheon guests in the White House in Washington ringing in his ears, he turned to Irish journalists accompanying him and said: "Listen, they love me".

All but his closest friends were bewildered by such comments, not knowing where self-mockery ended and seriousness began. Haughey's moods often changed with disconcerting rapidity. He would lose his temper suddenly over something apparently trivial, tossing papers about, slamming down phones and abusing people with foul language. Alternatively, he could be very charming. He hated to be thought of as ungracious or mean-minded, as evidenced by the fact that he was genuinely upset that a young backbencher like Mary Harney would think he had cut her out of his Christmas card list. His desire to control events — to be the producer as well as the actor — led him to behave in a bullying fashion. He treated some of his ministers and some of his underlings with contempt, humiliating them before their peers. Those who stood up to him, however, were not subjected to such treatment. While he delved into the detail of departmental matters, he could a moment later dismiss some other important issue with a wave of his hand. His erratic behaviour sometimes left his staff uncertain about what had happened or what it was they were supposed to do. Before an official visit to France in 1980, he agreed to grant an interview to the Irish correspondent of the most prestigious French newspaper, *Le Monde,* on condition that he was given advance notice of the questions. The questions were duly sent to his department and brought to Haughey's attention. He never looked at them but had them before him when the interview began. When the journalist asked him a question that was not on the list, Haughey threw a tantrum and demanded an explanation from his press secretary, Frank Dunlop.

Haughey's attitude to the media demonstrated many of his traits. He believed that there was a conspiracy behind most events: everything happened because somebody made it happen and for reasons that were not always apparent. He saw the most lowly report in any newspaper as having being inspired by someone and having being selected, edited and printed for a reason. If it was a reference favourable to Haughey, then it had been done by friends: if it was unfavourable, it had been inspired and placed deliberately by an enemy. But the media had been central to his political success. His image had been fixed in the 1960s when he and cabinet colleagues like Brian Lenihan and Donogh O'Malley had acted like young aristocratic "rakes" of a century earlier. He revelled in a life style that hinted at roguishness and spawned rumour upon rumour. He lived like a country squire, delighting in the pastimes of the displaced aristocracy, hunting, breeding horses, patronising the arts and enjoying the high life. He developed and retained a playboy reputation, consciously promoting a macho image and remaining one of "the lads". As party leader in the 1980s he could still raise a laugh and knowing smiles by interrupting a meeting of the Fianna Fáil financial committee to ask a fundraiser if he was "screwing" a named businesswoman. His interest in the sexual exploits of others was matched by gossip about his own sexual activities. In political circles and at some levels of Dublin society, his lengthy liaison with a married woman was widely discussed.

During his first decade in politics he had become a wealthy man, partly through the accountancy practice he had set up in the early 1950s with his school friend, Harry Boland. He never explained how he made his money but it was widely assumed, with some reason, that it came through the construction boom that hit the country during the same period. It became an election issue in 1969 when Conor Cruise O'Brien, a new recruit to the Labour Party, picked upon the sale of Haughey's Raheny home and 40 acre farm for £204,000, four times more than he had paid for it. The added value was partly as a result of the planning permission attached to the land: it was quickly covered in housing estates after the sale. Haughey moved, several jumps ahead of the encroaching suburbs, to the Georgian mansion, Abbeville, at Kinsealy in North Dublin. The twelve bedroom mansion, complete with four reception rooms and a ballroom, was designed by James Gandon, the architect who also gave Dublin the Customs House. The estate included stables and covered 280 acres. Haughey later added to his property by buying one of the famous Blasket Islands, Inishvickillane, off the Kerry coast and building a holiday refuge there.

His wealth, his behaviour, his political attitudes and his style of living did not impress many people in Fianna Fáil, notably the party founder, Éamon de Valera. After the arms crisis, President de Valera told a member of the then Fianna

Fáil Cabinet that Haughey would wreck the party. That de Valera was suspicious of Haughey was confirmed by the attitude of his regular companion and faithful supporter, Frank Aiken, who retired from politics in 1973 in a private protest over the fact that Haughey had been ratified as a Fianna Fáil candidate.

Haughey had many political acquaintances, many supporters and some political debtors within Fianna Fáil by the time he became Taoiseach in 1982. He had no close friends within the parliamentary party, however. Those, like MacSharry, who were generally perceived to be his closest associates within the party and within the government did not consider themselves to be his friends. Haughey's friends were a group apart, mainly people who had stood by him over a long period and especially after the 1970 sacking. Like a retinue to royalty, they gravitated around his house at Kinsealy. On major occasions, they were evident around Leinster House, awaiting news of his political fate. On less traumatic occasions, they sometimes moved alongside him when he was Taoiseach, accompanying him from meeting to meeting and waiting outside while he attended to official business. They, consciously or unconsciously, adopted Haughey's mannerisms, responding to situations and to outsiders as he might himself. Among his closest friends in this group was his solicitor and election agent, Pat O'Connor.

Chapter Six

Confusion is very understandable
Michael Morgan, April 1982

Nobody was closer to Charles Haughey than Pat O'Connor.

O'Connor's father was national director of elections for Eamon de Valera and Pat O'Connor was election agent for Haughey. O'Connor's daughter, Niamh, worked in Haughey's home helping with his constituency business. The O'Connor family lived just down the road from the Haugheys in Mabestown House, an attractive and well-maintained home on the main road from Kinsealy to Malahide in north County Dublin. The two families treated each other's homes as though they were their own: Haughey's children were frequently down at the O'Connors' and vice versa.

Pat O'Connor, a solicitor by profession, had been at school with Haughey, and when Haughey became an accountant and went into property, O'Connor handled the legal side of his dealings. There was nobody who knew more about Haughey's business affairs than Pat O'Connor. O'Connor ran a large and successful legal practice at Ormond Quay, not far from the Four Courts where his brother, Ciaran O'Connor, was a barrister.

Pat O'Connor's expertise as a solicitor was not confined to the areas of company law and conveyancing, however. During the arms trial, for instance, he was on Haughey's legal defence team. Physically, he was a very large man and at the time of the trial, photographers confused him with Haughey's bodyguards. It was a measure of how little was known of him in 1970, and public knowledge of him was hardly any greater in 1982. Pat

O'Connor had virtually no public profile except in the areas of Malahide and Kinsealy, where he lived, and among Fianna Fáil activists in Haughey's constituency.

The O'Connors and the Haugheys lived in the Dublin North constituency, a key marginal where Fianna Fáil took just one of the three seats in the June 1981 general elections. In that contest, a second Fine Gael candidate, Nora Owen, was elected just 166 votes ahead of her nearest rival, a Fianna Fáil candidate. Haughey saw Dublin North as one of the constituencies where Fianna Fáil could take a seat from Fine Gael if the local organisation made the effort. He let them know that they were to pull out all the stops. There was considerable pressure on the party's lone TD in the constituency, Ray Burke, to come up with results. The next opportunity was the February 1982 general election and local activists used every trick they knew to muster votes. Some Fianna Fáil activists had themselves photographed on a fishing trawler in Howth harbour. The picture was published with the claim that the people shown were local fishermen who supported Fianna Fáil.

Pat O'Connor's political work was mainly in the neighbouring constituency of Dublin North Central where Haughey was the best known TD of any party. But Fine Gael activists in Dublin North knew O'Connor well. They had been surprised in the June 1981 election to find that two families, including the O'Connors, were listed twice on the electoral register — in the Kinsealy section and again in the Malahide section. The error had probably arisen because the O'Connor home was about half way between Kinsealy and Malahide and those members of the O'Connor family entitled to vote ended up being listed twice. The double entry on the register did not, however, confer a right to two votes.

In the February 1982 election, Fine Gael activists in Dublin North were aware that on the figures of the previous contest, Nora Owen could lose her seat if less than 90 voters switched their allegiance to Fianna Fáil. Election workers were briefed that on polling day they were to keep a special eye out for anyone who might attempt to vote twice and also people who might try to vote in the name of other people, an offence known as personation.

Charles Haughey and his wife, Maureen, were among the first people to vote when polling began at 9 a.m. on election day, February 18th. They called to their local polling station at Kinsealy National School. The presiding officer, Michael Morgan, gave them ballot papers and Haughey posed by the ballot box for the ritual photograph of him slipping his paper inside.

Members of the O'Connor family were also up early that morning. Within an hour of the polls opening, Pat O'Connor and his daughter Niamh walked into John Paul II School in Malahide, which was also being used as a polling station.

They approached Enda Byrne, the presiding officer there. She recognised Pat O'Connor because in previous elections he had voted at Malahide. Mark Farrell, the polling clerk, noticed Pat O'Connor particularly — he was a big man. O'Connor and Niamh showed their polling cards and Farrell looked down at his copy of the electoral register: the O'Connor family was listed under the heading MABESTOWN. Pat O'Connor was number 1660 and Niamh O'Connor was number 1665. Farrell drew a line through their names and Enda Byrne gave them both ballot papers. The procedure was observed by Garda Seamus Gallagher, a local officer on duty at the school for the election.

The O'Connors then went to the small booth where voters marked their ballot papers in private, selecting the candidates of their choice. A few seconds later, they walked over to the ballot box, a black metal container, its lid firmly shut down and sealed with sealing wax. They put their ballot papers into the box through the slit in the lid.

They were watched also by Elizabeth Byrne, one of Fine Gael's personation agents on duty at Malahide polling station. She knew Pat O'Connor to see and she knew Niamh well. Elizabeth Byrne's job was to ensure that nobody attempted to vote twice or to vote in the name of another person. Personation was a serious crime — it carried on conviction a prison sentence of up to six months or a fine not exceeding £500. Such a conviction for a man of Pat O'Connor's standing in the community would be very damaging. The Incorporated Law Society, the governing body for solicitors, might have to strike him off their register, with the result that he would be prevented from practising his profession.

After voting at Malahide, Pat and Niamh O'Connor drove to Kinsealy National School. It was a journey of about two and a half miles and they were watched going into the polling station by Garda Hugh Smith, posted there for election duty like his colleague in Malahide.

The O'Connors approached the presiding officer, Michael Morgan. Morgan's poll clerk, Ann Craddock, was close by him. Dearbhla Egan, aged 15, was Fine Gael's personation agent and she watched Pat and Niamh O'Connor walk up to Morgan. Egan knew members of the O'Connor family well to see — they lived in the same area. The O'Connors handed over their polling cards. Egan watched and ticked their names off her copy of the electoral register. The O'Connor family was listed under the heading MABESTOWN, MALA-HIDE; Pat O'Connor was number 391 and Niamh O'Connor was number 388. Egan saw Morgan hand ballot papers to Pat and Niamh O'Connor.

A minute or two later, Garda Smith watched the O'Connors leave the polling station.

Fine Gael's sub agent for Dublin North was John Corry. He was at Malahide polling station in mid-morning when he spoke with Pat Walsh, the party's joint organiser in the Malahide area. Walsh told Corry that some of the O'Connors had voted at Kinsealy. Corry immediately checked the register in Malahide. The names of Patrick O'Connor, Joan O'Connor (his wife) and Niamh O'Connor had been crossed off the register used by Elizabeth Byrne, the personation agent. Corry told Walsh to go to Kinsealy and personally check that the same three people had voted there.

At around 10.45 a.m. Walsh spoke to Michael Morgan. Morgan told him that he had stamped ballot papers and given them to Pat and Niamh O'Connor. Walsh returned to Malahide and told Corry that the names of the O'Connors had been crossed off the Kinsealy register. Corry went into Malahide polling station and instructed Elizabeth Byrne to challenge any other members of the O'Connor family who presented themselves.

Back in Kinsealy National School, another member of the O'Connor family, Cormac, one of Pat and Joan O'Connor's sons, presented himself to presiding officer Morgan at around 11.30 a.m. John Boland, the outgoing Education Minister and Fine Gael's senior TD in the constituency, was in the polling station at the time and saw Cormac O'Connor go up to Morgan. O'Connor presented his polling card to Morgan and Boland interjected. He demanded that O'Connor be challenged. Dearbhla Egan, the Fine Gael personation agent, also said that she wanted to challenge O'Connor. Morgan made a move to get something. O'Connor seemed annoyed.

"Are you not going to let me vote?" he asked.

Nobody replied.

"Will you not answer me?" said O'Connor, and he walked out, watched by Garda Smith.

A short time later, Cormac O'Connor entered the Malahide polling station and presented his polling card to presiding officer Enda Byrne. The polling clerk, Mark Farrell, looked at O'Connor and thought how much like his father Pat O'Connor he appeared. Like him, Cormac was easily recognisable, thought Farrell. Enda Byrne called out the number on O'Connor's polling card and Farrell looked down at his copy of the electoral register.

"Cormac O'Connor" he called out in response,

"I would like to challenge this man", said Elizabeth Byrne, the Fine Gael personation agent.

Enda Byrne prepared herself to ask O'Connor a short series of formal questions.

"Are you the same person as the person whose name appears as Cormac O'Connor on the register of electors now in force for the constituency of Dublin North?" asked Byrne.

"Yes," said O'Connor.

"Have you already voted at this election?"

"No," replied O'Connor.

"Have you reached the age of 18 years on the date of coming into force of this register?" asked Byrne.

"Yes," said O'Connor, "do I look over 18?"

Elizabeth Byrne said she was not satisfied and that she would prefer if O'Connor was asked to take an oath. He readily agreed and Enda Byrne reached for a Bible. O'Connor put his hand on the Bible and repeated after Byrne: "I swear by Almighty God that I am the same person as the person whose name appears as Cormac O'Connor on the register of electors now in force for the constituency of Dublin North and that I have not already voted at this election and that I had attained the age of 18 years on the date of coming into force of this register."

Byrne stamped a ballot paper. Farrell crossed his name off the register. O'Connor went to a booth, marked his preference on the ballot paper and put it into the ballot box. It was just after 12 midday and Garda Seamus Gallagher watched Cormac O'Connor leave the polling station.

Sergeant Michael McGlynn of Malahide garda station was on patrol car duty in the area at about the same time that Cormac O'Connor was swearing his oath. Suddenly, the car radio spluttered out a message that he should go to Kinsealy National School. When McGlynn got there, he met his colleague, Garda Smith. Smith told him that he had received an allegation of personation. McGlynn got back into his patrol car and drove to Malahide polling station where he met Garda Gallagher. Gallagher reported more allegations of personation — McGlynn said he had just been speaking to Smith and knew all about it. He drove off to Malahide garda station and telephoned Coolock station. His call was taken by Inspector Pat Mulroy and McGlynn passed on the allegations.

Mulroy telephoned the office of the Director of Public Prosecutions and spoke to Ian Candy, one of the lawyers there. Between them, they agreed that the people working in both polling stations should give statements in Coolock garda station after polling finished at 9 p.m.

It wasn't long before the newspapers heard of the allegations. It was incredible — Haughey's election agent voting twice: nobody could quite believe it. Fine Gael election workers who claimed to witness the alleged double voting were careful about what they said. They told the story as they knew it in precise and exceptionally detailed terms. Walsh had a statement prepared for reporters which was also striking for its detail. It contained precise times and electoral register numbers which turned out to be accurate when they were checked. All the Fine Gael people involved refused to comment or make sweeping claims: they simply stuck to the details of their allegations.

Early afternoon editions of the *Evening Herald* carried the story on the front page under a large headline. Fianna Fáil headquarters in Mount Street was asked to comment but refused. People there were very gloomy when they heard the allegation. It could be extremely damaging to Fianna Fáil's performance at the polls if it became widely known before voting finished. Haughey said nothing but he appeared to people in headquarters to be very downcast. Nobody offered any explanation for what was alleged to have happened.

One person said of O'Connor: "He's only a big baby."

The outgoing Justice Minister, Jim Mitchell, was in his Dublin West constituency when he was eventually tracked down by officials from the Department of Justice. Reporters were hounding them for comment on the allegations against O'Connor, they told Mitchell. He decided to go into his office to check out what was happening. He read the *Evening Herald* and was able to obtain confirmation from the gardai that the allegations had been made and were going to be investigated. He decided to make no public comment because it would be politically inappropriate. In any event, there was enough mud flying around without Mitchell getting involved.

Just after 2 p.m., Pat Walsh, Fine Gael's organiser, called to Coolock garda station accompanied by Maria O'Brien, Fine Gael's publicity officer for the Dublin North constituency. They were met by Inspector Mulroy and Superintendent William Byrne, the senior officer in the station. Walsh and O'Brien gave their version of events: they alleged that Pat O'Connor, Joan O'Connor, Niamh O'Connor and Cormac O'Connor were guilty of personation.

O'Connor was Haughey's best friend and Superintendent Byrne was a former classmate of Haughey's at St. Joseph's Christian Brothers school in Fairview. While Haughey pursued his career in business and politics, Byrne joined the Garda Síochána. By the time that Haughey had assumed the office of Taoiseach in 1979, he had risen to the rank of Inspector. Most of his experience was in the fingerprint section of the Technical Bureau in garda headquarters. He had been in charge of it until the late 1970s.

Byrne became involved in a row in the fingerprint section during the investigation into the murder in 1976 of the British ambassador to Ireland, Christopher Ewart-Biggs. The ambassador and his secretary were killed when a remote control bomb exploded under their car shortly after it left Ewart-Biggs' home at Sandyford in south Dublin. The gardai came under tremendous pressure to catch the killers. An officer in the section, Sergeant Michael Diggin, examined a workman's helmet found at the scene but there were no fingerprints on it. Diggin was surprised to learn later that another officer in the section afterwards examined the same helmet and identified a mark on it. Concerned that he had missed a mark, Diggin checked the identification and disagreed vehemently with his colleague. A dispute over the mark split the fingerprint section into rival camps: Diggin was supported by a colleague, Sergeant Pat Corless, and the officer who made the wrong identification was backed by Byrne.

The upshot of the row was the assignment of the four main participants to other duties. Corless and Diggin were transferred to Dublin district detective units in Pearse Street and Store Street garda stations. Byrne was transferred to the Special Branch in Dublin Castle. When Haughey became Taoiseach in 1979, Byrne was occasionally seen with him as part of Haughey's security entourage. Just before Haughey left office after the June 1981 election, Byrne was promoted on the approval of the Cabinet to the rank of Superintendent. He was posted by the garda authorities to Coolock, Haughey's local garda station.

Now, in February 1982, Byrne found himself with the unenviable task of supervising an investigation into double voting allegations against the best friend of his old schoolmate

Charles Haughey — the man who was probably going to be Taoiseach again shortly.

Throughout the day, other members of the O'Connor family voted at Kinsealy. Dearbhla Egan was there when Maureen O'Connor, Niamh's sister, came in to vote, accompanied by Eimear Haughey, the Fianna Fáil leader's only daughter. When she presented herself to Michael Morgan for a ballot paper, Morgan asked her three questions. She answered each and was given a paper. Then both she and Eimear Haughey voted.

Meanwhile, Fianna Fáil election workers in the constituency concentrated on keeping local voters ignorant of events. Some of them drove around newsagents trying to buy up the entire edition of the *Evening Herald.* Shortly after 9 p.m. when the polling stations closed, a car screeched to a halt outside Fine Gael's election offices in Malahide. Somebody got out of the car and threw a bundle of *Heralds* through the door, then jumped back into the car which sped off into the night. Efforts to stop local voters reading about the allegations were useless however. Hundreds of commuters bought their newspapers in the city centre and took them home.

Just before RTE television's teatime news was about to be broadcast, large areas of Malahide were put into darkness by an electricity failure. It was said locally that someone had cut the supply by throwing a bicycle into a transformer, causing it to short circuit. If it was an attempt at sabotage, it made no difference, because RTE failed to carry the story. The BBC, however, carried reports on its news bulletins. RTE was criticised but said that their failure to report the allegations and name O'Connor was "normal practice" and they would not give a report until a person had been brought before a court. By the time polling finished at 9 p.m., the gardai were investigating the allegations.

Inside Coolock garda station, four inspectors took statements. Shortly before 10 p.m., Inspector Mulroy saw a man in the hallway of the station. Mulroy didn't know who the man was but he was carrying a large black metal box, a ballot box, and Mulroy knew he must be one of the presiding officers. Michael Morgan introduced himself and Ann Craddock, his polling clerk, to Mulroy. Mulroy ushered both into the superintendents's office and made arrangements for the lorry collecting ballot boxes from the polling stations to call and collect Morgan's box as well.

One of Mulroy's colleagues, Inspector John Geary, came into the office and the four casually discussed the allegations against Pat O'Connor while waiting for the lorry to come and take the ballot box away.

Geary and Craddock remained in the room while Mulroy took a formal statement from Morgan.

"Just tell me exactly what happened," said Mulroy, "that is all I want to know."

Morgan explained that he was a national school teacher but that for election day, he had been presiding officer at Kinsealy. He told how he had the school opened a half an hour before voting at 9 a.m. and how there was just one booth and one ballot box in the polling station. He mentioned the people who worked with him during the day, including Craddock and Egan. He said that voting had been normal, as in previous years.

"At what time did Pat O'Connor vote?" asked Mulroy.

"Sometime between 9.15 a.m. and 10.30 a.m. Mr. Pat O'Connor, Streamstown, Malahide, who is well known to me came into the booth and applied for a ballot paper," said Morgan. "He presented a voting card. I stamped and issued him with a ballot paper. I did not see him cast his vote. I can not now recall the number of the voting card he presented, but I was satisfied through my poll clerk that it was correct and in accordance with his number on the register of electors for the constituency of Dublin North."

Mulroy wrote it all down. Morgan said that at around 11.30 a.m., one of O'Connor's sons had come in to vote but had been challenged by John Boland. Morgan said that Boland instructed him to ask the questions outlined in his presiding officer's manual.

"I went to a room next door to fetch the manual, telling him (O'Connor's son) before I left that I would have to ask him the three questions formally. On my way back with the manual I met him going out in disgust," said Morgan.

He went on to tell Mulroy about other members of the O'Connor family who came in to vote. He was unable to remember the Christian name of an O'Connor woman but he recalled that she was challenged and then issued with a ballot paper. Morgan said that apart from the O'Connor man who left the polling station when challenged, everyone who applied for a ballot paper was given one and that the names deleted from the register accurately reflected the list of people who had voted.

Mulroy read the statement over to Morgan. One or two small amendments were made and when he finished reading, Mulroy asked Morgan if he wanted to make any further amendments. It was correct, replied Morgan, and he signed.

The last sentence of the statement was: "I have heard this statement read over to me and it is correct."

Elsewhere in the garda station, other people were giving statements or waiting to be called into one of the interview rooms. Ray Burke, Fianna Fáil's TD in his constituency, only heard about the allegations against the O'Connors late in the evening. After the polling stations closed and people from Kinsealy and Malahide went to the garda station, he organised a solicitor to call into the garda station to speak with two Fianna Fáil personation agents who were there waiting to make statements. The solicitor came into the garda station and spoke briefly with the two agents. After a few minutes they left the station with him and did not make statements to the gardaí.

Other people did, however. Enda Byrne, the Malahide presiding officer, and the Fine Gael personation agent there, Elizabeth Byrne, both gave statements to Inspector Dan Murphy. Inspector John Stapleton took a statement from Dearbhla Egan, Fine Gael's personation agent in Kinsealy. Mark Farrell, the poll clerk in Malahide, gave a statement to Inspector Mulroy. After Mulroy had taken the statement from Michael Morgan, Morgan left and the way was clear for Inspector Geary to take a statement from Ann Craddock, the poll clerk in Kinsealy.

Craddock first outlined the events of the day in a preliminary conversation. Then Geary took her formal statement. She explained that her job as poll clerk was to delete from the electoral register the names of the people handed ballot papers by the presiding officer. She said that at about 11 a.m. she became aware of a query as to whether or not Pat O'Connor and Niamh O'Connor had voted.

"I then checked my register of electors and saw that I had the names of these two persons deleted from the register. This indicated that Patrick O'Connor and Niamh O'Connor had already voted at Kinsealy National School," said Craddock.

She, too, described the incident involving John Boland and one of Pat O'Connor's sons. She also mentioned that around 1 p.m. and 5 p.m. other members of the O'Connor family came in and were issued with ballot papers.

The last sentence on her statement was: "I have heard this statement read over to me and it is correct."

The O'Connors did not make statements on election night but a reporter who called to their home was told by Joan O'Connor that the allegations were part of "another malicious smear campaign" by Fine Gael. The following morning, Friday February 19th, the O'Connor story was reported prominently by all the newspapers: much space was given to the election itself, but the O'Connor incident was the most extraordinary story to emerge from the poll.

Superintendent William Byrne was not directly involved in the previous night's investigations but on Friday morning in the garda station, he met Inspector Mulroy. Mulroy told him he was off to interview the O'Connors. Byrne told him not to. He said he would do it himself.

In the immediate aftermath of the general election, reporters pursued the O'Connor story. Although the focus of political attention shifted quickly from the election results to Fianna Fáil's internal difficulties and the challenge to Haughey from Desmond O'Malley, there was a considerable degree of public interest in the double voting allegations. The gardaí and the Department of Justice were asked by reporters if the allegations had been investigated and if anyone was going to be charged. Elsewhere in the country, at about the same time, people charged with personation were brought before the courts and dealt with. But there appeared to be no moves in the case of Haughey's election agent.

Pressure mounted on the Department, and early in the week after the election, Jim Mitchell asked his officials to inquire from the gardaí what was happening to the case. He was told that it appeared very little was happening. The Minister instructed his officials to contact the office of the Garda

Commissioner, Patrick McLaughlin, to request that the O'Connor case be investigated speedily. Neither he nor the Attorney General, Peter Sutherland, wanted an embarrassing contrast to develop between the handling of the O'Connor case and other alleged instances of double voting.

The case was proceeding, however. On Wednesday evening, February 24th, while political attention was focussed on the O'Malley camp as its members began their last round of meetings, Superintendent Byrne called out to the O'Connor house at Mabestown. In less than an hour, he interviewed Niamh and Cormac and their mother, Joan O'Connor. He told each of them in turn about the allegation that had been made about them. He asked them if they wished to make a statement and gave them, each in turn, the official caution: "You are not obliged to make a statement unless you wish to do so, but anything you may say will be taken down in writing and may be given in evidence."

Each of them replied separately: "I have no comment to make."

The following day, Superintendent Byrne interviewed Pat O'Connor at his office in Ormond quay in Dublin. He repeated what he had said the previous night to the members of O'Connor's family and also cautioned him. O'Connor replied: "I have no comment to make."

The garda file on the O'Connor case now appeared to be substantially completed: all that remained was for Superintendent Byrne to write his report, sign the file and despatch it to the office of the Chief State Solicitor in Dublin Castle. At that point, however, Superintendent Byrne went off to the garda training centre in Templemore, County Tipperary, to attend a course for superintendents. He did not sign the O'Connor file before he left Dublin, which meant there would be further delays in processing the allegations.

Deputy Commissioner Larry Wren intervened, however. He ordered Byrne to return to Dublin from the course. Byrne did so and the file was sent to Dublin Castle in the first few days of March where it landed on the desk of Kevin Matthews, head of the district court section in the Chief State Solicitor's office. The Chief State Solicitor, Louis Dockery, sent a copy of the garda file to the office of the Director of Public Prosecutions.

Matthews considered the statements and reports compiled by the gardaí at Coolock and, on Friday March 5th, wrote to the DPP seeking a direction on whether or not to prosecute. He suggested that there was enough evidence to bring charges against Pat, Niamh and Cormac O'Connor; there was not enough evidence against Joan O'Connor. He drew up lists of queries he believed needed to be answered before going to court: they ran to more than four pages and included numerous technical points about proving the appointment of presiding officers and clerks at the polling stations in Malahide and Kinsealy. He recommended that the DPP appoint a barrister to prosecute the case on account of the people involved, the publicity the case would generate and the likelihood that the O'Connors would be defended by a senior counsel.

The following Monday, March 8th, his proposals arrived in the DPP's office and were attended to immediately. A legal assistant to the DPP wrote back to Matthews that day and told him that Pat and Niamh O'Connor should be prosecuted under Section 3 of the Prevention of Electoral Abuses Act of 1923. Cormac O'Connor was not liable for prosecution because he appeared to have applied for a ballot paper at one polling booth and to have voted subsequently at another. A draft charge against the other two accused them of having acted the other way around: of applying for a ballot paper, having already voted once.

The DPP, Eamonn Barnes, decided that the prosecution would not be conducted in court by a barrister. Charges under the electoral laws were handled usually by solicitors and Barnes argued that normal practice should be adhered to in this case. Matthews subsequently asked him to reconsider his decision but Barnes refused again to appoint a barrister. It was decided eventually that Matthews himself would prosecute, a decision that they agreed was sufficient recognition of the importance and sensitivity of the case. As head of the district court section of the Chief State Solicitor's office, Matthews did not usually appear in court himself.

By the time the coalition government left office on March 9th and was replaced by Charles Haughey's minority administration, the accusations against the new Taoiseach's election agent were lodged firmly in the legal system. There was no reason why the law should not take its course.

Haughey was concerned for his friend and discussed the case with several people. Among some members of the new cabinet, there was a strong belief that Sean Doherty had been given the task of looking after the case as his first job as Justice Minister. Haughey maintained a close interest in the progress of the prosecution and had at least one meeting with Doherty and several other people during which they discussed the issue.

Approaches were made to several people in order to try and influence the manner in which the case was conducted, first in the district court and, later, when it was brought before the High Court. They included a statutory consultation between the DPP, Eamonn Barnes, and the Attorney General, Patrick Connolly. Although it was an offence under the Act setting up the DPP's office for anyone but those involved to canvass him about a case, the law provided for consultations between the Attorney General and the DPP. The holder of either office was entitled to approach the other to discuss anything he wished.

Pressure was brought to bear as well on the Chief State Solicitor's office. A barrister should be appointed to prosecute the case, it was suggested. The particular barrister wanted was not named, but Haughey's friends had in mind someone who could be relied upon to prosecute O'Connor with less than the usual vigour. The DPP and the state solicitor stuck by their earlier decision that the case should be prosecuted by Kevin Matthews.

The case continued on its way to a court hearing.

On Tuesday, March 30th, Garda Andrew Molloy from Malahide garda station called to Mabestown House, the O'Connors' home. The door was opened to him by Michael O'Connor, another of Pat O'Connor's sons. Garda Molloy handed him summonses for his father and his sister Niamh: they were to appear in Swords district court on April 20th on charges of alleged breaches of the Electoral Act.

Meanwhile, Inspectors Pat Mulroy and John Stapleton were clearing up some untidy ends of the case. The mapping section at garda headquarters provided a map of north County Dublin with arrows indicating the O'Connors' home and the polling stations at Kinsealy National School and John Paul II National School. Stapleton measured the distance between the

O'Connors' and Malahide polling station and from there to Kinsealy National School. The clerk of the Dáil, Michael Healy, certified copies of the electoral register which showed the duplication in the Mabestown area. The County Sheriff for Dublin, John Fitzpatrick, produced a certificate to the effect that there had been a general election on February 18th and gave details of the relevant polling stations and who had been employed in them. Most of it was technical information that might be required as evidence in court.

Inspector Stapleton also took a second statement from Enda Byrne, the presiding officer at Malahide. It covered technical details, such as the fact that she had been appointed a presiding officer and could produce, if required, her letter of appointment. That statement was made on April 8th. Unknown to either Inspectors Mulroy or Stapleton, other key witnesses had also made second statements several days earlier.

The statements were taken by Superintendent William Byrne from three people who had been in Kinsealy National School: Ann Craddock, the polling clerk; Dearbhla Egan, the 15 year-old Fine Gael personation agent; and Michael Morgan, the presiding officer. All three had made statements on the night of the election, after the polls had closed.

On the afternoon of Friday, April 2nd, Ann Craddock met Superintendent Byrne at Malahide garda station. Her first statement said that she had checked her register of electors about 11.00 a.m. on the morning of the election and had noticed that the names of Pat O'Connor and Niamh O'Connor had been crossed off. "This indicated that Patrick O'Connor and Niamh O'Connor had already voted at Kinsealy National School," her first statement said.

In her second statement to Superintendent Byrne, she said she did not know either Pat O'Connor or Niamh O'Connor to see. "I do not remember either Mr. Pat O'Connor or Niamh O'Connor coming into the polling booth at Kinsealy on the 18th February, 1982...The reason I had marked both names off the register is that I presumed but cannot prove that they had voted."

She added that it was not correct to say, as her first statement had, that she was satisfied that she had deleted the names of each person who voted at Kinsealy as they were handed ballot papers by the presiding officer. "I am now satisfied that I could easily have made an error in striking off names, including Patrick O'Connor and Niamh O'Connor from the register of electors."

She explained her earlier statement: "I did not realise what I was really saying in my statement to the guards at Coolock on the night of the elections as I was too tired and hungry from work and newspaper men and all I wanted was to get out of the station and go home." Her second statement concluded: "This statement has been read over to me and is now fully correct."

The following Monday, April 5th, Superintendent Byrne called to the home of Dearbhla Egan and, in the presence of her parents, spoke to her about the statement she had made on election night. She repeated precisely the same details about Pat and Niamh O'Connor entering the polling station and being handed ballot papers by Michael Morgan. She said she had not seen them cast their votes, a point not made specifically in her first statement.

The following day, Superintendent Byrne met Michael Morgan at his national school in Kinsealy. He signed a second statement which was witnessed by Byrne. It recalled that he had been told on election day that he had to go to Coolock garda station to make a statement. "When I arrived," he continued, "a Mr. Mulroy wrote out a statement purporting to come from me, to which I agreed as I was tired and weary after a 14 hour day without a decent meal. I now repudiate that statement as I am quite capable of making and writing my own statement."

He added: "I understand now that I should not have been told I had to go to Coolock garda station to make a statement. Even criminals are accorded the luxury of remaining silent." About the alleged O'Connor incident, he said he could distinctly remember giving voting papers to three gentlemen, Mr. Haughey, an elderly incapacitated gentleman and an illiterate gentleman. "I cannot recall being presented with a voting card or tearing off and handing a voting (ballot) paper to Mr. Pat O'Connor or 400 others. Mr. O'Connor is a familiar figure on election day only and as such is just another 'Sean Citizen' in Kinsealy polling booth."

Morgan said that he had relaxed and taken no more than ordinary notice of all voters after Haughey had voted. After

11.00 a.m., when they were alerted that something amiss had happened in Malahide, he took a more than ordinary interest in the O'Connor family. He could recall three other members of the family voting between 12.30 p.m. and 5.00 p.m. Two of them were challenged.

He concluded: "I am not a very politically motivated person, being more likely to vote for a good candidate rather than a party. Incidentally several people who had voting cards for both Malahide and Kinsealy handed their extra voting cards to me for destruction.

"Events of February 18th and June 1981 are now very unclear due to the proximity of the two elections and so confusion is very understandable."

Superintendent Byrne's decision to seek second statements from the three witnesses came as a surprise both to Kevin Matthews and to the DPP's office. Neither had asked specifically that the gardaí should return to any of the witnesses. The list of additional queries drawn up by Matthews and his comments on the case had been sent to the gardaí in the normal course of events. Many of the points raised were covered by certificates from the Dublin County Sheriff about the appointment of presiding officers and poll clerks. They were not received until after the second interviews, however.

The second statements from Michael Morgan and Ann Craddock, the presiding officer and poll clerk at Kinsealy, prompted new statements from the two garda inspectors who had interviewed them on the night of the election. Inspector Pat Mulroy and Inspector John Geary had been with Morgan and Craddock in the Superintendent's office. They had all chatted while awaiting a lorry to collect the ballot box from Kinsealy which Morgan had with him.

Inspector Mulroy said that Morgan struck him as careful and rather reluctant to commit himself. But Morgan had said: "I'm not involved anyway. He (Pat O'Connor) did nothing wrong in my place. Kinsealy is his proper place to vote. He always votes there. If he did anything wrong it was in Malahide." Inspector Mulroy said in his statement that it was clear from the conversation that O'Connor was well known to Morgan and that he had voted at Kinsealy that day.

After the ballot box was collected, Inspector Mulroy took a

more detailed statement from Morgan. He said he put questions to Morgan and the resulting statement was largely based on Morgan's replies. "I can clearly recall one question I put to him: 'At what time did Pat O'Connor vote?' ", Inspector Mulroy's statement said. "He was careful to stress that Mr. O'Connor 'applied for a ballot paper' rather than say he 'voted'."

Inspector Mulroy said that he read the statement over to Morgan when it was finished. Some small amendments were made and Inspector Mulroy said he asked Morgan if he wished to amend it further and Morgan replied: "It is correct." Morgan signed the statement and initialled the small amendments as the Inspector requested.

Inspector John Geary said in his statement that he had taken down a statement from Ann Craddock on the night of the election. Her statement had been made freely and no pressure was put on her to make it then and there. "She did not inform me that she was tired and hungry and evidence that she was fatigued did not come to my notice while I was taking the statement from her," Inspector Geary wrote.

He added that he saw Inspector Mulroy writing down Michael Morgan's statement. "This statement was freely made by Michael Morgan who did not appear to have any difficulty in recalling to mind the facts perceived by him in relation to the matter. I did not see any evidence of Michael Morgan being tired or weary on the occasion."

After Morgan had left the garda station, Inspector Geary read the statement that Inspector Mulroy had taken down. He pointed out to his colleague that it omitted what Morgan had said in preliminary discussions — that Pat O'Connor had voted at Kinsealy at previous elections.

On Tuesday, April 20th, a number of the prosecution witnesses were driven to court by Superintendent Byrne. Swords district court was packed with people when District Justice Donal Kearney took his place on the bench to try the case against Pat and Niamh O'Connor. Kearney was an experienced district justice. He had been one of the Dublin metropolitan justices some twelve years earlier when he had presided over the preliminary hearings that led to the so-called arms trial. In what was probably the most controversial case to come before him or any of his colleagues, he had returned four people, including Charles Haughey, for trial in the central criminal court and had decided that Neil Blaney did not have a case to answer. By 1982, he was the justice in number 10 district which covered north County Dublin and parts of County Meath.

Pat and Niamh O'Connor were not in the courtroom and the hearing began with an application from the prosecuting solicitor, Kevin Matthews, that they be instructed to appear so that witnesses could identify them. The counsel for the defence, Denis McCullough, argued that a person was not required to appear in court in person to answer a summons and was not required to make or assist a prosecution case. District Justice Kearney accepted the prosecution argument and adjourned the hearing briefly to allow the O'Connors time to attend.

Over the next few hours, the court heard evidence from more than 20 witnesses for the prosecution. The two officials at the Malahide polling station, Enda Byrne and Mark Farrell, gave evidence that the O'Connors had presented voting cards to them and had been given ballot papers. The Fine Gael personation agent at Malahide, Elizabeth Byrne, said she had seen both of them voting. The corresponding officials and personation agent from Kinsealy also gave evidence.

Dearbhla Egan, the Fine Gael personation agent at Kinsealy, said that Pat and Niamh O'Connor had received ballot papers there between 9.30 and 10.00 a.m. Ann Craddock, the poll clerk, said that the names of the O'Connors had been crossed off the official register used by her. But, she said, she could not remember the time of day she had done that. She agreed with the defence counsel that it would have been possible that a wrong name could have been crossed out in the course of the day.

Michael Morgan, the presiding officer at Kinsealy, took the witness stand. Because of his second statement to the gardaí repudiating what his first statement had said, the prosecution applied to the judge to have him treated as a "hostile" witness which meant, in effect, that the prosecution could cross-examine him, even though he was a prosecution witness. Morgan explained the difference on the grounds that he had gone to Coolock garda station on election night after a 14 hour day without a proper meal and he was anxious to get home for a bite to eat. "What I wrote that night was more in an effort to get out fast," he said. He added that a garda officer had had notes drawn up when he arrived at the station.

He agreed that he had said that Pat O'Connor had come into the polling station and applied for a ballot paper. But he said in evidence that O'Connor had come in some time during the early morning but he did not remember him applying for a vote. Matthews pressed him to explain the differences in his statements and if he had known when he made his second statement that summonses had already been issued against the O'Connors. "Mr. Byrne, can you answer that?" Morgan replied.

After the evidence was all completed and the lawyers had made their submissions, District Justice Kearney delivered his verdict. The advance press publicity about the case had given him an opportunity to look in to the law relating to the offence, he declared. He had found that they carried a mandatory sentence of not less than two months imprisonment and not more than twelve months, plus a fine not exceeding £500. That was a very severe penalty, he noted.

He went on to say that there was no way of proving that a person had voted in an election. Ever since a case had been brought "by Miss Mairín de Burca or another lady" about five years ago, the practice of keeping counterfoil records of ballot papers had ceased because of the High Court decision. Thus there was no way of proving that a person had voted at all. "I am ruling that the prosecution has not proved, and could not prove as the law stands, that these defendants or any defendants committed this offence of double voting or whatever the word is," he announced. There was no case to answer: he dismissed the summonses.

District Justice Kearney was correct when he said that it was no longer possible to prove that someone had actually voted. But he was wrong in the High Court case he cited as ending the practice of keeping counterfoils of ballot papers with voters' registration numbers on them. The case was not taken by Mairín de Burca or any other woman: it was taken by Niall McMahon. It was not heard some five years earlier. It was initiated in 1969 and a final decision was given by the Supreme Court in October 1971. The case was detailed on page 69 of the

Outside the courthouse, Pat O'Connor told reporters that the judgement was "excellent."

Not everyone agreed, however. Nine days after the hearing, the DPP instituted a procedure that required the district justice to set out the facts of the case and explain to the High Court why he reached the decision he did. The procedure, known as a "case stated", was tantamount to an appeal by the DPP against the dismissal of the charges.

In January 1983, District Justice Kearney drew up for the High Court a formal report of the proceedings in Swords district court. He listed a series of facts which, he said, had been proved by the prosecution in relation to the charges against Pat O'Connor. These included the following: "On 18th February, 1982 the Defendant (O'Connor) entered John Paul II National School, he presented a voting card at polling booth No. 3 there, his name was then called out and crossed off the electoral register, he was handed an official ballot paper and he subsequently put a folded ballot paper into the ballot box.

"On 18th February, 1982 the Defendant entered Kinsealy National School, he presented a voting card bearing his name at the sole polling booth there, his name was then crossed off the electoral register, he was handed an official ballot paper and he went to the voting compartment."

District Justice Kearney said there was insufficient evidence to establish whether or not O'Connor visited Malahide before Kinsealy or vice versa.

In deciding the case, District Justice Kearney said that the Electoral Act of 1923 defined a vote as a ballot paper which indicated clearly a first preference and was not spoiled. Therefore, the ballot paper must be produced in court to show whether it was accepted and counted as a vote or whether it was rejected as an invalid or spoiled ballot paper. But, the Electoral (Amendment) Act 1972 made it impossible for the prosecution to produce a specific ballot paper in court and therefore it was impossible for the prosecution to prove the offence with which the defendant was charged. "I determined the proceedings by granting the direction applied for and dismissing the charge," District Justice Kearney said.

The High Court case dragged on for more than a year and

became bogged down in an argument over procedure. It ended on May 10th, 1983 when the court's president, Mr. Justice Thomas Finlay, dismissed the DPP's appeal on a technicality. O'Connor's lawyers claimed that they had not received proper notice from the DPP about the appeal to the High Court. It was argued on behalf of the DPP that they had been properly notified by way of letter. Mr. Justice Finlay, in his judgement, said it was clear that O'Connor's lawyers could have been under no real misapprehension about what was going on when they received the letter. If he had any discretion he would without hesitation find in favour of the DPP. But in this instance he was bound by a specific law and so, he said, he was forced to hold that the DPP had not complied with statutory requirements.

Immediately after the hearing in Swords district court, the DPP had also asked Commissioner Patrick McLaughlin to institute an inquiry into the handling of the investigation of the allegations against the O'Connors. One of the main points of concern was the reason why Michael Morgan had changed his statement. The request led to a row between the Commissioner and the DPP — which also carried on beyond the lifetime of the then government — over the appointment of Superintendent Byrne's immediate superior, Chief Superintendent Maurice Connor, to carry out the new investigation.

Later, in 1983, a further inquiry was conducted after the appointment by the subsequent coalition government of Larry Wren as Garda Commissioner. It was carried out by the head of the community affairs section in garda headquarters, Chief Superintendent Owen Giblin. His report included an account of an interview in which he asked Superintendent Byrne why he had returned to three of the witnesses who had already given statements to the gardai. Superintendent Byrne told him that he had gone back to Ann Craddock and Dearbhla Egan because of the second statement from Michael Morgan. In fact, the dates on the documents produced at the time showed that Morgan was the last of the three to give second statements.

The DPP decided on the basis of Chief Superintendent Giblin's report that there was insufficient evidence to take any action. But the whole sequence of events that followed the allegation against Pat O'Connor on the day of the February general election helped to poison relations between the DPP and Fianna Fáil.

At the time, the O'Connor affair did Charles Haughey's new government no good. His election agent was ridiculed publicly by being referred to as Pat O'Connor Pat O'Connor and the incident seemed to set the tone for the new administration.

Even stranger things were to happen, however.

Chapter Seven

Tolerance of wrongdoing in some matters can have an immunising effect on society so that gradually greater wrongdoing can come to be condoned.

Seán Doherty, March 1982

The law was taking its course in Roscommon.

Michael Keaney and the eleven people found drinking in his pub after closing time were facing prosecution. The fact that the garda raid had taken place during the February general election campaign had annoyed Keaney but he was enormously cheered by the election result. Fianna Fáil was back in office and Seán Doherty — customer, friend and popular local TD — had been appointed Justice Minister. Doherty, the man to whom Keaney had turned for help after the raid, was now the boss of the gardaí. Keaney's attitude was that the gardaí worked for the government, so when Fianna Fáil was in government the gardaí were on Keaney's side. When the opposition held power, the gardaí worked for them and their friends.

Gardaí Tim Griffin and Jim Mooney didn't see things quite like that. They went about their business and Griffin reported the facts of the raid to his superiors in Boyle garda station. Inspector Martin O'Shea told him to prepare summonses in the usual way, and recorded his instructions in the case file. In the meantime, Doherty had taken over as minister. Shortly afterwards, O'Shea called for the file and examined his decision. With the help of Tipp-Ex fluid, used by typists to blot out mistakes, O'Shea deleted his original decision and wrote in new instructions.

"It is understood that a political meeting was held on the

premises on the night in question and it is policy not to prosecute during election time," he wrote. "However, the licensee should be cautioned that the law will take its course should any further breach be detected".

The change didn't please Sergeant Tom Tully, Griffin's immediate superior in Boyle garda station. It was the first that Tully had heard of a policy not to enforce the law during election campaigns, and it was irrelevant whether or not a party political meeting had been taking place. He told O'Shea what he thought of the decision but O'Shea said he stood over it. Tully was away when the change was made but he had no doubt that Doherty was behind it. Tully had been Sergeant-in-Charge at Boyle since his transfer there from Dundalk in 1978. He was not ambitious and had been appointed Sergeant-in-Charge at the station against his own wishes. But his superior officers wanted a man who could get things moving again in Boyle — the station had become very lax. Tully was a typically good sergeant: a stickler for detail, he demanded good, honest work from his men and while he imposed discipline on them, he displayed leniency and compassion when the situation called for it.

Tully became annoyed when anyone tried to interfere in his work and it was in this context that he had come to know Doherty during his term as junior Justice Minister. Doherty, or officials under his control in the Department of Justice, regularly contacted the station and asked for charges against constituents to be dropped. Sometimes Doherty would make the call himself and give a direct order to the guards. In one case, a woman driver had been arrested with more than double the legal limit of alcohol in her blood and Doherty tried to intervene in the case. Tully resisted, however, and the woman was successfully prosecuted. In another incident in December 1980, Doherty had succeeded in stopping a prosecution against Keaney's where, yet again, after-hours drinkers were discovered.

Now, a matter of days after Doherty became minister, Tully was again feeling his hand in the day-to-day work of the station. He had been considerably annoyed and frustrated when the earlier charges against Keaney and the others were dropped. Tully had been pushed far enough and he made a vow: the next time Keaney's had to be raided, he would do it himself and he would ensure personally that charges were brought if the law was being broken.

Doherty became Justice Minister at a difficult time. The widespread public concern over crime was reflected in the opinion polls at election time. As an issue it was nowhere as important in voters' minds as unemployment, but it was important enough for the politicians to react to it. The level of serious crimes committed in 1981 rose by 22% on the previous year and there was nothing to indicate a fall would occur during 1982. Dublin people in particular felt they and their homes were under attack and whole areas of the inner city were thought best avoided — day or night.

Fianna Fáil promised a campaign against crime and vandalism. Charles Haughey showed a personal interest in the problem and said that, once back in office, his party would see to it that 2,000 more gardaí were recruited. He also promised more garda stations for Dublin and party advertisements sought to turn anxiety into votes. "Fianna Fáil will take fear from the streets", proclaimed an advertisement which showed a dark, gloomy and threatening urban street scene. Fine Gael promised 1,400 more gardaí over four years and the outgoing Minister for Justice, Jim Mitchell, spoke of a garda authority, garda community councils to tackle the roots of crime and a complaints tribunal. He described Dublin as "bandit country".

Doherty's appointment as Minister drew mixed reactions from the gardaí. Some felt a certain pride that one of their own had climbed so high. They believed he would understand their problems better than his predecessors. Some Fianna Fáil politicians wondered how an ex-garda would relate to the Commissioner, and how the Commissioner would relate to him.

Three weeks to the day after his appointment, Doherty addressed the annual conference of the Association of Garda Sergeants and Inspectors in Bantry, Co. Cork. The AGSI was the smaller of the two main garda representative bodies but its 2,000 sergeant and inspector members held ranks around which the rest of the force pivoted. If they liked Doherty, he stood a better than even chance of good relations with the rest of the gardaí. The AGSI had also emerged as a progressive, at times radical, group and its leaders had become prominent in moulding public opinion. If Doherty got on well with them his public image would be enhanced. The conference was held in the West Lodge Hotel and Doherty was to make an after-lunch speech on the second day.

Shortly after mid-day uniformed gardaí, conference delegates and hotel staff began pushing cars out of the car park directly in front of the hotel. Once the area was clear, a large "H" was painted on the ground. An Air Corps helicopter appeared in the distance, low on the horizon just above the mountain tops. It advanced on the hotel and swooped low and fast over the roof. Circling back in an arc it swooped over the hotel once again before turning, approaching for a third time and hovering above the "H" in the car park. Slowly it lowered itself down amid the noise and dust thrown up by the rotating blades. The engine was switched off, the door opened and out hopped Doherty. He strode over to shake the hands of Derek Nally, general secretary of the Association and Phil Callanan, president. Doherty was followed by his private secretary, Richie Ryan. He was in good spirits, and smiled, chatted and slapped backs as he was led into the hotel and to an upstairs room for pre-lunch drinks.

After lunch, Doherty made one of the longest speeches of his entire career. It ran to 13 foolscap pages. He reminded delegates that he had been a garda and said he hoped the coolness and caution taught to him during his training would stand him in good stead as Minister. He mentioned the drugs problem, the need for good community relations, the problem of run-down garda stations and over-crowding in prisons and he promised that law reforms were "at an advanced stage of preparation". He quoted from the Bible. He dwelt on the erosion of standards of integrity and honesty. He made a brief reference to extradition — Ireland's position was no different from that of the United States and France, he said.

The delegates applauded but did not appear to be very impressed. The promise of early law reforms was welcome even though it had been made often enough before without any action following. But they were prepared to give Doherty a chance — he was, after all, just three weeks in office. Time would tell. Before he left the conference hall, Doherty insisted on being introduced personally to every delegate. He shook hands with every one of them and he had a few words with most. He was eventually ushered out of the conference hall and debating was resumed.

Back upstairs, Doherty had a couple more drinks with his hosts and gave a brief press conference where he repeated some of the points in his speech. Time dragged on and by 5 p.m. the helicopter pilot was threatening to take off without the Minister. A refuelling stop would have to be made in Shannon, and the helicopter was not supposed to fly at night. Eventually Doherty was helped aboard and whisked away at 6.15 p.m. Just before he left, however, he told Nally that he wanted himself and Jack Marrinan, leader of the larger Garda Representative Association, to join him on a nationwide tour of every garda station. They could do it by helicopter, Doherty suggested eagerly. The Minister seemed to have a thing about helicopters.

The following day, Wednesday March 31st, the sergeants and inspectors debated extradition. Two branches had put down a motion calling for a review of the constitution and of the definition of a "political crime" in connection with extradition proceedings. For over a decade, extradition had been the single most contentious issue in Anglo-Irish relations, apart from the central territorial dispute over Northern Ireland. Some British politicians and Northern Ireland Unionists were enraged by the "safe haven" they said the Southern courts had created in the Republic by not extraditing people accused of terrorist crimes in the North and Britain. Ironically, it was the British courts in the last century which had created the concept of a politically motivated crime and the consequent immunity bestowed on the accused.

The Criminal Law Jurisdiction Act of 1976, enacted simultaneously by the Republic and Britain, was an effort to find a workable compromise. The Act was the result of the Sunningdale Agreement of 1973 which set up a commission to examine the problem. From the outset, the British wanted full extradition but the Irish argued for an all-Ireland court. Both sides eventually agreed on the concept of extra-territorial jurisdiction under which people accused of certain crimes in one country could be tried and convicted in the other. The Act called the bluff of the British and the Unionists — if they produced the evidence, people hiding in the Republic would be convicted. The enactment of the new law produced no great rush of evidence from the Royal Ulster Constabulary against the hundreds of terrorists it was claimed were hiding in the Republic. RUC officers argued, however, that they needed to question suspects in order to be able to gather all the evidence necessary to bring charges.

In recent years, close ties had developed between the AGSI and the Police Federation of Northern Ireland. AGSI activists had grown to admire the professionalism of the RUC and had developed considerable sympathy for the difficult situation in which the RUC operated in Northern Ireland. Many gardaí would have been quite happy to see people wanted by the RUC extradited to Northern Ireland. Indeed, they believed that the growth of violent crime in the Republic, including the murder of gardaí, was directly linked to the growth of violence in Northern Ireland. Many gardaí had come to regard themselves as being on the same side as the RUC.

The sergeants and inspectors debated the problem at length. The motion was supported by the AGSI executive and Derek Nally went a step further when he said that consideration should also be given to allowing RUC members to enter the Republic to question people in garda custody. The motion was carried unanimously.

The following morning's newspapers published extensive reports of the debate and Charles Haughey read them carefully just before attending a meeting that day with the Garda Commissioners. The meeting was Haughey's first with the Commissioners since he had become Taoiseach again on March 9th. During his previous term in office, Haughey had established a precedent of regularly meeting his Justice Minister and the Garda Commissioner, Patrick McLaughlin, plus his assistants. Following one of the first of these meetings in 1980, the government announced a £100 million package to fight crime. Included were a dozen light planes and helicopters plus 2,000 more gardaí over the next 18 months. The planes never materialised and the promise of helicopters was dusted down for the February '82 general election. By holding meetings with McLaughlin and the other Commissioners, Haughey was deliberately trying to involve himself in the Justice Ministry and the workings of the force.

McLaughlin had been appointed Commissioner in 1978

when the Lynch government sacked Edmund Garvey. When McLaughlin took over, there was something of a sigh of relief among gardaí and a considerable amount of goodwill was at his disposal. He had been assistant commissioner with responsibility for the Dublin Metropolitan Area and rose through the ranks by hard work.

McLaughlin had two deputy commissioners under his command — Larry Wren and Eamonn Doherty. Wren was the senior deputy and three assistant commissioners were supposed to report to him — John Fleming, John Paul McMahon and Joe Ainsworth. Fleming was in charge of all gardaí activity in the DMA, an area stretching from Swords in the north to Greystones in the south, and west to Lucan, with headquarters in Dublin Castle. McMahon was responsible for crime prevention and detection everywhere outside the DMA and Ainsworth was head of the Intelligence and Security Branch. This was the former C3, the section of the gardaí which specialised in counter-intelligence in the international sense, intelligence on domestic subversion and general surveillance of political activists outside the established parties. ISB was without doubt the most sensitive section of the entire force.

While Wren was essentially an administrator over these three, Eamonn Doherty was even more closely involved in the administration of the force. His assistants — Michael Enright, Patrick Power and Frank Davis — were in charge of garda training, research and planning and personnel. Immediately under the nine commissioners were chief superintendents, superintendents, inspectors, sergeants and gardaí making a force of some 10,000 men and women. If the chain of command within the Garda Siochána was clearly established, so too, in theory, was the link between the force and the government. By precedent, the commissioner dealt with the Minister for Justice through the Department of Justice. Officials in the department were supposed to be a buffer between the political establishment and the law enforcers. Regular meetings between the Minister and the Commissioner would be expected to take place but only to discuss general policy matters or, on occasions, a major crime. Day-to-day running of the gardaí was solely the responsibility of the commissioner and his team. Jack Lynch did not have meetings with the commissioners. Haughey was different: he wanted to know everything that was going on and he wanted some senior officers to feel directly responsible to him.

It was a coincidence that Haughey's first meeting with the commissioners since he resumed office took place the day after the AGSI conference ended. Haughey, accompanied by Seán Doherty, was extremely annoyed by what had been said during the extradition debate. He told the commissioners that the debate was political, that the subject was no business for the gardaí and he wanted the sergeants and inspectors brought back into line. Their conference had been the most political meeting of gardaí since the force was set up, Haughey maintained. He instructed the commissioners to ensure that nothing like it happened again. The rest of the meeting was taken up with a discussion on crime with particular reference to the drug problem. Later that evening, Doherty addressed the annual conference in Ennis, Co. Clare, of the Garda Representative Association. He told the delegates that the meeting had agreed "a major programme of measures to combat crime". This included an unspecified number of new gardaí, more money to give the gardaí "whatever extra new facilities they needed" and the helicopters were promised yet again. He made no mention of extradition and Jack Marrinan pointedly declined to support his AGSI colleagues and their call for an examination of what constituted a "a political crime".

A few days after Haughey's meeting, Derek Nally and the entire AGSI executive were called to McLaughlin's office in garda headquarters. When they arrived, Ainsworth was the only other commissioner present. Haughey's views on the extradition debate were repeated and both McLaughlin and Ainsworth demanded retractions. They wanted the next issue of *Horizon,* the AGSI magazine, to retract some of the comments made during the debate, and also retract Nally's call for consideration to be given to joint questioning by the gardaí and the RUC. Nally and his colleagues left the office amazed and not a little annoyed. Everyone had been told well in advance what was going to be debated at the conference, the Minister's office had been given fair warning in the hope that he might make some comment during his speech and nobody had discreetly warned them off any topic.

Haughey, McLaughlin and Ainsworth got their answer in the April edition of *Horizon*. The magazine reprinted the entire speech on extradition by Inspector Tom Hughes, a member of the Executive, and beside it there was a small statement. The statement included the text of the motion — "conference instructs the national executive to seek an urgent review of the constitutional and legislative conditions governing the extradition laws and in particular where they relate to political crimes" — and reiterated that joint garda-RUC questioning had been raised by just one speaker. The magazine said the statement was being made "following some queries" but there was no retraction. Instead there was a lengthy editorial entitled "Freedom of Expression". It noted that the Association had a legal role to represent gardaí "in all matters affecting their welfare and efficiency". The AGSI had no doubt that if their members were attacked by people already on the run from the RUC or British police, it was a matter affecting their welfare. The editorial went on to say that gardaí were entitled to freedom of expression, guaranteed by the constitution, and that it was a healthy sign that gardaí were concerned enough about their work to make constructive proposals for change.

By the time *Horizon* was published, Doherty had other things on his mind. He was concentrating on making himself a household name.

Fianna Fáil's ten-point election programme had included a commitment that if elected the Government would "undertake an urgent national campaign to defeat crime and vandalism . . . ". In practice, the campaign was to revolve around a major publicity effort. Once in office, Doherty set about this task with energy and enthusiasm. He contacted Fianna Fáil's general secretary, Frank Wall, and asked who should help him to create and run the publicity campaign. The whole idea had been cleared by Haughey on the condition that the package was shown to him before it was launched.

Wall got on to Des O'Meara and Partners Ltd., a firm which dealt in public relations, advertising and marketing. Des O'Meara had an association with Fianna Fáil going back to before the 1977 general election. At that time, Fianna Fáil decided to use a number of advertising agencies and public relations firms to sell itself to the electorate. During the '77 campaign, O'Meara's handled the party's youth and agriculture policies, the Peter Owens Advertising & Marketing Agency looked after press advertising and the main publicity contract was given to O'Kennedy-Brindley, an advertising agency which had a long-standing association with the party. Since the '77 election, O'Meara's had developed their links with the party and in the February '82 campaign expanded their brief to include some press advertising.

Wall told O'Meara that Doherty wanted to see him about a campaign and a meeting was arranged.

This first meeting was held before the end of March. It took place in the Department of Justice and O'Meara brought along Colm Cronin who worked with Profile Ltd., one of O'Meara's offshoot companies. Present with Doherty was Richie Ryan, his private secretary. No other officials from the Department were present or involved in the meeting.

Doherty told O'Meara and Cronin that he wanted a publicity campaign to draw attention to the crime figures and the problem of vandalism. Almost 90,000 serious crimes had been committed in 1981 and malicious damage payments had cost the state around £9 million in the same year. He wanted these facts brought home to people and ways suggested in which they could help the gardaí. He particularly wanted the message got across to people living in urban areas because such problems were worst there. Doherty said he was not quite sure how a campaign of this nature was run but he told O'Meara he had confidence in him because he had worked for the party before. Wall had recommended him and Doherty said he would go along with whatever he and Cronin suggested. They should not hesitate to contact the gardaí for background information and help — Deputy Commissioner Wren was at their disposal.

O'Meara and Cronin went off to dream up their campaign.

It was decided to rely on television, radio and newspaper advertising. They would concentrate on the two Dublin evening newspapers and the *Evening Echo* in Cork. Later it was agreed to use selected provincial newspapers for the launch of the campaign. Cronin had further meetings with Doherty either in the Department of Justice or Doherty's office in

Leinster House. In the early stages of planning the campaign, Tony Fitzpatrick, Fianna Fáil's press officer, was often present. He made one or two suggestions but it appeared he was there to represent the party's interests and make sure Doherty did not agree to anything that would embarrass Fianna Fáil.

Cronin was familiar with public service advertising campaigns in Canada and Scandinavia and thought the idea would work well in Ireland. He proposed a campaign in four phases: the first would concentrate on crime and vandalism, and phase two would highlight drugs. Phase three would deal with drunken driving and the final phase would concentrate on the problem of car thefts. Doherty's personal involvement was planned from the beginning. The television advertisements would illustrate the problems, then Doherty would make an appeal to the public. Out of this grew the idea of a letter. Doherty would write to every household in Dublin; it would be part of his personal appeal.

Doherty — known to his friends as "the Doc" — was extremely conscious of his public image and on occasions, his need to appear important affected his colleagues in government. To be assured of re-election in Roscommon, Doherty believed he had to maintain a high profile locally. His status as a minister ensured he got more coverage in the local newspaper than an ordinary TD and he was also in great demand to attend local party functions. But his running mate in the constituency, Terry Leyden, was a junior minister — a lower status but one which ensured that he too got better than average publicity and was also in demand. Both were entitled to state cars but Doherty was able to exercise a degree of control over the cars because they were operated from garda headquarters and he was Justice Minister. Doherty had the usual black Mercedes but he issued a directive that Leyden was never to be given a Mercedes. When Doherty drove through the constituency, he wanted everyone to be in no doubt about who was in town.

Leyden was allowed to have a Peugot 604.

As campaign planning progressed, Doherty became increasingly worried about the wording of the appeal he was going to make. Under no circumstances could he ask people to "inform" the gardaí about things they knew. He could not be seen to be encouraging "informers", he insisted. At the same time, there was a danger that any encouragement to the public to do something positive about crime in their area might be interpreted as an encouragement to vigilantes. The dilemma was never properly resolved: in his letter to householders, Doherty told people they could help to prevent an act of vandalism "by acting on the spot"; but in the statement launching the campaign, he said people "should not endanger themselves by acting on the spot . . .". The problem about using a word like "inform" and all the connotations it had for Fianna Fáil, the Republican Party, was resolved with the simple request that people "talk" to their local gardaí.

Cronin and O'Meara believed that if the campaign was to have any lasting effect, each phase would have to be implemented. They hoped to launch the first phase in the spring and follow it up with phase two on drugs in the autumn. The bill for the first phase was £164,550 and a similar cost was expected for each of the other phases. Included in the £164,550 was an allocation of £8,500 to pay for advice on speeches that Doherty would make and for monitoring press reports. This was interpreted as payment for services specifically designed to boost Doherty's public image. Doherty agreed to the campaign and signed the contract without reference to his officials in the Department of Justice.

Work on the campaign was proceeding when the Dublin West by-election was called. Suddenly O'Meara's were told to bring forward the launch date to one week before polling. Filming had been sub-contracted and the producers were told to have the television commercial finished and ready for broadcasting on Wednesday, May 19th — seven days before the election. They were told bluntly that if they were unable to finish on time another producer would be found. The first batch of Doherty letters, headed with the official state seal and addressed "Office of the Minister for Justice", were delivered by a private courier firm before polling day to homes in Dun Laoghaire and the Dublin West constituency. In all, some 380,000 letters were delivered during the campaign and each one had Doherty's signature.

The television advertisement was made at Ardmore studios in Bray, Co. Wicklow. Plans were changed slightly and it was decided to include the problem of car thefts in the first phase of the campaign. The finished commercial showed a giant sledgehammer smashing into a house, a flowerpot, a telephone and the destruction of a car. The film then showed Doherty walking confidently towards the viewer appealing for an end to vandalism and for help for the gardaí. He had to do it a number of times before the director was happy. Like most people, Doherty was awkward in front of a camera—it took a number of dummy runs before he was able to walk and talk at the same time.

The campaign was launched on May 17th at a press conference in the Department of Justice. Officials in the Department were told about it a few days before and were mildly surprised. None except Doherty's private secretary was in attendance at the press conference. Present were: Doherty, Garda Commissioner McLaughlin and Deputy Commissioners Wren and Doherty. The conference was orchestrated by Cronin and statements were handed out. They were printed on government information service paper although no-one from the GIS was present. The GIS officer with responsibility for the Department of Justice, Mary Sheerin, was not informed that the conference was taking place.

The statement outlined the campaign, called the National Campaign Against Crime and Vandalism. Apart from the publicity generated by advertising on television, radio and in the newspapers plus the letters (all of which projected Doherty as much, if not more, than the campaign message itself), the package involved lectures to schools and community groups. The gardaí were told that sergeants and inspectors would have to be provided to give the lectures. The only other items in the campaign were a competition for schoolchildren (write an essay/design a poster) and a "suggestion scheme". Justice department officials were somewhat startled to learn that they, along with the gardaí, would judge the efforts of the schoolchildren.

Doherty read the statement while the three commissioners and his private secretary sat expressionless.

When the television commercial was finished, a copy was rushed to government buildings for approval by Haughey but he was tied up at a meeting. An official from his office, Brendan O'Donnell, and the government press secretary, Frank Dunlop, examined it instead. O'Donnell expressed the same fears as Doherty — no way could they suggest that people "inform" to the gardaí. But there were no problems. Haughey saw the commercial later and sought no changes. It was being broadcast by the time the Dublin West electorate cast their votes and Haughey was joking that Doherty was a star. By the time the votes were counted, Sean Doherty was a national figure.

*   *   *

While Doherty basked in the bright light of publicity, the senior garda officer with whom he had most contact was scarcely known to the public.

He was Joe Ainsworth, the Assistant Commissioner, head of the Intelligence and Security Branch. Ainsworth was a force to be reckoned with in the gardaí and some of his colleagues in garda headquarters spoke of him as the real commissioner. The ISB was based in a two-storey block beside an ivy-covered mansion inside the headquarters complex. People entering had to pass through a door opened and closed from the inside. On the left was a conference room and on the right was Ainsworth's office. A window overlooking the parade ground was fitted with bullet-proof glass and Ainsworth himself carried two guns. He was known as Two Gun Joe. The office walls displayed souvenirs of meetings with policemen in other forces — commemorative plaques and plates. One wall had a large bookshelf with volumes on international terrorism, subversion, legal manuals and reports. It was quite a small room, but too neatly kept to be cluttered.

Behind Ainsworth's desk there was a bank of telephones and on his left a red computer terminal. By pressing the keys Ainsworth could call up on the screen any of the information contained in the huge ISB computer which was housed in a room above him on the first floor. The computer had been installed in 1981 and had far more capacity than Ainsworth's intelligence and security operation used. Near the computer room there was another room occupied by the telephone tap transcribers — the team of people who listened to the tapes of telephone calls recorded by post office engineers. The rest of the building was occupied by the thirty or so people who specialised in monitoring communist groups in Ireland, Middle Eastern terrorist groups and American affairs. Such sections had names like the Red Desk or the Arab Desk. The bulk of ISB's work, however, was with domestic subversion. When Ainsworth took over the branch in 1979, it was known simply as C3.

He came from Castlebar in Co. Mayo and joined the gardaí in 1946. The family had strong links with Fianna Fáil — his brother Jude was one of the party's local councillors and family members were friendly with the party's TD for the area, Michael Ó Moráin. Ainsworth spent a brief spell at the beginning of his career stationed in Cork and some rural areas but he was soon transferred to garda headquarters in Dublin. There, he worked hard and rose through the ranks. Like every other member of the Garda Siochána (and especially those in headquarters), Ainsworth was acutely aware that all promotions above the rank of inspector needed cabinet approval. Successive governments had used the promotion system to reward officers whom they regarded as especially loyal. The result was distinct factions within the gardaí — certain senior officers were known to be Fianna Fáil men, others were Fine Gaelers and some, a few, avoided political associations altogether.

Ainsworth's first big break came in 1968 when he was promoted Chief Superintendent. The promotion was made on the personal instruction of O'Moráin, who was Justice Minister at the time. The Commissioner, Patrick Carroll, objected and recorded his disapproval in a letter to O'Moráin. But the promotion went ahead and Ainsworth became barrack master. He earned a reputation as an efficient administrator but by now some of his colleagues regarded him as highly politicised. His career stood still during the years that Edmund Garvey was Commissioner. Garvey was seen to have strong leanings towards Fine Gael and after his dismissal in 1978, he became actively involved in that party. It was when Garvey's replacement, Patrick McLaughlin, took over, that Ainsworth's career prospects brightened once again. He became McLaughlin's personal assistant and in 1979 was promoted assistant commissioner by the Lynch government.

He was just six months into his new job as head of C3 when Haughey took over as leader of Fianna Fáil and Taoiseach. Part of Ainsworth's brief was providing protection for certain politicians, judges, civil servants and diplomats. He was very concerned that the new Taoiseach should have proper protection and saw to it that extra security guards were placed around the grounds of Haughey's home. Ainsworth called regularly to make spot checks to ensure they were doing their job. He would often meet Haughey and the two would chat. As communications between them became more and more frequent, Haughey began to receive what amounted to security briefings from Ainsworth. Previous Taoisigh got such information via their cabinet security committee but Haughey's relationship with Ainsworth by-passed that system. Haughey also valued his link with Ainsworth because at the time he did not have the men of his choice in Justice or Defence — George Colley's veto had seen to that.

It was not until March 1982, when Haughey had Sean Doherty, his own man, in Justice that he could once again involve himself deeply in security matters. Shortly after he became Taoiseach, he called Ainsworth to his office in government buildings for a private meeting. Haughey brought up the question of leaks from the cabinet and the civil service. Certain delicate items had appeared in the newspapers which were causing him concern. He gave no specific details and didn't ask for an investigation, but it was clear that he expected results. He spoke mainly of "potential leaks" and a "potential problem". In his relationship with Ainsworth, Haughey rarely gave specific orders but he always required results. Ainsworth set about trying to find if indeed there had been "leaks" but he had nothing to go on: he needed a marker, a starting point. He got it from Doherty.

Within a month of Doherty taking over in the Department of Justice he was having regular meetings with Ainsworth. In April he had a lengthy discussion about security and Doherty told Ainsworth there was a serious problem of "leaks". Information from government departments was getting to the media — possibly even information from the cabinet as well. Doherty referred to certain political correspondents, but he was particularly concerned about Bruce Arnold, parliamentary correspondent of the *Irish Independent*. Arnold, British-born but resident in Ireland for most of his adult life, wrote a weekly column in which he analysed and commented upon current events. Doherty wanted to know if Arnold had links with newspapers abroad or foreign press organisations. Arnold had been increasingly critical of Haughey since the Dublin Castle summit with Margaret Thatcher in 1980. When the government changed its policy on the conflict between Britain and Argentina over the Falkland Islands, Arnold was particularly critical.

Doherty pressed Ainsworth about the "leaks" at a further meeting but this time he specified that Arnold was a problem. He told Ainsworth that Arnold's phone should be tapped. The tapping began on May 10th — five days after Arnold criticised the government for breaking ranks with other EEC countries by deciding to discontinue economic sanctions against Argentina.

Chapter Eight

We must always continue to conduct Anglo-Irish relations on
a constructive, mature, responsible basis.
Charles Haughey, May 1983

Just over three weeks back in power Haughey's government faced a series of difficult foreign policy decisions over the Argentine invasion of the Falkland Islands. The troops who landed on the island in the early hours of April 2nd set off a number of reverberations in Ireland. It was clear immediately that the crisis would toss the three main strands of Irish foreign policy into the one cauldron. Bilateral relations with Britain were clearly at risk. EEC solidarity was certain to come into question. And Ireland had an unusually central role to play at the United Nations through its temporary membership of the security council.

The dispute between Britain and Argentina struck obvious chords in Ireland and set off echoes of old slogans about Britain's difficulty being Ireland's opportunity. Parallels with Northern Ireland were not direct but they were close enough to excite interest. Argentina claimed the Malvinas just as the South claimed the North. The 1,800 inhabitants of the South Atlantic islands had a veto over any change in the sovereignty of their area, just as the majority of the North had. To the incredulity of most foreign observers, Britain was preparing to dispatch a naval task force 8,000 miles to enforce that veto. On the other hand, could Ireland support Argentina's military solution to the sovereignty problem when successive governments had rejected force as a means of solving the Anglo-Irish dispute?

Relations with Britain were already tetchy. Charles Haughey's first speech in the Dáil on March 9th had stressed a tough attitude towards the North; he pledged himself to work actively for British withdrawal. He confirmed that stance during a St. Patrick's Day visit to Washington when he urged President Ronald Reagan in an after-lunch speech at the White House to put Irish unity high among America's international objectives. The British had responded to both statements with antipathy. The exceptionally good relationship between Haughey and British Prime Minister Margaret Thatcher, which was one of the more unexpected aspects of his first period as Taoiseach, had turned very sour.

On his election as party leader and Taoiseach in December 1979, Haughey had declared the North to be the first political priority of his government. Given his background in the arms crisis and his cultivation of Fianna Fáil's nationalist wing, his election forced the British to take closer account of developments in Dublin. Nobody was sure how Haughey would react to the question of security co-operation on the border; this had been one of the main domestic criticisms of Jack Lynch during his final months as party leader. Various hints from Britain indicated, however, that London might be prepared to do business with Haughey.

In practice, Haughey's election helped the possibility of a new accord in Anglo-Irish relations. He was the only likely candidate for Taoiseach who could do a deal without the fear that he would leave himself open to internal criticism within Fianna Fáil on the "national question". Thatcher occupied a similar position within the British Conservative Party. She was so far to the Right that she was in no danger of being out-flanked by any substantial body of opinion on that wing of her party. That position had allowed her to resolve the Rhodesian problem in a manner which would, under a moderate British leader, have probably provoked vigorous criticism from the Right.

The peaceful transformation of the illegal white regime in Rhodesia into black majority rule in Zimbabwe within a year of Thatcher's election in May 1979 had created considerable interest in Ireland. Haughey set out to see if a similar style conference to the Lancaster House negotiations on Zimbabwe could be arranged for Ireland. His policy on Northern Ireland insisted that the problem had to be resolved by the two sovereign governments concerned. Towards that end, he spent much of his first year in office being nice to the British. Co-operation between the security forces on both sides of the border improved and he toyed with the idea of abandoning Irish neutrality in favour of a defence pact with Britain which might help shift Thatcher towards Irish unity.

Defence arose as a possible factor because of Thatcher's reputation as a cold war warrior and because it was perceived to be an issue that carried considerable weight with her. Suggestions, apparently inspired officially, in British newspapers seemed to confirm the view that defence could be the key to a breakthrough. Haughey had no basic objections to a defence agreement with Britain and could cite a common misconception about Ireland's neutrality as a reason for an agreement. When the then Foreign Minister, Seán MacBride, turned down an invitation to join NATO in 1950, he had given the continuation of partition as the reason why Ireland could not join the same military alliance as Britain. Instead, he had offered to sign a bilateral defence treaty with the United States but the Americans, eager to extend NATO, were not interested in bilateral deals.

From then on neutrality became closely allied to unity and not an end in itself. That view was further bolstered in the 1960s when the then Taoiseach, Sean Lemass, stressed that Ireland was neither politically nor ideologically neutral. His emphasis may have been prompted by a need to reassure the original EEC partners of Ireland's suitability for membership at the time of its first application to join. But these views of neutrality were not necessarily what Éamon de Valera, Fianna Fáil's founder, had in mind when he established the policy in practice at the outbreak of the Second World War. When offered Irish unity in return for the abandonment of neutrality, he demanded instead a united and neutral Ireland. Arguably, he did not consider the unity offer to be serious but he did lay down another reason for neutrality at that time. Ireland did not have the resources to protect its people against attack.

As part of the extensive preparations for his second summit meeting with Thatcher in 1980, Haughey instructed that the defence question be examined. Various aspects were looked at by the Department of Foreign Affairs, down to the possibility that a defence pact could be used to back up political guarantees for both communities in the North because it could allow British and Irish troops to patrol the six counties. Haughey appeared, at one stage, to be so eager to offer Thatcher a treaty that he was advised to take it slowly. But the extent to which he subsequently pursued the possibility with Thatcher herself is uncertain.

She arrived in Dublin on the Feast of the Immaculate Conception, December 8th 1980, at the head of the most highly-powered British delegation ever to visit the Republic. It included three other cabinet ministers, Lord Carrington, the Foreign Secretary and architect of the Zimbabwe agreement, Sir Geoffrey Howe, the Chancellor of the Exchequer, and Humphrey Atkins, the Northern Ireland Secretary. The day-long meeting did not appear to be taking place against the most propitious of backgrounds. In the North, tensions had been raised by a hunger strike in the Maze prison, formerly known as Long Kesh, by militant republicans seeking the return of the political status their colleagues had previously enjoyed. The status had been withdrawn as part of a new British policy of treating members of paramilitary groups as ordinary criminals. One of the hunger strikers, Sean McKenna, was becoming dangerously ill.

But the eight-point communiqué issued after the meeting devoted only one paragraph to the hunger strike. The remainder described the outcome of what the statement said had been "extremely constructive and significant" discussions. It committed both leaders to devote their next meeting to "special consideration of the totality of relationships between these islands". In preparation for that, they commissioned joint studies into a range of issues including "possible new institutional structures", citizenship rights, security matters, economic co-operation and measures to encourage mutual understanding. It added that development of "the unique relationship" between the two countries offered the best prospect of improving relations. And it said that they accepted the need to bring forward policies and proposals to achieve peace, reconciliation and stability.

It was far from being the normal bland communiqué issued after such meetings. But nobody was too sure what it all meant. British diplomats implied that it was all extremely significant. One of them repeatedly drew an analogy with a train leaving London for, say, Aberdeen. If one boarded it in London one could go all the way to Aberdeen: alternatively, one could get off at an earlier stop. The first step on the journey to Irish unity had been taken. But it was not certain by any means that the journey now begun would lead inevitably to reunification.

Haughey added greatly to the confusion. At a press conference as Thatcher left Dublin, he said that everything barring the Republic's return to the Commonwealth was now on the table. Anglo-Irish relations had been brought onto the new plane which he had declared, since becoming Taoiseach, to be necessary. Later, at an off-the-record briefing for the political correspondents of Irish newspapers, he was even more fulsome in his descriptions. The agreement was "an historic breakthrough", he declared. He was to deny ever using that phase at a later stage but everybody present heard him utter it. It was that comment more than any other which prompted the newspapers to report the outcome in the ringing tones they adopted.

On her return to London, Thatcher had put a much less dramatic interpretation on the communiqué's more opaque statements. She declared, for instance, that the "uniqueness" of the relationship between the two countries was based on the fact that the Republic was the only country with which the United Kingdom shared a land frontier. Later Atkins, the Northern Ireland Secretary, insisted that the agreement had nothing whatever to do with the North's constitutional position as part of the UK.

By any yardstick, however, there had been a major development in Anglo-Irish affairs. One could spend hours debating Britain's motives — were they trying to neutralise Haughey over the hunger strikes, to buy him off with kindness, to put pressure on Unionists to concede power-sharing with Northern nationalists, or had they decided that unity was the only option after all? But there could be no argument that something significant had taken place. In the world of Anglo-Irish discussions where developments were normally measured by millimetres, there was a new situation.

Haughey's own attitude did not help to resolve the confusion. As he stood at a first-floor window in Dublin Castle watching the British politicians leave by helicopter, he was euphoric. Yet he remarked to some of those present that the communiqué was the last thing they would ever get out of Thatcher. At his subsequent press briefing for political correspondents, Brian Lenihan, the Foreign Minister, and Michael O'Kennedy, the Finance Minister, both thought that he was overselling the outcome. Three days later, Haughey made an extremely cautious statement to the Dáil which stuck rigidly to the terms of the communiqué and denied vigorously that there was any disagreement between Thatcher and himself.

Members of Haughey's cabinet were as bemused as the general public about what had happened. Most ministers had not been involved in the preparations for the summit and, apart from Lenihan and O'Kennedy, none had any direct experience of the talks. At a cabinet meeting just afterwards, Haughey sounded quite offhand when asked what had transpired. He was not pressed about it but at the following cabinet meeting George Colley asked if they were going to be given a report on it. Haughey's response left everybody bewildered. He slapped his forehead with his hand and said he had forgotten about it but a briefing would be arranged. Then he added: "I can tell you, between these four walls, that what's been going on is nothing." The other members of the cabinet were never given a briefing on it.

The meeting in Dublin Castle had lasted for more than five hours. Haughey and Thatcher had had a private discussion lasting an hour and twenty minutes and nobody but the participants and the two senior civil servants who attended knew what had transpired. Defence, for example, had not been raised at any of the plenary sessions but it was not known if it had been mentioned at the tête-à-tête meeting. Most of the arguments about the significance of the summit revolved around the phrase "institutional structures". Haughey's friends hinted heavily that of course this meant the constitutional connection between the North and Britain. Lenihan eventually said as much in an interview with *The Sunday Tribune* when he suggested that constitutional and institutional were interchangeable words. If the totality of relationships was to be discussed, then, it was argued, the future of the North was to be discussed.

While the opposition parties in the South remained sceptical, the Northern Protestant leader, the Reverend Ian Paisley, was more than willing to take Haughey at his word. He launched himself on his self-styled "Carson Trail" to save the North from a united Ireland, cloaking himself with the mantle of Sir Edward Carson, the father figure of modern Unionism. He announced a new "third force" and revived the spectre of militant unionist resistance by holding nighttime rallies of men on remote hillsides. Instead of arms, they waved gun licences, indicating the availability of weapons and declaring a willingness to use them to keep Ulster British. Haughey's supporters pointed to Paisley's actions as proof that something was afoot: Paisley preferred to believe the sounds from the South rather than the reassurances from Thatcher who felt obliged to pay one of her rare visits to Belfast to calm Unionist fears.

Haughey appeared determined to reap whatever political advantage there was to be had. In the spring of 1981 he was facing into his first general election as Taoiseach and the "historic breakthrough" was an important element in his re-election programme. He abandoned his usual caution when talking publicly about the summit in a speech prepared for that year's Fianna Fáil Ard Fheis. The road to unity, he declared confidently, would be clearly visible within a year.

The studies conducted jointly by British and Irish civil servants were continuing but it was becoming evident that Thatcher was increasingly exasperated with the interpretation put on events in Dublin. Her next opportunity to speak directly to Haughey was at an EEC meeting in Maastricht in Holland, at which the Anglo-Irish bilateral session was expected to be one of the routine side-shows at such events. The British had made clear their unhappiness in advance, especially over Lenihan's interview. But Haughey appeared taken aback by the vigour of Thatcher's attack when they met. He emerged from the meeting after five minutes or so and declared glumly:

"She's very upset". He stayed silent, slumped in his seat, for the two-hour flight home.

Domestically, the opposition parties concentrated their attention on neutrality, eventually forcing the first-ever Dáil debate on this crucial issue of foreign policy. Haughey was questioned repeatedly and harassed relentlessly by the Labour Party leader Frank Cluskey. Apart from saying that Ireland still was not able to join NATO because of partition, he took refuge in the confidentiality of his private conversation with Thatcher. Unable to confirm or deny the persistent reports of defence discussions, he helped to fuel the issue. Thatcher herself publicly closed off the prospect of a bilateral defence arrangement by suggesting that, as Britain was a member of NATO, anyone who wanted a defence agreement with her would have to talk to NATO. Haughey later admitted privately that he had miscalculated badly the public support for neutrality.

Meanwhile, a second series of hunger strikes was getting under way in the North. The first strikes had been called off shortly after the Dublin Castle summit when Sean McKenna, the most seriously ill of the protesters, lapsed into a coma. The Provisional IRA leader in Long Kesh, Bobby Sands, ordered the others to end the protest and set about discussions with the prison authorities to resolve their differences. The talks became bogged down quickly in acrimony and obfuscation by the authorities. Sands led a new hunger strike with IRA and Irish National Liberation Army prisoners going on the protest at regular intervals to maintain maximum pressure on the British government.

Haughey, too, came under pressure to use his "special relationship" with Thatcher to win some concessions from the British. He tried desperately to persuade Britain to compromise but to no avail. In public, he remained silent apart from the occasional statement expressing concern. The hunger strikes and the imminent death of Sands persuaded him to postpone a general election on several occasions. Sands died on May 5th but the public reaction in the South was not as dramatic as anticipated. Haughey decided to go to the country in June. But the death of Sands and other hunger strikers gave Sinn Féin and other republican groups an issue around which to fight. For the first time in more than 20 years, two republican prisoners were elected to the Dáil in the constituencies of Louth and Cavan-Monaghan. Haughey blamed them and, by extension, Thatcher for his loss of power in 1981.

During his period in opposition, Haughey accused Garret FitzGerald of allowing the momentum of his Northern initiative to be lost at a meeting with Thatcher in November. He castigated FitzGerald for failing to insist on the immediate formation of a parliamentary tier to the Anglo-Irish council, the title given to ministerial meetings, which was set up at the summit. Haughey appeared to equate the parliamentary body with a round table conference on the future of Northern Ireland which had been the goal of Fianna Fáil policy for most of the previous decade. But his main concern was over a plan to hold elections and set up a new assembly in Belfast. The first hints of the plan had emerged before the June election from Humphrey Atkins. Haughey had reacted strongly, criticising any such move as pointless and contrary to the spirit of the Dublin Castle accord. Under a new Northern Ireland Secretary, James Prior, the assembly plan was progressing. By the time Haughey returned to power in March 1982, it was about to be unveiled.

His criticisms had become more vigorous by then and he persuaded the Social Democratic and Labour Party, the main political representatives of Northern nationalists, to go along with his outright rejection of the assembly plan. His objections were twofold. The assembly was an attempt at a settlement within the borders of Northern Ireland which he repeatedly described as "a failed political entity". Secondly, the assembly was contrary to what he believed to have been a central part of the Dublin Castle agreement — that Britain and Ireland were to produce proposals jointly for Northern Ireland. Britain was pushing the assembly plan unilaterally. There was no discussion with Dublin about it, never mind joint consideration of new proposals.

By coincidence, James Prior produced his assembly plan just four days after Argentina had invaded the Falklands.

Gerry Collins had had a busy three weeks in his new post as Foreign Minister. He accompanied Haughey to Washington for his St. Patrick's Day lunch with President Reagan and had been coming to terms with the intricacies of the EEC. During the last week of March, he had his first meeting with James Prior in London. It was totally unsuccessful: Collins made a last ditch attempt to dissuade Prior from his planned elections and assembly but he was rebuffed. Collins, however, was determined to make his mark in Foreign Affairs. A reputation as a Tammany Hall-type operator still lingered around him from his student days, more than 20 years earlier. He was undoubtedly shrewd but he was also a subtle politician who had shown his ability by coming through four years as Minister for Justice more or less unscathed. He was to be less fortunate in Foreign Affairs where he quickly found himself caught between the Taoiseach's Department on one hand and the Department of Foreign Affairs on the other.

Haughey had a special interest in the North and there was no love lost between him and the diplomats in Iveagh House, the headquarters of Foreign Affairs. During his American visit, Haughey had made his dim view of Irish diplomats both clear and public. At one press conference, he criticised Irish diplomatic missions for not having stressed sufficiently the case for Irish unity. He clearly held them responsible for the policy they enunciated, rather than the governments which gave them political direction. It was an extraordinary remark, ignoring all the conventions and realities of the relationship between governments and civil servants.

Haughey had another reason for distrusting the diplomats: they had inflicted a very public defeat upon him during his first term as Taoiseach. In 1980 he had decided, in response to urgings from people like Neil Blaney, to reshuffle Irish diplomats abroad in order to remove Sean Donlon from Washington. Donlon, a 41-year-old career diplomat, had been head of the Anglo-Irish section in Iveagh House before being appointed ambassador to the US by Jack Lynch. He had been extremely successful in Washington in building up the moderate Irish-American lobby and had run — on instructions from Dublin — a determined campaign to detach the IRA from its American funders and backers. His efforts had created many opponents in the Irish-American community. Haughey believed that all Irish-American opinion should be united because the various camps were essentially on the same side.

Haughey planned to move Donlon from the US to the United Nations and a sequence of consequential changes were prepared. Many of those involved were informed of their new postings. But resistance to the moves and particularly to the motives perceived to be behind them was exceptionally strong. Eventually, Donlon's Irish-American friends — influential people like Senator Edward Kennedy and the Speaker of the House of Representatives, T.P. "Tip" O'Neill — made it clear to Haughey that their relationship with Dublin would suffer if he persisted in his plans. Haughey backed off and Lenihan, then Foreign Minister, was left to deny publicly that any changes had been contemplated.

By 1982, Donlon was back in Dublin as secretary of the Department, promoted by Garret FitzGerald's government. Tension between the Taoiseach's Department under Haughey and Foreign Affairs became apparent soon after the new administration took over. Haughey's advisor on Northern Ireland, Martin Mansergh, sought direct access to Foreign Affairs files. The assistant secretary in charge of the Anglo-Irish section of Foreign Affairs, David Neligan, resisted. The Department did not like the idea of a northern specialist in the Taoiseach's Department who could disrupt the pattern of contacts and complicate everybody's life. The dispute went on over two months and covered information about the Falklands conflict. It was resolved eventually by a compromise whereby Mansergh would ask Haughey or Collins for the information he required: they would get it through the normal channels and pass it on to him. The dispute was both symptomatic of the relations between both Departments and a further irritant.

The Falklands conflict served to bring to a head this type of sparring, these mutual suspicions and differing approaches to foreign policy. Ireland's initial response to the invasion on April 2nd was left mainly to the diplomats: few Irish politicians knew much about the dispute between Britain and Argentina or about the islands and their inhabitants.

On two occasions at the UN, Ireland had supported Argentina's claim to sovereignty over the islands but had altered its stance in the mid-1970s. After the military take-over in Argentina and the so-called "dirty war" in which thousands of Argentinians simply disappeared, Ireland abstained as a protest against the régime's attitude to human rights. The initial response to the invasion was to avoid taking sides on the issue of sovereignty over the islands. In discussions among the ten EEC members, Ireland took a firm line that the community should not involve itself in the rights and wrongs of who owned the islands but Ireland opposed the use of force to settle the argument.

This approach had considerable support among the ten, many of whom did not want to take sides either. The Foreign Ministers of all the member states, including Collins, approved a two-paragraph statement that condemned Argentina's armed intervention and appealed to it to heed a call by the UN Security Council to refrain from using force. The UN appeal had been made the previous day when it appeared that Argentina, after several weeks of sabre-rattling, was about to invade. But it was too late by then to stop the invading forces.

On April 2nd, as well, the UN Security Council reconvened and Britain tabled a resolution demanding an end to hostilities, that Argentina withdraw its forces and that a diplomatic solution be sought. Britain did not want any modifications to the resolution: it had to be voted on as it stood. Ireland's Ambassador at the UN, Noel Dorr, cautiously condemned the use of force in defiance of the unanimous call by the Security Council the previous evening. Ireland had good relations with both countries involved but her duty as a member of the Council was to uphold its authority and the rule of law, he said. Dorr stressed that Ireland was not taking sides on the basic issue. His speech was clearly in line with the position adopted by Ireland and the other EEC countries and did not say explicitly how Ireland would vote on the resolution. As events transpired, voting on the British resolution was postponed until the following day to allow Argentina's Foreign Minister, Nicanor Costa Mendez, time to travel to New York.

The invasion of the Falklands was the main news item in all the Irish newspapers on Saturday, April 3rd. Details of the British resolution at the UN were reported along with indications that Ireland and most other Security Council members would back it. Charles Haughey was at his Kinsealy home that day and was kept informed of developments by Donlon who was also in contact with Dorr in New York. In the light of subsequent accusations about Dorr's actions, Haughey's involvement in the policy at that stage was of crucial importance. An impression was created at the time and fostered by his supporters subsequently that he had played no part in deciding the policies. In fact, he was kept abreast of developments that day and sanctioned the casting of Ireland's vote in favour of Britain's resolution at the Security Council. The resolution, number 502, was adopted by ten votes to one and with four abstentions. None of the permanent members of the Security Council used their veto: the Soviet Union abstained.

When Neil Blaney complained later to Haughey about Ireland's stance at the UN, Haughey excused himself by claiming that he did not know what Dorr had said at the meeting. Close associates of Haughey maintained that he only became aware of the Irish position through media reports. Stories were circulated among Dublin newspapers that Dorr had acted without full-scale consultation with Dublin. After the *Sunday Independent* printed the accusation, other civil servants in Iveagh House reacted furiously. The newspaper published a retraction the following week. But the claim that Dorr had made the policy persisted among Haughey supporters although some of them were careful to say that they were not accusing Dorr of exceeding his powers or responsibilities.

Dorr, a meticulously precise diplomat, was acting on the terms of the EEC statement, sanctioned by Collins, when he made his first post-invasion speech. On April 3rd, Dorr spoke again to announce that Ireland would vote for the resolution which, he declared, aimed to return to the pre-invasion status quo. Ireland insisted that both countries avoid force and negotiate, he added. Haughey was unhappy about the first statement but he condoned the second one and sanctioned the vote in favour of the resolution. He appeared to change his mind again later, especially when the British set about using Resolution 502 to good propaganda effect and, ultimately, for justifying their military retaliation against Argentina.

Even then, however, Britain was assembling a naval task force which set sail the following week as the focus of diplomatic attention shifted back to the EEC. Thatcher sent a personal message to Haughey and other EEC heads of government on Tuesday, April 6th, seeking support for trade sanctions against Argentina. Haughey's response was cool. He, Collins and Sean Doherty discussed the Falklands and the Prior assembly plan at a meeting the next day. The cabinet discussed the sanctions issue but a decision was avoided. No decision was taken either at a second cabinet meeting.

At that stage, a majority of the Ten were less than enthusiastic about sanctions. Britain had rarely shown any great desire for community solidarity and, at the time, was involved in another rearguard action over farm price increases as part of its unrelenting campaign to cut its contributions to the EEC budget. Britain was delaying the introduction of new agricultural prices, a strategy that was costing Ireland a considerable amount of cash and costing Haughey's government even more in terms of farmers' goodwill. Haughey hinted at various times that the farm prices and the Falklands policy were linked.

But the sanctions question was also a major test for Irish foreign policy. Britain was pulling out all the stops in the search for support and was demanding solidarity. If the EEC failed to grant it, the process of political co-operation (as the attempt to co-ordinate the foreign policies of the Ten was known) could be set back severely. If Ireland went along with it, she could be sucked into supporting British military action in a colonial-style situation. It was the first time that EEC sanctions had been sought in a situation where one of the member countries was involved militarily. That would have implications for Irish neutrality and, of equal importance, for domestic politics.

On balance, Iveagh House recommended that Ireland should support the sanctions. Its main argument was that the Irish interest in good Anglo-Irish relations — which had been the cornerstone of Haughey's Northern policy — would best be served by that course of action. By Good Friday, April 9th, the balance within the EEC had shifted and Ireland had come around to favouring sanctions. The permanent representatives of the Ten met in Brussels under the chairmanship of the Belgium Ambassador, Paul Noterdaeme. He suggested that a total ban on trade be introduced. Five countries, including Ireland, agreed immediately: the others, including West Germany and France, were more reluctant. The British pressed the issue and the doubters capitulated.

The following day the Ten issued a formal statement announcing the ban on Argentine imports and emphasising that their actions were intended to achieve the implementation of Resolution 502. Collins, in a statement in Dublin, reiterated that the government believed that Resolution 502 was the best means by which further fighting could be avoided and the rule of law upheld in international relations. EEC solidarity had been maintained. The British were delighted and Thatcher wrote to Haughey thanking him for Ireland's support.

But Haughey was deeply uneasy about the whole position. There were occasional murmurs of opposition within Fianna Fáil. Blaney had made his objections known in strong language to Haughey. In Argentina, the federation of Irish Argentine societies took full-page advertisements in newspapers to dissociate themselves from Ireland's UN stand. Collins continued to defend the policy in public, rejecting suggestions of horse-trading over the North or over farm prices. In one television interview he declared: "We support something if it is right and proper to support it and this we have done now."

While Britain's task force steamed southward, a bizarre and unconnected incident occurred in the Irish Sea. A fleet of Irish trawlers was fishing in international waters some 30 miles off Dublin Bay on Sunday, April 18th. A 75-foot trawler from Clogherhead in Co. Louth, the *Sharelga,* was fishing for prawns when it was suddenly pulled backwards at speed for some two miles. It then turned turtle and sank. The five crew members were tossed into the sea and rescued by other trawlers. The fishermen were convinced that a submarine had caught in the trawler's nets and sunk the *Sharelga.*

Haughey personally ordered the naval service to investigate. A spotter plane was dispatched to the area immediately and the fishery protection vessel *LE Aisling* steamed from her station off the north west coast. A second vessel and three more aircraft joined in the search next day. There was widespread scepticism at the submarine story: some experts maintained that the *Sharelga's* engines had probably gone into reverse, hauling her backwards over her own nets and sinking her. The *Aisling* recovered some of the *Sharelga's* gear with grappling hooks, including a severed hawser that had attached the nets to the trawler.

Almost two weeks after the incident the British Ambassador in Dublin, Sir Leonard Figg, called to the Department of Foreign Affairs on Saturday, May 1st, and formally accepted liability for the sinking of the *Sharelga*. Contrary to initial impressions, a British submarine had been responsible. The admission may have been prompted by a desire to keep on friendly terms with the Irish government or by a fear that British involvement was about to be discovered. But the delay and the timing of the announcement on a Saturday evening did not create a friendly atmosphere. The government demanded further explanations for the submarine's failure to surface and sought assurances that there would not be a repeat. The affair helped to sour relations with Britain but Haughey's mind had changed on the Falklands again by them.

Haughey's unhappiness over Ireland's position had increased steadily as the British task force neared the end of its 8,000 mile journey. Britain had tried towards the end of April to get EEC backing for efforts to persuade third world countries to impose sanctions on Argentina. Haughey was already concerned at the way in which the EEC sanctions were being portrayed as support for military action. At one stage, Martin Mansergh protested to the Belgians (who held the EEC presidency) about their suggestions that the sanctions gave implicit community support for Britain to re-take the Falklands by force. Ireland insisted that the sanctions were in support of diplomacy, not of military action.

Britain had retaken the remote island of South Georgia, where the crisis had begun, on April 25th. Collins hinted afterwards that the EEC would reconsider the sanctions — which were in force until May 17th — if there were any further outbreaks of violence. Ireland's position up to then had been "correct and proper", he added. By the end of April, however, it looked as if further military clashes were inevitable. The American Secretary of State, Alexander Haig, abandoned his attempt at shuttle diplomacy and the US came off the fence onto Britain's side. On May 1st, the RAF dropped ten tons of explosives on the Falklands main airport near Port Stanley. Jets from the aircraft carriers in the task force followed up with further raids.

Ministers gathered in Dublin on Sunday, May 2nd for a cabinet meeting to discuss the situation. They heard detailed briefings on the background to the conflict and the discussions ranged over the parallels with the North and the questions of neutrality. The echoes of colonialism had become more marked with the prospect of a military escalation. The *Sharelga* incident helped to personalise the conflict in the South Atlantic for some of those present. The main points were agreed for a statement which would shift the government around to a position with which Haughey would be more comfortable.

The statement said that the government was "seriously concerned at the escalating military situation in the South Atlantic."

It went on: "From the outset of the Falklands crisis, the policy of the Irish Government, both at the United Nations and within the European Economic Community, has been directed to preventing a wider conflict and promoting a negotiated, honourable settlement by diplomatic means.

"An adequate framework already exists within which such a settlement can be achieved if the parties demonstrate the political will to do so.

"It is important, therefore, that the possibilities offered by the United Nations should be fully exploited and further military escalation which would only make negotiations all the more difficult avoided. Ireland is ready to help in any way it can, through its current membership of the Security Council, to advance a diplomatic solution."

Haughey's main reservation since the crisis began had revolved around the demand in Resolution 502 that Argentina withdraw its forces from the Falklands. In the statement which followed the cabinet meeting, he finally imposed his will in relation to that demand. A draft of the statement included a mention of 502: Haughey cut it out of the final version. The statement released referred to the existence of "an adequate framework" within which a settlement could be achieved. Later, when pressed to explain the absence of any reference to

161

Resolution 502, Haughey maintained that this phrase was a reference to the Resolution. He also insisted subsequently that the three aspects of the Resolution — Argentine withdrawal, cessation of hostilities and diplomatic solution — were fully supported by Ireland and that that support had not altered. The statement concluded that the government wished to "reaffirm Ireland's traditional role of neutrality in relation to armed conflicts".

It was clear from the statement that the government was changing course. Its timing, as events were to prove, was also impeccable. About 8 p.m. (Irish time) on that day, May 2nd, the single most controversial military action of the Falklands war took place outside the so called "exclusion zone" which Britain had declared for 200 miles around the island. Three Argentine vessels, two destroyers and the cruiser *General Belgrano,* were heading back towards the Argentine when the *Belgrano* was hit by two conventional torpedoes. They had been fired without warning by a British nuclear submarine, HMS *Conqueror,* which had received an order from Thatcher's war cabinet to sink the cruiser. More than 200 of the 1,000 strong crew were killed immediately: the final death toll was 368 Argentine sailors killed.

The scale of the slaughter did not become apparent until well into the next day. There was a sense of relief and even of self-congratulation among ministers in Dublin. They had made their decision just in time: there was no question now but that Ireland would move as far away from any appearance of support for Britain as it possibly could. The caution of the Sunday statement was abandoned by the Defence Minister, Paddy Power, who gave vent to his feelings at a Fianna Fáil meeting in Edenderry, Co. Offaly. He accused Britain of telling lies and behaving like a hit-and-run driver over the *Sharelga* incident. Britain was now the aggressor in the Falklands, he declared. Ireland would take up a neutral stance immediately. The party members present gave him a standing ovation.

The new policy was completed on Tuesday, May 4th, at a cabinet meeting. The government declared afterwards that it would seek the withdrawal of EEC sanctions against Argentina and that it would seek an immediate meeting of the UN Security Council to put forward a new resolution demanding a cessation of hostilities. There was no mention, implicit or explicit, of Resolution 502 or that Argentina should withdraw its forces from the islands. In the Dáil, Garret FitzGerald drew attention to the omission and asked if Power's statement represented official government policy. Haughey said it did not but it was understandable in the circumstances.

Haughey himself took over responsibility for enunciating in public the new policy, thereby helping to give credence to the erroneous belief that somebody else had been in control till then. EEC sanctions had been designed to avoid military actions and conflict, he declared. They had not succeeded in their objective. But Haughey's UN initiative ran into an immediate hiccup. Responsibility for policy had now shifted totally from Foreign Affairs to the Taoiseach's Department, where the new statement had been drawn up. But somebody had overlooked one of the consequences of the demand for an immediate UN meeting.

Normal practice at the UN meant that if any Security Council member sought an immediate meeting they got it. But the Secretary General, Javier Perez de Cuellar, did not want an immediate meeting. Two days earlier, he had begun a delicate attempt to find a solution by putting proposals to both Britain and Argentina. He had informed the Council members privately of his moves and the information had been passed from the Department of Foreign Affairs to the Taoiseach's Department. The Irish request for a meeting threatened to disrupt his plans. He appealed to Ireland privately not to press the request. Haughey agreed and the government's request for "an immediate meeting" was re-written as "an immediate request" for a meeting. Perez de Cuellar's attempt at negotiations very nearly succeeded over the following weeks: he persuaded Britain to agree to the appointment of a UN governor for the islands, the withdrawal of troops and a deadline for talks.

The Irish change of direction had been announced in the immediate aftermath of the sinking of the *Belgrano* and before Argentina retaliated. Just after lunch on May 4th, two Argentine airforce jets launched two sophisticated Exocet missiles at several of the British ships. One of them hit the destroyer *HMS Sheffield* which was on picket duty twenty miles ahead of the rest of the fleet. The crew of the *Sheffield* never saw the plane which launched the missiles, but the ship was crippled and thirty people killed. News of the attack was broadcast on BBC television's main evening news later that day. The shock to the British psyche was immense: one of their most modern battleships had been put out of action by people whom they had come to see in racist and derisory terms as being unable to stand up to the military might of a developed western nation. Many British people realised, perhaps for the first time, that the task force could be defeated at a huge cost in lives and materiel.

Britain was intensely angry over Ireland's change of position. The coincidence of it coming on the same day as the attack on the *Sheffield* helped to heighten the antagonism of British public opinion. Many Britons believed that the move was motivated solely by anti-British sentiments within Haughey's government. Britain's official hostility to the Irish moves was communicated quickly and directly to Dublin. The official anger was prompted primarily by the demand for an immediate UN meeting. Once it had won acceptance for 502, Britain wanted to keep the Falklands issue out of the UN. It knew that any other resolution would weaken the terms of 502 which, it believed rightly, were the most advantageous it could get.

During the following weeks, British resentment was felt by Irish exporters and individuals. It clearly went much deeper and lasted longer than the response of British public opinion to IRA or INLA attacks in London or other English cities. Haughey denied that his actions had been motivated by any spirit of animosity towards Britain but by a desire to help. "The people of this country are deeply attached to our neutrality and they are not prepared to see it eroded," he told the Dáil.

Garret FitzGerald maintained that neutrality was a phony excuse. Ireland had backed League of Nations sanctions against Italy in 1935 and against Iran in 1980 over the holding of American diplomats as hostages. To argue that it was a breach of neutrality to back sanctions after hostilities broke out was inconsistent with tradition and with Haughey's own previous actions. FitzGerald accused Haughey of merely seeking temporary popularity at home at the expense of Ireland's international reputation and of Anglo-Irish relations upon which Haughey himself had placed such importance in 1980 and 1981.

Ireland and Italy opted out of the Common Market sanctions when the renewal of the trade ban was considered on May 17th. Four days later, as British troops went ashore at San Carlos in the Falklands, Haughey instructed Dorr to reactivate Ireland's request for a Security Council meeting. At the meeting, Dorr reviewed developments since the start of the crisis but merely suggested that the Council give the Secretary General a formal mandate to continue his efforts. Perez de Cueller's attempt at mediation had almost succeeded but had collapsed in a welter of recriminations between Argentina and Britain. At a second meeting, Dorr put forward a draft resolution which sought a three-day ceasefire to give Perez de Cuellar time to arrange a more permanent cessation and to continue his negotiations with a new mandate. The British were outraged at the ceasefire proposal: their troops and vessels had been under sustained aerial attack at San Carlos for four days. A ceasefire would, they believed, allow the Argentinians time to re-group and prepare a counter-attack while preventing Britain from consolidating its toe-hold on the islands.

Britain made it clear that it would veto any proposal demanding a ceasefire and Ireland dropped it. Instead, Ireland became a joint sponsor with five non-aligned countries of a modified resolution which did not call on the parties involved to cease hostilities but requested the Secretary General to try and arrange a ceasefire. The resolution was passed on May 26th but, to the surprise of nobody, it had no effect at all on the war in the South Atlantic.

Shortly afterwards, Argentina suggested privately to Ireland that Dorr should introduce another resolution demanding a ceasefire. British troops were advancing on Port Stanley and had re-taken the settlement at Goose Green in a vicious battle. Argentina appeared to have doubts about its prospects of victory and clearly wanted to switch the conflict back onto the diplomatic plane. Britain, on the contrary, wanted nothing to interfere with the progress of its forces. The Argentinian request was turned down by Haughey, presumably in the belief that it would further damage Anglo-Irish relations and stood little chance of success anyhow.

Two other Security Council members, Panama and Spain, moved the ceasefire motion, and Ireland voted for it. "We want to say 'stop' one last time", Dorr told the Security Council. Britain used her veto to defeat the proposal but controversy erupted over America's actions. The US Ambassador, Jeane Kirkpatrick, had urged her government to abstain and it had finally come around to her view. But the instruction was relayed to the UN meeting too late: she had vetoed the resolution but she explained afterwards that the US had meant to abstain. By then, however, all diplomatic efforts to solve the dispute had been exhausted and the war continued until the capitulation of the Argentine garrison at Port Stanley on June 14th.

Anglo-Irish relations were now at an extremely low level. Haughey insisted that if there had been any deterioration it had been caused by the British insistence on pursuing their assembly plan for the North. The British had side-stepped and downgraded the Anglo-Irish process and the parliamentary council, he complained. Britain retorted that there had never been any commitment to consult with Dublin over matters affecting Northern Ireland. The Irish Ambassador in London, Eamonn Kennedy, was called to the Foreign Office to be told by a junior minister, Douglas Hurd, of the British view. The message was reinforced by Thatcher herself in the House of Commons.

It appeared for a time as if the verbal hostilities would escalate to an unprecedented level. There were demands by the right wing of the British Conservative party for the removal of the franchise from Irish citizens in Britain and campaigns by *The Sun* newspaper to boycott Irish butter, and there was now a straight dispute which threatened to overturn the tacit understanding that had existed for a decade about Dublin's role in relation to Northern Ireland. Irish officials disputed Thatcher's interpretation of the consultation process by pointing to the joint communiqué issued after the Dublin Castle summit which had spoken of "bringing forward policies and proposals to achieve peace, reconciliation and stability" —a phrase which in Haughey's eyes meant Irish unity but probably something less to Britain. In addition, they claimed that a memorandum of understanding drawn up in January 1982 had outlined the proposals for the Anglo-Irish Council and said that consultations would take place under its aegis.

Haughey and Collins insisted, however, that relations were not as black as they were being painted. They could point to the continuation of ministerial contacts under the Anglo-Irish Council. But such meetings were few and far between and at a low level, dealing with non-contentious and routine issues. Collins, however, took the opportunity of the adjournment debate in the Dáil in mid-July to review foreign policy, including the Irish response to the Falklands crisis and the current state of Anglo-Irish relations. In the course of it, he noted that Anglo-Irish co-operation on politics, economics and security was "a two-way process", a reference that was interpreted by some commentators to imply a threat of withdrawing security co-operation on the border. Collins added: "We cannot accept a selective or inconsistent approach to mutual co-operation."

Haughey's aides suggested that Collins' remarks were a reminder to the British rather than a threat, but the very fact that reminders of that nature were thought to be necessary underscored the extent to which Anglo-Irish relations had deteriorated. Over the following months, the atmosphere continued frosty as the British pursued their assembly plan and arranged for elections in October. The SDLP, nervous at being outflanked by Sinn Féin with its new emphasis on political action, decided to contest the elections but to boycott the assembly. Haughey and his advisors would have preferred the SDLP to boycott the actual elections in the belief that such a move would have killed the initiative before it got off the ground. But the government refrained from putting too much pressure on the SDLP as Haughey continued his attempts to kill the assembly plan.

In two years, Anglo-Irish relations under Haughey had gone from the heights of good neighbourliness and optimism to the pits of mutual suspicion and ill feeling. Haughey could not be held solely responsible for that change but he had contributed considerably to it. He had helped to undermine the potential gains he had achieved in his Dublin Castle meeting with Thatcher by over-selling the results. On the Falklands, he had ignored the advice given to him about the effects of his policy on Britain and dismissed them as untrue or unjustified when they turned out as predicted. The over-selling of the Thatcher agreement casts doubt on whether Haughey really believed it contained the seeds of history: if it did why put it at risk for immediate political gain?

The Falklands crisis, on the other hand, laid down an important marker for the continuation of Irish neutrality. The policy would have been weakened considerably had Haughey allowed continued support for Britain's use of force to retrieve the Falklands. He had called a halt to the erosion of a policy which he himself had considered to be expendable some eighteen months earlier. But the price he paid was to demolish for the time being his own declared policy of seeking a solution to the Northern problem through a relationship between the British and Irish governments.

The Falklands crisis returned to the UN in the autumn of 1982 when twenty Central and South American countries, including such strange bedfellows as the marxist Cubans and the right wing military dictators in Chile, sponsored a resolution calling on Argentina and Britain to resume negotiations on the sovereignty of the Falklands. Britain was none too pleased, least of all when the United States supported the resolution. Ireland, however, abstained. Dorr explained that, by calling for negotiations, the resolution tilted somewhat towards the position of one of the parties.

The reason was scarcely convincing. Ireland had consistently demanded negotiations at the beginning and at the height of the war. The new resolution specifically cited Resolution 502 and Resolution 505 (which Ireland had co-sponsored in May). The Irish abstention made no sense whatever in view of its earlier voting record at the Security Council. Haughey, however, had decided on abstention and Dorr was once again, following instructions. The reason appeared to be a desire to mend fences with the British, a pragmatic response that he had rejected the previous summer.

Chapter Nine

*People can now produce evidence to justify their cynicism
and their low opinion of politicians.*
George Colley, June 1982

On the first weekend in May, as the government was altering its
approach to the Falklands crisis, Charles Haughey set out to
ease the precarious Dáil position that voters had given him in
the general election. He and his cabinet ministers descended on
Dublin West in a determined bid to translate his audacious
decision to give Fine Gael's Dick Burke the EEC Commissioner-
ship into an extra Dáil seat. Fine Gael, demoralised by Burke's
acceptance of the offer, also launched their campaign. It was
clear from the beginning that both sides were going to pull out
all the stops. Garret FitzGerald's leadership of Fine Gael could
be at risk if he lost, it was speculated. Haughey's "stroke"
would be completed if he won: if he lost, the Fianna Fáil
government would not be much worse off and would have
benefited from a couple of parliamentary weeks when the
opposition was short of Burke's vote. Haughey, it appeared,
had everything to gain and nothing much to lose.

On the surface, the odds should have been against Fianna
Fáil. The party's share of the first preference votes cast in
Dublin West in the previous two general elections had been less
than that won by Fine Gael. But Fine Gael's lead in the February
general election had been a mere 354 votes. The Labour Party
had won 2,617 votes, most of them falling into the anti-Fianna
Fáil camp. The Workers' Party had passed out Labour with
3,285 votes for its leader Tomás MacGiolla. When preferences
had been shared out after his elimination from the count, they

had gone in almost equal numbers to Fianna Fáil and Fine Gael. The Workers' Party was now supporting Haughey in the Dáil, had helped to elect him as Taoiseach and voted for his government on March 25th. Fianna Fáil could be hopeful that the Workers' Party attitude in the Dáil would pay by-election dividends with a greater share of MacGiolla's transfers going to the government candidate.

Fianna Fáil was seen to have by far the stronger candidate in Eileen Lemass, a 49-year-old political widow related by marriage to Charles Haughey. Like him, she had married one of Sean Lemass's children, Noel, whose Dáil seat she won in the 1977 general election. She retained the seat in the 1981 general election after beating her party colleague, Liam Lawlor, to the last of the constituency's five seats. In February 1982, however, Lawlor had turned the tables and taken the fifth seat. By contrast with her Fine Gael rival, Lemass was an experienced candidate and had a solid political base in the Ballyfermot area. The Fine Gael candidate, Liam Skelly, was a political novice who had joined the party formally the day before he was chosen at a selection convention. He was 40, a native of Inchicore, Dublin and a successful businessman. But his main political asset was the fact that he was backed by Jim Mitchell, Fine Gael's local strongman who had built up a secure base through hard constituency work. Mitchell had agreed to take Burke into the constituency and had helped to get him elected to the Dáil twice. He was extremely upset at Burke's defection.

Fianna Fáil threw everything it had into the by-election. Cabinet ministers were allocated sub-sections of the constituency for which they would be held responsible. Haughey was reputed to have told the party that no TD was to go home until after polling day, May 25th. Ministers were told to speed up the announcement of projects which their departments planned for the area, and other ministerial business was occasionally sacrificed to the immediate political needs of the by-election. But Haughey and his ministers withdrew temporarily from Dublin West on Sunday, May 2nd, to hold their cabinet meeting to discuss the Falklands situation and afterwards to stress Ireland's traditional neutrality in military conflicts. Everything, even government policy on the Falklands, appeared to be part of Fianna Fáil's all-out campaign to persuade the voters of Dublin West to give the government that extra seat that would make its future more secure.

There were minor embarrassments along the way for Fianna Fáil. Under pressure from the opposition, it produced a new Bill to close the double voting loophole revealed by the Pat O'Connor court case in April. The Prevention of Electoral Abuses Bill was debated and passed in a single day, making it an offence for anyone to apply for a ballot paper if they had already received one. It would no longer have to be proved in court that a person had attempted to vote, merely that they had requested a ballot paper in their own name when they had already obtained one earlier. Fine Gael and the other opposition parties did their best to embarrass Fianna Fáil over sharp practices in causing the by-election and in the way it was fighting it. Fianna Fáil retorted by accusing Dick Burke of having deserted the electors of Dublin West with unseemly haste. It urged voters to give it the seat and end the political instability which had caused two general elections within nine months.

The government's economic policy had also been thrown back into the melting pot by the by-election. Having inherited most of the budget from the coalition government, Fianna Fáil introduced its own budget on March 25th. It dropped the most contentious of the coalition's proposals, including the plan to add VAT to the price of clothes and shoes and to cut subsidies on food. It also set the new government a lower target for its budget deficit for 1982 of £679 million. Fianna Fáil appeared to be maintaining that it could sort out the country's economic problems quicker than the coalition and in a considerably less painful fashion. But its proposals were not completely painless. There had been a hefty increase in the percentage of income that employees had to pay for their Pay Related Social Insurance. The PRSI rate had gone up from 4.75% to 7.5% of gross pay from the start of the new tax year in April, and this rise cut immediately and directly into the take-home pay of those affected. Trade unions increased their pressure for reform of the general taxation system with marches and other protests. The Finance Minister, Ray MacSharry, announced on April 19th that no change was possible in the system: three days later the government capitulated and announced a new tax allowance of £312 a year for those paying the higher PRSI rates.

The result was to cut the deductions for social insurance from pay packets by half.

Around the same time, the government headed off a threatened increase in mortgage rates by offering building societies indirect subsidies in the form of cheap loans and lower taxes. Increases in children's allowances, due to be paid in July, were brought forward to May. Haughey's critics complained bitterly that he was trying to buy the by-election with these moves. His internal critics in Fianna Fáil thought much the same but said nothing in public. Economic commentators noted that the budget projections were already in tatters.

The voters of Dublin West were receiving more individual attention. A new factory for the American forklift company, Hyster, was announced for Blanchardstown. Community centres were promised for various places and at least nine new schools, five primary and four post-primary, were to be built, residents were assured. The new Education Minister, Martin O'Donoghue, pledged £300,000 for a sports centre in Ballyfermot. He also found a way to solve the expense of heating a school in Ballyfermot. The heating grant was based on the number of pupils, not the physical dimensions of the school, and one particular building suffered because the number of children had declined while it still needed as much money as ever to heat it. The school got the money it needed under the guise of a grant to carry out a study into the bureaucratic problem from which it suffered.

Brian Lenihan, Agriculture Minister and Dublin West TD, took a hand in a row over education in Lucan. Residents of a middle-class estate wanted a community school to be built in the Esker area in place of a community college which would have been run by the VEC as a replacement for a vocational school. On the eve of the poll, letters signed by Lenihan were distributed to all houses in the area promising that the community school would be built. Haughey had sanctioned the letter but O'Donoghue was not told of it in advance. The move angered other locals, including vocational school teachers, and culminated in a protest march to the Esker polling station on the following day.

Ray Burke, the Environment Minister, was busy meanwhile cutting the sod for a by-pass road around Palmerstown which turned out to be a little premature. The chairman of Dublin County Council, Sean Barrett, who was also a Fine Gael TD from Dun Laoghaire, complained that contracts for the road had not been signed. Besides, he had not been invited to the ceremony. Ray Burke, in a speech distributed to newspapers, held out the prospect of a new road linking Chapelizod to Kilcock and by-passing Lucan, Leixlip, Maynooth and Kilcock, with the advantage to local residents of taking heavy, western-bound traffic out of those villages.

Seán Doherty had speeded up his national campaign on crime and vandalism to make maximum use of the state-sponsored publicity measure for Fianna Fáil's benefit. As well as a house-to-house distribution of leaflets in Dublin West, the connection between the party's election efforts and the government-run publicity campaign was underlined by newspaper advertisements which showed Doherty talking to Eileen Lemass in front of a garda motorcycle. The week before polling, the Revenue Commissioners also took advertising space in the newspapers to remind employers to increase tax-free allowances in line with the PRSI concessions. On the eve of the poll, Haughey and Lemass were pictured in ads that appealed to voters to "strengthen the government's hand". In the same newspapers, the Department of Health advertised the fact that people earning less than £9,500 a year were now entitled to free hospital services.

But the ultimate example of the Fianna Fáil approach to the election was provided by Ray Burke in a housing estate in Clonsilla. Party canvassers had been inundated with complaints from residents about the condition in which the estate had been left by the developers. Trees had been promised but were not provided. Burke, through his contacts as Environment Minister, organised to have the trees provided. The night before the poll, several JCBs moved into the estate with a squad of workmen and a truck loaded with young trees. The trees were planted throughout the estate, presumably as a visual encouragement to support Fianna Fáil when residents came out to vote next day. But the trees also illustrated the illusory nature of some political promises; the day after the poll, the people from whom they had been borrowed dug them up and took them away again.

Early indications suggested that Fianna Fáil was winning. Opinion polls conducted privately by Fine Gael added to the sense of demoralisation in the party. Their candidate, it was clear, was totally unknown and the party vote could suffer against the heavyweight and highly visible Fianna Fáil campaign. Lemass ended up as a three-to-one favourite with the bookmakers but many within the party were not impressed with her campaigning style. She relied heavily on her status, as a widow without any other income, to win sympathy and votes. But people were clearly not impressed by that line of argument, especially when their own complaints about cuts in their take-home pay were met by the candidate's insistence that they were much better off than she was. Fine Gael put enormous effort into getting its candidate known throughout the area.

When the votes were counted Lemass headed the poll, pulling the Fianna Fáil vote up above that of Fine Gael with 39.7% against 38.9% for Liam Skelly. But her lead fell far short of the margin she would have needed to overcome the two-to-one advantage that Skelly received from the other candidates. MacGiolla doubled his share of the votes from the February general election, virtually wiping out the Labour Party and leaving its candidate a poor fifth and trailing among several other left wing contenders. Seven candidates were eliminated after the first count and their 2,800 odd votes distributed. Skelly got 959 to Lemass's 476 and went into the third count fractionally ahead of her. MacGiolla's transfers confirmed the same pattern: Skelly got 3,652 and Lemass received 1,635. Skelly won the seat without reaching the quota with 21,388 votes to 19,206 for Lemass.

Garret Fitzgerald declared the result to be a "damning interim verdict" on the government and claimed that it had shown that people wanted to keep a check on an administration they did not trust. Charles Haughey noted that the position was the same as it had been after the February general election. He still needed Neil Blaney and Tony Gregory to keep him in power. But it was not as simple as that. There was a brief flurry of speculation that Haughey would go for broke and call another election and there was some vague talk of another internal challenge to Haughey's leadership. It was clear that the result would have significant consequences for Haughey and his administration.

His "master stroke" had come unstuck. The strength of the main parties was precisely the same as it had been after the general election, but Fianna Fáil had given away one of the plum jobs available to a political party under the spoils system as it operated in Ireland. In return, it had had something of a parliamentary respite for two months, including the Easter break of almost four weeks. But the main implications of the Dublin West result were the effects on the national economy and on the government policy towards it. The by-election had cost the exchequer, directly or indirectly, an enormous amount of money. The PRSI concession could not be said to have been caused solely by the by-election but the atmosphere created by the impending poll helped to bring it about. That cost the State £45 million in lost revenue. Commitments to subsidise mortgage rates until the following September and to speed up payments of children's allowances also disrupted the budget targets.

The government had come into office promising a new economic approach. MacSharry had spelled it out in a memorable phrase when he set about creating an atmosphere of "boom and bloom" to replace the "doom and gloom" of the coalition. The budget of March 25th had put what ministers termed a more humane face on the economic framework established by the coalition. Almost immediately after its introduction, however, the government began to row back on the less popular elements of its economic policy. Determination to win the by-election overshadowed many of the government's decisions in its first two months in office. Economic policies were particularly vulnerable to that pressure. Haughey was behaving as he had in his first administration, caving in before resistance to any of his unpopular measures.

The political tables were quickly turned on Haughey. He was forced onto the defensive in the Dáil by Fine Gael which returned, with its new deputy for Dublin West, in a triumphant mood. Three weeks after the by-election the oldest member of the Dáil, John Callanan, died, leaving Haughey short another vote. From then until a by-election was held in his safe Fianna Fáil constituency of East Galway, the government needed the Workers' Party to give it a Dáil majority. George Colley renewed his attacks on Haughey from within Fianna Fáil with a statement criticising the government's conduct over the Gregory agreement, the Dick Burke appointment and the use of ministerial posts as a method of keeping backbenchers in line. Haughey was clearly the main target of his accusations about politicians who put survival above all else and exhibited the unsavoury side of Tammany Hall, the infamous Irish-American political machine. Colley elaborated on his statement, issued on Saturday, June 5th, in an interview in *The Sunday Tribune* with its political correspondent, Geraldine Kennedy. It was obvious that the interview had been set up and conducted well in advance of the statement's public release.

Haughey responded to the greater parliamentary uncertainty in typical fashion: he made an effort to persuade the Labour Party to form a loose alliance with his government. At a ball for the Grand Duke of Luxembourg in Dublin Castle, Haughey casually mentioned to Michael O'Leary, the Labour leader, the possibility of his party supporting Fianna Fáil. O'Leary replied that Labour would listen to any proposals he had to make. Haughey subsequently invited O'Leary to meet him in the Taoiseach's office in Leinster House. O'Leary took the precaution of bringing the chairman of Labour's parliamentary party, the Kildare TD, Joe Birmingham, with him. Haughey, who was alone, spoke in general terms about the problems facing the government. The Labour men offered to put any proposals he had to their party but Haughey made no specific suggestions. Shortly afterwards, the *Sunday Tribune* reported that Haughey had offered O'Leary a three or four year arrangement at a secret meeting. The information left O'Leary in trouble with his party who had known nothing of the meeting and forced him to explain that he had told nobody because there was nothing specific to tell.

The change in Fianna Fáil's political fortunes came at a particularly bad time for the government. In the Dáil, it was about to move its Finance Bill to give force to the budget's provisions. The Bill contained some changes from the budget announced by MacSharry, alterations which mainly benefited people who were better off. But the mood in the cabinet had also changed after the by-election. At a weekend meeting in mid-June, Haughey suggested that there should be a review of the situation and that they should map out their economic policy for the remainder of the year. He appeared to have an open mind on the policy to be pursued and the majority of ministers present quickly made it clear that the government should alter the course that it had been following. MacSharry knew from the Department of Finance that the budget targets were seriously at risk and that the state's income from taxation was certain to fall short of the amounts predicted in his budget speech. Martin O'Donoghue argued that the government should have kept its £45 million concession to PRSI payers for all the good it had done Fianna Fáil in Dublin West. Padraig Flynn suggested that they should nail their colours to the mast by taking a strong line. Albert Reynolds also favoured a new approach.

After several discussions along the same lines, the Taoiseach suggested that a cabinet sub-committee be formed to decide future economic policy and to draw up a plan which had been promised during the February general election. The eight-member committee was made up of Haughey, MacSharry, Reynolds, O'Donoghue, Des O'Malley, John Wilson, Ray Burke and Brian Lenihan. It began to operate shortly before the Finance Bill came before the Dáil, amid a flurry of newspaper speculation that the government faced defeat. The committee and the discussions which had given birth to it set the tone of the government's response to the demands for changes in the Bill from the Workers' Party and, to a lesser extent, the Labour Party and Fine Gael. There were to be no major concessions.

MacSharry had three meetings with the Workers' Party to discuss their proposed amendments. Several minor proposals were accepted but MacSharry would not agree to any alterations on major issues. The government simply did not have the money, he said. In the Dáil, MacSharry admitted that the proposed deficit for the entire year of £679 million would be used up by the end of June. But he insisted that the target for the year could still be met by bringing forward VAT and corporations profits tax payments to the Revenue Commissioners. The last of the series of meetings with the Workers' Party took place in Leinster House shortly before deputies voted on the second reading of the Bill. The Workers' Party and

Tony Gregory abstained and Fianna Fáil had a two-vote majority.

The danger to the government was far from over. A week later, on June 24th, the Dáil was due to debate the committee stage of the Bill, the point at which specific amendments would be tabled and decided. Defeat of the government on any one of them could cause an election. Numerous amendments were tabled, mainly by the Workers' Party and the Labour Party. Fine Gael's front bench had decided that its main aim was to bring down the government and the Finance Bill offered the best prospect of doing that; the party's attitude to the Bill was dictated by purely political motives rather than differences over Fianna Fáil's current economic policy. Labour had also decided to do its utmost to bring down the government even though many of its members were not enthusiastic about a general election.

Fianna Fáil was not unduly worried about the chances of its survival. The party's chief whip, Bertie Ahern, had a well-informed contact who kept him abreast of the deliberations of the árd chomhairle of the Workers' Party which decided the actions to be taken by its three Dáil deputies. Ahern was told that the árd chomhairle had taken a decision not to bring down the government on the Finance Bill. MacSharry's hand was strengthened by this information in his talks with the Workers' Party deputies. Fianna Fáil believed in effect that there was little parliamentary risk in taking a stern line against the Workers' Party's demands.

But the preparations for the committee stage of the Bill threatened to disrupt their understanding of events. The Workers' Party and the Labour Party tabled separate amendments about the same issues and it became apparent quickly that the government could be defeated as much by the procedure of the Dáil as by the intent of a majority of its members. Everything hinged on the first two amendments to the Bill which were to be debated on June 24th. The Bill proposed that couples earning less than £4,400 a year would be exempt from paying income tax; the first amendment, tabled by Labour, proposed that the limit be raised to £4,800. The second amendment was tabled by the Workers' Party and upped the limit to £5,000.

The usual procedure followed in the Dáil meant that amendments were not actually voted on directly. On most occasions, the issue that was voted on was the relevant section of the Bill. The Ceann Comhairle, when calling a vote on an amendment, proposed that the words in the Bill — usually those proposed by the government — should stand. Thus, government deputies vote "Tá" and opposition members vote "Níl". Assuming the government wins, the amendment is declared to have been defeated.

As the Dáil assembled for the debate, it became evident that it was going to be a particularly tetchy day. Nerves were clearly strained and tension grew throughout the morning. The government suddenly appeared to be in trouble, mainly because of the Dáil's procedure. Labour's Barry Desmond had been reassuring Fianna Fáil people privately that they had nothing to worry about. Labour would oppose the Workers' Party amendment, and presumably the Workers' Party would vote against Labour's amendment; both sets of amendments would be defeated and the government would be safe. In the Dáil chamber, however, Desmond and other government deputies were quick to point out that Labour's amendment should be taken first. That meant there would be a vote on the government's wording of the Bill, and the Workers' Party would have to vote against that in order to support their own amendment. The Workers' Party would be trapped by a procedure into voting against the government; their only alternative would be the embarrassing prospect of voting against their own amendment.

The debate on the Labour Party's first amendment was interspersed with bad-tempered remarks and exchanges. Labour and the Workers' Party sniped at each other constantly. Desmond was forced at one stage to withdraw a reference to "so-called deputies" in the Workers' Party. The Workers' Party also attacked Fine Gael for opportunism. MacSharry, for Fianna Fáil and the government, attacked the amendments on the grounds of the extra cost they would impose on the State. If Fine Gael voted for them, he declared, it would be voting against the very principles it had been expounding for a long time. John Bruton, Fine Gael's shadow Finance Minister, got to the crux of the matter when he declared that the issue was whether or not Fianna Fáil should remain in government. "We want them out," he said.

Elsewhere in Leinster House, Tony Gregory went to see Haughey and told him he intended to support the Workers' Party amendments. He would vote against the government. Gregory made it clear to Fianna Fáil that there was no prospect of changing his mind through any negotiations. The government, impressed by the clarity of his statements, took him at his word: no new deals were attempted. The Workers' Party was told by MacSharry and Ahern that Gregory would back their amendments. Desmond still suggested privately that Fianna Fáil would be all right because the amendments would be taken separately. Ahern spread the word around Leinster House that the government was almost certainly gone. But senior Fianna Fáil people still did not believe that to be true because of Ahern's information about the Workers' Party intentions. The Workers' Party was in a spot but, they believed, one of its members would not turn up for the crucial vote if the government was about to be defeated.

Back in the Dáil chamber, opposition members were beginning to complain about a government filibuster as Fianna Fáil backbenchers joined in the debate in an apparent attempt to delay the vote. All the participants were given an hour's respite at 2.30 when the debate was interrupted to allow for the normal question time. Shortly after the resumption, Joe Sherlock of the Workers' Party sought a ruling from the Ceann Comhairle, John O'Connell, on the procedure for the voting. Confusion followed for a time after O'Connell declared that the first vote would be on the Labour amendment and the Workers' Party could then move its amendment. Fine Gael and Labour members fought with each other to protest against this apparent change of heart. O'Connell become confused himself but finally conceded the point. He called a vote on whether or not the government wording of the Bill would stand. The Workers' Party would have to vote against that.

Deputies gathered in the Dáil chamber as the bells rang throughout the building summoning them to the vote. Fianna Fáil suddenly realised that it was about to be defeated. All three Workers' Party TDs were there, sitting in their usual place in the back row on the opposition side of the house. Gregory was sitting beside them. None of them had got lost or locked out accidentally: if all three were there, they would all have to vote and they would all vote against the government. Ahern told Haughey it looked like they were going to be beaten. On the backbenches the Workers' Party men were furious. They believed Barry Desmond had cornered them and Fianna Fáil by seeming to agree that the amendments would be taken separately. Instead, Desmond had been among those in the house who attacked the Ceann Comhairle when he tried to implement that idea. The Workers' Party deputies desperately urged Gregory to change his mind and vote with Fianna Fáil.

Haughey walked up the central steps in the chamber to vote, looking pale and tense. As he passed the Workers' Party and the Independents he looked straight ahead. He did not make his customary comment to them, a casual remark as he passed by. At the top of the steps he turned left to vote "Tá" while Fine Gael and Labour members filed right to register their "Níl" vote. The last two deputies to vote were Gregory and Sherlock. They stepped out onto the stairs together and side by side, mounted the single step to the top. As they stepped up to the top, Sherlock whispered desperately, "Wheel left". Sherlock himself turned right into the "Níl" lobby where his party colleagues were already. Gregory changed his mind at the last second. He turned left and the government was saved.

The vote was 80 for and 80 against. O'Connell declared that his casting vote should not be used to defeat the government, and the amendments were declared to be lost. Fianna Fáil was jubilant. Fine Gael was downhearted. "What did Gregory get in the last hour?" Fine Gael's Gerry L'Estrange shouted. As O'Connell sought to carry on with the next amendment, another Fine Gael backbencher demanded to know when the house would be informed of the latest Gregory deal. But Gregory had not sought and had not negotiated any new deal. He had taken his decision literally at the last moment for purely practical reasons. The measures which he wanted from the 22nd Dáil were not yet implemented and, almost certainly, would never be implemented by a new Dáil. He, personally, would not bring down Haughey's government.

Gregory and the Ceann Comhairle saved the government on two more occasions that day. But the sting had been taken out of the debate: it was clear that Gregory and the Workers' Party did not want the defeat of Fianna Fáil. After the near disaster on the opening amendments, all of them took care to avoid a recurrence. Nevertheless they all combined six days later to defeat the government on a motion tabled by the Labour Party demanding that a towelling factory in Kilkenny be re-opened by the state taking a share in it. Fine Gael added a demand that the necessary steps be taken in 1982 and supported the action in spite of Fianna Fáil accusations that it now favoured the nationalisation of ailing industries. The support for the motion of Gregory and the three Workers' Party deputies defeated the government by 80 votes to 78. But it was not an issue of confidence, not an issue on which the government would fall. Immediately after the result was announced, however, Garret FitzGerald declared that Fine Gael was tabling a motion of no confidence in the government.

The Fine Gael ploy appeared to have been based on a misapprehension. Shortly after the debate began the next day, July 1st, the Workers' Party made it clear that it would support the government. But some members of Fine Gael apparently convinced themselves that Haughey's more determined opponents within Fianna Fáil would withhold their support from the party leader. FitzGerald devoted a significant part of his speech to the point that a large majority of the Dáil's 166 deputies did not have confidence in Haughey. The anti-Haughey Fianna Fáil people were part of the "moral majority" within the Dáil, he said. And he warned those who voted confidence in Haughey that they would be responsible for whatever followed. "History will not be kind to them," he added.

Haughey confined himself to a defence of his government, particularly his stand on the Falklands and Ireland's right to have an independent foreign policy. The budget had been a measure of social concern, he said, and an economic plan was already at an advanced stage. It would propose "vigorous and disciplined" measures to eliminate the budget deficit and the trade deficit, contain a policy of high investment and encourage the substitution of Irish-made goods for imports. Besides, he argued, the country did not want the turmoil and upset of a general election. Long before the debate was concluded, the outcome was clear. Nobody in Fianna Fáil broke ranks, the Workers' Party and Tony Gregory voted with the government and Haughey won easily by 84 votes to 77, the same margin by which he had been elected Taoiseach.

The result confirmed that those who had put Haughey into government had not changed their view of the situation. The heat went out of the parliamentary crisis and it looked as though Fianna Fáil was probably secure until the 1983 budget. Political attention switched to Galway East where the by-election campaign caused by the death of John Callanan got under way. Haughey adopted a strongly nationalist tone at the convention to select the Fianna Fáil candidate. Fianna Fáil would not become the party of appeasement, a party that undermined the legitimate aspirations of Northern nationalists in return for hollow praise from doubtful quarters, he declared. FitzGerald, at his party's convention, attacked the government for being "anti-rural" and complained of the growing gap between poverty and wealth in the country.

Unlike Dublin West, Galway East was a safe Fianna Fáil area. In the previous two general elections Fianna Fáil had won more than half of all the votes cast. It was expected to do the same again, thereby guaranteeing election for the Fianna Fáil candidate on the first count. The government, however, was taking no chances with the outcome. Ministers descended on the area in force. On this occasion, the emphasis of the canvass had switched away from concessions; in line with the new approach which had been decided by the cabinet and revealed publicly during the Finance Bill debate, there were few handouts on offer from Fianna Fáil. The party stressed the need to secure the government by returning the Fianna Fáil candidate. A private opinion poll conducted by Fine Gael showed that the Fianna Fáil message was having an effect.

When the votes were cast on July 20th, Fianna Fáil's candidate, Noel Treacy, a 29-year-old auctioneer, was elected on the first count. He won 50.2% of the votes against 41.2% for Fine Gael, and 5.4% for Labour. In the constituency concerned it was not a spectacularly good result for Fianna Fáil: the party vote had dropped but not by enough to cause serious alarm. It neither confirmed nor denied Haughey's strength as a leader in electoral terms but gave him the Dáil vote he needed to return to the status quo of that parliament.

Although the new economic policy was apparent in the by-election, the short campaign also disrupted the cabinet's deliberations on that issue. Once the election was over, ministers returned to the question in earnest. The sub-committee on the economy concentrated primarily on drawing up the medium-term economic plan by the end of July. But the more immediate problem of the 1982 budget was becoming increasingly urgent. MacSharry knew by now that there was no prospect of the original targets being met unless drastic action was taken. He had re-organised the government's debts as far as possible to save money but that kind of re-jigging did not make much impact on the overall problem. The government's £45 million concession on PRSI in April had still to be met and the amount of money being collected in taxes generally was far short of the budget targets. The only option was severe cuts in expenditure and the cabinet set about wielding the knife at the end of July. The proposals were finalised over two and a half days of meetings in the last week of the month and announced publicly on Friday, July 30th.

The package was intended, the announcement said, to cut £120 million from government bills for the remainder of the year. A 5% pay rise for public servants, due in November, would be postponed until January 1983: special pay increases and recruitment in the public service would be halted: subsidies on flour and margarine would be abolished and the subsidy on butter would be reduced: spending by every single government department was to be cut. The ministry most affected was the Department of Health, where cuts of £12 million came on top of an earlier reduction of £20 million. The Department of Justice was to prune its spending by £8 million, most of it to be saved by a cutback in garda overtime. The package was released in Dublin by civil servants but MacSharry defended it in a prepared speech later that evening. The only alternative would be increased taxes, he said, but higher taxes would slow down economic recovery, The Labour Party condemned the cut as "arbitrary and indiscriminate". The Workers' Party described them as a confidence trick that was bound to affect its relations with the government. Fine Gael thought some of the proposals were reasonable, but dismissed others as mere bookkeeping. Several economists predicted that the plan would cut less than £120 million from a deficit that had been heading for £950 million. The target of £679 million still would not be reached.

Most ministers, however, had not waited in Dublin to hear the reaction. As the details were being announced, many of them took off on holidays. Haughey went to his private island.

Chapter Ten

My record of stewardship on security is impeccable.
Charles Haughey, March 1982

Routine work in the Department of Justice piled up. Sean Doherty was sometimes absent for days on end, and showed little interest in dealing with the everyday affairs of the ministry. Files on matters needing his approval or examination were sent to his office, but officials waited in vain for instructions and grew anxious when it became apparent that he would only deal with matters requiring an immediate decision. Everything else was put on the long finger. As a politician, Doherty had progressed well in a very short time but, as a cabinet member, he had a primitive understanding of the power at his disposal.

As a county councillor in a relatively tight knit community in Roscommon, Doherty had been able to operate successfully on a "you-scratch-my-back-and-I'll-scratch-yours" basis. In a small community where everyone knew almost everyone else, public representatives could often carry out their business by dealing directly with the people concerned. To a large extent, politicians were judged according to how successful they were at getting results and jobs for their supporters and friends. When Doherty was made a junior minister, he applied the same methods to his daily affairs. As a minister, he acted as though he believed he had absolute power in his area of responsibility.

With an entire Department under his control, he was able to operate the patronage system throughout the whole country. A garda station anywhere could be contacted on behalf of a friend or party member and anything he wanted done in the

Department could be done if he ordered it to be. At cabinet, he made little impression. He was seen to be very close to Haughey but some believed that he had been appointed just to do the Taoiseach's bidding. Prior to the meetings which Doherty attended between Haughey and the Garda Commissioners, he did not seek relevant files from his department or briefing documents from his officials. Doherty paid a lot of attention to his constituency. He tried his best to look after the interests of those who supported him and did not take kindly to anyone getting in his way.

Sergeant Tom Tully from Boyle was an equally determined man with a strong distaste for anyone who put themselves above the law. At the end of May, Tully again inspected Keaney's pub. It was half an hour past midnight. Tully was accompanied by a sergeant from Keadue station and a garda from Boyle. This time there were six people drinking after hours. Summonses were duly prepared and Michael Keaney got his on July 15th.

Thirteen days after the summons was served, Tully was on holiday at his mother's house when he got a telephone call. He was told that he was being shifted to a garda station on the border — Ballyconnell in Co. Cavan. He later received a copy of the transfer order, signed by Assistant Commissioner Frank Davis, the man in charge of personnel. The reason given was the standard explanation for all transfers; it was "in the best interests of the force".

Doherty used every opportunity to show the Roscommon electorate how important a man he was. He hoped towards the end of the summer to be present for the official opening of Boyle garda station. The building had been in use for some years but never officially opened, and would provide a splendid opportunity for the local TD and Minister to be the centre of attention. In July, Doherty flew by helicopter to Castlerea in Co. Roscommon to unveil a memorial plaque on the second anniversary of the shooting dead of two local gardaí, John Morley and Henry Byrne. The ceremony was attended by the men's widows and their children and was a poignant reminder of the dangers regularly faced by gardaí. A committee had organised the commemoration. The plaque cost £250. The reception afterwards in a local hotel, attended by Doherty, some senior garda officers and local people, cost £850.

Doherty's personal commitment to providing helicopters for the gardaí was never in doubt. First promised by a Fianna Fáil government in 1980, the whole project was never properly researched and costed. The coalition government of June 1981 to March 1982 attempted to have it examined adequately before endorsing the commitment. Doherty attacked the Justice Minister Jim Mitchell and said that any good hayshed erector could build hangars for the helicopters. When Doherty took over as Justice Minister and reaffirmed his commitment to helicopters, his personal use of the machines seemed to reflect this.

He used them to fly to conferences, to the garda training centre in Templemore, Co. Tipperary, and even to make a tour of the border with Commissioner McLaughlin. The commitment to buy helicopters for the gardaí became "The Aerial Wing" and a senior officer was put in charge, Chief Superintendent Patrick Culligan. Nobody was ever told what The Aerial Wing did without a plane or helicopter to fly. The gardaí continued to get air support from the Air Corps whenever cover was needed to assist escorts of large amounts of cash, and Doherty continued to hitch rides on Air Corps helicopters. The idea of an Aerial Wing was shelved for financial reasons in August. At the end of that month, Doherty had a lengthy meeting with Culligan about a "new offensive" on the drugs problem. A few days later, Doherty announced that Culligan had been given overall responsibility for the "new offensive". A statement announcing the appointment said it had been made by the Commissioner at Doherty's request.

Doherty maintained a good relationship with the Garda Representative Association, the group which spoke for rank-and-file gardaí. Throughout the year, he had a number of meetings with their general secretary, Jack Marrinan, and the executive. Doherty was generally very positive when they raised problems like the atrocious conditions in some garda stations. His dealings with the GRA got off to a good start at the beginning of his ministry. At the Association's annual conference in April, Doherty departed from his prepared speech to promise delegates that a new uniform would be issued to them soon. Commissioner McLaughlin later unveiled a prototype at the same conference to the delight of delegates. The uniform problem had been a big issue in garda politics for many years and, to those present, it seemed as though something was going to be done finally to give the force a more comfortable outfit and one which was the same colour and style for all ranks. Doherty, however, had not discussed the new uniform with his officials before the announcement and nobody had worked out what it would cost. Estimates ran up to £6 million but no funds had been allocated.

In May, Doherty inspected the proposed new headquarters for Dublin gardaí with McLaughlin and Assistant Commissioner Ainsworth. The new building in Harcourt Street would replace the existing accommodation used by gardaí in Dublin Castle. Doherty promised the rebuilt 40 Harcourt Street to the GRA but the bulk of the complex, the centre block, was to go to Ainsworth for his ISB operation. Ainsworth was at first cautious about moving from garda headquarters but he became enthusiastic about the new building. Detailed plans were drawn up to adapt it for all of ISB's accoutrements and high technology gadgets. There was talk of re-arranging the traffic flow around Harcourt Street, Camden Street and Kelly's Corner for "security reasons" and to allow easier access for the gardaí.

The inspection of the building was also part of the follow-up publicity to the national campaign against crime and vandalism. The campaign as such rapidly fizzled out after the burst of radio and television advertising which coincided with the Dublin West by-election. No more money was available to pay for the other phases envisaged when the campaign was launched. More than a year later, officials in the department and a couple of garda officers dealt with all that remained of the £164,550 campaign by judging the pile of essays and posters submitted for the competition by schoolchildren.

Ainsworth and Doherty got on well together. Doherty was very demanding but Ainsworth worked hard to see that everything requested was carried out. As with Haughey, his first dealings with Doherty included the special security that had to be provided for the Minister for Justice. Irrespective of which political party formed the government, certain people were always given above average protection, including the

Taoiseach, the Minister for Justice and the British Ambassador. A judge presiding over a trial in the Special Criminal Court would also be given extra special protection for the duration of the case. When Doherty was appointed minister, it was Ainsworth's responsibility to ensure that he was adequately protected. He assigned his second-in-command, Chief Superintendent Steven Fanning, to go to Doherty's home in Cootehall to examine what was necessary. Fanning knew the area well — he came from Knockvicar, just a few miles away, and was acutely aware that Cootehall was close to the border with Northern Ireland.

Doherty's home was a rather plain bungalow, built in a style which had come virtually to dominate house building in rural Ireland since the late 1960s. It was on the side of a small hill and had a commanding view over a broad expanse of the Boyle river, a tributary of the Shannon. The place was something of a security nightmare; it was very exposed and no trees or walls afforded protective cover. It could easily be attacked from almost any angle and a public road was only a hundred feet or so from the front of the house. The building was quite new and workmen had not yet finished a low boundary wall.

Fanning recommended that a high fence made of wire be erected behind the house. Similar protection would also have to be given to one side of the house and two small garda huts would have to be put inside the site. One uniformed garda and a plainclothes man would have to be on duty 24 hours a day which meant that eight extra men would have to be drafted into Boyle garda station. The house was also to be floodlit. The recommendations were no more than were expected — a compromise between turning the place into a fortress and showing a garda presence. Any alterations would be carried out by the Office of Public Works.

The job wasn't finished by the autumn and Doherty was taking a personal interest in what was going on. He had a meeting at his home with gardaí, the Board of Works man from Sligo and his own brother, Colm Doherty. Somehow, a simple security fence had become a wall, the same wall that was being built around the site in the first place. The area in front of the house sloped steeply down to the road and a retaining wall was needed if an attractive landscaped lawn was to be laid out. Entrance gates would also have to be built.

Colm Doherty got the contract. The "security wall" was finished and a retaining wall built in front of the house. The gates never materialised. The security wall would hardly have impeded an assault by a 10-year-old, let alone an IRA attack, but the retaining wall made the place more attractive. The cost was around £15,000.

Joe Ainsworth took enormous care to ensure that he himself was not an easy target. He was driven to and from work by an armed guard and was accompanied by a car containing more armed guards. His home was floodlit and a garda was permanently on duty outside. His telephone number was changed every three months. Such was Ainsworth's concern about the safety of himself and his family that it inevitably gave rise to stories among his colleagues. It was said, for instance, that his driver telephoned the house from a phonebox just before he was due to arrive to collect him. When the car drew up outside the house exactly according to plan, the passenger door swung open at the same time as the hall door of the house and Ainsworth rushed into the car fast enough to avoid lurking snipers. The truth or otherwise of such stories was irrelevant —Ainsworth was a legend within the Garda Síochána. If he was the subject of a certain amount of joking however, he took his work very seriously.

He believed in specialisation and setting up special units to deal with specific problems as they arose. When gardaí Morley and Byrne were murdered, Ainsworth responded by setting up eighteen Divisional Crime Task forces, one for each garda division outside Dublin. These were mobile patrols in Granada cars manned by armed plainclothes detectives. They constantly drove around their areas and were able to rush instantly to bank robberies, post office hold-ups and ambushes. The main use of the patrols was to combat armed crime but they were also able to watch known subversives, especially in border counties. The Security Task Force, based in Dublin Castle, was not formed by Ainsworth but came under his control. Its main function was to provide instant reaction to hijackings, kidnappings and such like.

Ainsworth was unpopular in some quarters largely because of the way he appeared to amass more and more control and more and more men under his command. Between the end of 1977 and 1982, the detective branch increased in numbers by over 122%. Of these, 80% were assigned to various units controlled by Ainsworth. By contrast, over the same period the uniformed section of the gardaí increased by just under 11%. While the strength of the force increased by some 2,000, there was little evidence of this on the streets and crime continued to rise by leaps and bounds. Few people knew where all the extra men had gone or what they were doing. Many were under Ainsworth's command but no information about their activities could be had from Ainsworth for "security reasons".

The man in charge of the Security Task Force was someone well known to Haughey, Superintendent Pat Doocey, who in 1970 had had the job of arresting Haughey on charges of conspiring to import arms. Doocey treated the case like any other and continued to work normally after Haughey and his co-accused were acquitted. He was one of the most experienced Special Branch officers in the Garda Síochána and almost his entire career had been spent working in counter-intelligence and anti-subversion. He was in charge of the day-to-day running of the branch and got a lot of job satisfaction from what he did.

On a Friday evening in June, Doocey was about to pack up for the weekend and head off home when he was told that he was being transferred to the Central Detective Unit, the section which investigated what the gardaí called crime ordinary — i.e. crimes which did not have a subversive aspect to them. Doocey was astonished at the order. He had not sought the transfer and he preferred working in the Special Branch where he had been for years and where most of his experience and talent lay. He asked why he was being moved but he was not told. When he went over to CDU he took charge of the Serious Crime Squad. Doocey's colleagues believed that he was moved because Haughey wanted revenge for the arms trial arrest, and because it suited Haughey to have someone like Doocey out of Special Branch. Haughey and others working for him were becoming more and more involved in the security affairs of the gardaí.

Charles J. Haughey. *(Derek Speirs/Report)*

The new cabinet after members had received their seals of office on March 9th 1982. Back row (l. to r.): Sean Doherty, Ray Burke, Martin O'Donoghue, Michael Woods, Brendan Daly, Albert Reynolds, Gene Fitzgerald, Padraig Flynn, John Wilson, and Patrick Connolly. Front row (l. to r.): Paddy Power, Desmond O'Malley, Brian Lenihan, Charles Haughey, President Patrick Hillery, Ray MacSharry and Gerry Collins.

Charles Haughey with one of his new Junior Ministers, Sean Doherty, March 1980. *(Derek Speirs/Report)*

Say Yes: Charles Haughey grudgingly passes the microphone to Desmond O'Malley to answer queries about Knock airport at a Fianna Fáil general

Doing business: Charles Haughey and Tony Gregory lending each other support.
(Peter Thursfield/Irish Times)

Patrick O'Connor leaving Swords district court on April 20th 1982, after the summons accusing him of double voting in the February 1982 election was dismissed.
(Kevin McMahon/Irish Times)

Sean Doherty (centre) with Joe Ainsworth (left) and Patrick McLaughlin inspecting the new Dublin metropolitan garda headquarters in Harcourt Street as part of the "National Campaign Against Crime and Vandalism" launched in May 1982.

Attorney General Patrick Connolly (left) with Education Minister Martin O'Donoghue at Áras an Uachtaráin to receive their seals of office, March 1982. *(Tony O'Shea)*

Malcolm Macarthur, in characteristic dress, being escorted by prison officers into the Four Courts, Dublin, in January 1983, where he was sentenced to life imprisonment for the murder of nurse Bridie Gargan. *(Paddy Whelan/Irish Times)*

Gerry Collins (right) confers with Desmond O'Malley after O'Malley and Martin O'Donoghue refused at a cabinet meeting to pledge loyalty to Haughey personally. Later that day, October 5th 1982, O'Malley and O'Donoghue resigned from the government. *(Derek Speirs/Report)*

Charles McCreevy is given a garda escort from Leinster House after his motion of no confidence in Charles Haughey was defeated, October 6th 1982. *(Derek Speirs/Report)*

Sean Doherty at The Way Forward press conference. Just before attending it, he had arranged for Assistant Commissioner Joe Ainsworth to supply garda bugging equipment to Ray MacSharry. *(Derek Speirs/Report)*

Bruce Arnold and Geraldine Kennedy reading the government statement confirming that their telephones had been officially tapped by the previous Fianna Fáil administration. *(Paddy Whelan/Irish Times)*

Ray MacSharry and Charles Haughey at a press conference to launch the government economic plan, The Way Forward, on October 21st 1982. MacSharry returned to his office afterwards to tape-record secretly his conversation with Martin O'Donoghue. *(Derek Speirs/Report)*

Deputy Commissioner Joe Ainsworth leaving the Department of Justice in the early hours of January 20th 1983 after he had offered his resignation to Minister Michael Noonan. *(Irish Press)*

Ray MacSharry attempting to explain why he bugged a conversation with a party colleague after his action was revealed in January 1983. *(Peter Thursfield/Irish Times)*

Ben Briscoe (left) and George Colley share a joke at the Fianna Fáil ard-fheis, February 1983. *(Derek Speirs/Report)*

Fianna Fáil parliamentary party chairman Jim Tunney meets the press after a crisis meeting of the party in January 1983. Standing in the background to his left is Ken Ryan, a party press officer. *(Tony O'Shea)*

Niall Andrews at the centre of an impromptu pro-Haughey rally outside Fianna Fáil headquarters in Dublin in January 1983 after the surveillance scandals had broken. *(Derek Speirs/Report)*

The suspicions of people in the Department of Justice were aroused by, among other things, the arrival early in May of a certificate from garda headquarters seeking a warrant to tap the telephone of Bruce Arnold. The system for initiating telephone tapping and processing the applications had been laid down over the years amid assurances from successive Justice Ministers that sufficient checks and balances existed to ensure abuses did not take place. Applications were received from the gardai and examined by the security section of the Department. Generally, the gardai were asked for some more information as to why the tap was wanted. The application was then given to the Minister who was also briefed and left to make up his mind. If he approved, a warrant was filled in detailing the particular phone number to be tapped and sent off to the Department of Posts and Telegraphs in the GPO. A room on the top floor of the GPO was linked by special telephone lines to the various Dublin telephone exchanges, the "01" area. In the exchanges the link lines were attached to the particular telephone line to be tapped and back in the GPO, the tape recorders were switched on. ISB couriers called regularly to the GPO to collect the tapes and bring them to the ISB offices in garda headquarters for listening and selective transcribing.

Tapping was supposed to be initiated by the gardai in the name of the Commissioner as head of the force. In practice, however, McLaughlin acted on the advice of his senior officers, two of whom could be expected to seek warrants from time to time. Joe Ainsworth needed them for his counter-intelligence work and John Paul McMahon occasionally needed taps when investigating a major crime, a large bank robbery perhaps, or a drug smuggling operation. But one of the problems in garda headquarters was that McLaughlin had long stopped seeking the advice of some of the deputy and assistant commissioners under him. Personality problems and faction fighting caused by political interference had destroyed the cohesiveness of the commissioners. Instead of regular discussions and the sort of common purpose that might have been expected, power politics and conspiracies had virtually paralysed their initiative.

Deputy Commissioner Eamon Doherty stood in for McLaughlin at social functions and was not regarded as a high-powered decision maker. The man closest in rank to McLaughlin, senior Deputy Commissioner Larry Wren, had been virtually ostracised. As the relationship between Ainsworth and McLaughlin grew, the proper chain of command was upset and Wren was occasionally frozen out of major investigations. This had happened dramatically in October 1981 during the kidnapping of Ben Dunne, heir to the Dunne's supermarket chain fortune.

The kidnapping was a nightmare for the gardai, the government and, not least, the Dunne family. As he crossed the border into Northern Ireland on his way to Newry to open a new store, armed men forced Ben Dunne out of his car, into theirs and drove south across the border again. Nobody knew whether the kidnappers had continued South or turned right and back into South Armagh, the most dangerous area in Northern Ireland for RUC officers, British soldiers, Protestant farmers and anyone else whom the Provisional IRA regarded as targets.

The first contact the Dunne family made with the gardai was through Wren. The contact was maintained through Wren in the immediate aftermath of the kidnapping. Because the crime occurred on the border and there were strong suspicions that Dunne was being held in South Armagh, the kidnapping had obvious subversive overtones. As the garda investigation got under way, it was natural that ISB should have become involved. Numerous telephones were tapped, locations were staked out and ISB men disguised as maintenance workers drove around Dundalk in a van trying to gather information. Gradually, the hunt for the kidnappers was taken over by Ainsworth but not to the satisfaction of Wren. Eventually, the Dunne family complained to McLaughlin and threatened to cease co-operating with the gardai unless Wren was returned to the forefront of the investigation. Ben Dunne was later released by his captors after gardai believed a ransom was paid.

When Sean Doherty asked Joe Ainsworth to tap the telephone of Bruce Arnold, Ainsworth discussed the request with McLaughlin. Although Ainsworth was only an Assistant Commissioner, his relationship with McLaughlin was such that some of the most important decisions in garda headquarters were taken by McLaughlin without reference to his two Deputy Commissioners. Despite the professed concern of Haughey and Doherty about "leaks", none was specified to Ainsworth when Doherty asked for the tap on Arnold. When Ainsworth spoke to McLaughlin, he also mentioned the alleged problem of "leaks". He told McLaughlin that "leaks" from the Cabinet were causing grave concern to the government and were regarded as a high security risk. McLaughlin went along with him and signed the application for the tap. When it arrived in the Department of Justice it specified Arnold's name and address. The usual explanation was offered; the tap was necessary to gather "useful information concerning subversive activity" which could not be got in any other way.

The application was processed by the security section of the Department. The head of the section, Jim Kirby, was worried when he saw Arnold's name and telephoned Ainsworth for more details. Kirby was told that Arnold was "anti-national" and might be in contact with people of a similar disposition. Kirby knew tapping was permitted only when necessary to investigate a major crime or to combat subversive activity. Ainsworth's explanation was an acknowledgement that the proposed tap on Arnold could not be justified according to the existing criteria. Kirby wrote down what Ainsworth had said and put it on file with the request for the tap. He then made his own recommendation that the application should not be granted and gave the file to Doherty.

Doherty overruled Kirby's recommendation and signed the warrant on May 10th. The warrant did not name Arnold — it simple gave his telephone number: 805575. After Doherty signed, the warrant was sent to the Department of Posts and Telegraphs and a copy was put on file in Justice.

Within days, tapes of Arnold's conversations were being collected from the GPO for the ISB listeners. The listeners were given no instructions on what they should transcribe; such instructions were generally not given on the basis that it was better to let the listeners use their own judgement and assess the importance of all they heard. They were used to hearing the voices of drug pushers, gangland criminals, political extremists and members of paramilitary organisations. Suddenly they were confronted with the Arnold family talking to their friends and Bruce Arnold chatting with politicians. Some of the listeners were perturbed and very few of the conversations were transcribed from the tapes. Most were simply rubbed clean.

Six weeks after the tapping of Arnold's telephone began, a public controversy about intercepting telephone calls blew up in Haughey's face. Fine Gael's former Justice Minister, Jim Mitchell, claimed in the Dáil on June 22nd, that during Haughey's first term as Taoiseach, a new telephone system had been installed in Leinster House which allowed Haughey to listen to other people's conversations. Haughey was shaken by the allegation and Doherty said it was part of a smear campaign against the Taoiseach.

The Leinster House telephones were operated by a Private Automatic Branch Exchange (PABX) located in the basement of Setanta House. There was nothing unusual about the PABX system — it was in use in hundreds of businesses around the country and simply allowed people with extensions to automatically obtain an outside line by dialling a number, usually nine. But some special console telephones, called SL 1s, had been added to the system. They allowed anybody who had one to eavesdrop on the conversations of people talking between extensions or on two people talking to each other via the main Leinster House telephone number, 789911. The eavesdrop mechanism was designed to allow business colleagues in a firm to interrupt each other or hold three-way conversations. In Leinster House, however, it could allow people to listen to their political enemies.

The first SL 1 was installed in January 1980 on Haughey's instructions. He asked for it a few days after he became Taoiseach following his close win over George Colley. Haughey held a meeting in his new office attended by Sean O'Kelly, an assistant secretary in the Department of Posts and Telegraphs. After O'Kelly left the meeting, instructions were issued in the Department and a blueprint was drafted which indicated that Haughey's telephone was to be the only one with the ability to eavesdrop, called an override. In the succeeding weeks, a total of 20 SL 1 console telephones were installed in the Taoiseach's office, the offices of the Minister for Finance and Haughey's room in the Fianna Fáil offices in Leinster House. All were part of the Leinster House system which in fact had extension telephones in a number of government departments, the homes of some senior civil servants and Haughey's home. Although

Haughey's SL 1 was supposed to be the only one with an override, the PABX was programmed so that seventeen of the SL 1s were capable of eavesdropping on other people's conversations.

The override could be used if somebody with an SL 1 dialled one of the other extensions in the Leinster House system and found it engaged. By pressing the override button on the console, the SL 1 user could listen to the conversation. Fine Gael had been suspicious of the telephone system in Leinster House since the autumn of 1980, long after the override SL 1s had been installed. Peter Prendergast, the party's general secretary, and John Bruton, Fine Gael's spokesman on Agriculture at the time, had had two separate conversations during which Prendergast heard voices on the line. The voices were not on a crossed line because they were not conversing —Prendergast heard them mention his name and one alerted the other that they (Prendergast and Bruton) knew they were being overheard.

Mitchell said the system was dangerous, alarming and should never have been allowed into Leinster House where the business of government had to be assured a degree of privacy. He and Garret FitzGerald demanded an enquiry with powers to call witnesses and order the production of papers. Haughey said that any suggestion that he used the system to eavesdrop was "absolutely ludicrous and preposterous". He called reporters to his office and showed them the button marked override on his desk telephone.

"I don't know about the override facility," he said. "It was just a button there on the console." It had never been pressed and he would certainly never listen to someone else's conversation, he said. Just then, there was a click and a whirr and someone joked that a tape recorder had been switched on. No, no, no, said Haughey, explaining that the noise was made by a fresh air machine installed to overpower smells from the Leinster House kitchens below his office.

The whole affair was investigated by the Dáil Committee on Procedure and Privileges which was unable to link Haughey directly with the instruction that the PABX be programmed to allow certain telephones to have an override. But Haughey was greatly damaged by the affair: cartoonists associated him with

Richard Nixon and linked Fianna Fáil to telephone tapping and tape recording conversations. Haughey never forgave Mitchell.

Meanwhile, the official tapping of Bruce Arnold's telephone continued. Cassette tapes were being collected from the GPO and given to the listeners in ISB. Even within ISB the tapping was kept very secret. Those involved were sworn to secrecy and transcripts were made on plain, unmarked paper. Only one copy was made and it was always given to Ainsworth. Some of those involved were apprehensive about what they were doing — they knew the purpose of the tap on Arnold had nothing to do with major crimes or subversion. They made few transcripts and all were of political conversations. The last conversation they transcribed was one in early July between Arnold and George Colley which centred around internal Fianna Fáil matters. When transcripts were given to Ainsworth, he occasionally asked for additional copies, but when he read the Arnold-Colley transcript he asked for the tape itself. He listened to it a number of times and then rubbed it clean.

Ainsworth made up his mind that no information useful either to himself or to Doherty was coming from the tapping. He showed the Arnold-Colley transcript to Doherty and asked for permission to remove the tap. Permisson was given and the tapping of Arnold's telephone stopped on July 12th.

Haughey and Doherty were still interested in Geraldine Kennedy. Doherty had mentioned her name to Ainsworth months earlier when he first spoke about "leaks". Nothing in the meantime had dissuaded him from his desire to have her tapped.

Early in July, Haughey tried to use an old friend to discover the sources for reports which Kennedy was writing in the *Sunday Tribune.* Hugh McLaughlin, proprietor of the *Tribune,* got a telephone call from one of Haughey's secretaries asking him to drop around if he had a few minutes to spare. Haughey had known McLaughlin for over twenty years through the accountancy firm of Haughey Boland. In the early 60s, McLaughlin had been one of the energetic brash businessmen whose style personified the era. In 1963, he launched *Woman's Way* magazine at a time when other people in publishing said that success was impossible. Haughey attended the launching ceremony. *Woman's Way* was a spectacular success.

McLaughlin dropped around to Haughey's office in the Taoiseach's Department at government buildings. Haughey said he did not like what the *Sunday Tribune* was doing. He was being wronged Sunday after Sunday by Geraldine Kennedy, and wanted to know where she was getting her information. The meeting lasted between 10 and 15 minutes.

McLaughlin contacted the *Tribune's* editor, Conor Brady, and told him that Haughey was concerned about Kennedy's reporting. Haughey had referred to her as "that Kennedy woman" and had asked McLaughlin to bring her "under control". Haughey had wanted to know her sources in Fianna Fáil and had asked McLaughlin to find out for him. McLaughlin asked Brady who Kennedy's sources were but Brady refused to divulge any information. McLaughlin pressed him but Brady broke off their conversation.

Haughey's interest in Kennedy went back some years. After he became Taoiseach in 1979, it was to her that he gave his first interview. He seemed to like her — Kennedy was a tough young reporter with a sharp political mind and a consuming interest in politics. She doggedly pursued stories and inevitably began to report on the opposition to Haughey within Fianna Fáil. The McCreevy incident in January was caused by remarks he made in an interview with her. It was she who had first reported after the general election that moves were afoot to ditch Haughey as Fianna Fáil leader. Her contacts with Haughey's opponents in the party developed until they trusted her above all other political reporters. In May, she revealed the businessmen behind the party by naming the members of the Fianna Fáil fund-raising committee. In June, George Colley gave her an interview in which he attacked Haughey's standards as a politician and in July she reported in detail the cabinet meeting which decided to change the government's economic policy. The report indicated that the change had been forced upon Haughey.

When Brady refused to help, McLaughlin tried another method of discovering Kennedy's sources. He instructed the *Tribune* telephonist to note the names of people ringing her and to pass the names to him. He need hardly have bothered — the government was already tapping her telephone.

The tapping began on July 28th when an application sent to the Department of Justice by the gardai was granted by Doherty. But the only people who were aware that the application referred to Kennedy were Doherty and Ainsworth, because her name did not appear on the application. The person named was Ronald Langan. Her address was given and also her telephone number: 280006. According to records in the Department of Posts and Telegraphs, Ronald Langan was the subscriber. In fact, he had long since moved out of the house and it was now rented to Kennedy. When one of Ainsworth's subordinates asked the Department of Posts and Telegraphs for the name of the subscriber of the telephone number given to him by Ainsworth, an out-of-date record was consulted and he was given Langan's name. Ainsworth did not choose to point out the error when he asked Commissioner McLaughlin to approve the warrant application. The reason for the tap was slightly different from that given in the application to tap Arnold's telephone; it had been necessary to tap him for "security purposes", but the tap on Kennedy was necessary for "national security", according to the application for the tap on her telephone.

The application was dealt with in the usual way by the security section of the Department. Jim Kirby was intrigued by the reference to "national security", and asked Ainsworth why the tap was needed. Ainsworth told Kirby that Doherty had all the details. He did not tell him the person to be tapped was Kennedy, even though Ainsworth knew this himself. The only reason advanced for the tap was that information about the Provisional IRA might be got through it.

Kirby was not satisfied. He wrote a note to Doherty stating that as he had no detailed reasons for the tap, he was unable to recommend either way that a warrant be signed. He said he was not satisfied that the standard reference to "security purposes" should be changed to "national security", and he recommended to Doherty that the application should not be granted.

Doherty overruled him and signed the warrant. It was sent to the Department of Posts and Telegraphs the same day, July 28th, and a tape recorder was connected to Kennedy's telephone via a link line from the GPO to the relevant exchange. Within a day or two, more tapes were being received by the ISB listeners. It didn't take them long to work out who was being tapped.

It was a busy time for Haughey and Ainsworth. Doherty was in almost daily contact with Ainsworth, and Haughey had regular meetings with him either in the Taoiseach's office in Government Buildings or his home in Kinsealy. Just before the application was made to tap Kennedy's telephone, Haughey spoke to Ainsworth about another special assignment; he wanted Ainsworth to brief a very important security meeting. The subject of the meeting was subversion and Ainsworth was to outline the extent of the problem and how the gardai were dealing with it.

The meeting was to take place on Thursday, July 29th in a conference room beside Haughey's office in Government Buildings. Those scheduled to attend included Ireland's Ambassador to the United States, Tadhg O'Sullivan, the Ambassador to Britain, Eamonn Kennedy, Foreign Affairs Minister, Gerry Collins, Doherty and Haughey. There would also be officials from a number of government departments: Sean Donlon, Secretary of Foreign Affairs; David Neligan, head of the Anglo-Irish section and Michael Burke, principal officer in the section; Kirby from Justice; Government Secretary, Dermot Nally. From the Taoiseach's office there were Wally Kirwan and Frank Murray; Haughey's right-hand man, Padraig O hAnnrachain, and his advisor on Anglo-Irish relations and foreign policy in general, Martin Mansergh.

Ainsworth had never been asked to brief such a gathering in his entire career.

Haughey wanted the briefing because he was not happy with the high level of security co-operation between the Republic and Britain and the Republic and Northern Ireland. In April, he had made clear to McLaughlin and Ainsworth his opposition to extradition when he complained about the AGSI discussion on the subject. Existing co-operation fell short of extradition but was most publicly demonstrated by the Criminal Law Jurisdiction Act under which a person accused of terrorist-type offences in Northern Ireland could be tried in the Republic and vice versa. The Act also amended a number of other laws, including the Explosive Substances Act which enabled courts in the Republic to try people accused of bomb offences anywhere. The Criminal Law Jurisdiction Act was brought in by the Fine Gael-Labour coalition government led by Liam Cosgrave and had been in force since mid-1976. It was all that remained of the Sunningdale Agreement reached in 1974 between the Irish and British governments. Sunningdale saw the setting up of a power-sharing executive administration in Northern Ireland in which Protestant and Catholic politicians from different parties worked together in government for the first time. The Agreement was supposed to lead to a Council of Ireland where politicians from the North and the South would work together. Some people believed this was the first step towards a united Ireland. Loyalist opinion in Northern Ireland was so bitterly opposed to the package that street demonstrations and a strike destroyed the power-sharing executive soon after it was set up. During negotiations for the agreement, British and Northern Ireland politicians argued for an extradition agreement with the Republic, but courts in the Republic refused to extradite people for what were regarded as politically motivated crimes. The Criminal Law Jurisdiction Act was a compromise solution.

It provoked a lengthy debate during its passage through the Dáil and was opposed by Fianna Fáil. Haughey spoke on the last day of the debate and complained that if enacted, the new law could provoke violence and disorder in the Republic. He said it could bring into question the impartiality of the police force and the courts, and implied that the government was betraying the Northern Ireland nationalists. When Justice Minister Patrick Cooney made his summing-up speech for the government, he made pointed reference to the fact that, unlike other Fianna Fáil speakers, Haughey had failed to endorse the objectives of the Bill. Neil Blaney also withheld support from the aims of the Bill. The Act was passed amid threats from the Provisional IRA that it would attack anyone in the Republic who operated it. Government ministers, judges and policemen were to become "legitimate targets" if the law was enforced.

The new Act differed from the main body of criminal law in

one small but significant way. The sections of the Act which allowed people accused of terrorist-type crimes in Northern Ireland to be tried in the Republic could only be operated if the Attorney General, a political appointee, gave permission. Nearly all other criminal laws were operated at the behest of the Director of Public Prosecutions, an independent office set up by legislation in 1974. The DPP, Eamon Barnes, gave the go-ahead for prosecutions on the basis of evidence submitted to him by the gardai. But in the case of a few Acts, the Criminal Law Jurisdiction Act and the Genocide Act included, prosecutions could only take place if the Attorney General allowed. Attorneys General were appointed by the government and remained in office so long as the government held power. Since the setting up of the DPP's office, Attorneys General served to advise governments on constitutional matters. Appointments were made on the basis of legal knowledge as well as loyalty to the party. The balance between the two was a matter for whoever made the appointment.

The Criminal Law Jurisdiction Act came into force simultaneously in the Republic, Britain and Northern Ireland on June 1st, 1976. There was no great rush from the RUC to have evidence presented in the Republic's courts against the hundreds of IRA terrorists it was claimed evaded justice in the North by seeking refuge in the South. Attitudes towards the Act within Fianna Fáil oscillated between a willingness to use it since it was now on the statute books and a belief that it should be repealed at the first available opportunity. Up to the end of 1978, no moves were made from either Northern Ireland or Britain to have cases heard in the Republic's courts. The first application was then made, concerning a crime committed in Northern Ireland allegedly by a person residing in the Republic. The Northern Ireland authorities wanted the person tried in a court in the Republic. The application was refused because the evidence was vague. The first application which was granted concerned James Lynagh, Laurence McNally and Aidan McGuirk.

Henry Livingston was a 62-year-old farmer who lived at Tynan in County Armagh, a mile or two across the border from County Monaghan. He arrived in his farmyard to feed his cattle shortly after midday on March 6th, 1980. There was a sudden burst of gunfire from the barn. At least two men were inside, firing at him with Armalite rifles. Livingston was hit twice and fell to the ground. Six more bullets tore into his abdomen as he lay there, already dead. The gunmen took his car and made off towards the border. Before crossing they abandoned it and continued on foot. Livingston was a Protestant and at one time had been a member of the Ulster Defence Regiment.

Less than two hours after the murder, gardai in Monaghan town noticed Lynagh, McNally and McGuirk with mud on their clothes and boots. They were arrested and taken to Monaghan garda station. Back at the farmyard, RUC forensic experts were making a plaster cast of a footprint found in the mud near Livingston's body.

Lynagh, McNally and McGuirk were charged under the Criminal Law Jurisdiction Act with murdering Livingston. The case was the first one given the go-ahead by an Attorney General in the Republic. The decision was made by Tony Hederman, the Attorney General appointed in 1977 by Jack Lynch, who continued to serve after Haughey took over in 1979. The trial took place in July 1980 in the Special Criminal Court in Dublin and evidence was given by gardai from Monaghan and RUC officers from Belfast. All three were acquitted when the court ruled that the prosecution had failed to establish a prima facie case against them. The evidence was purely circumstantial — there was nothing to link the mud on their clothes and boots to Livingston's farm.

The first people convicted in the Republic for crimes committed in Northern Ireland were Robert Campbell and Michael Ryan. On July 10th, 1981, Campbell and Ryan plus four others, Angelo Fusco, Dingus Magee, Anthony Sloan and Michael McKee, shot their way out of Crumlin Road jail in Belfast. Campbell and Ryan were the first two caught in the Republic and were tried in the Special Criminal Court in Dublin in December. They were sentenced to ten years' imprisonment for shooting at an RUC officer during their escape, and five years for the escape itself. Fusco, Magee, Sloan and McKee were also caught, and tried in the Special Criminal Court on similar charges in February 1982.

Each was sentenced to ten years for shooting at an RUC officer, three separate terms of eight years each on related gun charges and five years for escaping from Crumlin Road jail. The sentences were to run concurrently. All of the charges were brought under the Criminal Law Jurisdiction Act after permission for the case to proceed was granted by the then Attorney General, Peter Sutherland.

Considerable publicity surrounded the next application of the Act. In May, a Northern Ireland judge went to Dublin and sat in the Special Criminal Court to hear evidence in a trial he was conducting in Belfast. The trial concerned the murders of James Stronge and his father, Sir Norman Stronge; a former Speaker in the Stormont Parliament. Both were shot dead in their home, Tynan Abbey in County Armagh.

Owen McCartan Smyth, a 29-year-old Republican from Monaghan was arrested in Northern Ireland and charged with counselling and procuring others to commit the murders. He was also charged with murder and membership of the Provisional IRA. The case was heard in Belfast before Judge Brian Hutton, but a number of witnesses from Monaghan said they did not want to travel to Northern Ireland to give evidence. Hutton was able to use a section of the Criminal Law Jurisdiction Act to adjourn the case in Belfast and come to Dublin to hear evidence from the Monaghan witnesses. McCartan Smyth was brought to the border by the RUC and handed over to the gardai while Hutton himself travelled South under heavy garda protection. In the Special Criminal Court, he sat beside High Court Judge Liam Hamilton who questioned the witnesses on his behalf.

As the evidence was being heard, an attempt was made to have McCartan Smyth released. Seamus Sorohan S.C. argued that McCartan Smyth was not in lawful custody. Sorohan's submission was rejected by Hamilton who said he was satisfied beyond any shadow of a doubt that McCartan Smyth was legally held.

"He is now in the custody of the Garda Síochána who are under obligation, by virtue of the Criminal Law Jurisdiction Act, to bring him as soon as may be to some convenient point of departure and deliver him into the custody of the police in Northern Ireland," said Hamilton.

It was a decision that smacked of extradition, as far as some Fianna Fáil people were concerned. McCartan Smyth was returned to the RUC and his trial resumed in Belfast. He was later acquitted of counselling and procuring others to murder the Stronges and the charge of murder was dropped on Hutton's instruction. However, he was convicted of being a member of the Provisional IRA and was sentenced to five years imprisonment.

Judge Hutton did not need the Attorney General's permission to enter the Republic and hear evidence in the McCartan Smyth case. The Attorney General's imprimatur was also not needed for the trial of Gerard Anthony Tuite which took place in Dublin in June and July. Tuite made legal history by being the first citizen of the Republic to be tried in an Irish court for a crime committed in England. The Attorney General's permission was not needed because Tuite was charged under the Criminal Law Jurisdiction Act only in so far as it amended the Explosives Substances Act. But his trial focussed more attention than ever before on the operation of the Criminal Law Jurisdiction Act.

Tuite was a member of the Provisional IRA based in London. He was arrested in England on charges connected to the Provisionals' Christmas bombing campaign of 1978. He was being held in Brixton Prison in London when he and two others escaped by tunnelling their way through their cell walls and scaling the perimeter wall. Described as the most wanted man in Britain, Tuite was arrested in Dundalk, County Louth, in March 1982. He was charged with having explosives at a flat in London between June 1978 and March 1979. During the trial in the Special Criminal Court in Dublin British policemen told how they found bullets, an Armalite rifle and a tape recorded "hit list" of British politicians and VIPs hidden in the flat. They also discovered maps of English cities and information about army barracks in Britain. Tuite was also linked during the trial to two car bombs in London.

The trial attracted widespread publicity in the Republic, Northern Ireland and Britain. Tuite's lawyers argued at the outset that the Special Criminal Court had no jurisdiction to try him but their objections were over-ruled. Hamilton said that Tuite had been properly charged and that the court had jurisdiction to hear the case. He sentenced him to ten years imprisonment on July 14th.

Provisional Sinn Féin, the political wing of the Provisional IRA, condemned the trial and jailing of Tuite but the Northern Ireland Secretary, James Prior, said it was a "remarkable event" and praised the Republic's Government. "We just hope it will continue," said Prior.

But while Prior complimented the Republic, Haughey made plans for the special security meeting in Government buildings on July 29th — just over two weeks after the Tuite verdict. Haughey called Ainsworth to his office a few days before the meeting and discussed at length what Ainsworth would say. Those who attended the meeting would not easily forget it. Someone who was there later described it as a "Royal Command Performance".

Ainsworth outlined the strength of subversive organisations in the country, their origins and what they stood for. He dwelt particularly on the Provisional IRA, its training camps, garda knowledge of the organisation and contact with it. He based his assessment on the number of camps and arms dumps discovered by his men. He said there was a serious problem and the question was how to contain it. He painted the picture in primary colours. The way to tackle things was to concentrate on seizing the materials, not the people behind them; prevention through seizures. It was more important to put the instruments of death out of action than it was to get the people connected to them, he said. In follow-up operations after the seizures, if one got intelligence leading to arrests, that was a bonus.

He outlined how the gardai were tackling the problem, the various sections of ISB, the numbers involved and the cost and the dangers facing his men. If the problem was not contained, it could overwhelm the entire country. Politicians said things from time to time which did not help, and sometimes had the effect of putting his men "on a war footing". He mentioned speeches by Northern Ireland politicians on extradition as an example of what could inflame passions leading to trouble.

"We've lost some good men," he said, "and some will have bullets in them for the rest of their lives".

Then he mentioned the Tuite case. He reminded everyone that when the Criminal Law Jurisdiction Act was passed, the Provisional IRA threatened to bring their war to the South if the government of the Republic operated it. Ainsworth said he believed this would happen if the government continued to use the Act and there were more cases like Tuite. Judges and politicians would become targets. His men were already overstretched, he said, and providing adequate protection to all who would need it would be a problem. He made it clear that he felt the Act should not be operated by either the gardai or the government and he pointed out that the Attorney General had what amounted to a veto over the use of large sections of the Act.

He finished, gathered up his papers and left the meeting.

The two ambassadors, Haughey, Collins, Doherty and their officials remained where they were. Some of the officials were shocked and dazed by what they heard and the way it had been told to them, others were frightened. They wondered how it was that an officer of the state, the head of intelligence, was in effect telling the head of elected government what laws would be used and what would not.

There was no doubt where Haughey stood. It was highly unlikely that the law would be used in future, for the reasons which Ainsworth had outlined. The ambassadors to Britain and the United States also knew the reasons and would be able to argue the Republic's position if and when an application to use the law was made and refused. There was no love lost between Haughey and the British in the aftermath of the Falklands war. By refusing to operate the Act, Haughey could take refuge in well-worn Republican dogma: the troubles in Northern Ireland were Britain's problem, the border was Britain's border in Ireland. Haughey's attitude was: why should we help them?

The remainder of the meeting dealt with the latest crisis in Anglo-Irish relations, on whether or not it had been agreed at the December 1980 Dublin Castle meeting between Haughey and Margaret Thatcher that in future Britain would consult the Republic on matters affecting Northern Ireland. The British said no. Haughey said yes. But while this was the issue under discussion, an extraordinary government statement put out afterwards concentrated on attacking Garret FitzGerald. It used the language of the Civil War and accused FitzGerald of "taking sides" with Britain and claimed he was acting "at the suggestion of British Ministers." It referred to FitzGerald's "recent activities . . . in London" where he met Prior "without revealing to the government or the public what was said at the meeting". The statement concluded by linking FitzGerald to the Duke of Norfolk, an elderly peer who had claimed in the House of Lords earlier in July that FitzGerald approved Prior's proposals for a Northern Ireland assembly. There was an hysterical note in the attack on FitzGerald and no reference was made to Ainsworth's contribution to the meeting and the decision not to operate joint security legislation with the British.

The collapse of Anglo-Irish relations and Haughey's personal antipathy towards the British had at last found expression in a clear change of security policy. The change was foreshadowed in a Dáil speech by Gerry Collins two weeks previously in which he said that security co-operation was a two-way process. When Haughey came to power in December 1979, his enemies feared that matters like cross-border security co-operation would be scaled down or possibly stopped altogether. They feared that Haughey's brand of republicanism would result in a change in the policies pursued by Lynch. Haughey's supporters hoped and prayed for just such a change. But during his first government, he went out of his way to please the British. He made much of his "unique relationship" with Margaret Thatcher, cemented by teapot diplomacy and the "historic breakthrough" at the Dublin Castle summit. Security co-operation between the Garda Síochána and the RUC was maintained and improved. Prosecutions were taken under the Criminal Law Jurisdiction Act and the first conviction was handed down the day before the June 1981 general election in which Haughey lost power.

Now, however, all that was gone. The "unique relationship" with Thatcher was but a brief flirtation. Haughey had his own men in Justice, Defence and the Attorney General's office. There was no Cabinet committee on security — an unique break with the past. The Cabinet Security Committee (normally including the Taoiseach, the Tanaiste, the Ministers for Foreign Affairs, Justice and Defence and the Attorney General) was supposed to be the forum for discussion on security matters. Its very existence was not admitted but it was yet another of the buffers between politicians and institutions like the gardai and the Defence Forces. Its use reduced the risk of security leaks from the Cabinet while at the same time maintaining collective responsibility for the actions of government.

When Haughey wanted to change security policy, he did so in a devious and secretive manner. Having orchestrated and manipulated behind the scenes, he saw to it that a secret meeting was presented with what amounted to a *fait accompli*. There was no discussion on the policy change and nothing was announced in public. Haughey's conduct seemed to confirm the fears his opponents had about him on security.

Chapter Eleven

I don't know what this is about, Malcolm, but whatever it
is you are on your own
Patrick Connolly, August 1982

Threats from the IRA were not the most immediate problem
facing the Garda Síochána as a whole at the end of July. The
country was experiencing a wave of murders that was
unprecedented. Between Saturday, July 24th and Monday,
July 26th, four people died as a result of violent attacks. Robert
Belton, a member of a well known Fine Gael family, had been
shot on July 16th when he tried to resist an armed raid on his
sub-post office in the Dublin suburb of Donnycarney. Hit over
the head and shot in the leg, he died in hospital of his injuries on
July 24th. In the early hours of the same morning, 20-year-old
Patricia Furlong from Dundrum in Dublin was strangled after
a summer festival in Glencullen, a tiny village in the mountains
just south of Dublin. The following day, Sunday, July 25th, a
27-year-old farmer, Donal Dunne, was found shot in a bog a
mile and a half from Edenderry, County Offaly. His body was
discovered by a family having a picnic: he had been killed by a
shotgun blast.

As details of each of the killings emerged, the most horrific
seemed to be the death of Bridie Gargan, a 29-year-old nurse at
St. James's Hospital in Dublin, who came from Dunshaughlin,
County Meath. Thursday, July 22nd, was hot and sunny in the
afternoon and Nurse Gargan was on her way home from the
hospital to her flat in Castleknock when she stopped to
sunbathe in the Phoenix Park, near the official residence of the
American Ambassador. Around the same time a man was seen

walking in the park. He was noticeable mainly because of his heavy clothes on a hot day and he was carrying a spade wrapped in a black plastic bag and a blue holdall bag. He wore a tweed, fisherman's style hat, and a heavy blue pullover, and had a well-trimmed beard.

In the holdall bag he had a lump hammer — a heavy hammer with a head similar to that of a sledge hammer — and an imitation pistol made from the firing mechanism of a crossbow. Near the residence of the American ambassador, he left down the packaged spade, took out the imitation gun and looked about to make sure there was no-one near. He went over to Nurse Gargan, pointed the "gun" at her and told her to get into the car. She looked up and asked: "Is this for real?". He told her he only wanted the car and ordered her to lie on the back seat. She got into the car but then she panicked. He took out his lump hammer and hit her several times on the side of the head.

His check that there was no-one around had not been very thorough. A gardener at the ambassador's home, Patrick Byrne, had watched the man approach the car and look around. He had seen the two people get into the car and then the man raising his arm in a hitting motion. He decided to investigate. As Byrne approached, the man pointed the "gun" at him and told him to go away. Byrne grabbed the arm holding the "gun" and the two tumbled to the ground. The man regained control, however, pointed the weapon at Byrne again and threatened to shoot him. Byrne stood back as the man drove off at high speed in a low gear along a jogging track. The gardener raised the alarm and drove around with a friend trying to find the silver-coloured Renault 5 again.

The car, meanwhile, was given an escort through the traffic. As it drove out of the Phoenix Park, an ambulance driver noticed the injured woman in the back seat, blood on the window and the parking permit for St. James's Hospital stuck on the windscreen. He concluded that the driver was a doctor taking an injured person to hospital so he signalled the car to follow him while he led the way through the traffic, with siren and flashing lights, to St. James's. The car followed the ambulance into the hospital entrance but left the grounds again. The man drove to the South Circular Road in Rialto and abandoned the car in a laneway, leaving the injured woman in it along with the hammer he had used to bludgeon her.

He noticed bloodstains on his sweater, pulled it off and tossed it into another laneway. He went into a travel agency, asked the staff for a glass of water and if they would phone for a taxi to take him to the suburb of Blackrock. A woman in the agency directed him to a bus stop. He took a bus and stayed on board as it crossed the city to Ballymun Avenue. He got off near the Fingal House pub, bought a packet of disposable razors in a shop nearby and went into the pub's toilets. Without any soap, he slowly shaved off his beard. When he emerged from the toilet, he asked the barman for change and phoned a taxi. It was two hours or so since the attack in the park and he asked the taxi driver to take him to the city centre. When they arrived there, he told the driver to bring him to the car ferry terminal in Dun Laoghaire.

Meanwhile, Bridie Gargan had been found in the back of her car in a critical condition. She was taken to the Richmond Hospital and put onto a life support system, but she died four days later. The gardaí were hard pressed to solve the case and the three other murder cases facing them at the same time. Public attention concentrated on the murder of Nurse Gargan because of the circumstances of the attack, the brutality of the assault and the bizarre manner in which the murderer and his victim had been escorted from the scene of the crime. The gardaí set about examining Nurse Gargan's car for fingerprints and other forensic evidence and tried to trace the purchaser of the Chinese-made hammer through distributors and hardware shops. They also tried to check records in psychiatric hospitals in the hope that they might find a lead to the killer.

Malcolm Macarthur did not have a psychiatric record or any other type of record that would emerge from these types of enquiries. He was 36 years old, the only son of well-to-do parents, brought up on the family's 180-acre farm near Trim in County Meath. His parents later separated and he went to live in the United States with his uncle, Jack Macarthur. While in the US he received a Bachelor of Arts degree from Davis University, a constituent college of the University of California. He returned to Ireland in the late 1960s.

Most of those who met him subsequently believed Macarthur

was an academic, highly qualified and intelligent. He was not interested in small talk and had few close friends. But he moved in a circle of Dublin society where the bohemian mingled with the strait-laced. They socialised in city centre pubs where professional people rubbed shoulders with prostitutes and homosexuals. Macarthur stood out, with his air of mild eccentricity which reinforced his image as an academic. As well as his upper-class accent, he adopted mannerisms which gave him an air of diffident superiority. His clothes added to the image: he regularly wore bow ties and fawn-coloured corduroy jackets and had silk handkerchiefs flowering from his breast pocket.

In the mid-1970s he began living with a woman called Brenda Little and through her became friendly with Patrick Connolly, a leading barrister who was appointed Attorney General by Charles Haughey in 1982 after Michael O'Kennedy had refused the post. Little, a native of Finglas in North Dublin, had got to know Connolly after a chance encounter in the city centre about twelve years previously. She was in Grafton Street collecting money for a new sports complex at Oldtown, not far from Finglas. Connolly was among the passers-by she approached for support. He quizzed her about the project. She explained what it was and then, to her astonishment, Connolly handed over £5 — a sizeable sum of money in those days. Only then did Connolly tell her that he had a family connection with Oldtown and that he was a trustee of the site on which the complex would be built. From this meeting, their friendship developed. They shared many interests over the years and accompanied each other to the opera and to the Irish Film Theatre. When she met Macarthur, Connolly in turn got to know him and they became friends.

Macarthur and Little had a son, born in 1975, to whom he was devoted. They were well off at the time; Macarthur's father had died and the family home was sold, leaving him an inheritance of £70,000. In 1980, the couple moved to a house on Iona Road in Glasnevin that had belonged to Macarthur's grandmother. The following year, the building was sold and he received £10,000 of the proceeds.

In the winter of 1981-82 the couple moved into a basement flat in Donnybrook, rented by Connolly. He had lived there himself for several years but was moving to a new luxury apartment he had bought in a development overlooking Bulloch Harbour near Dalkey, in south Dublin. Macarthur and his son stayed in the Donnybrook flat until May 23rd 1982 when they left with Brenda Little on a package holiday to Tenerife. Connolly, who saw them off at the airport, stopped renting the flat shortly after the couple left the country.

Brenda Little was keen to stay on in Tenerife but Macarthur was less enthusiastic. His finances were running low and he decided to return to Ireland. Macarthur never had a job but had lived comfortably off the money he had inherited from his father and the proceeds of· his grandmother's property. Apparently, he now decided that the easiest source of cash lay in armed robbery in Ireland. There had been a major spate of armed robberies in the country several years earlier and considerable publicity about the phenomenon, but the numbers had dwindled because of the success of armed special garda squads in catching raiders. Macarthur's attitude, however, illustrated his mental state: he suffered from a severe personality disorder.

His perception of reality was defective. He acted as though things that happened could be made unhappen by believing that they had not happened. Conversely, one could make things happen by simply declaring them as fact or as reality. His relationship with society in general was badly adjusted. He wanted to be separate from society — as evidenced partly by his demeanour and his style of dressing — but he was courteous to people. He appeared to be very alert and quick to grasp ideas and suggestions, but he was living up to an image that was not based in reality. He was not, as many of his acquaintances believed, an academic. Neither had he, as some believed, attended Trinity College in Dublin or King's College in Cambridge. His grasp on reality, however, was about to be loosened even further and he was about to slip into a psychotic interlude.

Macarthur arrived back in Dublin on July 8th and put his plan into action. He avoided his usual haunts and acquaintances and booked into a guest house in George's Street, Dun Laoghaire. He grew a beard, and bought a hat and a pair of spectacles to use as disguises. He decided that he needed a gun and he bought a crossbow from which he fashioned an imitation weapon. But he was unhappy with the effect and determined to get a real shotgun.

On July 17th, he went off to a clay pigeon shoot near Swords in County Dublin in the hopes of stealing a shotgun. He wandered around the shoot for the afternoon and tried to engage some of the participants in conversation, but failed to get any opportunity to take a shotgun. He tried again the following day at another shoot near Ashbourne in County Meath but without success. At the same time, he kept an eye on newspaper advertisements for shotguns for sale. Eventually he found what he wanted: a farmer in Edenderry, County Offaly was offering a shotgun for sale.

Macarthur decided that he needed a car as well. On July 22nd, he went by bus into the centre of Dublin from Dun Laoghaire and wandered down the quays. Arriving at the Phoenix Park, he wandered around looking at parked cars. He thought he had found what he was looking for when he saw a silver-coloured Renault 5 parked near some trees. The driver's door was open and there was someone lying alongside it in the long grass: he could not tell whether it was a man or a woman. He put down the spade he carried around (in case anyone got killed and had to be buried), took out his imitation gun and, carrying the hammer he had bought as a weapon, he approached the car.

Back in his guesthouse after the attack on Nurse Gargan, Macarthur noticed more bloodstains on his shirt. Eventually he threw it and a pair of trousers into the sea, and got rid of the imitation gun by tossing it into Bulloch Harbour. The day after the attack in the Phoenix Park, Macarthur telephoned Brenda Little in Tenerife and told her he was in Ostend in Belgium. He made the call from Dun Laoghaire and he told her he would be back in Tenerife a week later.

Macarthur still had not got a car but he was also looking for a gun. The following weekend he hitch-hiked to Edenderry in response to the newspaper advertisement offering a shotgun for sale. He arrived on Saturday, July 24th. He slept overnight under a canal bridge near the town. Next morning he met Donal Dunne by prior arrangement in the town and Dunne drove out to a local bog used occasionally for clay pigeon shooting to demonstrate his double-barrel, over and under, shotgun. He gave it to Macarthur to fire. Macarthur shot him in the face.

He left Donal Dunne's body in the bog, partially hidden by undergrowth, and stole his car to drive back to Dublin. He abandoned Dunne's Ford Escort car in Temple Lane, off Dame Street. It was found by gardaí within 24 hours. They appealed to anyone who had noticed it being driven to Dublin the previous day to contact them. With the deaths of Bridie Gargan, Donal Dunne, Patricia Furlong and Robert Belton over the one weekend, the gardaí were under severe pressure to get results.

Each of the murder cases was being investigated separately: there was no reason to link any one with any other. Inevitably, the gardaí concentrated on looking for a personal motive for each of the killings, apart from the Belton murder. Their inquiries into friends and associates occupied a considerable amount of time but yielded no results. One acquaintance of Nurse Gargan became the prime suspect for her killing because of discrepancies in his replies to questions. He was questioned on several occasions but was cleared of suspicion by forensic evidence.

The high level of public interest also meant that there were numerous reports of "sightings" of suspicious-looking men who answered the generalised description of Nurse Gargan's attacker. The knowledge that the attacker was now without his beard upset the initial eye-witness description. A photofit picture of the attacker was assembled from the descriptions given by witnesses but was not released. It bore little resemblance to Malcolm Macarthur.

A week after the two murders, however, detectives were beginning to link the killings of Bridie Gargan and Donal Dunne. Initially, there was nothing much on which to base the belief other than a vague similarity between the crimes such as the fact that the killer fled the scene in the victim's car. Once it became apparent that the victims had no previous connection with the killer, the probability of a link increased.

The search for Gargan's murderer moved to north Dublin. Gardaí traced the public house in which he had shaved off his beard, and were also contacted about a man seen acting suspiciously at the clay pigeon shoots in Ashbourne and Swords. But several other pieces were about to fall into place. Macarthur had made no further progress in his quest for easy money in the meantime. He carried the shotgun in a case and met at least one acquaintance who later looked back fearfully on the encounter. Macarthur wore thin rubber gloves when they met, explaining that he had a skin problem, but he later took them off and settled down to a meal with other members of the acquaintance's family. His hands appeared to be all right to the others.

By Wednesday, August 4th, Macarthur's financial problems had become acute and he resolved to take desperate action. He searched his memory for someone he might have known briefly and casually and who might be of use to him now.

Harry Bieling was a former United States diplomat based in London who, in the late 1960s, came to Ireland to visit friends and liked the country enough to settle down permanently. He bought a small, solid-looking house in Killiney, County Dublin. It was called Camelot, and was built of granite blocks like the much larger house a few yards down Victoria Road for which it used to be the gate-lodge. Harry Bieling's house had a commanding view of Killiney Bay and, further south, along the coast to Bray Head and the Sugar Loaf mountain in Wicklow.

At around 5.45 in the evening of August the 4th, Bieling heard a knock on the door. He opened it and standing on the pavement was a man carrying a case whom he thought he knew but whose name he couldn't quite remember.

"Hello," said Macarthur, "do you remember me? I was at the party here about eight years ago."

Bieling, embarrassed in case the caller was someone he really *should* remember, fudged the answer as Macarthur continued to talk. He said he was interested in photography and remembered there was a fine view from the living room window; he had noticed it particularly at the party. He wondered if he might take a photograph of the view. But, said Macarthur, he really did not want to intrude. Were there any visitors? he asked. No, said Bieling, he was alone. He invited Macarthur inside.

Macarthur entered and turned left into the living room. To the right, through a very short passage was a circular dining room and above it, by spiral staircase, a bedroom. Macarthur admired the view but Bieling wondered out loud how he would be able to take a photograph with all the haze that was about that day. Macarthur said it had been just like that when he first saw the view; that was exactly how he would like to picture it.

The two of them chatted about mutual acquaintances. Macarthur mentioned Mrs. So and So and, Oh Yes what about that chap from Donegal. He recalled the party, reminding Bieling that, at the time, he was being pursued by "some slut from Ballymun". Bieling couldn't remember most of the people Macarthur mentioned and those he could, he hadn't seen for years. But they chatted for a while, Macarthur with the case by his side and seeming very relaxed and calm. Bieling brought up the photographs the man wanted to take.

"I hope you have a sense of humour", Macarthur said as he opened the case and produced a shotgun. He motioned to Bieling to sit down and sat down himself with the gun on his lap pointing at Bieling. Bieling decided it was time for a stiff drink and asked Macarthur if he had any objections. Macarthur said no, so long as there was not a gun in the drinks cabinet. Bieling said he could come over with him and watch as he poured a large vodka. Macarthur followed Bieling over and watched, declining the offer of a drink himself. Both men returned to their respective seats, Bieling clutching his glass.

They sat there for a few moments, Bieling looking nervously down the barrel of the gun and not knowing what to say.

Macarthur said he wanted money.

"Have you been doing this for long?" asked Bieling.

"About a year," replied Macarthur.

Macarthur said he expected Bieling to provide him with several hundred pounds. He recalled how he used to spend a thousand pounds a week in Dublin — he said he expected at least that much from Bieling. Macarthur said he had been having financial problems ever since his patrimony ran dry. Bieling said he had no cash but that he thought he had a cheque book upstairs. Most of his money was in the Educational Building Society, he told Macarthur. They discussed how Macarthur couldn't have that because to get it, Bieling would have to withdraw it personally. A cheque seemed to be the only option.

"How are you going to get away with it?" asked Bieling. Macarthur asked if he could use the telephone: Bieling said he could, but pleaded with him not to pull the lead out of the socket. It would take six months to get it fixed, said Bieling. Macarthur said he wanted to call his accomplice who would be able to guard Bieling while he, Macarthur, went to have the cheque cashed in the morning. They spoke a little about accomplices. Macarthur said his current partner was his second. It was very difficult to get reliable people these days, he said. Bieling reminded him that, so far, he had not committed a crime and that if he left, nothing more would be said of the matter.

It was clear that Macarthur had no intention of leaving. Bieling fixed himself another stiff vodka and they continued to chat about money, friends and cheques. At 7 o'clock Bieling decided he would try to provoke a resolution of the situation. He told Macarthur that his housekeeper, Bridget, was due in half an hour to cook his dinner and he had better get this cheque book, which was upstairs.

Macarthur followed him to the other end of the living room, through the short passage, past the hall door and into the dining room. Bieling went up the spiral stairs with Macarthur following, gun in hand.

Clothes, shoes and papers were strewn around the bedroom. Bieling apologised for the mess and rummaged through the drawers. He must have made a mistake, he said, the cheque book wasn't there, it must be downstairs. Macarthur got agitated, and accused Bieling of trying to trick him. Look for yourself, said Bieling, but Macarthur refused to touch anything.

Bieling went first down the stairs again, a few steps ahead of Macarthur. At the bottom, he siezed his chance and rushed for the door. Out on the street, he turned left and ran for his life. He was gone before Macarthur could do anything about it. Macarthur went back to the living room, and put the shotgun back into the case. He went down the road, knocked on the door of one of Bieling's neighbours and asked if he could use the telephone. The woman sensed something suspicious about him and slammed the door in his face. Macarthur turned back out onto the road and managed to hitch a lift from a man going in the direction of Dalkey.

Patrick Connolly was in his apartment in Dalkey — number 6, Carnsore, Pilot View — when Macarthur arrived that evening, August 4th. The last he had heard from Macarthur was about two or three weeks previously. Macarthur had telephoned him and said he was calling from Liege in Belgium. Connolly was delighted to see his friend again but told him that Brenda Little had telephoned a few days earlier from Tenerife wondering where he was. Connolly had telephoned her back the previous day, August 3rd, and indeed earlier that day as well. When told that Little was trying to contact him, Macarthur said to Connolly that she must have misunderstood his last call to her from Ostend, that he had tried to call her that evening but had failed to get through. He told Connolly that he expected to be in Ireland for a few days sorting out some financial matter. Connolly assumed it was to do with his grandmother's estate and offered him a bed in his flat if he wished to stay. Macarthur hesitated. He said he didn't want to intrude. Connolly assured him that he was not intruding and he was welcome to stay.

Macarthur decided to avail of Connolly's generosity. He moved in.

Harry Bieling meanwhile had told the gardaí that he had been almost robbed by a man with a shotgun. He gave gardaí in Dalkey a detailed description of Macarthur but was unable to provide a name. Macarthur never told him who he was and Bieling couldn't remember, try as he would. That night, he asked a friend around and together, they drank a bottle of whiskey as shock began to affect Bieling. He eventually got to sleep at around 5 a.m.

His telephone rang at nine the following morning. Bieling, hungover and feeling rotten, groped for the handset. He picked it up, put the receiver to his ear and listened. Somebody was playing Beethoven's 7th Symphony.

"Hello, this is your friend from yesterday," said Macarthur, calling from Connolly's flat. "Why did you run?". Bieling didn't know what to say. "Oh, you must have been scared. Silly joke gone sour," said Macarthur.

He asked Bieling who should call the gardaí to tell them it was just a joke. Bieling said Macarthur should do it and Macarthur agreed he would. He then asked if he could call around next week.

"Yes," said Bieling before he hung up, "but telephone first".

Macarthur called the gardaí in Dalkey station. He gave his name and a false address in the centre of Dublin and mentioned the incident at Bieling's house. It hadn't happened, he told the garda who answered the telephone, there was no need for them to worry. It was just a joke, he said.

Although Macarthur had now identified himself, the gardaí were not much nearer to locating him. However, the focal point of the search was beginning to shift to the Dun Laoghaire area. As well as the Bieling incident, detectives on the murder investigation were now presented with a valuable source.

John Monks, a newspaper seller who operated in the centre of Dun Laoghaire, walked into the garda station there on Friday, August 6th, the day after Macarthur had made his telephone call to Dalkey gardaí, and told a detective about his suspicions of a man who had regularly bought papers from him. The man wore heavy clothes even though the weather was hot, he had had a beard but shaved it off recently, and he wore glasses which he removed or looked over when reading newspapers. Monks identified a heavy, military style sweater, similar to the one that Bridie Gargan's killer had discarded, as being like the one worn by his customer. Gardaí decided to stake out Monks's newspaper stand and on Saturday they set up another unit in Dun Laoghaire to pursue the case.

On Sunday, the Kilkenny and Galway hurling teams met in Croke Park for the all-Ireland semi-final. Connolly, a lover of the game, had arranged to go with his brother, Anthony Connolly, manager of the Irish Sugar Company factory in Carlow, and his nephew, Stephen. There was room enough for Macarthur and all four were chauffeured across the city by garda sergeant Joe Doherty, the driver of Connolly's state car. Connolly and his brother had places in the VIP box, where coincidentally, the Garda Commissioner, Patrick McLaughlin, was watching the match. Macarthur and Stephen had seats in the stand.

Unfortunately for the murder investigation team in Dun

Laoghaire, Macarthur did not return to John Monks's news stand. While living in Connolly's flat he made full use of the advantages available to him. He tended to telephone the taxi rank on Marine Road in Dun Laoghaire and ask drivers to bring newspapers to him in Pilot View. He occasionally ordered the *Irish Times* and the English satirical magazine, *Private Eye;* another time he called a taxi to go to an off-licence in Sallynoggin and bring him a bottle of Perrier water. Apart from his ride in the garda-driven state car to Croke Park, Macarthur accompanied Connolly in it on a number of mornings on the Attorney General's way into work.

But the net was beginning to close on him. On Monday, August 9th, the gardaí quizzed Harry Bieling at his home about the description he had given to the gardaí in Dalkey the night Macarthur had attempted to extract money from him. Bieling began to realise just how narrow his escape had been.

The detectives asked Bieling if he knew any Attorneys General living in Dalkey and if he knew anything about Pilot View. Bieling said he didn't but he went over the names of the acquaintances that Macarthur had mentioned to him. Over the next few days the gardaí tried to track down the people named by Bieling.

On Wednesday, Bieling was asked to go to Dun Laoghaire garda station for a further session with the murder squad. This time it lasted five hours. They kept asking Bieling about Pilot View: did he know anyone living there? And Attorneys General who lived in Dalkey: did he know any? They mentioned the murder of Charles Self, a homosexual who had been brutally killed in his Monkstown flat the previous January. They asked Bieling if he thought Macarthur was homosexual. They made it clear to him that they thought they were onto a series of murders involving the gay community. They asked Bieling about Bridie Gargan and Donal Dunne — did he know them? He said he didn't. But the questioning went around in circles and back to Pilot View and Attorneys General in Dalkey. Bieling didn't know any.

As each bit of the jig-saw was put into its proper place, the gardaí moved one step forward. On Friday, August 13th, Macarthur was driven into the city with Connolly in his state car, but returned later in the day to Pilot View by taxi. The gardaí, meanwhile had traced him to the flat in Donnybrook that he had occupied and that had been rented by Connolly. The owner of the flat was called upon by detectives, brought to Dun Laoghaire garda station and questioned in detail about the occupants of the Donnybrook flat. He told them that Patrick Connolly had been the tenant until several months earlier. Other detectives searched the Donnybrook flat while another group kept an eye on Connolly's new home in Pilot View. Inside, Macarthur telephoned the taxi rank and asked the driver who answered to bring some hack-saw blades to the flat. When the driver arrived, he was surrounded by armed detectives, questioned briefly and then told to go away quickly.

Connolly's flat was in the upper two floors of the block named Carnsore which detectives watched, front and back. A man was spotted at the window but when the intercom bell on the downstairs door was pressed, nobody answered from Connolly's flat. Around 5 p.m. the detective leading the murder investigations, Superintendent John Courtney, along with the man in charge of the Dun Laoghaire unit, Detective Inspector Noel Conroy and Detective Sergeant Tony Hickey, managed to get inside the main entrance door to the block by ringing the bell of another flat. The three decided to remain there until Connolly arrived home.

Meanwhile Connolly was clearing his desk in Government Buildings. Tomorrow, Saturday, he was off on his holidays to America and he had to be sure there was nothing left over that would need attention during his absence. He was looking forward to his trip; he planned to go first to New York, then on to New Orleans, Phoenix, Salt Lake City and Washington. The journey had been booked several weeks in advance and was costing around £2,000. Connolly was an extensive traveller and since he had become Attorney General had had less time at his disposal than when he was a senior counsel practising law. Earlier in the year, he had hoped to holiday in Argentina but that plan had been upset by the Falklands war.

He left his office at around 6 p.m. He planned to spend the evening packing and then get to bed early for a good night's sleep before the journey ahead.

When he arrived at Pilot View, Connolly was met by Courtney, Conroy and Hickey. They asked him if there was a man in his flat. He said there was, his friend Malcolm Macarthur. They told him that Macarthur was wanted in connection with an armed robbery in Killiney. Connolly was astonished and shocked. They explained to him what had happened and each reassured the other that the name was correct — it was Malcolm Macarthur the gardaí wanted for the robbery and it was Malcolm Macarthur in Connolly's flat. Connolly tried to contact Macarthur on the intercom but he didn't answer. Then he went to a neighbour's flat and telephoned him but there was still no answer. He conferred with Courtney and Conroy. They warned him that Macarthur might be armed but Connolly said he didn't believe somebody he knew as well as Macarthur would harm him. He gave the keys to the two detectives and they went up the stairs to his flat.

At the top of the stairs, they turned right and walked the few paces to Connolly's door — number 6. Courtney and Conroy knocked but Macarthur would not open the door. They tried the keys but inside Macarthur had left a key in the deadlock and so the door could not be opened. Eventually, Macarthur said he wanted to speak to Connolly. Courtney and Conroy called Connolly and he came up the stairs to them. They passed on Macarthur's request. Connolly went to the door and asked Macarthur to open it. Macarthur said he would. Connolly stood back as Courtney and Conroy took up positions directly in front of the door ready to storm inside. Conroy had his gun poised just in case.

As Macarthur opened the door, they rushed inside, spread-eagled him against a wall and frisked him. He was unarmed. Connolly walked in. It was five past seven. He looked at Macarthur.

"I don't know what this is about, Malcolm," he said, "but whatever it is, you are on your own".

Connolly told Courtney and Conroy that they could question Macarthur in the living room but that he was going upstairs. The detectives asked Macarthur if he had a gun in the flat; he said he had and would show them where it was. He led Courtney and Conroy up the stairs to a storage compartment just under the roof of the flat. There he showed them a refuse bag and, inside it, the shotgun. The three of them went to Connolly's bedroom and showed him the gun. Connolly was amazed. He had had no idea the gun was in the flat. He watched as Macarthur was led away by Conroy, his arresting officer, to Dun Laoghaire garda station for questioning.

More gardaí came into the flat and began a detailed search. Connolly showed them Macarthur's bedroom and some of his belongings there, plus some other items which he had stored for him when he went to Tenerife. Connolly then went back to the living room quite shocked at the thought that a trusted friend had been involved in an attempted armed robbery and had used his home to hide a shotgun. He telephoned his brother Anthony in Carlow and told him the news but said he thought that everything was all right. His brother wanted to come to Dublin to be with him. As yet, Connolly had no idea of the other charges facing Macarthur — the murders of Bridie Gargan and Donal Dunne. He was eventually told by Superintendent Pat Doocey, head of the Serious Crime Squad. With this news, Connolly's sense of shock grew and grew. He was horrified at the prospect of telling Brenda Little what had happened and he also thought that somebody would have to tell Macarthur's mother. He telephoned his brother again and told him of the murder charges. Anthony said he was definitely coming to see him and would be there in about an hour and a half. The enormity of the events began to sink in on Connolly. He spoke to the gardaí in his flat. It was clear to them that Connolly was completely innocent and although they wanted to question him to establish Macarthur's movements, if nothing else, it was apparent that there would be a problem. Connolly told them he intended going on his holidays the following morning, Saturday. He explained that he had booked a long time ago, and that he would be flying out early from Dublin to London. The problem of when the murder investigating team could interview Connolly was not resolved that evening.

After Connolly's brother arrived, he decided to face the ordeal of telling Brenda Little. He telephoned the apartment block in Tenerife where she and Macarthur had been staying. His call was taken by someone in the entrance hall and Connolly left a message for her to call him back urgently. She did and Connolly told her everything. They had a very difficult conversation; Little disbelieved what Connolly was saying, and he was distressed at the hurt his news was bringing. Little told him that Macarthur's mother was probably staying with friends in Mullingar but Connolly decided to wait until the morning to call her. There was somebody else he should contact first.

Haughey had a telephone on Inishvickillane and Connolly attempted to reach him at around 10 p.m. He had great difficulty getting through and when he did, the line was very bad. He told Haughey what had happened but Haughey didn't seem to grasp the significance of events or didn't hear properly on the bad line. Connolly told him that he was going on his holidays the following morning and Haughey didn't tell him not to. Haughey thought he was just being informed about the arrest, perhaps because he should congratulate the gardaí.

Connolly spent the rest of the evening talking with his brother and packing his bags. He went to bed in the early hours emotionally drained and exhausted.

The gardaí had cause to feel pleased with themselves that night. One of the most trying murder hunts for years was over. They had the killer in custody and he was co-operating with them. Macarthur gave them a lengthy statement in which he confessed to the killings of Bridie Gargan and Donal Dunne and the incident at Bieling's house.

Despite the obvious importance of the case, nobody in the gardaí had kept the Department of Justice informed of the most recent developments. The gardaí were not obliged by regulation to keep the Department, and hence the government, briefed on developments of operational matters but it was well established by precedent that informal links were maintained with certain officials so that policitians were kept up to date. Under normal circumstances, the gardaí would have told the Department on Monday, August 9th, when they were questioning Bieling about Macarthur's friends, Pilot View and Attorneys General in Dalkey, that they were following a definite line of enquiry. By Wednesday, August 11th, when they questioned Bieling in detail about Pilot View and Attorneys General, they should have been able to inform the Department that an arrest could be expected shortly. And by Friday afternoon, they were in a position to say that an arrest was imminent. They need not have mentioned Connolly — his role could have been explained immediately after the arrest. But by August 1982, these lines of communication had broken down. The critical information was not passed on.

Courtney and Conroy called to Pilot View early on Saturday morning but Connolly was in no mood to talk to them. They said they wanted a statement and pressed him. He refused and a row ensued, peppered with sharp language. Connolly argued that he was an innocent party to the affair, that he was Attorney General, about to leave on his holidays, and could just as well make a statement when he returned. But they had to treat him like any other citizen; they said they needed to question him as to why a man about to be charged with double murder had been living in his flat. Connolly was unmoved, and eventually Courtney and Conroy were forced to accept that he would make a statement when he returned.

By the time Connolly caught his mid-morning flight to London, the newspapers were onto the story. Nobody could quite believe it: the man who had bludgeoned a nurse to death and blown the head off another man had been living with Haughey's Attorney General, who was leaving the country a few hours after the arrest. It was the most sensational story for years, and it came in the middle of August when little else was happening.

Shortly after Connolly was met at Heathrow Airport by an official from the Irish Embassy in London (a courtesy accorded to all holders of diplomatic passports), Macarthur appeared before a special sitting of Dun Laoghaire district court. He was charged with the two murders and aggravated burglary (burglary with a weapon). His address in the court was the same as Connolly's — 6, Carnsore, Pilot View, Dalkey, Co. Dublin. He was remanded in custody until the following week and taken out by detectives for the journey to Mountjoy Prison with a jacket pulled over his head. A crowd of people in the narrow laneway leading from the court booed and jeered as he was taken away.

Meanwhile in London, an Irish embassy car had delivered Patrick Connolly to his hotel, the Cavendish, off Jermyn Street in the West End. By then, too, Haughey had been fully briefed by telephone by Seán Aylward, his private secretary. He was told where Macarthur had been arrested, what the charges were and the fact that a shotgun had been found in the flat. Haughey understood the political implications immediately and ordered that Connolly be contacted in London.

Connolly was out for the evening and returned late to his hotel room. He telephoned his brother in Carlow and was told that Haughey was trying to contact him. There was also a message for him at the embassy. Connolly called and Haughey asked him to return to Dublin. Connolly said he didn't want to, insisting that he was on holidays and was about to go to the United States. He told Haughey that he could ring him again when he landed in New York and Haughey agreed, apparently having got the impression that Connolly was about to board a flight. Connolly, however, stayed overnight in London and only flew to New York the following day, Sunday.

The Macarthur story dominated the front pages of each of the Dublin Sunday newspapers. The *Press* and *Independent* played it low key, sticking deadpan to a report of Macarthur's court appearance in Dun Laoghaire the previous afternoon, but each also stated that he shared the same address as the Attorney General. *The Sunday Tribune* went to the heart of the story. "Double murder suspect held in A-G's flat", said the headline. Late editions of the paper had a stronger headline. "A-G flies out as murder suspect charged", said the new headline. Haughey knew that all hell was about to break loose and that Connolly would have to return, by order if necessary.

By the time Connolly's plane touched down at Kennedy Airport in New York, late on Sunday, Irish time, all hell had indeed broken loose. It seemed that no matter how far he went from Ireland, the crisis followed him. He was met at the airport by Ireland's deputy consul general in New York, Donal Hamill, and was besieged by reporters. Connolly could see for himself that things had got out of hand and he knew that it was likely that he would have to return to Ireland to offer an explanation. Hamill drove him to his hotel, the Roosevelt on Madison Avenue and 45th Street. Haughey telephoned him there from Kinsealy and, this time, Connolly accepted that he would have to fly back to Dublin. Haughey told him it was imperative that he should return. The situation was drastic, he said. Connolly agreed without argument.

On Monday morning, the *New York Post* announced

Connolly's arrival in the city with a report headlined: IRISH BIGGIE FLEES HERE AFTER SLAY SCANDAL. The *Post's* rival, *The New York Daily News,* was slightly more restrained. IRISH LAWMAN IN SHOCKER, the *News* declared. Both headlines illustrated the distorted understanding of Connolly's position, created in part by the fact that neither he nor Haughey had made any public statement since Macarthur's arrest.

In Dublin, journalists were demanding explanations from the Government Information Service. Suspicions were exacerbated by the false information issued through the GIS. On Sunday, for instance, the GIS said that Haughey would return from his island the following day, Monday, for a previously arranged meeting with trade unionists: in fact, Haughey returned on Sunday. On Sunday evening, a GIS spokesman said that Haughey's first contact with Connolly after the arrest of Macarthur had been on Sunday evening when the Taoiseach spoke by telephone with him in New York. In fact, Haughey had spoken twice with Connolly by then, first on Friday night immediately after the arrest and again on Saturday when Connolly was in London. At that stage Haughey knew exactly what the charges were against Macarthur and also that a shotgun had been found in the Attorney General's flat.

Connolly left it to Hamill to make the arrangements for the return to Dublin. The quickest way was by Concorde, the British Airways supersonic jet, to London and from there to Dublin. The Concorde flight left New York on Monday and Connolly could be back in Dublin late on Monday night. If he were to wait for the next Aer Lingus flight, he would not get back until Tuesday. And so on Monday, after just one night in New York on the first day of his holiday in the United States, Connolly boarded the Concorde for London on the first leg of his journey home.

The consulate in New York furnished Connolly with copies of that morning's British newspapers which he read on the flight with no great relish. He requested some notepaper and a stewardess brought him a few sheets of airline paper. Connolly began to write his statement of explanation.

He said he wanted to "allay any public disquiet which may have arisen". He had known Macarthur socially for a number of years, his fiancée and members of her family for many years. Macarthur had degrees from Cambridge and the University of California. Since May, Macarthur had been in Tenerife with his fiancée and their child, said Connolly. He said that Macarthur had arrived at his flat on August 4th and told him that he had been in London and Belgium on business. Connolly said he had invited him to stay.

He said he had had no knowledge at any time that the gardaí were searching for Macarthur and that his arrest and the charges against him were a surprise and a very great personal shock. Connolly said that his holiday had been arranged for almost two months and the gardaí had said it was in order for him to depart.

"I had already furnished them with all the information I had concerning Mr. Macarthur's presence in my home", he said, despite his row with Courtney and Conroy, and the fact that he had not made a formal statement to them.

He said that when he went to London on Saturday, he was contacted by the Taoiseach who suggested he should return. Connolly said that he told Haughey he would prefer to discuss the matter from New York but when he arrived in New York, the Taoiseach contacted him and asked him to return to Dublin to "discuss the situation that had arisen".

The final few sentences of the statement were not written by Connolly as he flew the Atlantic back to Ireland. He arrived in Heathrow Airport, London, and was again besieged by reporters, who were even more insistent that he answer questions. The story had grown to such dimensions that BBC television had an outside broadcast unit filming Connolly's arrival at Heathrow live on its main evening news. But Connolly refused to say anything and boarded the Irish Air Corps plane sent to London to take him on the last leg of his journey back to Dublin. The 10 seat Beechcraft plane was piloted by two Air Corps officers. Connolly sat at the rear, alone with his thoughts and nine empty seats as the small plane flew through the night to Casement Aerodrome near Dublin. Haughey was in Kinsealy waiting for Connolly to turn up. He had summoned the government press secretary, Frank Dunlop, and the deputy head of the GIS, Ken Ryan, to his house. Haughey didn't appear upset or anxious but late in the evening said he was hungry. He asked Dunlop to drive him down the road to Pat O'Connor's house, for something to eat.

They got into the car and went down the avenue to the entrance which was cluttered with reporters waiting for Connolly to appear. Haughey told Dunlop to drive on, not to stop under any circumstances. Dunlop had to slow down because he was entering a major road and the reporters swarmed forward to the car. But the road was clear, he put his foot down and the car surged away towards O'Connor's house. Haughey told Dunlop not to stop outside O'Connor's but to slow down, let him jump out and then speed off again towards Malahide. Dunlop did as he was instructed and Haughey disappeared running up O'Connor's driveway. Later Dunlop brought him back in time to receive Connolly. Reporters were told that Haughey had gone to commiserate with one of his aides, Pádraig O hAnnracháin, whose house had been damaged by fire.

By the time that Connolly's car drove through the gates of Kinsealy, his every movement was being relayed around the world by news agencies, radio and television stations. When he saw the reception waiting for him at Baldonnel and Kinsealy, he knew that he would almost certainly have to resign.

He spoke with Haughey for about half an hour. The two were of one mind on Connolly's position as Attorney General; resignation was the only option under the circumstances. Connolly explained to Haughey all that had happened and his role in the events. While they spoke, a typist prepared his statement and the remaining sentences were added. They referred to his innocence in the affair but that, because of his unique position under the constitution and the law and the embarrassment caused to the government, it was his public duty to tender his resignation. The Taoiseach accepted it.

Connolly hoped that some of the information in the statement would put a stop to the more lurid rumours in circulation about his relationship with Macarthur and Brenda Little. All were untrue. There was no prior connection between Macarthur, Bridie Gargan and Donal Dunne. The friendship between Connolly and Macarthur, such as it was, had come about through Brenda Little. Macarthur had never met Haughey. Nevertheless, the bare facts of the case were so apparently unlikely that it was scarcely surprising that rumours of sinister undercurrents should proliferate.

Connolly's statement was telephoned to the newspapers in the early hours of Tuesday morning, August 17th, and Superintendent Billy Byrne from Coolock garda station distributed it to reporters waiting at the gates in Kinsealy. Connolly went home to Pilot View, a private citizen and, in the immediate aftermath of his resignation, took refuge among his family and friends. On Wednesday, August 18th, he finally made his statement to the gardaí.

The following day, August 19th, Macarthur appeared in court again, this time in Dublin district court. The brief hearing was uneventful: Macarthur was dressed in a light-coloured sports coat and bow tie and said nothing while he was again remanded in custody. Outside, however, a crowd of people had gathered to see him being led from the Bridewell building. Again, they booed and jeered and some jostled him as the handful of detectives and uniformed gardaí on duty tried to hurry him to a waiting vehicle.

The atmosphere of cover-up and crisis was fuelled by the inept handling of the affair by Haughey and his aides. Frank Dunlop was on holiday when Macarthur was arrested and did not return to Dublin until late on Monday. In his absence, the media was reliant on Ken Ryan, a former reporter with the *Irish Independent* who was appointed to the GIS by Haughey after offering to help with the negotiations with Tony Gregory earlier in the year. Ryan was under intense pressure from the media and issued some statements that added to the air of crisis.

But the biggest gaffe was made by Haughey himself. Later on Tuesday, after Connolly had resigned, Haughey hosted a press conference on public sector pay negotiations which was inevitably dominated by questions on the Connolly-Macarthur affair. Haughey was caught off guard a number of times and admitted he had spoken to Connolly on the night of Macarthur's arrest and that when he spoke to him in London, he knew all the facts of the case. He was asked why nobody in the government had congratulated the gardaí on their work.

"It was a very good piece of policework", said Haughey, "slowly, painstakingly, putting the whole thing together and eventually finding the right man".

At the time Macarthur was an innocent man until proven guilty of the charges against him. Haughey was clearly in contempt of court. His aides pleaded with reporters not to publish or broadcast the remark. Those working for Irish newspapers and RTE were unable to in any event because if they did, they would have been just as guilty as Haughey. Foreign media were not subject to the same restraints, however, and when broadcast in Britain the remark was heard by people living along the east coast of Ireland — the area from where any jury trying Macarthur would be drawn. Macarthur's lawyers later attempted to have Haughey cited in the High Court for contempt. They failed when the judge accepted that Haughey had made a *bona fide* mistake. It did not stop some people thinking that the remark was part of a huge conspiracy to keep the case out of the courts and thus protect certain unnamed people, politicians and lawyers. Haughey, acting Justice Minister at the time and indeed himself a former Justice Minister, knew exactly what he was doing, they claimed.

The Macarthur affair caused immense damage to Haughey's government. Some of his own adjectives to describe it — grotesque, unbelievable, bizzare, unprecedented — were apt, and led to the invention of a new word, GUBU, coined by one of his critics of old, Conor Cruise O'Brien. GUBU followed Haughey wherever he went and was widely used to describe some of the strange incidents which continued to dog his government. Public suspicion over the Macarthur affair in fact transcended the life of Haughey's administration. In January 1983, Macarthur was sentenced to penal servitude for life when he pleaded guilty to Bridie Gargan's murder in a hearing in the Central Criminal Court which lasted about five minutes. No evidence was given in court because the judge ruled it was irrelevant since the accused had pleaded guilty. There was an immediate public furore and more accusations of conspiracy and cover-up. In fact, what had happened was normal legal practice.

By the time Macarthur came to court, there were four charges against him: the two murders, aggravated burglary and possession of a firearm with intent to endanger life. The evidence against him on three of the charges (the Gargan

234

murder, the burglary and the arms charge) was overwhelming. The charge of murdering Donal Dunne was less easy to prove because there were no witnesses. But without doubt, Macarthur was going to be sent to jail for a very long time on any of the charges against him. The defence and prosecuting lawyers "plea bargained", a routine occurrence outside the courts but one which the legal profession was reluctant to admit existed. From the point of view of the defence, almost any bargain was in the interest of their client. As far as the prosecution was concerned, the less opposition there was from Macarthur's lawyers the easier their job would be.

Macarthur's senior counsel, Patrick MacEntee, offered a plea of guilty to manslaughter to both murder charges. Prosecuting senior counsel, Harry Hill, turned down the offer after consultations with the Director of Public Prosecutions, Eamonn Barnes. MacEntee offered a guilty plea on the Gargan murder and a manslaughter plea to the killing of Dunne. Again, Barnes rejected the offer on the basis that it would be unfair to the Dunne family. Instead, it was agreed that Macarthur would plead guilty to the murder of Bridie Gargan and the other charges — the murder of Donal Dunne, aggravated burglary at Harry Bieling's home and possession of a firearm — would be set aside for the time being. If Macarthur forfeited his right to appeal by failing to lodge an appeal within the time allowed after his conviction for the Gargan murder, then the prosecution would not proceed with the other charges. There would be no point: Macarthur had only one life and ten life sentences would not change that. There was also a chance that Macarthur might be acquitted on a charge of murdering Donal Dunne because of the lack of witnesses. In July 1983, the DPP duly entered a *nolle prosequi* on the remaining charges and the case against Macarthur was closed, as far as the state was concerned. Many people believed, however, that justice had not been seen to be done in the case.

The ensuing public outcry was not abated by those who pointed out that Macarthur's treatment by the courts was not unusual. Those who believed there was a conspiracy and a cover-up had their convictions confirmed. The fact that the case was still of consuming public interest a year after Macarthur's arrest was an indication of the depth of interest the affair aroused when it erupted in August 1982. In the immediate aftermath, public confidence and trust in Haughey's government plummeted. Very little the government said or did was accepted at face value and the scandals which continued to surface afterwards convinced many people that their suspicions were well founded. Unlike other scandals, however, there was no cover-up.

Chapter Twelve

The things that happen to people are like the people they
happen to.
Editorial in *The Irish Times,* September 1982

Events were moving rapidly in County Roscommon; the
conflict between Sergeant Tom Tully and Sean Doherty was
reaching a climax.

The chain of events that followed the raid on Michael
Keaney's pub on the Boyle to Ballyfarnan Road during the
general election campaign in February had led to the order to
Tully, on July 28th, to move to Ballyconnell, County Cavan.
Tully sought an interview with Commissioner McLaughlin and
appealed against the move. On August 10th, he was told his
request for a meeting had been rejected and that his appeal had
failed; he was to go to Ballyconnell two days later.

Tully considered taking his case to the High Court, and
sought legal advice. In anticipation of court action he prepared
a draft affidavit outlining his case and the background of
political interference in garda work in County Roscommon.
The six-page document gave details of five cases to back up
Tully's central assertion that, as he put it: "I am the victim of a
vicious piece of victimisation at the hands of the Minister for
Justice and some garda officers because I would not yield to
political pressure to square serious violations of the law."

Tully was persuaded, however, to use the review body
within the force which adjudicates on disputes over such
matters as transfers. This body consisted of Deputy Commissioner Larry Wren, Liam Breathnach, an assistant secretary
in the Department of Justice, and Michael Boyle, a member of

the executive committee of the Association of Garda Sergeants and Inspectors. Tully also agreed to take his case to the AGSI, the body which represented his interests as a sergeant.

Little time was lost in arranging a hearing for Tully in the Department of Justice. It took place in late August in a conference room at the Department's headquarters in St Stephen's Green in Dublin. Tully was accompanied by another member of the AGSI executive, Mick Murray, who represented him at the hearing. They argued that there was no proper reason for the transfer and detailed Tully's record within the force. Tully did not speak and his draft affidavit was not presented to the review body. The Commissioner's side of the argument had been presented to the body earlier, so the hearing lasted less than fifteen minutes.

As he left the Department, Tully and Doherty met by accident. Tully was walking out the main door: Doherty had just alighted from his official car and was walking up the steps to the door. He had to stand aside while Tully came out the door. They knew each other well from years of casual encounters in the Boyle area. Neither said anything.

The review body made its decision there and then to overturn the order instructing Tully to move to Ballyconnell. The decision was both unanimous and, for the AGSI, unprecedented. It was the first time the AGSI had won a case before the review body. But of greater surprise was the unanimity of the decision: Deputy Commissioner Wren clearly disagreed with the decision of the Commissioner to transfer Tully. News of the result became known unofficially later that day, although Tully was not formally told of the decision for a week. Doherty was furious. That night he phoned Wren and Breathnach at their homes to castigate them. Next day he summoned both to his office separately to reinforce his complaints about their decision. He demanded to know of Wren why he had seen fit to overturn a decision of the Commissioner, his senior officer. Breathnach left the meeting muttering to colleagues that he was not sure if he had just lost his job or not.

Against all the odds, the local sergeant from Boyle had bested the Minister for Justice. Rumours and reports of what had happened spread through the garda force but, as yet, the public at large knew nothing of the trial of strength that had been going on. Doherty called off his plans to carry out the official opening of Boyle garda station, one indication of the consequences for his standing in the area. In some sections of the Garda Síochána it also raised hopes that the growth in abuses and irregularities over recent months could be halted. The main result of Tully's victory — as with the Macarthur affair — was a psychological effect out of all proportion to the situation that had given rise to it. It opened up another crack in a floodgate that was about to burst.

Doherty had other things on his mind as well. He was faced with a hunger strike in Limerick prison over an overtime dispute by prison officers. Doherty had agreed to give prisoners extra recreation, but the warders declared that they would work the necessary overtime only if they were paid for their lunch-hour as well as for the new duties. Doherty refused the lunchtime payment on the basis of the cost and the precedent it might set for the rest of the public service. The dispute included reports of threats to the lives of the warders but Doherty stood firm. A stopgap compromise was worked out eventually; the hunger strike ended and the overtime dispute dragged on in the background for months.

The publication in September of the official crime figures for 1981 brought a lengthy comment from Doherty as Minister. The record figures demonstrated the seriousness of the situation, he declared, in a statement that went on to detail the measures he was taking. Recruitment of gardaí was being accelerated; operating procedures improved; modern equipment provided. A new radio network and computer facilities would give any garda on the beat anywhere in the state access to centrally stored information. Legislation to amend garda powers would probably be brought before the Dáil during the next session, he said.

By mid-September Doherty was contemplating a return visit to the annual race meeting in Listowel, County Kerry. He and three friends from Carrick-on-Shannon had gone to the five-day holiday event the previous year. One of them, Desmond Cox, a chemist from Carrick and a keen racegoer, had booked four rooms in the Mount Brandon Hotel in Tralee for the week beginning September 20th, Listowel race week.

Before that, however, Doherty had one item of business to look into.

His brother-in-law, Garda Tom Nangle, was due to appear in court in Dowra, on the border between County Cavan and County Leitrim on September 27th, accused of assaulting a man in a bar in Blacklion, County Cavan, the previous December. Nangle was a young garda and the brother of Doherty's wife, Maura. At the time of the alleged assault, he had been stationed in Blacklion, one of a strong complement of gardaí who manned a checkpoint between Blacklion and its twin village a few yards across the border, Belcoo.

On Thursday, September 16th, Doherty told a female secretary in his ministerial office to contact Jim Kirby, head of the security section in the Department of Justice. She was to ask Kirby to initiate an enquiry through the gardaí with the RUC about James McGovern who lived just across the border from Blacklion in County Fermanagh. She passed on the message to Kirby but he did not act immediately. He waited until the next day when he queried the instruction with Doherty: the Minister confirmed that he was to make the enquiry.

Kirby telephoned Chief Superintendent Tom Kelly, one of the senior officers in the Intelligence and Security Branch of the gardaí. He asked Kelly to contact the RUC and enquire about James McGovern. Kelly did so and was told by the RUC that McGovern was "clean". He relayed the information back to Kirby.

Jimmy McGovern was aged 33 and lived with his parents and brothers at the family home in Marlbank, a corner of County Fermanagh in the foothills of the Cuilcagh mountains. From Marlbank, with its spectacular views northwards, to Blacklion in County Cavan was a few miles along an unapproved cross-border road: by approved border crossings it was considerably further. On Tuesday, December 21st, 1981, Jimmy McGovern drove down to his local pub, the Bush Bar in Blacklion, where the annual Christmas draw was due to take place. The Bush Bar was owned by another family named McGovern who were not related to the McGoverns in Marlbank.

Jimmy McGovern had left the Bush Bar and crossed Blacklion's only street to a pool hall before closing time. But he returned to the bar around closing time to get change of a £1 note for the pool tables. Garda Tom Nangle, who had also been in the Bush that night, was leaving the building about the same time but stopped off at the bar to get some more drink. He was having an argument with Seamus McGovern, the barman and son of the owner, as Jimmy McGovern came in. Jimmy passed a remark. The next thing he knew he was lying on the ground, dazed. He was taken off to hospital in Enniskillen and treated for a cut on his head. Meanwhile two McGoverns from the Bush brought Nangle up the street to the garda station and complained to Sergeant Michael Forde that he had assaulted a man in their pub.

The following night Jimmy McGovern made a statement to the gardaí about the incident. About a month later, as the case was still being processed, three men called to Jimmy's home. They were Seamus McGovern, the barman from the Bush Bar, and two brothers, Frankie and Joe Maguire. Frankie Maguire was a cattle dealer for whom Jimmy McGovern's brother, Philip, drove a truck. Joe Maguire ran the Lough MacNean guesthouse across the road from the Blacklion garda station and he was a peace commissioner appointed by a Fine Gael Minister for Justice, Patrick Cooney. His close contact with the gardaí as a peace commissioner and as a neighbour made him anxious to settle the argument between Tom Nangle and Jimmy McGovern.

The three men asked Jimmy McGovern if he would be prepared to settle the case privately. There would be less trouble for everyone: Nangle could lose his job in the Garda Síochána if he was convicted, they suggested. Jimmy's family urged him to agree but he still felt sore about the incident. He said he would settle for £2,000, that Nangle's job must be worth that much to him. The others said Nangle would not have that kind of money. They suggested he come to Blacklion and meet Nangle himself.

Jimmy agreed and went to Blacklion with them but Nangle was not free to see them. Joe Maguire, Seamus McGovern and Tom Nangle, in plain clothes, subsequently drove across the border to Jimmy's home. Maguire went into the house and asked Jimmy to come out to the car. He did and they all had a discussion. After some bargaining, a deal was struck. It was agreed that Nangle would pay Jimmy McGovern £400 and Jimmy, in return, was to go to the garda station in Blacklion and withdraw the statement he had made. Joe Maguire and Seamus McGovern witnessed the arrangement.

Jimmy McGovern went to the garda station to withdraw his complaint but he was told that it was out of the hands of the local people at that stage. He told Joe Maguire what had happened. Eventually, however, he signed a statement retracting his complaint and gave it to a garda from Blacklion station. But he never got his £400. He met Tom Nangle on two occasions shortly afterwards and asked for the cash: Nangle said there was no word from Dublin about the case.

Shortly after the incident, Nangle was transferred from Blacklion to Ballymote in County Sligo and his brother-in-law became Minister for Justice. In mid-July 1982 he and Jimmy McGovern bumped into each other accidentally in a hotel in Bundoran, County Donegal. Jimmy asked again for his money: Nangle gave his stock answer that there was still no confirmation that the case had been dropped.

Some six weeks later, Jimmy McGovern discovered that the case had not been dropped. He was crossing the bridge and the border between Blacklion and Belcoo when a garda handed him a summons to appear in Dowra District Court on September 27th.

Meanwhile, Sean Doherty had gone off to the races in Listowel with his three friends from Carrick-on-Shannon. On the day the meeting began, September 20th, members of the Irish National Liberation Army planted explosives at a radar station on top of Mount Gabriel in West Cork and put it out of action on the grounds that it was part of NATO's western defences. But the attack, the main violent action by a paramilitary group south of the border in 1982, did not immediately disturb Doherty's plans.

On Tuesday, September 21st, the four friends went to Listowel, accompanied by Doherty's strong ministerial body-guard. As well as his armed driver, Doherty was accompanied by two other detectives from the Intelligence and Security Branch who were armed with handguns and carried Uzi sub-machine guns in their car. They travelled in a separate car from the Minister. In Listowel, the two detectives accompanying the Minister were Donie Dunne and Peter Fallon. They travelled in a green Ford Granada car which they took turns driving.

After the day's racing, the ministerial party moved on to Ballybunion, the traditional-style holiday resort in north Kerry, to the Ambassador Hotel there, one of the main centres of post-racing socialising. Doherty was not the only cabinet minister in the area; Albert Reynolds, the Minister for Industry and Energy, was also there. By 9 p.m. or so, the group left for the Fenit area and a meal in the Tankard restaurant. The party had increased substantially in numbers by then. Two women, one of whom worked with the garda drug squad in Dublin Castle and the other with the Department of Justice, had joined up with the group in Ballybunion. In the restaurant, the party divided into two. A group of seven people, including Doherty and his three friends from Carrick and the local Fianna Fáil TD, Tom McEllistrim, occupied one table. The protection detail — Detectives Dunne, Fallon and Doherty's driver, Detective Garda Michael Tierney — occupied another table with the two women.

It was about 4 a.m. when they all left. Desmond Cox picked up the restaurant bill for the seven diners at the table. They all got back to the Mount Brandon Hotel in Tralee about 4.30 a.m. but Doherty and his protectors were not destined to get much sleep. Doherty was due back in Dublin later that morning for a meeting in the Department of Justice about the Mount Gabriel radar station bombing and for a cabinet meeting. First, however, there were some problems to be sorted out. One of the party had left his car in Ballybunion and the two women had to be driven back to their hotel in the holiday resort.

A squad car was summoned from Tralee garda station and Detective Garda Dunne asked the uniformed driver, Garda Michael O'Donovan, if he would take the women to Ballybunion. Garda O'Donovan refused. Dunne went to his colleague, Detective Garda Peter Fallon, and asked him for the keys to their Ford Granada. He left Tralee shortly before 5 a.m. with the women in the car for the twenty-mile drive to Ballybunion. Garda O'Donovan also went to Ballybunion in the squad car with a local detective, Michael Coote, who was on security duties with the Minister while he was in the Tralee area.

Detective Garda Coote picked up a car in the carpark of the Ambassador Hotel in Ballybunion and drove it back to Tralee. Garda O'Donovan followed behind him in the squad car. Four miles or so from Ballybunion, on the Tralee side of the village of Ballyduff, they saw the headlights of a car in a field on the left-hand side of the road. There was a bad right-hand bend at the spot and marks on the ditch beside the road showed where the car had gone through it. The car was on its roof. Garda O'Donovan found Detective Dunne standing beside the overturned Granada, looking shocked and dazed.

He brought Dunne back to Tralee. What happened when they arrived in Tralee was disputed later in a court case. Garda O'Donovan said under oath that he arrested Dunne because he believed he was too drunk to drive. Dunne, according to Garda O'Donovan, retorted: "To hell you are", jumped out of the squad car and ran up the road to the Mount Brandon Hotel. He went to Desmond Cox's bedroom where Doherty and other members of the party were.

Dunne, also on oath, denied that Garda O'Donovan had ever attempted to arrest him. He said he was driven in the squad car to the Mount Brandon Hotel. A jury at Tralee Circuit Court in June 1983 found him not guilty of two charges of escaping from lawful custody and of frustrating a prosecution under the Road Traffic Act.

Dunne's return to the hotel prompted the three other detectives guarding the Minister for Justice to leave their charge. Garda Fallon from ISB, Garda Tierney, the Minister's driver, and Garda Coote, the local detective assigned to the Minister, all left the Mount Brandon Hotel and drove back to the crashed car. They collected an Uzi sub-machine gun and Dunne's handgun from the Ford Granada. About 7.30 a.m. Doherty and his protection detail left Tralee for Dublin and a cabinet meeting.

While rumours and gossip began to develop in Kerry after the Minister's departure, a much more damaging and serious scandal for Sean Doherty was still in the making in Dublin. On Friday, September 24th or Saturday, September 25th, the RUC was contacted again by a senior Garda officer — not Chief

Superintendent Tom Kelly — about Jimmy McGovern, the Fermanagh man due to give evidence against Garda Tom Nangle in the District Court at Dowra on the following Monday. The RUC headquarters in Belfast ordered that McGovern be taken into custody but a Special Branch officer in the Fermanagh area, Detective Inspector Ian Carter, questioned the order. His views were overruled, however, and the order was confirmed by Assistant Chief Constable Trevor Forbes.

In Blacklion, meanwhile, the impending court case had created enormous interest among the gardaí stationed there. Some had gone out of their way to issue summons for minor traffic offences to ensure that they would be able to travel the ten miles to Dowra for the Nangle hearing. Jimmy McGovern, too, had made preparations to take the day off. He was employed at the time with a contractor who was busily laying concrete driveways into farms. The business was booming, thanks to an EEC grant for farmers to have the work done. The grant was about to end and there was pressure on them to complete as many concrete laneways as possible. As he had to take a day off for the court, McGovern decided to make an appointment with a dentist in Enniskillen for 4.30 p.m. He reckoned the court case would be well finished by then.

On Sunday night, September 26th, Jimmy McGovern left home to cross the border to Blacklion to meet some friends. They went drinking and later went to a football club dance. Among the people he met was Seamus McGovern, the barman at the Bush bar, and they arranged to drive together to Dowra the next morning. Jimmy McGovern changed his mind about going home: he decided to stay with a cousin, John McNulty, in Belcoo. He arrived at McNulty's house, close to the local RUC station, about 3 a.m. and knocked up his cousin.

The RUC arrived at his family home at Marlbank about 6 a.m. They looked through the house casually and asked who was the normal occupant of the empty bed. The policemen sought instructions by radio when they were told Jimmy wasn't there. Nobody in the house knew where he was. The police took Philip, one of Jimmy's brothers, with them: he was taken to the interrogation centre at Gough barracks in Armagh and questioned before being released that evening.

Half an hour later the RUC arrived at McNulty's house in Belcoo. They asked McNulty, who was not getting much unbroken sleep that night, if anyone other than his family was staying there. He told them about Jimmy McGovern: they showed no interest in anyone else. Jimmy was woken up by an armed and uniformed constable pulling at the blankets on the bed and telling him that he was under arrest as a suspected terrorist.

Jimmy said he couldn't go with them because he had to be in court in Dowra. The constable said he was going to Armagh. Two other policemen were waiting outside with a Ford Cortina and they drove off with their captive, still protesting about his court appearance in Dowra. They drove into the heavily-fortified police station in Enniskillen and one of the RUC men went into the building. He emerged within five minutes, and said that he had left a message to be relayed to the gardaí about McGovern's detention.

On the way to Armagh, the policemen did not talk but they and Jimmy McGovern exchanged cigarettes. Shortly after 9 a.m. they arrived at Gough barracks. His pockets were emptied, he was examined by a doctor and placed in a cell. Some two hours later, two detectives brought him to an upstairs room where his fingerprints were taken. Jimmy told them about the court case in Dowra and his story about the alleged assault. They joked that he would be a great guy for getting the brother-in-law of the Justice Minister. One of the detectives said he would notify the gardaí and later told Jimmy that he had done so. Then the interrogation began in a low-key fashion.

Unknown to them, a senior officer in the RUC telephoned a counterpart in ISB at garda headquarters. The special request from the South, which they had spoken of a few days previously, was being looked after, he said.

Meanwhile, the detectives asked McGovern if he was a member of the IRA or knew any Provos. He said he was not and did not. They asked him about attending H-Block demonstrations and about the murder of a UDR man in Florencecourt, close to Marlbank, several years earlier. Jimmy McGovern admitted being at a few H-Block rallies and working at a polling station in Blacklion for Kieran Doherty, the IRA hunger striker in the North who had been elected to the Dáil in the June 1981 general election and was one of the ten republicans who died during the prison protest. After three-quarters of an hour, he was taken back to his cell for lunch.

After 3 p.m. he was taken to a different interview room where there were two detectives, one of whom he had seen in the morning. They told him they had good news for him: he was not being held any longer. But they could not release him immediately because they did not have a car available to take him home. He told them about his 4.30 p.m. appointment with a dentist in Enniskillen: one said he would phone and cancel the appointment for him. After a casual conversation about smuggling in Fermanagh, he was taken back to his cell, given a medical examination and released about 7.30 p.m. Three different RUC men drove him home to Marlbank.

The courthouse which shared a solid building with the garda station at Dowra had been packed for the hearing of the Nangle case. Sergeant Michael Forde told how Garda Nangle had been brought into the Blacklion garda station by Seamus McGovern and his father, Vincent McGovern, who accused him of assaulting a man in their pub. When he went down to the Bush bar, the sergeant saw James McGovern being treated by a number of people and he saw a cut on his head.

Garda Tom Nangle was defended by another brother-in-law, Kevin Doherty, a solicitor and brother of the Minister for Justice. He asked Sergeant Forde in cross-examination if James McGovern had made a statement the next night and if he had made a further statement on January 21st. The sergeant said that the general gist of what McGovern had said in the second statement was that he did not want to go ahead with the complaint. "He didn't wish to pursue it?" Doherty asked. "He gave reasons for not wanting to pursue it", Sergeant Forde replied.

Vincent McGovern, the owner of the Bush bar, and his son, Seamus, told the court that Nangle had asked for more drink as he was leaving at closing time. They refused to serve him any more drinks. They saw Jimmy McGovern come in and they saw Nangle hit him. Seamus McGovern agreed under cross-examination that it was possible that Jimmy McGovern had tried to strike Nangle and he had not seen it.

Nangle, in evidence, said he had asked the McGoverns for a take-away as he was leaving but was refused. He alleged that James McGovern said to him: "Fuck the guards, they should all be in H-Block". He said he turned around but saw James McGovern raise his left hand and he felt that McGovern was going to strike him. "In self-defence I put up my hand and it connected with him and he fell down"; Nangle said. He said he felt threatened because of his previous dealings with Jimmy McGovern whom, he said, he had interviewed about H-Block acivities some six months earlier.

Nobody mentioned in court why Jimmy McGovern was not present. The local Garda Superintendent said afterwards that he had been told by a local member of the force when he arrived at the court that Jimmy McGovern would not be attending. He had not been given any reason, he said.

District Justice John H. Barry said that cases like this one were always unpleasant and uncomfortable for the courts when gardaí were involved. It was extraordinary that every time there was a question of assault connected with guards there was "the question of so-called patriots". The court must have the best evidence available, he said. "The best evidence is that of James McGovern, but, for what reason I don't know it was not forthcoming". He dismissed the charge of assault.

When the case was over the prosecution and the defence witnesses drifted out to a local pub, McLoughlin's. Nangle remarked that there he was, having a drink while poor Jimmy was locked up in Gough. Later in the day, when the court had finished its sitting, there was a farewell party for District Justice Barry in McLoughlin's. He was due to retire several weeks later and September 27th was his last day to sit in the courthouse at Dowra.

Next day, the floodgate burst. Sean Doherty's brother-in-law had been cleared of assaulting a man who had been unable to give evidence because he had been detained for the day by the RUC. Suspicion was rife. Jimmy McGovern told the *Irish Press* that his arrest had been a "cover-up" designed to stop him appearing in court. His father maintained there was something very fishy going on: "It looks like the RUC and the gardaí are working hand in hand." Doherty was quoted as saying: "I deny any knowledge of the affair; the whole thing is crazy".

The Director of Public Prosecutions, Eamonn Barnes, began an enquiry into the decision by the district justice to allow the case to go ahead in the absence of the main prosecution witness. He eventually took the issue to the High Court on the grounds that the decision by the district justice to acquit the accused man was not in line with the evidence he had heard. In June 1983, however, the High Court upheld the decision reached by District Justice Barry in the case. There were no grounds for the High Court to interfere in the case, it decided.

But the political repercussions at the time were immense. The suspicion on every politician's mind, that somehow Doherty had been involved in using both the Garda Síochána and the Royal Ulster Constabulary to interfere with the court case, carried huge implications. It appeared to be the ultimate "fix", but at what cost? For a Fianna Fáil Minister to allow the RUC to have such a favour to hold over the gardaí and the Irish government demonstrated an extraordinary lack of concern for the political consequences, and an extreme insensitivity to the traditions of his own party. That he could do so after attending meetings like the July 29th session, at which it was decided not to operate the Criminal Law Jurisdiction Act in future, was extraordinary. The RUC insisted that Jimmy McGovern's message about his detention had been transmitted to the gardaí. The gardaí claimed that the senior officer on the spot was only told that the witness was not going to turn up and was not given a reason. Two reporters who were in court for the hearing said that no mention had been made of the reasons for the failure of the main prosecution witness to appear.

Fine Gael's shadow Justice Minister, Jim Mitchell, demanded explanations from the Garda Commissioner and called on the DPP to investigate all the circumstances surrounding the dismissal of the prosecution and to publish his findings. Fine Gael, he added, might demand Doherty's resignation unless the facts of the case were established satisfactorily within a short time. Labour's Justice spokesman, Dick Spring, said there was serious public disquiet about the case and he too called for a full statement from the DDP.

Doherty responded with a formal statement denying that he had any prior knowledge of, or involvement in, the detention of McGovern or any of the circumstances surrounding that detention. In an interview with RTE, he said he had only been informed a few days earlier that Nangle was appearing in court. He added: "My brother-in-law — I'm not his keeper. It's as simple as that". Doherty also asked Commissioner McLaughlin to investigate the circumstances in which the case proceeded without a key witness. McLaughlin appointed Chief Superintendent Steven Fanning, the second in command of the Intelligence and Security Branch to Assistant Commissioner Joe Ainsworth to carry out the task.

Meanwhile, in the border town of Blacklion, Jimmy McGovern was receiving more offers of financial inducements to stay away if the case ever came to court again. A Fianna Fáil activist from County Sligo approached Joe Maguire, the peace commissioner and guesthouse owner in Blacklion, and said he was a friend of Nangle. Maguire's sister and Nangle's sister, Maura Doherty, had been at school together, he pointed out. He said that he and a friend were prepared to put up some money to have the case settled. Maguire agreed to ask Jimmy McGovern about the offer but McGovern asked for £25,000 in sterling. The talks fell through. Another tentative offer was made later through Seamus McGovern, the son of the owner and the barman at the Bush bar. If the case went to court again, a sum of £6,000 was to be left at the Bush Bar for Jimmy McGovern. He could collect it the day after the hearing — provided he did not turn up in court to give evidence against Nangle.

A year after the incident in the Bush Bar which started the whole affair, Jimmy McGovern was back in the pub for the 1982 Christmas Draw. This time he did the carrying out — he won the draw and took away a huge seasonal hamper.

The assault charge against Nangle was not tried again because the High Court upheld the original decision of District Justice Barry. The toing and froing around Blacklion eventually quietened down and Jimmy McGovern was left pursuing a complaint against the RUC. Before the controversy lost steam, however, Charles Haughey's government was to run into many more problems.

Chapter Thirteen

It's time to shit or get off the pot.
Charles McCreevy, October 1982

Niall Andrews, the 44-year-old Fianna Fáil deputy from Dublin South, had fought two tough general elections during the previous fifteen months. They were particularly tough for him because he had been almost mangled by his party and constituency colleagues, Seamus Brennan and Síle de Valera, but he had managed to keep his first preference vote just above that of de Valera and thereby secured his seat in both elections. Andrews believed that the fame of his running mates — who symbolised the two wings of Fianna Fáil — endangered his political future. He set out to create his own image: he adopted strong positions on foreign policy issues and was rapidly becoming the party's liberal, especially on questions like apartheid in South Africa and right-wing repression in Central America.

On September 23rd, however, he dealt with issues much closer to home in a speech he prepared for a Fianna Fáil meeting in his constituency. Controversies over the Falklands and James Prior's initiative in Northern Ireland proved that there was a well-organised pro-British lobby in Ireland, he declared. This lobby was a threat to the sovereignty and independence of the state, and its chief spokesmen were Conor Cruise O'Brien; Bruce Arnold, the *Irish Independent's* columnist; and Jim Kemmy, the Democratic Socialist Party TD from Limerick. They were allies of Fine Gael in their "obsessive vendetta" against the Taoiseach. But they did not oppose Charles Haughey because of his social and economic policies: they opposed him because he was the republican leader of a republican party. "In the same way and out of the same motives, with the help of Irishmen, British Tories hounded Parnell and harassed de Valera", he concluded.

It was a view that was gaining ground rapidly within Fianna Fáil and particularly among the embattled supporters of Charles Haughey. He and his government were under increasing pressure from all sides. Scandals were multiplying and many had not yet surfaced in public. Ministers were beginning to blame each other in public for the failure of their confident predictions of earlier months to come true. Albert Reynolds, the Energy Minister, blamed Des O'Malley, the Trade, Commerce and Tourism Minister, for a rise in petrol prices double what he, Reynolds, had insisted it would be. The government as a whole faced an extremely rough parliamentary time over its spending cuts when the Dáil resumed. Trade unions in the public service were still threatening dire consequences over the postponement of their November wage rises.

Within Fianna Fáil there were rumblings of serious discontent. Haughey had hinted he wanted to re-draw constituency boundaries which hampered the party's ability to win an overall Dáil majority. After the 1977 general election, when the electoral boundaries drawn up by a coalition government rebounded upon them, Jack Lynch appointed an independent electoral commission to take the drafting of divisions out of the hands of governments. The commission did its job so well that the proportion of seats won by each party was closer than ever before to the proportion of votes each received. But that meant that Fianna Fáil no longer received a bonus in seats that hitherto had helped it enormously.

Haughey was wrestling with the problem of re-drawing the boundaries without having to abolish the commission and take the procedure back into political hands. That would be a dangerous exercise politically: it would be quite apparent that he was trying to change the ground rules because he suspected he could not win an election with the existing arrangements. On the other hand, it was extremely difficult to draw up terms of reference for the commission which would achieve the effect he required without making them so blatant that he might as well abolish the commission.

His hints of changes caused consternation among some Fianna Fáil backbenchers. They were concerned primarily with their own seats, not the overall party position. But they did not want anything done during the summer recess and behind their backs. Their protests won them a promise that nothing would happen before the first meeting of the Fianna Fáil parliamentary party after the summer holidays. It was due to be held in Leinster House on October 6th, but it never got to debating that issue in detail.

Charles McCreevy was a politician in the Haughey mould. Professionally, he was an accountant who, like Haughey, had carved out a comfortable living for himself. Like Haughey too, he was interested in horses. Politically, his instincts and temperament were similar to Haughey's; he came from a strongly republican backround. It was not surprising, therefore, that he was a Haughey supporter from his election to the Dáil in the Lynch-led landslide in 1977. But his opinion of Haughey turned sour; he had not lived up to McCreevy's expectations that he would provide decisive leadership. His criticisms culminated in his *Sunday Tribune* interview with Geraldine Kennedy in December 1981 which marked the first major break in Fianna Fáil ranks since George Colley had defined the concept of loyalty to the party leader after Haughey's election to that position.

In mid-September McCreevy began to put his own plan into action. He gathered several people around him and told them of his intentions and his plans. They included George Colley, Hugh Byrne, the 39-year-old TD from Wexford, in the Dáil for just over a year, and Tom Fitzpatrick, a deputy from Dublin South Central since 1965, Seamus Brennan and Bobby Molloy. McCreevy put his idea to Colley first and the two of them invited the other four to a meeting in Tom Fitzpatrick's house in Dublin. McCreevy was not seeking their approval but merely telling them for their information and hoping for their support.

He had decided that the best strategy was to table a motion of no confidence in Haughey as party leader and as Taoiseach. That would force the parliamentary party to vote on Haughey as leader and not for or against any other contender. McCreevy told the others that he was determined to go ahead with or without their support. He was insistent that his motion would be pushed to a vote: there would be no repeat of the February backdown, whatever happened. He wanted the group to canvass support for the motion but it was clear that the idea was McCreevy's, the initiative was his and that control over the challenge rested with him. It was time, McCreevy told his colleagues to: "shit or get off the pot".

On Friday, October 1st, McCreevy dropped a copy of his motion into the office of the party chief whip, Bertie Ahern, and sent another copy by courier to Haughey's Kinsealy home. Haughey was just leaving by helicopter when the messenger arrived but Ahern had already told him of the motion tabled for the party meeting the following Wednesday. It did not come altogether as a surprise to Haughey and his closest colleagues. There had been hints of a leadership challenge in recent weeks but discreet soundings by Haughey's supporters had failed to unearth anything definite. Haughey carried on as planned that evening, flying to Rockwell College in County Tipperary for a ceremony to commemorate the centenary of Éamon de Valera's birth.

Ahern phoned all the members of the cabinet who were available and told them of the motion. Des O'Malley was on holiday in Spain, but was due home the next day. Martin O'Donoghue knew nothing about the motion until the next day, when it was widely publicised. Other likely opponents of Haughey knew nothing of the plan either: Joe Walsh, a backbencher from west Cork who was known to be anti-Haughey, first heard of the challenge when the *Irish Press* phoned him. He told them that the motion would not get much support.

Most of Haughey's supporters were taken by surprise as well. But the main question on the minds of most Fianna Fáil deputies was whether or not McCreevy was a stalking horse and, more importantly, for whom. Most of Haughey's backers reckoned that this was George Colley's bid for power. Some told others that it was all a joke, but McCreevy was not joking. He was busy organising a second group of disaffected backbenchers to canvass support as well as his inner circle.

On Saturday, October 2nd, ministers began to line up

behind Haughey, led by Ray MacSharry and Brian Lenihan. Some, however, were non-committal in public, giving rise to more and more speculation that Haughey could be in deep trouble. Haughey himself did not think so but several of his associates were not so sure. They believed they had used up quite a number of political debts during the February challenge by O'Malley and that it might be difficult to ward off another attack.

McCreevy issued a statement declaring that he no longer considered Haughey to be the man for the job as Taoiseach. The days of political strokes, deals and "convulsion politics" had to end, he added. He went on to accuse Haughey of making reckless and daft economic proposals for electoral gain and of presiding over the lowest morale ever experienced in Fianna Fáil. Twice in the statement he mentioned that the vote on his motion would be by secret ballot.

Haughey went on the offensive the next day. In an interview on RTE radio's "This Week", Haughey laid it on the line. The dissidents were a small minority within Fianna Fáil but they were not for the party. They would have to stand up and be counted this time, he declared. Using a horse-racing analogy, he added that they had better be prepared to go the full course if they came up to the starting tapes on this occasion. He announced that he would insist on a roll-call vote so that constituency organisations would know how everyone voted. He would also demand the total support of his cabinet.

Haughey's supporters were delighted with his performance, but it also confirmed his critics in their opposition to him. Haughey was trying to scare them into obedience by going behind their backs to their constituency organisations. It was a tactic that he had used against them individually in the past and it had worked very well. Most backbenchers were, at the least, apprehensive at the prospect of having to do battle with their own organisations. But the issue raised a fundamental point as to whether Dáil deputies, sent to Leinster House by the electorate at large, should be subjected to the will of their local party organisations. That would mean, for instance, that a deputy could be mandated to vote for or against anything within the parliamentary party, or even in the Dáil. Haughey supporters ignored that point but continued to insist that he was entitled to the support of all party members because he was their democratically-elected leader. His opponents argued that the point was central to the debate now raging within the party.

The argument about Haughey's leadership was fought, in public, over the secret ballot issue and the method by which deputies would vote on McCreevy's motion. It quickly became a code for the central issue of confidence. Those who opposed Haughey could signal their position by declaring their support for a secret ballot; those who supported him saw no need for secrecy. Haughey had also given the dissidents another piece of ammunition with his insistence that his cabinet should pledge their loyalty to him as leader.

McCreevy hoped that at least one minister would resign from the cabinet before the meeting. That would raise the stakes and help create a momentum against Haughey. By his radio interview, Haughey had ensured that there would be at least one resignation. Listening to the interview, Martin O'Donoghue decided that he had to give up his cabinet seat as Minister for Education. Haughey's insistence on personal loyalty to the party leader was not democracy, he believed. This was a party matter, not a government matter, and Haughey had no right to look for loyalty on it. It was merely a political tactic which had no basis in party rules. O'Donoghue's mind was made up.

McCreevy replied to Haughey's interview with a statement that carried several barbed comments. Roll-call votes were once used by British landlords and the aristocracy who feared secret ballots in Ireland, he said. The linking of Haughey to the British colonial regime was clear enough but there was another little barb buried in the comment; Haughey owned a horse called Aristocracy and that was the main reason the word was added into the sentence by McCreevy.

Constituency organisations throughout the country began holding meetings. They discussed the McCreevy resolution. Some took no decision on what the deputy or deputies in their constituency should do; others, like Dublin South, passed motions ordering their TDs to vote for Haughey. Niall Andrews was committed to backing Haughey. Seamus Brennan, the other local TD, was determined to oppose him: he was told that he would not be re-selected as a candidate for the next general election unless he changed his mind. In Fianna Fáil headquarters in Dublin's Mount Street, party executives declared that thousands of messages of support for Haughey were coming in from all over the country.

The dissidents were also getting messages, some of them genuine, others merely unpleasant. The abusive telephone calls were made, generally, by people who refused to give their names or gave false names and addresses. As often as not they were made at all hours of the night and were clearly designed to unsettle and intimidate the recipients. The better-known dissidents had experienced something similar the previous February, during the days leading up to O'Malley's challenge to Haughey. Obscene phone calls were made to members of Seamus Brennan's and George Colley's families: Mary Harney's family was informed by phone that she was spending her time in Leinster House in unorthodox ways.

But the climate among the opponents of Haughey had changed. Some had received similar calls and come under the same kind of internal party pressure in February and had borne it quietly. Afterwards, their complaints sounded like sour grapes, and several had felt bad ever since about yielding to intimidation. On this occasion, they were not prepared to suffer in silence. David Andrews from Dun Laoghaire, Hugh Byrne from Wexford and Tom Bellew from Louth announced publicly that they had received intimidatory calls. Their public statements were an illustration of a very important element in this challenge — the sense among Haughey's opponents that they were salvaging their self-respect after the debacle in February.

Meanwhile, Haughey was orchestrating his response to the McCreevy motion. He met party officers on the morning of Monday, October 4th, in preparation for a meeting of the party's national executive that evening. He was confident of victory at the parliamentary party meeting but he was not leaving anything to chance. The 84-member executive met in party headquarters in Dublin that night and the session went very much as Haughey had planned. Speaker after speaker got up and declared his or her confidence in the leader. But there was a handful of people who dissented. George Colley told the meeting that he did not think it was appropriate for the executive to pre-empt the decision of the parliamentary party: it was not the executive's function to issue mandates to the parliamentary party.

The toughest and most surprising speech was made by Eoin Ryan, a son of one of the party's founders, Fianna Fáil leader in the Senate and a pillar of the country's financial establishment. Ryan declared his opposition to Haughey in no uncertain terms: the party leader was an electoral liability, he said. But Haughey was in near total control of the executive although he emerged from the meeting only with a vague resolution which declared support for the Taoiseach and the government in their efforts to bring the country safely through difficult times. The executive made no attempt to tell the parliamentary party how to vote.

The outcome heartened Haughey's critics as well as his supporters: both sides saw it as a victory. But the main attentions of the party were focused on a cabinet meeting scheduled for the next morning, Tuesday October 5th. O'Donoghue and Des O'Malley were expected to resign, but would they? And would anyone else?

Before the meeting, Haughey attempted to head off one resignation at least. He had a private discussion with O'Malley at which he suggested that there was no need for O'Malley to resign. He, Haughey, wanted to be rid of O'Donoghue whom he believed was involved up to his neck in the plot. O'Malley was non-committal but, as subsequent events demonstrated, he was far from convinced that he should resign from the government. He was in a corner. He had not known about McCreevy's motion until he returned from holidays the day after it was tabled. Seamus Brennan was supposed to phone O'Malley in Spain beforehand but he had not done so because he believed it was better that O'Malley should not know about the plot until he returned home. O'Malley arrived home to a *fait accompli* in which he had no part and the wisdom of which he doubted strongly. Yet he could scarcely vote confidence in Haughey and he could not declare, as a cabinet minister, his loyalty to Haughey personally.

Once the cabinet meeting began, it was clear to everyone present that O'Donoghue was there to resign. He arrived without his ministerial files. Haughey was anxious to get the issue out of the way and to produce a statement of unanimity. Most ministers indicated that they stood firmly behind Haughey but O'Donoghue and O'Malley expressed reservations. Haughey wanted a statement out in time for the RTE lunch-time news on radio. An announcement was agreed by the cabinet to the effect that it backed Haughey but that two members had expressed reservations. It was released in time for the bulletin. O'Donoghue and O'Malley were not named in the statement but their identities were easily guessed. The cabinet ended its discussion of the issue with the agreed statement and a promise that the two members with reservations would discuss their situation with each other and with Haughey later in the day.

O'Malley was still not convinced that he ought to resign. Relations between himself and O'Donoghue were still extremely bad: they had not spoken since the abortive challenge to Haughey by O'Malley the previous February. O'Malley still felt that O'Donoghue had betrayed him then in spite of his magnanimity towards O'Donoghue in public in the aftermath. Neither man had had any inside knowledge of McCreevy's challenge before it emerged in public but they were thrown together now by the circumstances McCreevy had created.

McCreevy kept his head down after he tabled his motion and issued two statements over the weekend. He was not giving interviews to the media and he was not canvassing anyone himself. He and O'Malley talked on Tuesday after the cabinet meeting. McCreevy reminded O'Malley that he, McCreevy, had been one of the few people who stood by him when the chips were down in February. McCreevy had been the conspirators' front man, appearing on radio and television programmes on the eve of that party meeting. He did not demand that O'Malley repay him by resigning but the implication was there. In McCreevy's view it was "shit or get off the pot" time for everyone.

O'Malley and O'Donoghue were talking again. They met during the afternoon and O'Donoghue said he was going to resign. They agreed that he would hold off his announcement so that both could announce their resignations together, if O'Malley decided to resign as well. O'Donoghue went off to attend his last ministerial function, the launching of an insurance scheme for teachers. Later, he went to the Olympia Theatre to see a performance of Hugh Leonard's play "Kill", a political satire which hardly bothered to disguise the fact that its central character was meant to represent Charles Haughey.

O'Malley had made up his mind that he, too, had to resign. McCreevy effectively cornered him with his motion: if O'Malley did not resign who else was going to put their careers on the line to stand up publicly to Haughey? O'Malley, however, was not the only one to seriously question whether or not he should support McCreevy's resolution. Several opponents of Haughey within the party were deeply unhappy about McCreevy's unilateral action and his behaviour after he had lodged his motion.

The central steering committee which McCreevy created around himself had also had a few moments of crisis during their meetings. After Haughey declared his determination to have an open vote, several of the dissidents wavered. They argued that they could not inflict such troubles on some of their more vulnerable friends. They were putting people on their own side under enormous pressure by going ahead with the motion if there was an open vote. Some could even lose their Dáil seats, possibly their livelihoods. But their resolve was stiffened by McCreevy's inflexibility: he declared that he was still going to put the motion and press it to a vote, secret or open. The incipient revolt among the dissidents passed.

After the theatre, O'Donoghue called around to O'Malley's house. O'Malley's decision to resign had already been announced publicly on RTE television by George Colley. O'Donoghue only stayed a few moments because he had another appointment to keep. Seán Doherty, the Justice Minister, had been looking for O'Donoghue earlier in the day, and left a message at O'Donoghue's home saying that he would like to talk to him. O'Donoghue went to Doherty's flat in Ranelagh.

Doherty and O'Donoghue were not close as cabinet colleagues but they had talked occasionally. During the previous month, O'Donoghue had spoken to Doherty about the party leadership in casual chats in Leinster House; he had alluded to the problem of the party's finances and the belief among Haughey's opponents that its lack of money was a product of his continued leadership. Doherty was seen as a supporter of Haughey's but not the member of the cabinet closest to the Taoiseach: at that stage of the year, the minister closest to the leader was Pádraig Flynn. Nevertheless, when O'Donoghue was told that Doherty wished to talk to him he concluded that the Justice Minister was probably acting as an emissary from Haughey.

Doherty urged him to consider carefully whether he should resign or not. Resigning would be very foolish and not part of Fianna Fáil's traditions. McCreevy and his motion were not to be taken too seriously, Doherty suggested. O'Donoghue told him that the decision was made by then. They had a cup of tea and chatted for a while with O'Donoghue outlining his criticisms of Haughey's leadership.

Earlier that day, Assistant Commissioner Joe Ainsworth had asked for photocopies of all the transcripts taken from the wire taps on the telephones of Bruce Arnold and Geraldine Kennedy. Only one copy had been made from the tapes of the phone conversations that were transcribed. But Ainsworth sought extra copies of some transcripts on several occasions. On October 5th, he got copies of the complete files on both the Arnold tap which had been lifted on July 12th and the Kennedy tap which had been in place since July 28th. There were relatively few transcripts, as the listeners in the Intelligence and Security Branch had decided that few of the conversations were of interest. Those that had been transcribed all contained party political material. Ainsworth gave the complete set to Sean Doherty.

After his meeting with Doherty, O'Donoghue returned to O'Malley's house where the two Ministers drafted a statement and then phoned Haughey at home to tell him of their decisions. Each talked to him in turn: Haughey just said in reply: "All right". The statement said that loyalty to a party and to a government did not mean loyalty to an individual. The leadership was a matter for the party, not for the collective responsibility of the cabinet. They supported a secret ballot, complained of intimidation and longed for a return to Fianna Fáil's former idealism, stability and integrity.

The announcement had little surprise value left. But the decision of both to resign guaranteed that the contest would come to a head on this occasion. The opponents of Haughey were committed irrevocably to a vote on the McCreevy motion. Among junior ministers, Sylvester Barrett withheld his backing for the party leaders, but did not offer his resignation, leaving Haughey the option of firing him if he wanted to. That was a tactic considered by O'Malley as well but ultimately rejected by him. Haughey never took action against Barrett.

After the two ministerial resignations, the organising committee of dissidents met again and planned their last-minute efforts to sway party members. Most of them believed that they could not win in an open vote. Their best estimate was 23 people in support of the motion in a roll call vote. In a secret ballot, they reckoned they would get up to 35 and there was an outside chance of having a bare majority of 41. Haughey supporters were confident of victory: their estimates of the support for the motion ranged from a derisory handful up to fourteen or so.

The party meeting on October 6th lasted twelve hours. It began with a wrangle over procedure: McCreevy refused to propose his motion until the method of voting was decided. A compromise was agreed. Both the resolution of "no confidence" and the method of voting would be discussed at the same time. When the debate was completed, they would vote if necessary on how they should take the vote on the motion. Then they would vote on Haughey's future as leader of Fianna Fáil and as Taoiseach.

It was the most extraordinary party meeting most of the participants had ever attended. It was the first time they had ever debated the leadership of the party openly and with few holds barred. It was also the first time that members of the 1982 parliamentary party ever spoke their minds openly to colleagues with whom they did not see eye to eye on the leadership. From every perspective it was entirely without precedent in Fianna Fáil that the party, while in government, should debate the fitness of its leader to continue in office and to continue as Taoiseach.

Jim Gibbons spent most of his time at the meeting taking notes on official Dáil notepaper of other speakers. One of Haughey's lieutenants, P.J. Mara, sat just behind him and watched his activities. Mara remembered some of the phrases which Gibbons attributed to speakers. When the same phrases appeared later in an extensive account of the private meeting in the *Sunday Tribune,* the Haughey camp believed they knew the source. Haughey and his friends wanted to keep tabs on everything.

McCreevy addressed Haughey directly and told him to watch the people behind him, not those who stood before him. Haughey's so-called friends were his real enemies, he declared. But the early part of the meeting was dominated by speakers declaring their support for Haughey, including most of his cabinet. John Wilson, the Transport Minister, declared that he had to oppose the motion because he was responsible through the collective responsibility of the cabinet for Haughey's actions. Michael Woods, the Health Minister, said that he would sink or swim with Haughey and he defended the cuts in the health service that had been foisted upon him by Haughey and the other members of the cabinet. Pádraig Flynn, the Minister for the Gaeltacht who had become one of Haughey's closest confidantes during the life of the government, complained that the motion played into the hands of Fine Gael, the British and their "media collaborators". Asking rhetorically who was pressing for this motion, he named three journalists — Bruce Arnold, Geraldine Kennedy and John Feeney, the *Evening Herald's* main columnist. They were trying to be divisive and, he asked, was the party going to be divisive for them?

Paddy Power, the Defence Minister, took up the issue of an open ballot and proclaimed that Fianna Fáil would be a better party without the dissidents, even if it was smaller. "We should flush them out", he said.

The meeting dragged on after lunch, mingling criticisms of Haughey personally with complaints about the government in general, merging attacks on McCreevy with vague references to outside forces and the spectre of unseen hands behind the whole affair. By late afternoon, Haughey's critics were in full flight, taking courage from each other and complaining in front of him about many of the aspects of his rule that they did not like.

Seán Byrne, a 45-year-old farmer from Tipperary South who was in his first Dáil, made a major impact on his colleagues with a speech in which he accused the party leadership of allowing Fianna Fáil to be destroyed. There was too much wheeling and dealing and too many things were being swept under the carpet. A senior minister had phoned him before the meeting and called him "a Jim Gibbons". In 1981 a minister and supporter of Haughey had approached him to rig a party convention and he dared the person concerned to identify himself.

George Colley told Haughey that he could decide whether Fianna Fáil stood or fell. There were people in the party, Haughey supporters, who were determined to take over the party. They would break it up and do so soon unless they were controlled. Bobby Molloy identified Haughey as the source of the divisions within the party and appealed to him to recognise that by resigning. Mary Harney challenged those members of the cabinet who said privately that Haughey was not the best man to lead the party to stand up and to be counted as well.

O'Malley argued that it was wrong to equate the personality of the leader with the whole party. Even if Haughey was not his personal choice as Taoiseach, he should be entitled to serve in a Fianna Fáil government. The question of loyalty was being misunderstood. O'Donoghue said that the cabinet in a healthy democracy should be made up of the different factions within a party. He had not been able in conscience to give the Taoiseach the pledge of support he had sought from his cabinet. But he believed that the motion was tabled at the wrong time and the leadership issue was presented in the wrong way. Nevertheless, it was there and the issue had to be decided.

By the time the meeting broke for tea, the dissidents were euphoric. As they emerged from the Leinster House party rooms in which the debate was being waged, some toyed with the idea that they could actually win. The mood of the meeting appeared to be changing. Haughey's critics were talking straight and openly and it appeared that anything could happen. But the mood was fractured when the meeting resumed and it became clear that the dissidents had spent their manpower and their ammunition. The tide flowed back in Haughey's favour.

Michael O'Kennedy, the backbencher who had resigned his EEC post to return to domestic politics, announced that he was supporting Haughey. In doing so, he was voting against a unanimous direction given to him by his constituency organisation in Tipperary North. He added that he regretted the references to having people cleared out of the party.

Eventually, a vote was called on the procedure for deciding McCreevy's motion. Fifty deputies raised their hands in support of a roll-call vote, 27 raised their hands in support of a secret ballot. Three members abstained. Then the names of all the party's deputies were read out in alphabetical order and each declared his or her support for the leader. Bertie Ahern was the first called upon to vote: he voted against McCreevy's motion. The last man on the alphabetical list was Pearse Wyse, who backed the motion. The result was clear long before they got to Wyse's vote, however: 58 deputies said they had confidence in Haughey, 22 said they did not.

It had been a long day and, for Haughey, a bruising one. Elsewhere in Leinster House scores of reporters and a handful of Haughey's faithful followers waited in enforced inactivity for the twelve hours. Both groups swung into action as the deputies emerged from the meeting. Members of the instantly christened "Club of 22" looked enormously pleased with the outcome and happily gave interviews. Haughey gave a press conference at which he refused to take any questions and which ended before most of the press arrived. In the corridors of Leinster House there was a brief period of bedlam.

In the car park outside the building, the Haughey supporters waited to give their opinions of his opponents. Jim Gibbons was struck by one of them as he made his way to his car. Mary Harney was jostled and subjected to verbal abuse. Charlie McCreevy rejected the urgings of gardaí and Leinster House ushers that he use a side exit. Heavily protected, he went out the front door to boos and jeers and shouts of "Judas" and "Blueshirt".

Chapter Fourteen

I think some people are quite paranoid about
this whole question of eavesdropping and telephones.
Charles Haughey, December 1982

Haughey's brief press conference was held in the Senate antechamber. He declared that it was now time to get back to the normal business of government. But there was an air of revenge and viciousness about the actions of some of Haughey's supporters.

Ciarán Haughey, one of the Taoiseach's three sons, approached Geraldine Kennedy at the press conference. "Miss Kennedy", he said to her, "you will pay for this". Kennedy was taken aback by the threat but shrugged it off as a careless remark made in the heat of the moment — tempers were frayed at the end of a long day. The threat was overheard by Kennedy's colleague from *The Sunday Independent,* Joe O'Malley. It might have been forgotten had it not been for a strange telephone call to her home the following morning. "We know where you are", said the anonymous male voice at the other end of the line. She got similar calls throughout that day and the following morning, Friday. On Friday night, she dined with a friend in the Quo Vadis restaurant in the centre of Dublin. Afterwards, she went to her car to drive home. There was a broken bottle and a note clipped to the windscreen by one of the wipers. "We are watching you", said the note.

Several days later, Kennedy mentioned her experiences to a Fianna Fáil man. He subsequently called her back and said he had talked to one of Haughey's close associates. The associate had said he would "Call the boys off" and she would have no more difficulties, the man reported.

A lot of people believed they were being watched around that time and many were becoming careful about what they said on the telephone. A number of Haughey's opponents (not only those among the 22) believed they were being followed by ISB detectives. So too did some senior civil servants, and some people who had permanent garda protection began to wonder if they were being guarded or watched.

Haughey's victory failed to confirm that his position as leader was unassailable. In fact, it had the opposite effect — the 22, the losers, were buoyant with hope. After all the intrigue and backroom plotting they were now out in the open. They were relieved to have finally got off their chests what had been bothering many of them since December 1979 and particularly since the previous February. A corresponding siege mentality developed among the victors. They believed their backs were to the wall and that they would have to use every means available to survive.

Among some of Haughey's supporters, paranoia replaced rational thought. They blamed the media for all their troubles. They said there was a combined Fine Gael-media conspiracy against them. Some of his close advisers, like Martin Mansergh, blamed the British. Mansergh, who came from an Anglo-Irish landowning family in County Tipperary and whose father was an historian of the British Commonwealth, firmly believed that since 1979, M16, British intelligence, had been plotting the political destruction of Charles J. Haughey. There was a growing tendency in Fianna Fáil to brand critics of the party, Haughey and the government as somehow anti-Irish and therefore by implication pro-British. "Anti-national" was a phrase already in official usage to describe one critic of the government.

It was an atmosphere which bred rumours and in the aftermath of the Macarthur-Connolly affair and the mysterious arrest by the RUC of Jimmy McGovern, there was little that the public was not prepared to believe. A small incident with a simple explanation could grow into a major issue when the politics of fix and cover-up were at work. Rumours which had been circulating for some time in Kerry concerning the crash of Doherty's escort car began to drift around the country. It was said that Doherty had been in the car with a well-known blond-haired singer. According to the rumour machine, she had received serious neck and spinal injuries and was spirited away into a hospital run by nuns. She was being moved from hospital to hospital by an Air Corps helicopter each time reporters came close.

The reality of what happened was simple, if embarrassing, Donie Dunne, one of Doherty's bodyguards, had used an unmarked garda car to leave home two women who were drinking late with the Minister's party. Dunne crashed the car on his way back and left a sub machine gun inside. The crash was not properly investigated at the time and questions only began to be asked within the gardaí when rumours spilled into the newspapers in mid-October. The gardaí contributed considerably to the rumour machine by not explaining promptly what happened and advancing "security reasons" as an excuse for not doing so.

Other incidents attracted the attention of reporters, and turned out not to be malicious rumours. In September, the *Sunday Independent* reported briefly on an inside page that a Sergeant Tom Tully of Boyle had successfully appealed a transfer order against him. The newspaper's news editor, Kevin O'Connor, was tipped off by one of his regular garda contacts that the Tully affair was worth examining in greater detail. There was a lot going on and people were scared of talking.

O'Connor travelled to Roscommon and began asking questions. He used a false name, Jack Dunne, when telephoning people to arrange meetings. Only when he met them in person did he reveal his identity and purpose. He guaranteed total confidence to anyone who gave him information and soon stories began bubbling to the surface. There was a litany of fixing and squaring cases that were pending against Doherty's constituents; the ordinary rule of law was on the point of breaking down in the area. It was widely known that charges could be dropped if the right man was contacted, and everyone knew who the right man was. Three gardaí gave O'Connor signed statements describing how Doherty had attempted to obstruct proceedings against a drunk driver. Another garda made a verbal statement in the presence of three garda witnesses. O'Connor also got detailed information about Tully's troubles. Back in Dublin, he continued his investigation among gardaí and politicians. Word began to spread that the *Sunday Independent* was about to publish a big story on Doherty. O'Connor hoped to have his report published on Sunday, October 17th.

On Friday, October 15th, O'Connor got a message to call one of his garda contacts but not to use a telephone inside the *Independent* building. He went to a public call box in Middle Abbey Street and dialled the number of his contact. The contact told him four things in quick succession: his telephone was being tapped; he was being followed; every effort would be made to stop publication of the Doherty report; and the "top man in the country" knew what material he had. O'Connor returned to his office and thought about the call. He had a lunch-time appointment in Mooney's pub in Lower Abbey Street with one of Haughey's ministers. He certainly didn't want to be followed to the rendezvous.

He left the *Independent* building by a side door and walked briskly down an alleyway, across a back street and into Woolworth's store on Henry Street. He left, walked across O'Connell Street and into Clery's, leaving again by a side door. He continued down O'Connell Street and entered Wynn's Hotel on Lower Abbey Street just opposite Mooney's pub. If anyone was following him, he thought he had probably lost them.

He crossed the street and went into the pub. The minister was sitting opposite the door and had a commanding view of anyone who entered. O'Connor indicated to him that they should both go downstairs to the toilet. They talked there, breaking off their conversation whenever anyone entered. The minister was able to confirm much of what O'Connor already knew. Later that afternoon, O'Connor spent three and a quarter hours with the *Independent's* solicitor going over the story. The solicitor passed it, largely because of the weight of evidence against Doherty supported by the signed statements of gardaí. He suggested only a few minor changes. O'Connor returned triumphant to the Oval Bar in Middle Abbey Street where he had arranged to meet Michael Hand, his editor. O'Connor told him that everything was all right by the solicitor but Hand said he had read the report and didn't want to publish it. He suggested that the report be held over for a while and told O'Connor that they would discuss it tomorrow, Saturday.

Political attention that weekend was not focused on the government but on the Fine Gael árd fheis taking place in Dublin. O'Connor was there on Saturday gathering material for his column, "Backchat". At the same time in Kinsealy, Haughey was holding another of his special meetings with senior garda officers.

Once again, Haughey was concerned about leaks to the newspapers. He had first raised this subject with Joe Ainsworth shortly after he became Taoiseach in March. He discussed it with him at a private meeting in his office in Government Buildings not long before Doherty raised the same subject and asked Ainsworth to tap the telephone of Bruce Arnold. On this occasion, however, Haughey was concerned about a specific leak. A report had been published in the *Irish Times* the previous day stating that the Attorney General in FitzGerald's government, Peter Sutherland, advised that if oil companies were forced to buy a fixed amount of their oil from the state-owned refinery at Whitegate, there was a danger that EEC laws would be infringed and Ireland taken to task in the European Court. Sutherland's advice had remained on file when Haughey's government came into office and his opinion had not been contradicted by his successor, Patrick Connolly, and his successor in turn, John Murray. The revelation, based on a copy of Sutherland's advice which had come into the possession of the *Irish Times,* was in sharp contrast to what Haughey's government was saying at the time.

The report was an embarrassment to Haughey and annoyed him. The meeting arranged the day after publication was to order an investigation into the "leak". Three garda commissioners were called to Kinsealy — McLaughlin, Ainsworth and the Assistant Commissioner in charge of crime investigations, John Paul McMahon. With Haughey was Attorney General Murray. Haughey told McLaughlin, Ainsworth and McMahon that he was worried about "leaks" and specifically the leak which had led to the *Irish Times* report. It was written by Olivia O'Leary and Haughey said he wanted an investigation carried out to find the source of the "leak". McMahon was to carry out the investigation. At the time of the meeting, the only journalist whose telephone was being tapped was Geraldine Kennedy but the warrant for her telephone was due to expire in about a week and a half.

By the time the meeting in Kinsealy was over, O'Connor had returned to the *Sunday Independent* office to speak to Hand about publication of the Doherty report. Hand argued that the evidence was flimsy and that the report was too hard on Doherty. The report dealt with the drunk driving case, a raid on Keaney's pub and the Tully affair. O'Connor said there was further background information which fitted into an overall pattern of abuse of power by Doherty but Hand was unmoved. He said the report should be held over for an unspecified length of time and that "one big exposé" should be done later. O'Connor told Hand that he might have to resign as news editor in protest. O'Connor's story was backed by the paper's political correspondent, Joseph O'Malley.

That night, O'Connor telephoned Tony O'Reilly, the proprietor of the Independent group of newspapers. O'Reilly was in the United States, where he worked for the Heinz food company in Pittsburg. He listened as O'Connor recounted the events leading to what he believed was the suppression of an important news story. O'Reilly said he would look into the matter. The following week, O'Connor spoke to several executives in the newspaper, none of whom supported him. He spoke to Hand mid-week and was told he was off the story, that his position as news editor was being reconsidered and that he was no longer writing "Backchat".

Despite his difficulties, O'Connor did not tell reporters in other newspapers. But rumours began to circulate among politicians that the *Independent* had a big story on Seán Doherty which, for some unknown reason, the newspaper was not going to publish. The rumours were part of the current political gossip when the Labour Party held its annual conference in Galway from Friday, October 22nd, to Sunday the 31st. In the bars, restaurants and corridors, politicians and reporters exchanged gossip. Two politicians separately told Peter Murtagh, security correspondent at the *Irish Times,* that some interesting things appeared to be going on in Roscommon. They were worth looking into, they said. Murtagh returned to Dublin and made an appointment to see one of his regular garda contacts.

The meeting took place in the man's office. He was relaxed and chatted over a cup of coffee. At the mention of the rumours and Sergeant Tully, his demeanour changed instantly. He became nervous, said it was impossible to speak in his office, and moved to another nearby room. There, he said it was not safe to talk at all in the building, that they would have to meet elsewhere. A colleague had a flat, he gave the address; he would be there at 4.30 p.m. People were being followed, so watch your route and look to see that nobody is behind you all the way, he advised. Do not use the telephone. The contact had already developed his own code for telephone conversations: Haughey was referred to as number one, Doherty was number two, Ainsworth three, McLaughlin four, Tully five and so on down a list to number twelve — Murtagh.

A few hours later, the contact was much more at ease sitting in an armchair in his colleague's flat. The colleague kept an eye out the window to make sure the house was not being watched by plainclothes gardaí.

The contact said that the Doherty story was much bigger than Tully, but that Tully might be the key to other things. The gardaí, he said, were slowly being taken over and turned into an instrument of Haughey and Doherty. Haughey had become directly involved at the highest level in the force by holding secret meetings attended by Ainsworth and other senior officers. The meetings sometimes took place in Kinsealy — Haughey knew everything that was going on. Doherty had become deeply involved in the day-to-day affairs of the force, and it was believed that McLaughlin merely did what he was told. People were being watched, gardaí seemed to be tailing other gardaí, and some people no longer felt safe. It seemed as though anyone who criticised or opposed was moved aside.

The contact detailed the happenings in Garda headquarters and some elsewhere in the force. There had been a series of strange transfers and appointments which seemed to have little to do with the talents or merits of the individuals concerned. They could only be explained, he said, in terms of a take-over of the force by people who saw it as an extension of their own political rule.

It had started, he said, with the Pat O'Connor affair. The

double voting allegation had been investigated in a way that was now the subject of a separate investigation on the orders of the Director of Public Prosecutions. Doherty's campaign on crime and vandalism had been a farce designed only to promote himself. The level of his interference in Roscommon and around the country was unprecedented and he didn't request things of the gardaí — he ordered that they be done. People were becoming very frightened and the contact believed it was only a matter of time before "accidents" began happening to people who were getting in the way of things. The gardaí had been directly involved in the Dowra affair and there was a cover-up on the Kerry car crash. Officers high and low in the force were subject to abuse if they did not do what they were told and Tully was just a small example.

There was a six-page document headed: "Statement of Sergeant T.A. Tully 12891 M, Boyle," which outlined his case. The document contained about two pages of personal details and four pages of detailed instances where Doherty had used his influence as Justice Minister or as a junior minister to interfere in proceedings against constituents. Several senior officers were named, including an Assistant Commissioner. The document was connected to Tully's successful efforts to fight his transfer order.

The contact said that if the information in the document came out it might prise open other aspects of the Doherty story. But he warned that if Doherty and certain garda officers felt threatened they might react fiercely. It would not be safe in future to meet in public or speak on the telephone. Any further meetings were to be arranged through the colleague.

Such was the contact's caution at the time that before deciding to speak to a reporter, he went to his solicitor to seek advice. He wanted to know the probable consequences of his disclosures and concluded that he would almost certainly lose his job if he was discovered. He decided to go ahead nonetheless. At the meeting with the solicitor, the contact's colleague waited outside in a car. He noted the registration numbers of a few vehicles that stopped nearby just to see if they were being followed. Later he checked the numbers with the garda computer and it transpired that two — a van and a car —were false. It was a regular practice of the ISB to use false number plates for undercover work. Such incidents bred paranoia.

The day after meeting the contact, parts of the story were checked with a senior civil servant at a meeting in his office. On hearing references to Tully, Dowra and O'Connor, the civil servant stood up from behind his desk, walked quickly to a nearby shelf and switched on a radio.

"One can't be too careful", he said.

He confirmed enough of each story to indicate that they were substantially true. On Thursday, October 28th, the *Irish Times* printed three reports on different pages. One told the story of Tully's successful resistance to his transfer and quoted from the document. Another said that Jim McGovern had been arrested in Northern Ireland as a direct result of contact between police intelligence services on both sides of the border and the third reported that the handling of the investigation into the Pat O'Connor case was the subject of an internal garda investigation ordered by the DPP.

Doherty's office was asked for a comment on the Tully story before it was published. His brother, Kevin Doherty, said that if the report was published, it could damage the Minister's "good name".

The day it was published Dick Spring, the Labour Party spokesman on Justice, attempted to raise the Tully affair in the Dáil, but he was prevented by the Ceann Comhairle. That night, however, Fine Gael's Justice spokesman, Jim Mitchell, put down a motion calling for a judicial enquiry into allegations of improper political interference in the gardaí over the previous two years and also allegations of improper activity by gardaí themselves.

Mitchell and Fine Gael were well briefed on the troubles in the Garda Síochána. About three weeks previously, Garret FitzGerald had been informed of Doherty's conduct and other disturbing matters concerning the force. The information came from a garda who had a secret meeting with FitzGerald in the home of Katherine Meenan, FitzGerald's personal assistant. The informant arrived for the meeting about fifteen minutes before FitzGerald to ensure that he would not be seen by FitzGerald's security guards.

In public, Doherty refused to say anything about the

allegations but he was furious and made strenuous efforts to get a copy of the document on Tully. His brother was also interested in it. Shortly after the report appeared in the *Irish Times*, Kevin Doherty bumped into a member of the executive of the Association of Garda Sergeants and Inspectors. Kevin Doherty mentioned to him that Seán Doherty was contemplating promoting him and, in the next breath, he mentioned getting a copy of the Tully document. In the eyes of the officer, the implication was clear — promotion in exchange for the document. The officer, who was already in line for promotion, refused to have anything to do with the suggestion.

Efforts were revived to have Tully removed from Boyle. A petition was organised in the station as part of a campaign orchestrated from garda headquarters in Dublin. As names were being sought for the petition, a senior officer in headquarters contacted a senior officer stationed in Roscommon to ask if the list was ready yet. The officer in Roscommon had known nothing of the petition until he got the call. Fourteen of the twenty-eight gardaí in Boyle signed the petition but no further attempts were made to transfer Tully.

More damaging facts about Doherty were to emerge. It was discovered that at the end of August, he had used his position as minister to apply considerable pressure to have a recruit garda passed out from the training centre even though the recruit had failed his final examination. The pressure was resisted and instructors at the centre threatened to strike if the man was allowed to pass out. The recruit happened to come from Doherty's constituency.

In Roscommon, there was widespread criticism amongst gardaí about Doherty's conduct locally. Many believed they were unable to do their job because people knew that if they were charged with a criminal offence, there was a chance that the charge would be dropped. Even those people who were convicted by the courts had an avenue open to them — they could petition Doherty's office for a reduction of sentence. It was known locally that a high number of petitions were successful. Much of what was contained in the Tully document proved to be true: Doherty had used his influence to have charges dropped against Keaney's and he had attempted to stop a blood sample of a drunk driver constituent being sent for testing. Many people around Boyle were frightened and refused to talk about certain things on the telephone.

The feelings of some people in Dublin were little different. They spoke of noticing cars following them, increased garda activity around their homes and strange noises on the telephones. Some of the Fianna Fáil dissidents believed their telephones were tapped. There were rumours that the telephones of Bruce Arnold and Geraldine Kennedy were tapped along with the telephones of either Olivia O'Leary or Dick Walsh, political correspondent of the *Irish Times*. It was suggested that conversations between these reporters and Desmond O'Malley, George Colley, Martin O'Donoghue, Seamus Brennan and Charlie McCreevy were to be recorded. Rumour had it that the tappers were gardaí and were very nervous. Garda and civil service contacts constantly warned of possible dangers. If the fears of some people seemed a little paranoid, there were indeed things happening in secret which confirmed that their concern was justified.

Shortly after the October 6th meeting of the Fianna Fáil parliamentary party, Martin O'Donoghue approached the leader of the Labour Party, Michael O'Leary, with a proposal which O'Donoghue believed would ensure the survival of the government in the short term while at the same time resolving the leadership crisis. O'Donoghue suggested that Labour support the government in the Dáil until the next budget in return for Labour participation in the budget. The deal would be conditional on Fianna Fáil getting rid of Haughey. O'Leary was astonished at the risk being taken by O'Donoghue, and tried to warn him obliquely. He also asked who would replace Haughey. O'Donoghue said that it could be either himself or Ray MacSharry. O'Leary did not commit Labour either way.

O'Donoghue was convinced that the result of the McCreevy motion had proved him right all along. The only way to get rid of Haughey was to have an agreed replacement and then force Haughey to resign in the face of united opposition to him in the party. But the only way this could be achieved would be for someone on Haughey's side to defect and turn against him. O'Donoghue tried to contact MacSharry immediately after the parliamentary party meeting but, unknown to him, MacSharry was in hospital for a couple of days. O'Donoghue had a chance meeting with Albert Reynolds and spoke about the problems facing the party. There were suggestions, said O'Donoghue, that certain people were continuing to support Haughey because they were financially compromised. He said there were rumours that MacSharry stood by Haughey because he had to. He said that money was available if people needed to be "uncompromised", freed from their obligation to support Haughey. Reynolds said he should talk to MacSharry; O'Donoghue said to tell MacSharry that he was looking for him.

It was not long before rumours began to fly about within the higher reaches of Fianna Fáil. It was said that £100,000 was on offer to MacSharry to change sides, that if he wanted to be Taoiseach, a house would be bought for him in Dublin, that Doherty could have £50,000 to ditch Haughey. It was also said that the only reason Haughey clung to the leadership was that his creditors were holding off because of his position. Haughey was one million pounds in debt to a bank, according to the rumour machine.

The government's precarious position in the Dáil was further weakened by the sudden death on Monday, October 18th, of the Clare TD, Bill Loughnane. A staunch supporter of Haughey, Loughnane was an old-style republican whose bitter opposition to Jack Lynch ingratiated him with the Haughey camp. He was 67 years of age and the oldest TD in the Dáil. His funeral took place on Wednesday, a day after another backbencher, Jim Gibbons, had a heart attack.

As the Fianna Fáil TDs and Ministers walked behind Loughnane's coffin and stood by his grave, some pondered the prospect of another general election. Padraig Flynn and Sean Doherty separately told MacSharry that O'Donoghue wanted to see him. There was mention of big money for him to abandon Haughey. MacSharry didn't like what he heard. He regarded himself as occupying several delicate positions — he was Tanaiste, Minister for Finance and the joint honorary treasurer of the party — and felt he was very vulnerable to such rumours. He had come a long way under Haughey.

In the mid 1970s, MacSharry was a relatively minor figure in Fianna Fáil. When the party was in opposition between 1973 and 1977 he was the front bench spokesman on the Office of

Public Works, a portfolio which did not offer many opportunities to develop a high profile either in public or within Fianna Fáil. MacSharry came to politics through business. He was elected to Sligo corporation in 1967 with the backing of the local Junior Chamber which felt it needed a voice in the local authority.

MacSharry owned about 75 acres of land, his home and a small haulage business. The haulage business involved three licenced trucks which contracted to transport goods. The business suffered a blow just before the 1969 general election in which he was elected to the Dáil. Two of the trucks, loaded with tomato chip baskets and parked waiting for transport to Northern Ireland, were set on fire and destroyed by vandals. It was a severe blow to such a small business and the damage was estimated at around £15,000 but MacSharry, conscious of his position as a local politician and now a TD, did not want to be seen to make a large malicious damages claim against the local authority. He sought £2,700 damages and settled for £2,300. He had hoped the balance would be covered by his goods in transit insurance but the policy did not cover trucks that were parked. The effects of the blow to the business were felt for some years and early in 1976, MacSharry negotiated a loan of £5,000 from Merchant Banking Limited, an off-shoot of the Gallagher property empire with which Haughey had dealings. Haughey also had accounts with the bank.

During this period, George Colley was opposition spokesman on Finance and had also resumed his work as a solicitor. At one stage, Colley was retained to recover £2,500 by a client who maintained MacSharry owed the money. Colley wrote to MacSharry and they met in Leinster House to discuss the matter. MacSharry suggested payment by post-dated cheques and a satisfactory conclusion was reached. Colley thought no more of the episode.

On the political front, Colley and MacSharry appeared to be quite close. Colley dissuaded him from pursuing his career in the European Parliament because he felt MacSharry was needed in Sligo and was a man of ability who should stay in Ireland. When Fianna Fáil was returned to power in 1977, MacSharry approached Colley and asked him to use his influence with Jack Lynch to get him an appointment. Colley recommended MacSharry and he was made a junior minister in Finance, Colley's department. Colley was the toast of the MacSharry family and was welcomed at the family celebrations in Sligo.

Over the following two years, MacSharry worked well and Colley believed he had promise. Then Jack Lynch resigned as Taoiseach. On the day before the crucial meeting of the parliamentary party to elect a new leader, MacSharry came to Colley and told him that Haughey wanted him to propose him. At that time only Pádraig Flynn among Haughey's supporters would publicly declare his allegiance but Haughey wanted a minister to propose him — MacSharry would do. MacSharry appeared to be in a quandary: he repeatedly told Colley that he supported him but he said he would have to propose Haughey. The impression which Colley gained from this interview was that some years ago Haughey had lent money to MacSharry, that the Haughey camp was now insisting that MacSharry propose or second Haughey, and that he could not refuse because Haughey had helped him when he was in financial difficulties. Colley said that MacSharry had to do what he had to do. But MacSharry indicated that even if he proposed or seconded Haughey, he would not necessarily vote for him.

The following day, MacSharry proposed Haughey for the leadership and subsequently became Agriculture Minister in the new cabinet.

In the autumn of 1982, MacSharry was extremely sensitive to any suggestion that he was financially compromised. By the time details of O'Donoghue's brief conversation with Reynolds reached MacSharry at Loughnane's funeral, they were embellished with specific suggestions, mainly that £100,000 was available. Doherty's earlier conversation with O'Donoghue seemed to fit into a pattern. MacSharry believed that O'Donoghue's persistent attempts to change the Fianna Fáil leadership provided enough evidence to have a charge of treason, a capital offence, laid against him. This wasn't a joke: some of Haughey's supporters really did believe that the dissidents were traitors in the legal sense and should be tried.

In Dublin the day after the funeral, MacSharry met O'Donoghue in a corridor in Leinster House around lunch-time. MacSharry told O'Donoghue that he heard he wanted to see him. O'Donoghue said he did and asked MacSharry when he thought he would be free. MacSharry said he would be busy for some time in the afternoon because the government's new economic plan, "The Way Forward", was being launched in the Burlington Hotel at 3 p.m. They agreed to meet around 5.30 p.m. in MacSharry's office in the Department of Finance, the block adjoining the Taoiseach's offices in Government Buildings.

MacSharry had lunch in the special ministers' dining room in Leinster House. He asked some of his colleagues if they had a tape recorder he could borrow. After lunch, Doherty telephoned Joe Ainsworth and said he wanted to borrow a tape recorder for MacSharry, describing in detail the type of recorder needed. Ainsworth selected a suitable model and a specially sensitive microphone which was an accessory to the main machine. It was similar to the tiny microphones which are clipped to the clothes of people interviewed on television. He also got some batteries and one of the special cassette tapes used by the recorder. The tape was capable of recording for two hours, one hour on either side. Doherty told Ainsworth that the equipment was needed before 5.30 p.m. by MacSharry in his office in the Department of Finance. Ainsworth said he would be passing that way going home and would make the delivery personally.

Doherty told MacSharry of the arrangement. MacSharry asked why Ainsworth was going to deliver the equipment and Doherty said he was passing MacSharry's office.

MacSharry attended the launching of "The Way Forward" in the Burlington Hotel and thought Haughey handled the press skilfully. He returned to his office around 5 p.m. to take delivery of the recorder from Ainsworth.

Ainsworth arrived and went to MacSharry's office, gave him the equipment and show him how to use it. He checked that the batteries were fitted properly and operating the recorder. He put the cassette inside and plugged in the special microphone. He showed MacSharry how to turn it on and off and then he left. When he had gone, MacSharry selected a place to conceal the recorder and microphone so that O'Donoghue would not realise he was being taped. There was a small filing cabinet beside his desk which was slightly lower than the top of the desk. MacSharry put the recorder into the top drawer of the filing cabinet and left it slightly open so there was just enough space for the wire connecting the recorder to the microphone. There were a couple of telephone directories on top of the cabinet and he hid the microphone by wedging it between the directories and the top of his desk. Everything was set.

As the time approached for his appointment with O'Donoghue, MacSharry received a delegation in his office. Running out of time, he hurriedly saw them out again by one door and rushed back to his desk to switch on the tape recorder as his private secretary came in by another door to announce the arrival of O'Donoghue.

"How are you, Martin?" asked MacSharry.

"Well, thanks", said O'Donoghue. "How did it go this afternoon?"

"Not so bad", said MacSharry adding that he had just received the estimates for 1983 and the figures seemed to be holding.

MacSharry then asked O'Donoghue what was on his mind. O'Donoghue said that so long as Haughey remained leader of Fianna Fáil, people in the party would be jittery at the prospect of fighting a general election. MacSharry said that the 58—22 split in the parliamentary party as a result of the McCreevy motion did not matter. O'Donoghue disagreed. He said the leadership problem remained and most people thought the government could not last beyond the summer of 1983 at the outside. But there was an alternative, said O'Donoghue, change leader.

"Well, you know my view on that", said MacSharry who went on to deny that he was involved in the moves in 1979 against Lynch. Their conversation was interrupted when MacSharry's telephone rang. He answered the call and spoke briefly. When he finished, O'Donoghue returned to the problem of how to remove Haughey and save the government.

"Well, let me give you the bones of it quickly. It seems to me that you are limping now and you are depending on Gregory and Blaney and you are always vulnerable", said O'Donoghue. "The other option is the Labour Party and now I know they appear to be in rags and so on, but there are about three or four different factions we all know and let's say that I am satisfied from each faction that they guarantee at least one year, and some of them would be interested in up to four years".

O'Donoghue said that once Haughey was removed, it would be up to the party to choose a successor and he hinted that MacSharry might be the man. He said the way to ditch Haughey was for a number of senior cabinet members to agree that he had to go. Then they would go to Haughey and tell him to resign and choose a new leader from among themselves.

"You would not see that happening", said MacSharry. "I could not see it happening. In the situation you have George and Dessie, you have Seamus Brennan and yourself".

"Seamus Brennan?" interrupted O'Donoghue, "forget it".

"You are talking of coming out of a room with a Pope", said MacSharry, "He is the Pope in his mind — you see this is the trouble".

"I just want to say quickly if Charlie goes, George goes and I think that is the price of it within the party", said O'Donoghue.

"Sure George won't go", said MacSharry.

They continued to talk about the leadership problem for a few minutes before MacSharry raised the matter of money which Albert Reynolds mentioned to him just before Reynolds had gone to America on official business.

"I really hit the roof when I heard my name mentioned in connection with money".

"I'm supposed to have been bought for £50,000 in February", quipped O'Donoghue.

MacSharry said he had overdrafts of £8,000 and £35,000 and documents to prove it, then returned to what Reynolds had said to him.

"I'm not too concerned but I mean I do not know whether it is true or not, but what he was talking about was arising from a conversation with yourself", said MacSharry. He had only heard bits and pieces and "£100,000 was being offered".

"I certainly did not say that", said O'Donoghue immediately.

Said MacSharry: "I do not know where the story came from but that is what he was talking about. I don't give a damn what was happening in Fianna Fáil and I could not care less if I was not there tomorrow or whenever the decision was made, but if I was to go round with the arse out of my trousers I would not take a brown penny from anyone".

O'Donoghue said he didn't think anyone implied that there was any substance in such suggestions. He mentioned again how he was alleged to have been paid £50,000 for his conduct during the O'Malley challenge to Haughey but he knew how true that was.

He continued: "What was being said was, if there was any suggestion of somebody being compromised financially, that it would be sorted out. But the money thing that I heard about town was that the Boss was in financial trouble and certainly again, if that was one of the problems, it would be better to organise some way of financing it".

MacSharry said there was no way that Haughey could be in financial trouble. O'Donoghue said there were persistent rumours that Haughey was under pressure to ensure that a highly controversial housing development in North Dublin was granted planning permission because so much money was at stake. It was claimed at the time that Haughey stood to gain if the development went ahead. MacSharry said that all Fianna Fáil politicians were accused of this sort of thing — the newspapers loved anything that hit Fianna Fáil, he said.

MacSharry again turned to the question of money. He said that all his dealings were above-board and he was concerned if anyone was suggesting, behind his back, that he was financially compromised.

"Yet if there is a compromise situation in relation to C.J. or myself or others, where is that money going to come from, where are we going to get it?" asked MacSharry.

"There is a lot of money around all right but not for C.J., not for him to stay", said O'Donoghue.

"You could never have a situation develop where there would be money around to move a political party in any kind of situation", said MacSharry.

"That is why I am not going after that aspect", said O'Donoghue.

The conversation reverted again to the question of Haughey's leadership and the split in the party. MacSharry said O'Donoghue did not have to resign from the cabinet when he did. O'Donoghue said it was clear that Haughey wanted rid of him. Haughey had spoken to O'Malley and referred to O'Donoghue as "that bastard O'Donoghue" when asking O'Malley not to resign, said O'Donoghue. MacSharry said that opposition to Haughey was wrong.

"If there is a group that will not support the leader, that is not part of Irish politics", he said.

O'Donoghue explained again that it would be possible in his opinion to remove Haughey and they returned again to McCreevy's motion and the split.

"One thing that had made Fianna Fáil the strength that it has is the protection of its leader", said MacSharry. "You go into any constituency: half the constituency would be for O'Donoghue and the other half would be for Andrews and they would fucking knife each other. Let's face facts, knife each other for and against but that is the way it is".

MacSharry again mentioned the alleged £100,000 for him to change sides. He said he had mentioned it to his wife and she was going to ring O'Donoghue.

"I would not blame her", said O'Donoghue.

MacSharry said he put her off and resolved to speak to O'Donoghue personally. The conversation then drifted once again into the joint problem of Haughey's leadership and the survival of the government. It was clear that both men were set in their convictions and neither was prepared to give way. The conversation ended by 6.30 p.m. and O'Donoghue left.

MacSharry examined the tape recorder hidden inside the drawer. It appeared to have worked fine. He unplugged the special microphone and removed the tape from the recorder.

Late that night he met Doherty in the Georgian Restaurant, a steak house near Portobello bridge on the edge of Rathmines. He gave the recording equipment back to him and Doherty said he could get the tape transcribed. He offered to stand over his secretary to ensure that nobody else learned of its contents. MacSharry gave him the tape which he said he wanted back plus one copy of the transcript. *No other copies were to be made,* he insisted.

The next day, Doherty telephoned Ainsworth. He told him he had a tape and he wanted it transcribed quickly. It was wanted at government, he said. The tape was dispatched to Ainsworth's office in garda headquarters. Ainsworth gave it to one of his officers for transcribing. It was a difficult task: many of the words were indistinct and the conversation was at times hard to follow.

The conversation was eventually transcribed onto twelve pages. Neither O'Donoghue nor MacSharry was named in the transcript. Their voices on the tape were identified simply as number one and number two; MacSharry was number one because he began the conversation. The pages were clear white sheets with no identifying marks on them. In the top left and bottom right hand corners the word SECRET was stamped on every page. The pages were then put between two covers — blue back and pink front — and clipped together with a slim plastic binder.

Ainsworth made three copies before telephoning Doherty to say the job was finished. Doherty said he would call him back and tell him where to deliver the transcript. He did and told Ainsworth to bring it to Government Buildings where he would meet him.

Ainsworth left one of the copies in his office and brought the other two around to Government Buildings from garda headquarters. He met Doherty there and was given back the tape recorder, microphone and batteries. He gave Doherty two copies of the transcript and the tape. Doherty thanked him and Ainsworth left.

Doherty later gave one copy of the transcript and the tape to MacSharry. MacSharry thanked Doherty and brought what he thought was the only transcript and the tape home with him to Sligo.

Doherty kept the third copy of the transcript. It made interesting reading. Its cover was dated "21st October 1982", the day the bugged conversation took place. There were six words on the cover —

SECRET
RESTRICTED TO GOVERNMENT
SPECIAL CORRESPONDENCE

Fianna Fáil
The Republican Party

MEATH - WESTMEATH

THATCHER
WANTS
GARRET

DO YOU?

SAFEGUARD IRELANDS NEUTRALITY

VOTE
Fianna
Fáil
The Republican Party

THE WAY FORWARD

Printed by Ratoath Printing Co. Tel. 256

Chapter Fifteen

In politics you never reach the end of the line
Ray McSharry, November 1982

Shortly after MacSharry bugged his conversation with O'Donoghue, Sean Doherty had another talk with Joe Ainsworth. Doherty returned to the subject of leaks and referred to the taps on the home telephones of the two journalists, Bruce Arnold and Geraldine Kennedy. The tap on Arnold's telephone had been off since July 12th, and the warrant governing the tap on Kennedy's telephone was due for renewal. The procedure required that, at the end of three months, the Garda Commissioner had to submit a new certificate declaring that the tap was "yielding results" if it was to be renewed.

With the noticeable increase in media reports about Doherty's own activities forming a background to their conversation, the Minister for Justice suggested that Arnold's telephone should be tapped again. Ainsworth, fresh from his recent meeting with Haughey about leaks to the *Irish Times,* demurred. The taps were of little use in detecting leaks, he argued; Doherty could see that from the transcripts already taken from them. Ainsworth had given Doherty an entire set of transcripts. Besides the record of Arnold's conversation with George Colley, there was another conversation of particular interest: Arnold talking with Derry Hussey, husband of Gemma Hussey, Fine Gael TD for Wicklow. Derry Hussey was chairman of Fine Gael's election strategy committee and was one of Garret FitzGerald's closest and most important advisors. Among the transcripts taken from the tap on

Kennedy's telephone was one of a conversation she had had with Peter Prendergast, a member of the committee and a former general secretary of Fine Gael. Doherty kept the transcripts for several days before returning them to Ainsworth.

It was decided to continue the tap on Kennedy's telephone. The certificate to have the tap renewed was sent from garda headquarters to the Department of Justice. It was signed by McLaughlin and said that the tap on telephone number 280006 was yielding results. Like the original application, the renewal certificate did not indicate that the telephone was rented by Geraldine Kennedy. As far as anyone in the Department of Justice knew, somebody called Ronald Langan was being tapped.

Neither Ainsworth nor Doherty, both of whom knew the true identity of the target, corrected the error. In fact, it worked to their advantage, Jim Kirby, head of the Security Section in the Department, didn't know that Kennedy was being tapped. Kirby had objected to the original application in July because Ainsworth refused to tell him why 280006 and Ronald Langan should be tapped. His objections to the tap might have been far stronger had he known that it was Kennedy's telephone.

The renewal certificate was sent to the Department of Justice just before the three-month life of the warrant ended. Doherty didn't have to authorise anything; he was merely informed that the gardaí were continuing the tap because they said it was yielding results. The warrant on Kennedy's telephone was renewed on October 27th. The *Sunday Tribune,* the newspaper for which she was political correspondent, was in liquidation. Publication had been suspended two days earlier, on Monday, October 25th.

It was only after Kennedy's tap was renewed that word began to filter back to officials in the Department that Arnold was not the only journalist being tapped. Kirby decided to check out the rumour and examine each of the eighty or so warrants on file to see if he could find Kennedy's. He checked each of them; telephone numbers against the named subscriber, the names against the addresses and so on until just one warrant stood out — Ronald Langan's. Kirby decided that Ronald Langan was really Geraldine Kennedy.

Meanwhile, Doherty was finding himself in increasingly hot

water over the disclosures about his conduct in his constituency and as minister. He, more than any other individual, appeared to be carrying an aura of scandal with him into the cabinet room. But he had the sympathy of most of his cabinet colleagues. Several were unhappy about the allegations that followed Doherty, especially over the Dowra affair, but most were persuaded that it was all a Fine Gael plot, backed by the media, to pick off government ministers one by one. Their attitude was that they had to stand together.

On a more mundane political level, however, Charles Haughey's government was clearly in trouble. The cuts in public spending which had caused difficulty since they were announced at the end of July were certain to dominate the new Dáil session that opened on Wednesday, October 27th. The government had managed to dissuade trade unions from taking action over the postponement of pay rises in the public service, but its cuts in spending, particularly on health, were still controversial. The Health Minister, Michael Woods, who had opposed the cuts strenuously in cabinet, was left by Haughey to defend them in public.

A week earlier, Haughey had launched a four-year economic plan which confirmed the turn-about in his economic approach from the early months of 1982. "The Way Forward" was mainly the work of the cabinet's economic sub-committee formed after the Dublin West by-election, and had been compiled largely by Padraig O hUiginn, the secretary of the Taoiseach's Department. In spite of its central message of austerity, it was published and launched lavishly. The 116-page document was bound in royal blue covers and the contents were laid out generously with section headings also printed in blue. The name of the printers responsible was not on the published document. It was printed by Irish Printers Ltd., a company that produced election material for Fianna Fáil and whose owner, Paul Kavanagh, was later to become the party's chief fund-raiser. The importance of the document was illustrated by the extensive public relations exercise surrounding it. On launch day, for instance, copies were specially delivered to the managers of the country's main businesses.

The new government policy promised to eliminate the deficit in the current budget by 1986 through a mixture of cuts in public spending, reductions in the public service, more taxes on sectors which paid the least income tax and cuts in social insurance like pay-related benefits. Haughey maintained that the plan had an inescapable and inexorable logic to it. But commentators noticed that, tough as the measures proposed were, the success of the plan was also based on an unprecedented rise in exports to give an annual growth rate of 5% up to 1987.

The document clearly had a political dimension in that it doubled as an election manifesto. It was becoming increasingly likely that it would be used in that role; the death of the Clare TD, Bill Loughnane, on October 18th deprived Fianna Fáil of a Dáil vote just as John Callanan's death had in June. But the Workers' Party could no longer be relied upon to back the government because of its new economic policy. They and Tony Gregory held the balance of power again.

Fine Gael's árd fheis the weekend before Loughnane's death was a low-key affair that tried to exploit Fianna Fáil's weaknesses by pointing to Fine Gael's solidity and reliability. Apart from a brief controversy over a motion dealing with plans to hold a referendum on abortion, there was little excitement at the conference. The party's strategists reckoned that the less they did the more they would benefit from the near certain collapse of Haughey's government. The Labour Party was in greater disarray as it went into its annual conference in Galway on the following weekend, preparing to do battle on the isue of electoral strategy and whether it should join another coalition or not. On the second day of the new Dáil session, Michael O'Leary resigned as party leader and as a member of the party because his approach had been defeated. Dick Spring, virtually unknown as a national figure, took over a seriously divided party.

Labour's divisions appeared to be the only potential bright spot for Fianna Fáil as the Dáil resumed on October 27th. Jim Gibbons, the deputy from Carlow-Kilkenny and Haughey's most implacable enemy since their paths had crossed in the witness box of the central criminal court in 1970, had suffered two heart attacks. He was in a stable condition but seriously ill in hospital in Kilkenny. It appeared unlikely that he would be able to attend the Dáil, which meant that the Workers' Party alone held the balance. An opinion poll published on the Dáil's opening day showed that Fianna Fáil and Fine Gael, probably for the first time ever, were neck-and-neck.

When the Dáil resumed, Fine Gael attacked from the beginning, forcing divisions on Haughey's selection of two junior ministers, Ger Brady and Denis Gallagher, to replace Martin O'Donoghue and Des O'Malley in the cabinet, and on his insistence on calling a by-election for Clare in mid-November. The government won both votes with the help of the Workers' Party, but in the first week of November Haughey appeared to have run out of time. He tried to fend off a vote on his economic plan and avoid defeat on a motion by the Labour Party, under its new leader Dick Spring, attacking cuts in the health services. Garret FitzGerald accused him of trying to stave off defeat by filibustering the economic debate until after the Clare by-election. On November 3rd, FitzGerald tabled a motion of "no confidence" and a two-day debate was arranged.

The Workers' Party announced its support for the "no confidence" motion and the debate became a platform to launch the general election campaign. In public, senior members of Fianna Fáil admitted that they had a problem but they did not concede defeat. In private, some, like chief whip Bertie Ahern, had their own election material printed and ready to distribute long before the final vote.

But they also pursued every conceivable angle that might change the odds in their favour and avoid defeat. Ahern had been told by his Workers' Party contact that the party's árd comhairle had decided some time earlier that they could no longer support the Fianna Fáil government. The party was now saying the same in public but Ahern arranged a meeting for Haughey and MacSharry with the three Workers' Party deputies. Haughey urged them not to take precipitate action; much could still be done, he suggested. Joe Sherlock, the Workers' Party leader in the Dáil, accused the government of having gone back on its word by switching its economic policy. Proinsias de Rossa told MacSharry that the government had reached the end of the line. MacSharry replied: "in politics you never reach the end of the line".

The Labour Party, its new leader less than two days in office when the debate began, was also approached to see if some arrangement could be reached. But that was ruled out by Labour on the morning of the second day of the debate. Neil Blaney, although his support was presumed, was not all that happy either about the turn-about in the government's economic attitude. A delegation from his organisation met Haughey after the publication of "The Way Forward" and complained about its emphasis on spending cuts. They threatened Haughey that Blaney would vote against the plan. In the event, Blaney stood by Haughey on the basis that he and his organisation could use Haughey as long as nobody had a Dáil majority and because they did not want an election.

In spite of the apparent certainty that Haughey faced defeat, most commentators were wary of predicting the outcome. Haughey had confounded his critics so many times and squeezed out of so many tight corners that nothing could be forecast with certainty.

As proof of his determination, Haughey and his associates continued their efforts to avoid defeat. (Sean Doherty's period as Justice Minister had taught him that, unfortunately, TDs could not be arrested on their way to Leinster House for a Dáil vote). It was known from the Finance Bill debates and votes in June that Tony Gregory alone would not be responsible for defeating the government. He had saved them in June and he might be able to do so again. Gregory, too, was unhappy about the new economic stance and particularly the proposed cuts in health spending. Michael Woods assured him that compromises were possible, but he believed the government would be defeated and announced that he intended to abstain.

Now MacSharry and Ahern tried to involve Gregory in one of their most ambitious plans to avoid defeat. It involved Jim Gibbons, still in hospital since suffering two heart attacks a fortnight earlier: Oliver J. Flanagan, the venerable Fine Gael TD from Laois-Offaly; Tony Gregory and the proposed referendum to insert into the Constitution an article banning abortion.

Fianna Fáil produced the wording for the referendum on Tuesday, November 2nd, and Haughey made it clear to his parliamentary party when informing them of it that it would be an election issue. Fine Gael's leadership had indicated at its árd fheis two weeks earlier that it favoured consideration of the abortion issue in the context of an overall review of the Constitution. Ever since Haughey and FitzGerald had given referendum commitments to "pro-life" compaigners in the summer of 1981, Haughey had stood by the strict terms of the proposal while FitzGerald had not. With the question ready to put to voters, Haughey clearly saw an opportunity of wrong-footing FitzGerald.

But the referendum might come to the party's aid before a general election and help it to avoid defeat. The idea had actually come to Fianna Fáil from some of the "pro-life" people who were enthusiastically in favour of the party's wording for a change in the Constitution. They suggested to Fianna Fáil that Oliver J. Flanagan might not be too happy with the leadership of his own party and, on this issue, might prefer to see Fianna Fáil stay in office until the referendum was safely held. It was unlikely, however, that Flanagan, the oldest member of the Dáil, would cross the floor of the house to vote confidence in Haughey.

But a possible scenario was put together which would involve Gibbons. If he were to leave hospital and travel towards the Dáil, Flanagan might agree to "pair" with him, in other words, to operate the system whereby deputies from opposing parties agree to cancel each other out by staying away for votes if one of them is prevented by circumstances from being present in the Dáil. That would leave the combined opposition — Fine Gael, Labour, the Workers' Party and Jim Kemmy — with 81 votes. Fianna Fáil, with the help of Blaney, would then have 80 votes. If Tony Gregory could be persuaded to come off the fence, the government would have 81 also. Gibbons need never appear in the Dáil on a stretcher: Flanagan could maintain there had been a misunderstanding when he did not turn up either. But Haughey would have survived again, against all the odds.

The likelihood of getting all these factors in place was remote, but Ahern set about trying it. He spoke to the Ceann Comhairle, John O'Connell, and got a promise from him that he would support the government if there was a tied vote on the confidence motion. He arranged to have a heart ambulance travel to Kilkenny to pick up Gibbons and he talked to the Gibbons family. All he wanted Gibbons to do was get into the ambulance and have it drive down the road: it could bring him back again almost immediately.

Obviously, Fine Gael would never have agreed to this "pair". But the scheme, its proponents believed. would be enough to tempt Oliver J. Flanagan to break ranks in order to keep Fianna Fáil in office to bring in its "pro-life" amendment. The arrangement in this instance would have effectively restored Jim Gibbons's vote to Fianna Fáil. The "pro-life" people wanted to suggest to Flanagan that it was in the interests of the amendment that he "pair" with Gibbons and this would help Fianna Fáil to survive in power. Bertie Ahern was very interested in the idea, if the "pro-life" supporters could pull it off.

On the morning of Thursday, November 4th, Tony Gregory was called to MacSharry's office in Leinster House and Ahern put the proposition to him. If there was a pairing arrangement between Flanagan and Gibbons, would Gregory vote with Fianna Fáil? Gregory said he wanted to talk to Flanagan before he would believe anything. Brendan Shortall, public relations officer for the Pro-Life Amendment Campaign and one of its leading strategists, spent most of the day in Ahern's office in Leinster House. By lunchtime, however, it was clear that the idea would not work. Jim Gibbons would do nothing to help Charles Haughey.

Meanwhile, in the Dáil chamber, Charles Haughey had opened the debate with an attack on Fine Gael for blatant political opportunism and an overwhelming desire for office. He claimed credit for having brought down the inflation rate by eight points to 13%, reduced interest rates and improved the balance of payments. His government had produced an economic plan that was approved by all the key financial and economic institutions, farmers, businessmen and a vice-president of the European Commission. Garret FitzGerald declared that more than a hundred of the Dáil's 166 members were now seen to have no confidence in the Taoiseach.

Most members of the cabinet who spoke made a point of complaining about the "smears and vilifications" against Haughey, and of attacking FitzGerald for hypocrisy and for orchestrating the campaign against Haughey and individual ministers. The individual minister most in the limelight — that morning's newspapers carried a statement from him about the car crash in Kerry — was Sean Doherty, who attacked ferociously. He revealed that a blood sample showing the brother of the previous Justice Minister, Jim Mitchell, to have an excessive level of alcohol had been lost in the post. Others, he said, had been involved in accidents in official cars and, he implied, had had relatives who were involved in stranger events.

He had been pursued and vilified in an attempt to undermine the credibility of the office of the Minister for Justice, the credibility of Fianna Fáil as a party and the credibility of the party leader, he said. But he did not refute any of the main accusations against him. He did not explain what had happened to the car driven by the protection detail in Kerry. On the Dowra affair, he merely repeated that he was not his brother-in-law's keeper. "I have no responsibility for the actions of someone else, in the same way as Deputy Mitchell is not responsible for the actions of his brother and Deputy (Peter) Barry is not responsible for the actions of his niece."

Doherty dismissed the accusations of political interference in the Garda Síochána. It was essential, justifiable and legitimate for Dáil deputies to make political representation. He added: "There is a considerable difference between representing one's constituents and using one's position to impose some type of duress on subordinates, whether gardaí or others, to bring about a decision contrary to the legal requirement".

FitzGerald, he went on, had left the country like the Scarlet Pimpernel and undermined "Anglo-Irish foreign policy"; he supported a situation that resulted in political chaos in Northern Ireland; he had pursued pluralist policies across the free world merely to popularise himself. FitzGerald, said Doherty, was prepared to abandon the Irish people, their traditions and Constitution and everything national and dear to them in order to achieve political popularity at home.

Ray MacSharry wound up the debate, defending the government's economic policies and complaining about a small cell within (he avoided saying Fianna Fáil at the last moment) Fine Gael which determined the party's behaviour. "We have this motion of confidence because Fianna Fáil refused to make any deals with anybody", he declared. The party's dissident wing made one last attempt to influence events. As the time for a vote on the confidence motion approached , Des O'Malley approached Charles Haughey in the Dáil chamber. The government need not be defeated, O'Malley remarked; if Haughey were to stand down, the Labour Party would back a Fianna Fáil government temporarily. Haughey retorted that it was too late for that.

There was no tension surrounding the outcome of the vote. The government had been falling for two days and everyone knew it, although most people wanted to have the votes counted before they could be certain. There were no last-minute surprises. The Workers' Party voted against the government, as it had said it would. Tony Gregory abstained, as he had promised. Neil Blaney voted with the government, as everyone had assumed he would. Jim Gibbons was not produced on a stretcher. Oliver Flanagan voted with Fine Gael. The result was 80 votes for the government, 82 against. There was a spattering of applause but no euphoria as Haughey went off to tell President Hillery that his minority government had collapsed. The third general election within eighteen months was fixed for November 24th.

Haughey began the campaign with an immediate challenge to FitzGerald to debate on television the reasons why he had forced an election. Fianna Fáil, he declared, would fight the campaign on the basis of its economic plan, its performance in government, its proposal for a referendum on abortion, its defence of Irish neutrality and its resolve to maintain Ireland's position in the world as a sovereign and independent nation.

It was apparent to the strategists in both parties that Fianna Fáil had to make the running, decide the issues and force the pace. In Fine Gael, on the other hand, the strategy was simply to do as little as possible in case its strong position was eroded. The opinion polls published just before the campaign indicated that the two parties were neck and neck. Satisfaction with Haughey's government was at an all-time low, dissatisfaction at an all-time high. Polls conducted privately for Fine Gael indicated that Fianna Fáil's base support was beginning to crumble: up to 9% of Fianna Fáil supporters did not intend voting for the party.

Given Fianna Fáil's change in economic policy, there was no obvious area of major disagreement. Fianna Fáil had come to accept both the analysis of the economy and the remedies proposed by Fine Gael. The issues, instead, were to be questions of trust and credibility. In his first campaign press conference, Haughey declared that he did not trust FitzGerald on the question of abortion. FitzGerald had responded to the publication of the Fianna Fáil wording for the referendum by welcoming the proposed constitutional clause as being "about as good a formula as you can get".

Nevertheless, Haughey tried to make it a central issue of the campaign. He promised to hold the referendum before Christmas 1982 if he was elected. FitzGerald pledged the Government he would lead to hold it before the end of March 1983. In spite of Haughey's best efforts, however, the abortion question fizzled out as a campaign issue. Fine Gael was also putting emphasis on trust, and more particularly credibility; Haughey's leadership was the issue "on which things turn", FitzGerald admitted at his opening press conference.

As the campaign progressed, Fianna Fáil turned towards the so-called "green" card, the use of nationalism to imply doubts about its opponents and to consolidate its own base support. Haughey's advisers had been telling him for some time that the British were behind many of the disclosures that were emerging in public. The collapse of Anglo-Irish relations over the Falklands war and the ill feeling over James Prior's Northern Assembly helped to encourage that belief. Fine Gael strategists had already anticipated that Haughey, faced with severe electoral defeat, would play this card. Yet the party walked straight into the ploy.

Gerry Collins, the Foreign Minister, set the ball rolling by claiming that FitzGerald had been used as an instrument of British policy in relation to Prior's plans for the North. He cited a speech by the Duke of Norfolk in the House of Lords in which he said that he had had lunch with FitzGerald and that the Fine Gael leader approved of Prior's devolution plan. The speech had been used by Fianna Fáil some months earlier to accuse FitzGerald of "an irresponsible intrusion" into an area that was properly the responsibility of the government.

FitzGerald now denied the accusation as a perversion of the

truth. He said he had met the Duke in order to persuade him to alter Prior's Bill to allow Senator Séamus Mallon, the deputy leader of the Social Democratic and Labour Party who had been appointed by Haughey to the Senate, to take his seat in the new Northern Assembly.

The controversy was fuelled by a report that Prior, on a visit to the United States, had revealed that FitzGerald would shortly be proposing the formation of an all-Ireland court and police force. His reported comment appeared to suggest a degree of collusion between FitzGerald and the British minister. Prior subsequently denied making the comment but admitted that he was aware of suggestions to that effect.

At an otherwise bland news conference in Leinster House a week into the campaign, Haughey threw down the "green" card. Britain, he said, should stop interfering in the Irish election campaign. British radio, television and newspapers were interfering in Irish affairs, he said. And he had a message to send to them: "Britain, stay out of our election. The Irish people are perfectly capable of deciding for themselves which government they want. They can choose for themselves".

The card was not an instant winner. Things were looking very bad for Fianna Fáil at that point in the campaign. An opinion poll showed that three-quarters of the electorate did not believe anything said by the party's politicians, a much greater credibility problem than other parties had. And one out of every ten Fianna Fáil supporters did not want the party back in government, it found.

FitzGerald, meanwhile, was preparing the only speech on the North that he intended to deliver during the campaign. He proposed to refer to the formation of an all-Ireland court and of a joint police force that could operate in border areas where problems of jurisdiction hampered security operations. He had floated the idea the previous May in the course of a lecture on BBC radio and television. It was only one point in a speech in which the main emphasis was on the need for a radical new approach by Britain to the North. He suggested that there should be a court and a police force, separate from the RUC and the gardaí, that would be common to both parts of the island and deal with crimes of violence. "Such a joint court and police force, under North/South control, would match the subversives' capacity to create a single entity of terrorism in this island", he said.

Against his advisers, FitzGerald went ahead with the speech and the security references. It appeared that the charges of collusion had some foundation: Prior had apparently said that FitzGerald would talk about the things he did talk about. The party spokesman on Justice, Jim Mitchell, fleshed out the joint policing idea in greater detail at a press conference on security policies. But Fianna Fáil translated the proposal into the introduction of armed RUC men onto the streets of southern towns and cities. Haughey recounted the worried query of an old woman who asked him if it meant the reintroduction of the Royal Irish Constabulary. Leaflets were produced in several constituencies, some bearing Fianna Fáil's name and others anomymous. In north Dublin, an anonymous leaflet asked: "Do you want the RUC policing our streets?" Another declared: "No to armed RUC patrols in Dublin".

In Meath and Westmeath, a leaflet with Fianna Fáil's name took its theme from a famous World War One recruiting poster depicting Lord Kitchener, declaring: "Your country needs you". It showed Kitchener pointing at the reader declaring: "Thatcher wants Garret. Do you?" It went on: "Safeguard Ireland's Neutrality. Vote Fianna Fáil. The Way Forward".

As the campaign moved into its last weekend, the opinion polls indicated that the "green" card was working for Fianna Fáil: the party's base support was solidifying. Haughey did all he could to maintain the momentum. On Saturday, November 20th, the party press officers handed out to reporters assembling for a press conference a brief biography of the Duke of Norfolk, taken from a news agency's biography, which included the information that the Duke was head of intelligence at the British Ministry of Defence at the time of his retirement in 1967.

Haughey was in typically buoyant mood when he arrived for the conference in the party's headquarters in Mount Street in Dublin. Tapping a picture of himself on the wall, he commented: "isn't he beautiful" and sat down. The conference meandered on until he was fed a question about the Duke of Norfolk: was he really only a doddery old Duke? Given his cue, Haughey launched into a renewed attack on Garret Fitz-

Gerald. "The fact is that Garret FitzGerald had lunch with a trained British spy, whether he knew it or not", he declared. And he accused FitzGerald of over-stepping his responsibilities by talking to the Duke about political initiatives in the North.

Haughey went on to dismiss as "laughable" FitzGerald's complaints that he was being vilified by Fianna Fáil. Fine Gael, he said, had been carrying on a "cold, calculating and vilifying character assassination of me". Later in the news conference, he said that various journalists were working for Fine Gael. Looking pointedly at Bruce Arnold, he appeared to reach for a file before him as if to open it and produce evidence of his accusation. He thought better of the move. But the incident and the entire press conference left some of those who attended with a feeling of deep unease.

Fine Gael, meanwhile, was doing frantic research to work out the effects on voters of the "green" card. Party activists reported that it was being raised by people on door-to-door canvasses. But opinion surveys of Dublin constituencies reassured the party's strategists that the damage was not too severe. They decided to try and make a virtue out of necessity; the longer the issue was dragged out the more ineffective it became for Fianna Fáil.

The Attorney General, John Murray, joined in the controversy with a statement to the effect that FitzGerald's policing proposals would undermine the effectiveness and independence of the forces of law and order and the sovereign institutions of the state. Fine Gael immediately demanded Murray's resignation.

The stage was set for a final confrontation between Haughey and FitzGerald in a live debate on television. FitzGerald underlined the total personal hostility that existed between them by refusing to allow himself to be pictured with Haughey before the debate. During the discussion, FitzGerald was clearly well briefed and well rehearsed. Either FitzGerald won or it was a draw: he had held his ground where he had lost it to Haughey in the last television debate between them during the February election.

As the votes were counted on Thursday, November 25th, it quickly became apparent that Haughey had lost the election. Overall, Fianna Fáil lost 6 seats, Fine Gael gained 7, Labour gained 1, the Workers' Party lost 1 and the one member of the Democratic Socialist Party, Jim Kemmy, lost his seat. The outcome was Fianna Fáil 75, Fine Gael 70, Labour 16, Workers' Party 2, Independents 3. But the playing of the "green" card had held Fianna Fáil's vote at 45.2%, almost the same as it had been in June 1981. Fine Gael, on the other hand, increased its share of the vote for the third election in succession to a record 39.2%. Labour had a very modest revival with 9.36% and the Workers' Party vote fell fractionally to 6.2%.

Haughey conceded defeat but looked surprised at the suggestion that he might reconsider his leadership of the party. Indeed, his critics within the party had not done very well in the election. The dissidents were blamed by the party leaders for the defeat and some of them suffered at the hands of the electorate as well. Several had lost their seats, including Martin O'Donoghue in Dun Laoghaire, Jim Gibbons in Carlow-Kilkenny, Sean French in Cork North Central, and Tom Bellew from Louth; others, like George Colley and Séamus Brennan, saw a drop in their votes. Haughey had, for the third election in succession, failed to win the party an overall majority but the first meeting of the new Fianna Fáil parliamentary party endorsed his leadership.

Fianna Fáil continued in office for another eighteen days until the new Dáil assembled on December 14th. The show was over, but Haughey's government still had several tasks it wanted to complete. The tap on Geraldine Kennedy's telephone had been taken off during the election campaign. On November 16th, a week before the election and almost three weeks after Commissioner McLaughlin had signed a certificate to say the tap was yielding results, a new application was sent to the Department of Justice to have it removed. The application was automatically granted. During the election, the *Sunday Independent* journalist, Kevin O'Connor, asked Haughey at several press conferences if the telephones of journalists were tapped and if he would introduce guidelines on phone tapping drawn up by the European Commission on Human Rights. Haughey promised to look at the Commission's proposals.

On Friday, December 3rd, the cabinet discussed a number of appointments to state bodies and promotions within the gardaí. It decided to appoint a former director general of Bord Fáilte, Joe Malone, to the organisation's board. Malone had always been close to Haughey and was chairman of a Fianna Fáil fund-raising committee at the time. A senior counsel, Vivion Lavan, was to be appointed a High Court judge and to take over the full-time post of chairman of the planning appeals board, An Bord Pleanála. At the age of 38, Lavan is believed to have been the youngest person ever proposed for a position on the High Court.

The appointment of Lavan ran into technical problems because, as Bruce Arnold revealed in the *Irish Independent,* there was no vacancy in the High Court. The chairman of An Bord Pleanála had to be a High Court judge but Lavan could not be given the post because there was no vacancy in the court. Haughey admitted the problem, described the rule as defective and said that Lavan was no longer interested in the appointment "for personal reasons".

A third appointment, announced by Seán Doherty as Justice Minister, was the promotion of Joe Ainsworth to the new post of Deputy Commissioner of the Garda Síochána. The post had had to be created for him because the two existing positions of deputy commissioner were already occupied. At a meeting between Ainsworth and Doherty several days later, it was agreed that Ainsworth would continue as head of the Intelligence and Security Branch. But his responsibilities were also to be extended to detectives covering ordinary crime; Ainsworth was to have control over all plain-clothes policemen in the state.

The appointments were severely criticised by Fine Gael and Labour. Garret FitzGerald warned that the new government would have to examine appointments made in these circumstances and he urged those offered positions to consider carefully the propriety and wisdom of accepting them. In the event, any appointments made by the outgoing government were upheld by the coalition administration that followed it.

On December 9th, RTE television's main current affairs programme, "Today Tonight" presented a lengthy report on allegations that Seán Doherty used his position as Justice Minister to interfere directly in garda matters in his Roscommon constituency. The programme looked into six cases in which Doherty was said to have used political influence on the gardaí locally. The cases included the attempt to transfer Sergeant Tom Tully to Ballyconnell after the raid on Keaney's pub, and alleged drunken driving offences. In most of them, the programme concluded there had been political interference. It also revealed that Doherty had used his power as Justice Minister to reduce fines for people from the area who petitioned him.

Doherty complained that the allegations were false and represented in an unfair and biased manner and said he would not submit to trial by RTE. He refused on a subsequent RTE radio programme to answer specific questions. He had never done anything wrong or injurious to the public interest, he added. He had made representations on behalf of his constituents and he would make no apology for that.

Some more of the actions he had taken in office were about to be revealed, contrary to the firm beliefs of those who had been involved in them.

Chapter Sixteen

You must as head of Government accept responsibility.
Charles Haughey, January 1983

Michael Noonan didn't know where his new office was on his first morning as Minister for Justice, and asked his driver if he knew where it was. The driver took him there to a characterless, modern office block on the south side of St Stephen's Green whose only redeeming feature was its panoramic views over the park. The hall porter was able to recognise him, welcomed him to the building and showed him to the lift. Noonan got out at the fourth floor and was met by Andy Ward, secretary of the Department. There was an immediate briefing for Noonan about the Department and the way it was run. He listened carefully to what Ward had to say before asking the question that was on his mind.

Were the telephones of Bruce Arnold and Geraldine Kennedy tapped? They were, replied Ward. Michael Noonan was about to have a political baptism of fire.

He was something of an unknown political quantity when Garret FitzGerald appointed him to what he knew was going to be one of the hottest ministries in the new government that he formed on December 12th. Noonan was 39 years old and had been TD for Limerick East since June 1981. He had made no impact as a national figure and spoke just four times in the Dáil during the life of Haughey's defeated government. But he was said to be very close to FitzGerald and was regarded by some Fine Gael people as a young man destined for great things in the party.

He joined Fine Gael in 1964, having been attracted by what

he believed was a new spirit in the party typified by Declan Costello's "Just Society" policy proposals. He graduated from University College Dublin, took a Higher Diploma in Education and returned to his native Limerick to become a teacher. He worked for Fine Gael during the 1968 by-election which saw Desmond O'Malley take the Dáil seat held by his late uncle, Donogh O'Malley. Noonan became involved in local politics and in 1974 was elected to Limerick county council. He continued to build a base for a Dáil seat but the 1980 re-drawing of constituency boundaries upset his plans. He scaled down his activities until the party constituency organisation in Limerick East asked him to work in their area. The following year, he was elected their TD in his first attempt to win a Dáil seat. FitzGerald and the party's backroom tacticians were very impressed with Noonan. He was shrewd, cautious and very intelligent but also extremely tough politically. During the life of the Fianna Fáil government, he was Fine Gael's spokesman on Education and also helped to advise the party strategy committee on which constituencies might yield extra seats for Fine Gael in a general election.

When Noonan came to Dubin in mid-December for the first meeting of the new Dáil, he thought that if he was lucky he might get a minor cabinet post, perhaps Defence. His friend and colleague, George Birmingham, the young Dublin North Central TD, speculated that Noonan might be made junior justice minister. The prospect of being Justice Minister had never occurred to Noonan.

On the morning the new Dáil assembled, Tuesday, December 14th, Noonan met Seán Barrett, Fine Gael's chief whip, who told him not to leave Leinster House for lunch. Noonan knew then that he was going to be in the cabinet — somewhere. He found out where shortly after lunch when FitzGerald called him to his office and offered him Justice. FitzGerald also said he had an immediate task for Noonan: he had information that the telephones of two journalists, Geraldine Kennedy and Bruce Arnold, were tapped and he wanted it checked out. Noonan was sceptical.

FitzGerald was elected Taoiseach in mid-afternoon and went to Áras an Uachtaráin to collect his seal of office. The Dáil adjourned until the evening while TDs, their wives, families and friends relaxed in Leinster House waiting for him to return and announce his cabinet. Some of the impending appointments became known to reporters and Peter Murtagh of the *Irish Times* approached Noonan. He asked Noonan to confirm that Kennedy and Arnold had been tapped by the outgoing Fianna Fáil government. Noonan was taken aback and wondered if he was the only person who had not known that tapping was going on.

Andy Ward's instant confirmation of the tappings without the necessity of having to check records indicated the concern that had been felt for some time in the Department of Justice. Officials who were aware of Doherty's conduct concluded that all they could do was to ensure that all files were kept up to date so that an accurate record existed if and when there was a change of government.

Noonan moved into his office, a large room on the fourth floor with an adjoining office for assistants and his private secretary. Officials had spent some time clearing files from the office after Doherty left. In the wake of his departure, there were hundreds of files piled up in a room awaiting the minister's attention. His going was greeted in the Department with widespread relief which quickly became tinged with apprehension when it was realised that the new man intended to conduct a thorough investigation. The programme published by the new government included a commitment to set up a judicial enquiry into allegations of political interference in the Garda Siochána over the preceding three years. Such an enquiry had implications for the Department as well as the gardaí. Initially, however, it was crucial to establish who had initiated the tapping — Doherty or the gardaí.

One of Noonan's immediate concerns was how he should react if the tapping was revealed in the newspapers. He was aware that the *Irish Times* had the story and so he prepared a statement in anticipation of publication and the inevitable calls for comment.

The report was published by the *Irish Times* on Saturday, December 18th. It was brief and gave the bare facts. Haughey's government had tapped the two journalists' telephones on foot of official warrants. Other newspapers eagerly took up the story. The Irish Council for Civil Liberties and the National

Union of Journalists made statements of concern and demanded a full explanation. Noonan responded with a carefully-worded statement. He said the alleged tapping was obviously an important matter but he could not comment, confirm or deny the report "at the moment". The statement indicated a possible departure from the standard government response to tapping claims, which was to refuse comment on the basis that such matters were "security". There had been just one break with that rule in recent years, when Jack Lynch assured TDs after the arms crisis that their telephones were not tapped. Noonan's statement bought him some breathing space and left him the option of making further, detailed comment.

On the same Saturday, an unusual meeting took place at Garda headquarters. The chief constable of the RUC, Sir Jack Hermon, and his Assistant Chief Constable in charge of the RUC Special Branch, Trevor Forbes, had discussions with their opposite numbers in the Garda Siochána — McLaughlin and Ainsworth. It was unusual for such meetings to take place on Saturdays and the agenda was quite extraordinary. There was just one item: any issues which might arise with the advent of the new government in the Republic. Ainsworth had been surprised when he read that morning's *Irish Times* report on the telephone tapping, but he thought he was in no danger so long as the government stuck to precedent and did not confirm it.

The meeting at Garda headquarters was not primarily about tapping, however.

Earlier in the week, the *Irish Times* had revealed that not only had RUC headquarters in Belfast ordered the arrest of Jimmy McGovern after contact with the gardaí but also that the order was resisted by an RUC Special Branch officer in Enniskillen. Forbes was linked to the arrest when the objections were overruled and he confirmed the order. A second report the following day revealed that garda contact with the RUC was initiated from Doherty's office in the Department of Justice. Both reports made certain garda and RUC officers very nervous.

McLaughlin and Ainsworth were worried about the whole Dowra affair and the possibility that a new investigation might be launched into it. The investigation carried out by Chief Superintendent Stephen Fanning after McGovern's arrest in

Northern Ireland in September was far from satisfactory, though through no fault of Fanning's. His appointment to the investigation raised eyebrows in garda headquarters and elsewhere. Fanning was deputy head of ISB, yet it was known that people in ISB had been involved in McGovern's arrest. Fanning was therefore investigating his own men and would of necessity have to question his superior officer, Joe Ainsworth. There was no possibility that an investigation carried out under such conditions could be properly executed. In the event, Fanning was unable to make a full enquiry. Somebody from outside ISB should have been appointed to the investigation and so long as any suggestion existed that Ainsworth had to be interviewed an officer of at least his rank should have been appointed.

The prospect of yet another investigation was not greeted with any relish by McLaughlin and Ainsworth. The affair was discussed with Hermon and Forbes. Hermon eventually offered to make a public statement on his return to Northern Ireland to the effect that the RUC had acted properly throughout the affair. This statement could be interpreted in the Republic as support for McLaughlin and it might help him if he was increasingly under siege.

When news of the meeting leaked out, the government promptly disowned it. Noonan made a statement discounting suggestions that Anglo-Irish relations or new cross-border police initiatives were discussed.

"The meeting was concerned with operational security matters and neither the government nor any minister had any part in arrangements for it to take place," said the statement. It did not say that the "operational security matters" discussed included the arrest in Northern Ireland of Jimmy McGovern. While it was normal for the Commissioner of the Garda Siochána and the Chief Constable of the RUC to meet and discuss ways of tackling their mutual security problem, the border, the fact that it was held behind the back of a government only a few days in office caused considerable annoyance to the new administration.

The next day, Haughey gave a lengthy post-election interview on the Sunday RTE radio programme, "This Week". The wide-ranging interview inevitably dealt with the allegations against Doherty and the question of telephone tapping of journalists. Haughey's response to questions showed he was clearly aware of the crucial point in the affair: he said he had never initiated a warrant for tapping when he was Justice Minister.

"I would only respond to a request for one from the garda authorities or the Revenue Commissioners or something in that area. I don't think any politician himself should ever initiate. That would be an abuse", he said. Haughey's understanding of the significance of a minister initiating a tap was apparent but his knowledge of which bodies could initiate taps was faulty. The Revenue Commissioners did not have the authority to request tapping. Haughey insisted twice in the interview that he knew nothing about the tapping. He said it would be "absolutely ludicrous" to tap journalists' telephones. He said that a judicial enquiry into the other allegations against Doherty should be set up and charged to investigate the tapping claims as well. He claimed again that he was the victim of a campaign against him in the media.

A number of Fianna Fáil politicians hoped that a judicial enquiry would be established immediately. They could then retreat into the well-worn sub judice refuge of "no comment". The initial effect of setting up a judicial enquiry would be to stifle all mention of the allegations against Doherty, the tapping and anything else it was feared might be revealed.

On Monday, December 20th, McLaughlin was asked formally by Noonan if he knew that Geraldine Kennedy's telephone was being tapped. He said he didn't.

On Tuesday, Haughey and most of the members of the old cabinet dined together at Johnny Oppermann's restaurant in Malahide, County Dublin. It was a social event, both pre-Christmas and post election, and the conversation was, for the most part, light. Doherty arrived late. When the dinner ended at around midnight, he and Haughey left together.

They went to Haughey's home in Kinsealy and, for up to two hours, they discussed in detail the telephone tapping and how they should respond to any further revelations. Weeks later, Haughey would claim publicly that this conversation was very brief and that it took place as they were walking out of a social gathering. It would also be claimed that Doherty simply replied to Haughey's query by telling him not to worry. The truth was that both men discussed the tapping in detail and their failure to state this later was part of an elaborate effort to minimise the political damage caused to Haughey by the revelations.

In the few days left before Christmas, Noonan concentrated on studying the evidence to hand in the Department of Justice. There were copies of both warrants, both applications from the gardaí for the warrants, the application for a renewal of the tap on Geraldine Kennedy's telephone and notes of Jim Kirby's reservations about both taps and his recommendation in both cases that the warrants should not be granted.

The investigation in the Department was relatively short and simple. The relevant documentation was on file. It was obvious that an investigation would have to be carried out in the gardaí but who could investigate the Commissioner and his newly-appointed deputy? The question was on Noonan's mind two days before Christmas when he attended his first passing-out ceremony at the Garda Training Centre, in Templemore, County Tipperary.

He arrived at the centre and was greeted by McLaughlin. They shook hands and chatted. Noonan inspected the 66 new gardaí and made one of the most innocuous speeches of his career. His brief address to the new gardaí, their families and friends was laden with clichés and platitudes but it was written exactly as Noonan had ordered in the Department. He wanted to say absolutely nothing that could in any way upset the investigation and his expected confrontation with McLaughlin. At lunch, he was in the awkward position of sitting beside McLaughlin. Noonan engaged in small talk and later went home to Limerick to ponder over Christmas how he could have the Commissioner and his new deputy investigated.

The best person to carry out the investigation in the Garda Siochána was the Senior Deputy Commissioner, Larry Wren. He was the obvious choice for a number of reasons. Firstly, there was his rank; secondly, he had a long career of practical experience as a policeman deeply involved in major investigations and was once head of C3, the forerunner of the ISB. His brief as Deputy Commissioner was crime and there was no suggestion that Wren had been involved in any of the matters which needed investigating.

After Christmas, Noonan spoke again to McLaughlin about the tapping. He said there would have to be an investigation inside the gardaí. Noonan suggested that Wren carry out the investigation but McLaughlin resisted. He said there would be a personality clash between Wren and Ainsworth. But Noonan pressed his case and eventually McLaughlin agreed. Wren began his enquiries in earnest in the first week of January, the first real opportunity after the Christmas and New Year holidays.

Wren reported to Noonan and Noonan in turn dealt with the cabinet sub-committee on security, made up of the Taoiseach, the Tanaiste, the Minister for Foreign Affairs, the Defence Minister, the Attorney General and himself. As the investigation progressed and Noonan had to take decisions, he cleared them with the committee and reported what progress was being made. Within the Department, Noonan relied upon Ward and Kirby for guidance and advice. Inside the gardaí, Wren was on his own.

It was evident even before Wren began his investigation that McLaughlin's continued position as Commissioner was in serious doubt. His admission to Noonan before Christmas that he did not know Geraldine Kennedy's telephone was being tapped indicated that he had not exercised proper control over the force. He could not evade his responsibility by pleading that the person named in the documentation presented to him was not Kennedy. In the case of Bruce Arnold, he willingly collaborated in the tapping simply because his head of security said the target was "anti-national".

Wren concentrated his investigation on a number of key people in the ISB — the listeners, transcribers, some of Ainsworth's senior colleagues (Stephen Fanning made a lengthy statement) and Ainsworth himself. Ainsworth wrote his own statement and gave it to Wren. It was passed in turn to Noonan. The statement was a rambling attempt to justify the tapping. Ainsworth mentioned his conversations in April with Doherty. He referred to Doherty's professed concern about leaks, his interest in Arnold and Kennedy and his request that they be tapped.

Noonan, Ward and Kirby studied the statement. They drew up about fifteen supplementary questions and fired them back at Ainsworth via Wren. The replies indicated that Ainsworth simply didn't understand the issues. He appeared not to see the significance of Doherty initiating the taps and he appeared not to understand that the use of taps in these particular circumstances was in fact an abuse. Noonan, Ward and Kirby decided that the transcripts of the taps would have to be read by them to see if, by some remote chance, there was anything in them which could justify the tapping.

Noonan went back to the security committee to discuss whether or not the transcripts should be read. Peter Sutherland, the Attorney General, advised that technically, anyone reading the transcript would become tappers by proxy: they would be committing the same invasion of privacy as had been committed by the tappers themselves. The solution was to have Arnold and Kennedy sign a release allowing the transcripts to be read.

Arnold and Kennedy were asked to come to Sutherland's office in Government Buildings to discuss the problem. Both signed agreements giving permission to the government to read the transcripts as part of the official enquiry. When Sutherland told Noonan that they had the go-ahead from Arnold and Kennedy, he asked Ward to write to McLaughlin for copies of the transcripts. McLaughlin responded immediately and copies were dispatched to the Department from garda headquarters.

The transcripts were in the special ISB pink folders favoured by Ainsworth. The word **SECRET** was stamped all over them. Noonan gave the copies to Ward, Kirby and FitzGerald. FitzGerald had to read them to be in a position to back up Noonan if and when there was a public controversy over the whole affair. They all agreed that the transcripts contained nothing that could be of use to the gardaí investigating serious crimes or subversion. They indicated an interest in party political matters of concern to Fianna Fáil.

Wren decided to investigate some of the other matters which had given rise to public disquiet including the Pat O'Connor incident, the Tully transfer controversy and the Dowra affair. McLaughlin was asked for information about

Dowra and procrastinated. He possessed the file and released information from it with great reluctance. Requests for the file resulted in a few sheets of paper contained in it being handed over. Further requests elicited more sheets of paper until eventually the entire file was extracted piecemeal. Papers were found in garda headquarters which indicated that McLaughlin was better informed about the Tully affair than he had previously indicated. There was also the lengthy correspondence between McLaughlin and the DDP, Eamonn Barnes, detailing the row between them over Billy Byrne's handling of the O'Connor double voting allegations. It was clear that if Noonan wanted reasons to question McLaughlin's stewardship of the gardaí, he had them.

Towards the end of the second week in January, Noonan decided he had enough information to write a report for the cabinet. The report had to explain what happened and how the guarantees given in the Dáil by previous Justice Ministers had broken down, and it had to examine the problem of public confirmation. If the government made a statement, should it be done in the Dáil chamber or through the media? And what was to be done with McLaughlin and Ainsworth?

Noonan was writing his report when rumours came from the gardaí about ISB equipment being used to bug a conversation between politicians. Somebody involved had confided in someone else and a rumour had started. Noonan asked Wren to investigate. Wren traced the rumour back until he found a person who had first hand knowledge of the bugging. A statement was made confirming the essence of the rumour. The statement was signed and Wren witnessed it. There was no proof however. The identity of just one of the two politicians involved was known, Martin O'Donoghue.

On Tuesday, January 18th, Wren decided that Ainsworth had to be confronted about the bugging. He asked him about it that evening at a meeting attended by Stephen Fanning. At first Ainsworth denied any knowledge of the incident. Wren used the sparse amount of information he had: he told Ainsworth he knew that such a conversation had been transcribed in ISB and that Ainsworth was given a copy of the transcript. Ainsworth then admitted his involvement.

At 7 p.m. Wren telephoned Ward and said that Ainsworth wanted to see Noonan. The meeting was arranged immediately and Ainsworth and McLaughlin went to Noonan's office in the Department of Justice. Wren accompanied them and armed himself with a pistol. They entered the room and Noonan was told that Ainsworth had something to tell him.

Ainsworth described what had happened, how Doherty had asked him to get a tape recorder and a specially sensitive microphone for MacSharry and how he later had the tape transcribed. He produced a tape recorder and showed Noonan exactly how it worked. Noonan asked what the conversation recorded by MacSharry had been about. Ainsworth handed Noonan a pink folder: Noonan could read the conversation for himself, he said. Noonan looked at the transcript in complete amazement. It was conclusive evidence of what just a day or two previously had been a rumour.

The meeting went on for several hours. Noonan and Ainsworth talked about the bugging. Ainsworth regarded the whole affair as a simple thing, an innocent request with which he had been pleased to assist. Noonan asked Ainsworth to write down all he had said. Ainsworth sat at the conference table in Noonan's office and tea was brought in. When Ainsworth finished, he left with McLaughlin and Wren.

Noonan called in Ward, Kirby and Liam Breathnach, the official who sat on the Garda Síochána review body when it had decided to overturn McLaughlin's order to transfer Tully. They discussed the latest development; their investigations were over. The telephone tapping and the bugging had been unravelled, the conclusive evidence in both instances having come from Ainsworth. Noonan told them he would have to rush over to Government Buildings where a cabinet meeting had been taking place all day. While Noonan had been interrogating the gardaí his cabinet colleagues had been grappling with the problems of framing the budget.

For most of the day, reporters had been told to expect a statement on the telephone tapping. They were waiting in Government Buildings when a short, strange but sensational statement was released at around 2 a.m. on Wednesday, January 19th. It said that a "miniature tape recorder, not involving telephone tapping, had been sought from a garda source and subsequently returned together with a tape of a political conversation which was transcribed using garda facilities". The statement promised that the government would make a further statement on the telephone tapping within two days.

This led to intense speculation throughout Wednesday. Fianna Fáil politicians accused the government of trying to distract attention from the economic problems facing the country, but in reality the government was being extra careful in case its next move landed it in the High Court.

Only two garda commissioners had ever been sacked by an Irish government. The first was General Eoin O'Duffy, who was dismissed by a Fianna Fáil government in 1933 and later went on to become leader of the Blueshirts, Ireland's contribution to the fascist movement which afflicted most European countries at that time. The second was Edmund Garvey who was summarily sacked by the Fianna Fáil government in 1978 and later went on to sue the government successfully in the High Court and Supreme Court.

One afternoon in January 1978, Garvey had been called into the office of the then Justice Minister, Gerry Collins. Garvey was a tough commissioner who demanded high standards of discipline from the gardaí. Some gardaí maintained his demands were unreasonable and there was considerable tension between Garvey and the garda representative bodies. Collins told Garvey he wanted his resignation but he wouldn't give any reason. Garvey refused and the government sacked him later that night. In the following days the government stuck to its refusal to say why Garvey had been sacked. Garvey sued, claiming that his treatment was contrary to natural justice. He won in the High Court, and the Supreme Court upheld his victory when the government challenged it. Garvey's legal team had included Peter Sutherland and FitzGerald's government knew what mistakes to avoid with McLaughlin and Ainsworth.

In the Garvey case the Supreme Court said the government was wrong not to provide him with an adequate opportunity of dealing with the reasons, which had to be given, for his dismissal. A garda commissioner could be sacked but he had to be told why and allowed an opportunity to reply or show that the accusations against him were untrue.

Throughout Wednesday morning and afternoon, January 19th, Noonan prepared statements on the telephone tapping and bugging with the help of officials in his department. The government was going to sack the two commissioners if they did not resign. It was certainly going to publish the findings of Noonan and Wren's investigations no matter what happened.

Between 7 p.m. and 9.30 p.m. that night, Noonan confronted McLaughlin in his office in the Department of Justice. Noonan went through a litany of criticisms over his handling of the Garda Síochána. He said that he would find it very difficult, if not impossible, to defend certain of McLaughlin's actions were they to become public. The criticisms included the investigation of the Pat O'Connor incident, the Tully transfer order, the Dowra affair, his relationship with Ainsworth and his apparent lack of control over him. McLaughlin was given time to think about his future.

Fifteen minutes after McLaughlin left, Noonan confronted Ainsworth until 12.30 a.m. He went through the same process, asking him to account for his actions. There was the telephone tapping, the bugging, the Dowra affair which had concerned his section, ISB, and his relationship with Doherty. Ainsworth offered his resignation there and then but Noonan said he should think about it overnight and talk to his wife and family. Ainsworth walked out of the Department of Justice that night a shattered man.

Before noon on Thursday, January 20th, Noonan received a short resignation letter from Ainsworth. After lunch McLaughlin's letter arrived. He too was resigning and in a separate letter delivered at the same time he offered some explanation. It did not affect his fate, however.

That night Noonan issued three statements at a press conference in Government Buildings. The first said that McLaughlin and Ainsworth would retire from their positions from February 1st, the second gave details of the bugging and the third confirmed that the previous government had been tapping the private telephones of two journalists. Several pages of further information were left out because of the retirements.

The disclosures threw Fianna Fáil into its most serious crisis for at least a decade.

Chapter Seventeen

The Fianna Fáil front bench express their deep regret that the irresponsible activities of the present government in the area of security have caused the resignation of Commissioner Patrick McLaughlin and Deputy Commissioner Joseph Ainsworth.

Fianna Fáil statement, January 1983

Charles Haughey was hanging on to the leadership of Fianna Fáil by a thread. Although he was not the sole focal point of attention, he knew that he was in serious trouble. He had admitted that it would be an abuse for a Justice Minister to initiate telephone taps: the government had revealed that Sean Doherty had done just that to two journalists. Haughey had accepted that he, as head of government, bore responsibility for the actions of his ministers. And those actions included the abuse of the State's security system and the bugging by one of his closest political allies of one of his party colleagues. The two separate cases illustrated graphically the mood that had prevailed within his embattled government.

Fianna Fáil's immediate response was to accuse the government of irresponsibility, causing the resignation of two dedicated and loyal garda officers and raising implications for the security of the State. The party's front bench declared that it was a matter of urgent public importance that a judicial enquiry be established into security surveillance and interference with the gardaí.

Behind the scenes there was intense activity. Ray MacSharry was in Sligo when he discovered from the government announcement that his cabinet colleague, Seán Doherty, had kept an extra copy of the transcript of his bugged conversation with

Martin O'Donoghue. Two days later MacSharry phoned Doherty at home and asked him if the report was true: Doherty admitted he had a copy. MacSharry demanded that Doherty return it to him. Doherty drove to Sligo from Cootehall and returned it.

As the disclosures unfolded on television on Thursday night, they were watched by a sombre gathering in Haughey's house in Kinsealy. Among those present were Doherty, Brian Lenihan, Ray Burke, Brendan Daly, Michael Woods and Padraig Flynn. Most of them, including Haughey, were taken aback by the extent of the new government's revelations, particularly by the wealth of detail released.

Haughey dispatched Woods and Flynn to the RTE television studios in Montrose to appear for Fianna Fáil on the "Today Tonight" programme. They had a thankless task trying to defend the actions of their administration. Back at Kinsealy, there was some discussion about how the damage might be contained. Haughey never asked Doherty, either then or later, about the telephone taps when other people were present. After some low-key discussions, the meeting broke up.

Afterwards, it was clear that Doherty would resign his position from the party's front bench. MacSharry also resigned his front bench position later in the day. Both men defended themselves in public statements; neither admitted that anything they had done was wrong. Their resignations were explained on the grounds that they wanted to be free to defend themselves.

Doherty maintained that the taps on the journalists' telephones resulted from discussions between him and the garda security chiefs because national security had been endangered through leaks of highly confidential government papers and memoranda. The taps had been properly initiated and followed the practices of other Justice Ministers. "My actions were motivated solely by my concern for the security of my country and were not at any stage discussed by the government or with the Taoiseach", he said.

Haughey, in a press conference for political correspondents, remained loyal to his colleagues. He was not going to censure them because they had suffered a great deal in the media and elsewhere. But he made it clear that he was not going to follow their example by resigning: "I propose to lead the party in opposition and back to government". He accepted that MacSharry had thought honestly that he should record the conversation but added that he himself would never record a conversation with an individual without their knowledge.

On the telephone taps, he suggested that he had been wrong when he had thought that ministers never initiated taps: Doherty had told him that was not true. He was not aware of the taps and had not seen transcripts of either of the telephone taps or the bugged conversation. He now believed, from what Doherty had told him, that jounalists had been tapped in the past but he had not known that when he had commented on it during the general election campaign.

He added that he had been extremely concerned about "leaks" from cabinet meetings and some disturbing incidents where government papers and memoranda made their way into the hands of the media. He had initiated an enquiry by senior civil servants into the arrangements for confidentiality. And he had asked his colleagues to be more careful. But, he said, he had initiated no other security processes.

Haughey made no mention of the talk he had had with Joe Ainsworth shortly after he assumed power in which he had raised the question of alleged leaks. He had told Ainsworth of his concern about "leaks" from the cabinet and from the public service in general. He did not specify any particular "leaks"; it was generally not his style to tell gardaí what to do, merely to mention problems. In his discussions with Ainsworth in April 1982, Sean Doherty gave explicit instructions to the gardaí to tap the telephones of Bruce Arnold and Geraldine Kennedy. The taps were required because of "leaks", said Doherty. Haughey also failed to mention his October 1982 meeting in Kinsealy when he had specifically requested three garda commissioners to investigate a "leak".

Haughey cancelled a six-months tour of constituencies planned to raise party morale after the election, and announced that he had brought forward the next meeting of the parliamentary party to the following Sunday, January 23rd. He also announced that he had set up a committee within the parliamentary party to enquire into both the telephone tapping and the bugging. It was headed by the chairman of the parliamentary party, Jim Tunney, and had three other members:

Bertie Ahern, the chief whip, Michael O'Kennedy, the former EEC Commissioner and David Andrews, the Dun Laoghaire deputy who was one of the 22 members of the old parliamentary party who had voted against Haughey the previous October.

The formation of the committee, however, was given little attention at the time. Most of the newspaper interest, for instance, was in the bugged conversation. Little was known publicly of the contents and the context in which it had taken place.

Ray MacSharry came to Dublin on Friday, January 21st, to talk to Haughey, meet O'Donoghue, issue a public statement and hold a press conference. MacSharry justified the bugging on the grounds that, in the words of his statement: "there were serious suggestions about financial arrangements which might be entered into, which I felt would affect my character and integrity". Asked at the press conference if these "serious suggestions" were something to do with his allegiance to Haughey, he replied: "not at all, it is not a matter relating to the party or the leadership".

At their private meeting earlier, MacSharry and O'Donoghue had agreed that neither would publish the transcript of the conversation. MacSharry had a copy of the transcript and the original tape which had turned up in his wife's jewellery box in their home. O'Donoghue did not have a copy and, indeed, had not read a transcript which had been shown to him by Larry Wren on the day that the government released its statements.

O'Donoghue arrived back in Dublin the night before the disclosures from the gruelling circuit followed by candidates for the Senate in their search for the votes of county and city councillors. He was due to leave the capital again on Thursday, January 20th, the day of the disclosures. That morning Wren called to his house and asked him to identify the transcript, which carried no names. O'Donoghue was tired and out of touch with day-to-day political events in Dublin. He was aware of the government statement earlier in the week that a garda tape recorder had been used to bug a political conversation. Neither he nor anyone else outside the government and the top echelons of the gardaí knew at that stage that MacSharry had been the instigator.

O'Donoghue identified the transcript as being that of a conversation between himself and MacSharry. But he did no more than glance at it: it did not occur to him that the contents of the transcript were about to become a major political issue. He went off that evening to a function in his former Dáil constituency of Dun Laoghaire and was in the RTE studios that night when he heard the government revelation about the bugging. He went on television to say he was "very angry" that the conversation had been recorded. The conversation was about internal party political matters, he said.

Contrary to O'Donoghue's expectation that the onus was on MacSharry to explain his action, subsequent developments forced O'Donoghue onto the defensive. The day after their meeting, Saturday, January 22nd, Haughey was attending a meeting of the party's directors of elections during the November general election. The meeting had been arranged as the launching pad for his post-election tour of the country but it had been too late to cancel it when the scandal broke.

Inevitably, scores of journalists turned up to see if Haughey or Doherty would be available to say anything about the scandal. The party's press officers were there as well. In the atmosphere of rumour, innuendo and tension that prevailed, it was said that Doherty was to issue a statement later in the day. This was to reveal that taps had been put on the telephones of journalists by a coalition government and on the Workers' Party, and that the coalition government in the mid 1970s had tapped telephones at the British embassy in Dublin; and it was to explain the background to the bugging. That was expected to include a reference to the £100,000 being offered to MacSharry to withdraw his support for Haughey.

The fact that a statement was expected, and the likely issues it would cover, was reported by RTE radio from lunchtime on. At the Burlington Hotel in Dublin where the directors of elections were meeting the Fianna Fáil press officer, Tony Fitzpatrick, told reporters that a room had been set aside for a press conference. As the day wore on, Fitzpatrick announced that Doherty would not attend but would issue a statement. Later, he said that Doherty had left for Roscommon and that they wanted to contact him to check details of a draft statement. By 6 p.m., another press officer, Ken Ryan, said that there was unlikely to be a statement until 9 p.m. because of problems with the Official Secrets Act and possible libel. Doherty wanted someone else to give a second opinion, he said.

A statement was never issued. The next day, Doherty denied that he had prepared a statement with any of that kind of material or information. Fitzpatrick said Doherty had never intended to make a statement on telephone tapping but that Doherty had told him he was considering a statement about events leading up to the bugging. The episode over the statement, however, was to have an effect on subsequent events.

Martin O'Donoghue heard the radio reports and was getting calls from journalists all afternoon asking about the £100,000 that was said to be available to bribe politicians. His main concern was still the Senate campaign: voting was due to take place at the beginning of the following week and he had a number of eastern countries left to cover. The previous day, after his meeting with MacSharry, he had gone off to meet councillors in County Louth. On Saturday, he was due to travel again and he was panicked into going live on radio to refute the reports in circulation.

He went into a fifteen-minute programme called "Any Other Business" which rarely dealt with highly contentious issues. But its presenter, John Bowman, was well used to dealing with political controversies. He began by replaying a segment of an earlier programme on RTE in which MacSharry denied that, in bugging the conversation, he was trying to trap O'Donoghue into making compromising statements.

O'Donoghue told Bowman that the bugged conversation was private and confidential. He added that he had accepted the explanation given by MacSharry for recording it although he was unhappy about the format of MacSharry's explanation. But, he went on in reference to the day's rumours, he had not offered MacSharry a six-figure sum to change his vote or anything. He had gone into the meeting with MacSharry to find out, among other things, if he had financial problems. He had heard rumours, he said.

And, O'Donoghue said, he was suggesting to MacSharry that they would see what could be done if he had been compromised in any way. In what way? Bowman asked. "If part of the financial problems of the party also included some personal financial problems, then that would be part of the, if you like, general problem to be dealt with", said O'Donoghue.

Bowman asked if that meant that money given to the party could be diverted to help individuals with financial problems. O'Donoghue made a distinction between money given to the party and the sums available to help individuals. There were precise sums, a precise manner of payment and so on. "That was what had been conveyed to me", he said. "I'm not going to disclose sources. I see it as perfectly reasonable". He continued: "I think there's a very important democratic distinction between setting out in the first instance to bribe people or intimidate them and, on the other hand, setting out — as I understood I was setting out — to see if that had happened and, if so, what we could do to overcome it and get rid of it out of the party. I see there's a very important political difference and, indeed, moral difference between the two. So I have absolutely no apology to make to anyone for behaving in the manner I did".

It was an ethical minefield, Bowman remarked. O'Donoghue agreed. The conversation then drifted into complaints by O'Donoghue about Doherty's apparent intention of becoming involved. There was no reason why party members should see the transcript. It was the business of no-one else but MacSharry and himself. "He gave an explanation", said O'Donoghue. "I accepted".

The interview added a whole new dimension to the controversy. O'Donoghue was admitting that there was money available to negate the effects of bribes, that this was what had been conveyed to him by people he refused to name. That implied that there were other people involved, people who were not alone prepared to give money to the party if it changed later but who would provide money to party members to help them do so.

The next morning, the former cabinet met at Fianna Fáil headquarters in Mount Street in Dublin to prepare for the crucial parliamentary party meeting in the afternoon. The consensus opinion was that the party leadership should keep back from the debate and watch how it developed. They agreed, however, that Martin O'Donoghue could come to the meeting.

The group broke off its discussion in time to listen, in party headquarters, to the RTE radio programme, "This Week". It featured a lengthy interview with Doherty and shorter interviews with O'Donoghue and MacSharry. Doherty revealed that the home and office telephones of Vincent Browne, the editor of *Magill* magazine, had been tapped by his predecessor and that he had continued the surveillance. O'Donoghue declared bluntly: "I did not offer Mr MacSharry a bribe". MacSharry said that his actions had been totally vindicated by O'Donoghue's admission that he had had conversations with others about money being available to change the leader. "Obviously they were considering financial compromise for some individuals including myself", he added.

In the *Sunday Press* that morning, the paper's new political correspondent, Geraldine Kennedy, revealed that Charles Haughey had attempted personally to find out her Fianna Fáil sources in a conversation with the proprietor of the *Sunday Tribune,* Hugh McLaughlin. McLaughlin subsequently asked the paper's editor, Conor Brady, who her sources were. Brady told him that such information was confidential and made it clear that he would not help him. McLaughlin later asked a switchboard operator in the newspaper office to log the names of people who called Kennedy, she revealed.

Charles Haughey opened the meeting with a review of developments and repeated the announcement about the party's internal committee of enquiry. There was some discussion about inviting Martin O'Donoghue, no longer a member of the parliamentary party, to the meeting. Most people favoured his attendance; several, including George Colley, argued that "outsiders" could be asked to comment later but should not attend the parliamentary party meeting. It was agreed to invite O'Donoghue: Bertie Ahern phoned him at home and asked him to come into Leinster House.

The meeting got underway, with Doherty under attack. Time and again he was asked questions about the phone taps and about the previous day's reports that he was to reveal all sorts of other security actions. Deputies developed a pattern of asking Doherty questions and, after he had replied, of commenting on the scandal. Haughey was forced to agree that he disapproved of disclosures like Doherty's on radio. He was questioned about the telephone taps and denied any knowledge of them. When he was asked about Kennedy's report in the *Sunday Press*, he asked rhetorically whether members believed the media or the leader of the party.

Doherty walked out of the meeting at one stage, in response to the constant pressure. He declared that he had to protect himself and mentioned seeking legal advice. At the time he was being criticised primarily for the previous day's reports or, as deputies called it, the "media cock-up". He returned shortly afterwards.

As the meeting dragged on into the evening, attention finally turned to the bugging incident. O'Donoghue spoke first, outlining the bones of the conversation as he remembered it. MacSharry followed him and turned what O'Donoghue had anticipated would be a defensive explanation into an attack on O'Donoghue.

Party members had been listening to the increasingly complicated exchanges in public between O'Donoghue and MacSharry during the previous two days. As far as most of them were concerned, the debate between the two men was taking place in a vacuum: very few people knew what was actually on the transcript. MacSharry now made a highly effective speech. He talked about his reputation, his family, the sensitivity of the posts he had occupied in government and in the party. He emphasised his concern when he heard that O'Donoghue was mentioning him to other people in the context of money. And he insisted that O'Donoghue had now confirmed that there were people available to compromise party members.

O'Donoghue, already tired and now taken aback by the effectiveness of MacSharry's statement, was becoming more and more confused about what was in the transcript. MacSharry had shown him the paragraph relevant to his case when they met the previous Friday; otherwise, he had no clear memory of the detail of the conversation three months earlier. In effect, the argument hinged on one sentence in the transcript where O'Donoghue was recorded as explaining: "What was being said was, if there was any suggestion of somebody being compromised financially, that it would be sorted out".

O'Donoghue maintained that the comment meant that there would be money available to help anybody who had been compromised and to free them of their problem, to counter the effects of the bribe. MacSharry maintained that O'Donoghue was simply telling him that a bribe was available for him. O'Donoghue accepted at the meeting that MacSharry had put that interpretation on the remark. In his efforts to explain his position, he agreed with MacSharry that it might have looked that way to him. But he denied that that was what he meant.

At one stage when a "six-figure sum" was mentioned during the meeting, O'Donoghue interjected that the amount involved was not that much. It was about half that, he said. O'Donoghue's friends within the party were appalled at the way he appeared to be incriminating himself. Deputies who had had open minds about the rights and wrongs of the bugging were coming to accept MacSharry's version of events and, more importantly, that his action might have been justified.

MacSharry's performance went a very long way towards clearing his name among his colleagues. Politically, he set the scene for Charles Haughey and his supporters to fight back. The fight began almost immediately. Haughey supporters expressed outrage at a party member and former cabinet minister involving himself as an "honest broker" between people with money who wanted to change the leadership and the views of Fianna Fáil deputies. They repudiated any suggestion that the party's policy and leader could be changed by anonymous outsiders. And they demanded to know who these people were?

The meeting ended with neither issue resolved and agreement that the Tunney committee investigate both and report back at the earliest possible date. O'Donoghue finally decided next day to seek a copy of the transcript. He asked the Justice Minister, Michael Noonan, if he could have a copy. Noonan agreed and promised to supervise personally the making of a copy from the Department's files. O'Donoghue received the copy and took it to a solicitor on Monday, January 24th and considered what action he should take.

He issued a cautious statement that evening and tried to explain his position and retrieve the ground he had already conceded to MacSharry. He read it out on "Today Tonight", but was once again in murky waters when he was questioned about the transcript. Afterwards, he met Des O'Malley, Seamus Brennan and Mary Harney. He let them read the transcript and they urged him to release it to the newspapers. He said he could not do that because of legal advice he had received about ownership of the document.

The issue was beginning to crystallise around Charles Haughey, and whether or not he should continue as leader. Most Fianna Fáil deputies believed Haughey when he said he had not initiated the telephone taps. But a significant number of them did not believe it was likely that he had known nothing about the taps until the government statement. Parliamentary party members had a convenient opportunity to test local opinion within Fianna Fáil about the affair during the first two days of the next week. Voting was taking place over those two days for the Senate elections, an event which invariably brought deputies and local councillors together. The message appeared to be that Haughey must go: many deputies returned to Dublin for the opening of the new Dáil session on Wednesday the 26th with that message.

In the Dáil, just resumed after its Christmas break, Fianna Fáil's front bench was in chaos. During question time, Brian Lenihan tried to harass the new government over the collective responsibility of the cabinet for statements and actions taken by individual ministers. Haughey was badly wrong-footed when he tried to criticise Garret FitzGerald for making appointments to his Department from outside the civil service. Haughey maintained he had never done that but he had to sink back into his seat when FitzGerald read out a list of non-civil servants Haughey had appointed less than a year earlier.

It appeared that such incidents were more straws in the wind. In among the rumours and speculation that enveloped Leinster House, several TDs went to Haughey to tell him they believed he must resign. None of them were numbered among the dissidents who had voted no confidence in the leader the previous October. It appeared that the middle ground which had stayed loyal to Haughey in 1982 was changing its mind.

Even Haughey's supporters were coming to believe that he was about to resign. Several were saying as much: one, with tears in his eyes, told a reporter that Haughey was actually drafting his resignation speech. The news went out on RTE and reverberated among politicians. Some of Haughey's most determined supporters were so convinced that he was on the point of going that they went to Neil Blaney to see if he could dissuade him.

Blaney did not want to compound Haughey's problems by being seen going to his office in Leinster House. He told the deputies who came to him to go back and argue with Haughey again. Some two hours later, shortly after midnight, Blaney talked personally to Haughey by telephone. Blaney told him he had a responsibility to Fianna Fáil and the country to stay. If he resigned without a clear successor to take over, Fianna Fáil would split into a number of factions. Haughey assured Blaney that he had no intention of resigning.

The next morning, Thursday, January 27th, the *Irish Press* published a two-page political "obituary" of Haughey. Most of the material had been already prepared in line with the practice of newspapers of keeping biographies of prominent people ready for publication. Other material had been put together the previous night as the rumours of Haughey's impending resignation multiplied. As the night wore on, the rumours became more insistent. While the first edition of the *Irish Press* was being printed an unusual editorial conference was called to decide whether or not to run the "obituary". All the indications pointed to Haughey's resignation and the latest information suggested that the Fianna Fáil leader would announce his retirement before 4 a.m.

The main argument in favour of publishing was the fact that the paper would have stolen a march on its rivals if Haughey resigned. It would be embarrassing, of course, if he did not. But it seemed to be worth the gamble. After a lengthy discussion and talks with the printers to make sure it could be done, the editor, Tim Pat Coogan, decided that it should go into the paper's city edition.

Haughey arrived for a party meeting in Leinster House that morning with some people convinced that he was going to declare his resignation: fewer believed he was going to fight off successfully any challenge that arose. Many were simply confused about his intentions. One of his closest supporters, P.J. Mara, asked him before the meeting what he was going to do. "The bottom line is that you are not going to resign. Right?" Mara asked. Haughey shrugged.

The meeting began with a discussion about Jim Tunney's announcement the previous day that he was resigning as head of the internal investigation and that the work of the committee was being suspended. Tunney said his decision was because of an article in the *Irish Independent* which described him as a supporter of Haughey and which he read as implying that he would not carry out an impartial enquiry. However, he was prevailed upon by the meeting to reconsider and to revive the enquiry.

Then the meeting turned to the leadership. Ben Briscoe, the 48-year-old deputy from Dublin South Central, recalled that Haughey had said a year earlier that he would resign the leadership if he felt that it was in the party's best interests. Briscoe maintained, regretfully, that that time had come. He went on to extol some of Haughey's merits, adding: "I love you, Charlie". Haughey replied: "I love you too, Ben". A voice at the back of the room groaned and commented: "I hope the papers don't hear about this". (They did, and the remarks were reported widely: Haughey's friends said that the leader's remark was heavily ironic, while some of his new opponents took it at face-value as an indication of his good humour and repartee).

Tunney, as chairman, said that the leadership could not be discussed without suspending standing orders. Ber Cowen and Liam Hyland, colleagues from Laois-Offaly, proposed and seconded the suspension. It was agreed immediately. Briscoe had nothing much more to say. Ray Burke, the former Environment Minister who had been seen as a Haughey supporter, made it clear that he had changed his mind. But he suggested that Haughey should be allowed to go in his own time, that he should not be pushed any further. The message was tempered only by repeated criticisms of the media for their saturation coverage of the party's deliberations and, in the case of the *Irish Press,* for its premature announcement that the Haughey era was over.

Haughey sat at the top table with handwritten notes in front of him. When he got up to speak and announced that the media would not hound him out of office, he promised he would discharge his duty and responsibility to Fianna Fáil and to the country in the way he thought was right. He would take, he said, his own decision in his own time. In the context of the discussion at the meeting, few deputies doubted that he intended to resign.

Haughey invited party members to go and see him throughout the day. That evening he presided over a meeting of the party's national executive, the same executive that had supported him with an overwhelming majority the previous October. The majority was now overwhelmingly in favour of his resignation. Numerous criticisms were voiced of the telephone tapping and the bugging and they all led to the same conclusion: Haughey should resign. The mood of the parliamentary party and of the Fianna Fáil organisation, as represented by the national executive, was as one.

When the executive meeting ended, Haughey wandered around the room, exchanging comments and shaking hands. Most of those present thought that he was saying goodbye to them. Few party members in the parliamentary party or in the executive thought he would still be leader when the árd fheis was held in Dublin at the end of February. It appeared that Haughey himself was about to cut the thread by which he retained the leadership.

Chapter Eighteen

You can't count moving heads.
Seamus Brennan, February, 1983

The race to succeed Charles Haughey was already on. Michael O'Kennedy was the first to throw his hat into the ring on Wednesday, January 26th, the day before the parliamentary party's meeting. His campaign to become leader, managed by his fellow Tipperary TD Sean McCarthy, was in full swing by the time the party meeting ended and most deputies believed Haughey's resignation was imminent.

Des O'Malley was clearly going to be a candidate even though he had not yet begun any kind of campaign. But some of his supporters were concerned enough to interrupt a dinner he was attending on Thursday evening, January 27th, to tell him to return to Leinster House. O'Kennedy was going full steam ahead and Haughey's resignation might come at any moment, they thought.

Gerry Collins joined in from his bed in the Mater Hospital in Dublin where he was convalescing after an operation a month earlier. In interviews with newspapers he projected himself as an agreed candidate to succeed Haughey. He said he did not want to get involved until the situation clarified itself but he was available to be leader if it would help unite the party. "I'm not looking for it but if it has to be done, it has to be done", he said.

A fourth candidate and another possible agreed nominee was John Wilson, the former Minister for Posts and Telegraphs and Transport and Power. He did not campaign but was waiting in the wings as a possible compromise to avoid another divisive leadership election.

But Haughey had not resigned yet. It was clear that he might have to go but equally clearly he did not want to give up what had been the ambition of his political life. After one bruising meeting, Haughey asked rhetorically of several of his friends: "How do I stop all this sewage coming out of the newspapers?" He added, also rhetorically: "Is there any God up there?".

His main card was that he was still leader of the party. It was now more than a week since the government had lifted the lid momentarily on the activities of its predecessor. The cabinet chosen by Haughey had tapped telephones for party political purposes and his Tánaiste had bugged a conversation with a colleague. Haughey, of course, still denied any knowledge of these actions. He was also trying to stave off the consequences of responsibility as head of government for the actions of his ministers.

Time was on his side, and he had succeeded in buying some time. Some of his friends like Liam Lawlor advised him to stay on, that events could be turned around to his advantage. As the crisis within Fianna Fáil headed into its second weekend, Haughey began to fight back.

Messages of support for Haughey began to trickle through after the first reactions of dismay at the surveillance scandals. Haughey and his friends threw themselves into a counter-attack. They decided that every caller to party headquarters who supported the leader was to be urged to telephone or call in person to their local TD and express their view that Haughey should remain. Telephone calls began to go out from Mount Street and Kinsealy to potential supporters trying to get meetings arranged and sympathetic motions passed by constituency organisations. Constituency activists were urged to call newspapers and announce their backing for the leader.

Haughey himself was active on the telephone as well. On Friday, January 28th, Haughey called several of the TDs who were perceived as occupying the "middle ground' in the party that was slipping away from him. He was getting a lot of messages of support from all over the country, Haughey said. They wanted him to stay.

Hints were emerging from the Haughey side that he would

continue as leader until the árd fheis. There was no longer any doubt about his intentions: he was not going to resign. Blaney talked to him again over the weekend, encouraging him to make a public statement to this effect. Haughey said nothing in public but Brian Lenihan went on radio to declare that Haughey would stay on. Those who opposed Haughey now knew that they had a fight on their hands. Some of them spoke about organising a petition but nothing was done at that stage.

If Haughey's intentions were clear, so were the weapons with which he was intending to fight. Some of the issues which had been overshadowed in the first week of the crisis now began to play an important part. The Tunney committee's enquiry was still underway and its report should be awaited before anything was done, Haughey supporters argued. That bought more time.

The Haughey camp focused its attention on Martin O'Donoghue and his admission that he had talked to people who were prepared to pay money to people to change the leadership of the party. The moral minefield of whether a bribe was still a bribe if it was intended to free someone from a bribe raised niceties that were trampled underfoot in the political battle now raging.

Lenihan led the attack on this issue. "The most serious issue is the attempt to corrupt people in public life", he said. "If there are funds available for this purpose it is a very serious moral as well as political issue". Lenihan added that he was "morally outraged", and astounded that the media had not turned their investigative talents to that issue.

Lenihan also featured in another prong of the campaign by declaring that he would be a candidate for the leadership if Haughey were to step down. MacSharry, among others, had worked out a strategy along the lines that Haughey's chances of survival were increased by the number of prospective candidates who put themselves forward. His supporters could then claim there would be a political bloodbath if there was an election for a new leader. Fianna Fáil would not be split two ways but anything up to half a dozen ways.

In pursuit of this line of argument, MacSharry deliberately encouraged the candidature of Wilson and Lenihan. Meanwhile, Haughey's counter attack had already paid dividends.

O'Kennedy, the first contender to declare his hand by his actions, now backed off very rapidly and very publicly. On the same radio programme as Lenihan, he said he had canvassed on the understanding that Haughey was resigning. When he found out he was wrong, he had explained to Haughey what had happened and assured him of his loyalty. "I would not be a party to undermining Mr. Haughey or any other leader", he explained.

The Haughey campaign was not proceeding smoothly, however. The Fianna Fáil press office distributed a list of deputies whom, it said, had pledged their support for the party leader and had urged him to continue in office. The fact that there were only twelve names on the list out of a parliamentary party of seventy-five was not very encouraging. It became even less helpful to Haughey when two of those named, Denis Lyons from Cork North Central and Michael J. Noonan from Limerick West, complained publicly that they had not authorised anyone to include their names on such a list.

By this stage, the entire Fianna Fáil organisation from the parliamentary party down to local branches was involved in the debate. It was partly a public relations battle, with columns of newspapers filled with the results of resolutions for and against Haughey passed by different units of the organisation. In several cases, such announcements sparked off conflicts within those parts of the organisation they were said to represent.

The secretary of the party branch in University College, Dublin complained at publicity that had been given to the fact that it supported Haughey. The branch had not decided anything, had not met at all and would not meet until after the parliamentary party decided the issue. Ógra Fianna Fáil, the party's youth organisation, announced its support for Haughey but was challenged subsequently by some members who accused Haughey supporters of stage-managing a meeting.

Still, the Haughey machine was working flat out to make maximum use of every ounce of support it could get. On the evening of Monday, January 31st, a rally was to be held outside the Mount Street offices in support of Haughey. It was organised by Liz Sheridan, a party activist from the Dublin Central constituency, whose name was distributed to callers by party officials at the headquarters. A "book of support" had been opened in the headquarters and those attending the rally were to sign it. There was vague talk as well of a mass rally to be held in the Phoenix Park at an unspecified date.

Such activities were already causing serious concern among members of the parliamentary party who had come to oppose Haughey. It appeared that he was willing to split the entire organisation in order to hold onto the leadership. Their concern was accentuated by the actual format of the Mount Street rally, the sentiments expressed and the atmosphere it evoked.

Several hundred people gathered outside the building, their numbers inflated considerably by party press officers giving exaggerated reports to journalists who were not at the scene. It was not a highly organised gathering. Placards attacked the media and extolled Haughey in quasi-religious terms. Some spoke of his "crown of thorns", another urged him to forgive his enemies who did not know what they were doing. A group chanted: "Charlie Haughey walks on water". Others sang: "He's got the whole world in his hands", a song that had come to be associated with Pope John Paul's visit to Ireland in 1979.

The only member of the parliamentary party to speak was Niall Andrews, the deputy from Dublin South. To persistent cheering, he announced that Fianna Fáil would not be bought by anyone outside the organisation but would be run by "you the people". He fuelled the belief among Haughey supporters that the parliamentary party was selling out the wider organisation. And he accused the media of "executing" Haughey, just as the leaders of the 1916 Rising had been executed.

Other events outside the party were also grist to the mill. Counting of votes in the Senate elections concluded the next day, Tuesday, February 1st, and the results were analysed for indications about the relative strength of Haughey's supporters and his opponents among the Fianna Fáil electorate. His opponents own the battle easily. Among those comfortably elected were Martin O'Donoghue and Eoin Ryan, the Senator who had opposed Haughey publicly as an electoral liability the previous October. Among those defeated was P.J. Mara, whom Haughey had nominated to the Senate during his period in government.

Meanwhile, the Tunney committee was continuing its enquiries. Altogether, the four-man group was to meet 28 times for a total of 80 hours, mostly in the office of one of its members, David Andrews, in the old College of Art building, sandwiched between the National Library and Leinster House. It met and questioned Ray MacSharry, Martin O'Donoghue, Sean Doherty, Albert Reynolds, Pádraig Flynn and the party's press officer, Tony Fitzpatrick, his assistant, Ken Ryan, and another assistant, Fionnuala O'Kelly. All the interviews were conducted in Andrews' office, except for the meeting with Haughey which was held in one of the party's main rooms in Leinster House. The committee had no power to call people outside the party and those who were questioned did not answer under oath.

The committee had decided initially to tape record all its proceedings. But the plan was abandoned shortly after work got under way because the tape recorder being used broke down. The members decided instead that they would all take notes of the accounts given to them by those involved. At the end of each day's sessions, they would compare notes.

Haughey, it was reported initially, would not give evidence at all. Tunney was said to have indicated that there was no reason why he should as there was no evidence that he had known anything about the telephone taps or the bugging. But it was decided eventually that he would. He was questioned by all the members of the committee, notably by Andrews.

Indeed, Andrews was in a difficult position on the committee. He had been identified for the previous year as an opponent of Haughey and had never made any secret of his views. He was one of the "Club of 22" dissidents in October and he had been named as a member of the committee deliberately as a gesture to the other side of the party and to increase the committee's acceptability to the party as a whole.

Once it became clear that the committee and its enquiry were part of Haughey's tactics in holding on to the leadership, Andrews was urged by his political friends to resign. They suggested that the committee's main purpose would be to exonerate Haughey of any responsibility for the scandals, particularly as it was restricted to members of the party and could not seek information from outsiders like gardaí or civil servants. Andrews, however, resisted the pressures.

On Tuesday, February 1st, one of the party's backbenchers, Clem Coughlan, was killed when his car collided with a truck on the main road from the west to Dublin, between the towns of Athlone and Moate. Coughlan, a 39-year-old deputy for Donegal South West, was on his way to the Dáil when the accident occurred. He was among the party members who had backed Haughey in 1982 but who had now changed their minds and believed that he should go.

His death brought to a halt the intense activity within the party and served to underline the pressures under which deputies were operating. It meant, as everyone recognised, that the party meeting scheduled for the next day would have to be postponed. Haughey had been given some more time, but his opponents were determined that the crisis should be brought to a head before the end of the week. Their determination was increased by Tunney's handling of the scheduled meeting.

When deputies gathered for the meeting on Wednesday, February 2nd, Haughey began with a tribute to Clem Coughlan. Tunney asked for a minute's silence and when it was over he walked quickly out of the room, declaring in Irish that the meeting was adjourned. Several people jumped to their feet, trying to raise other questions, demanding that he return. Tunney kept going. But people continued to talk after his departure. George Colley suggested that anyone who wanted the meeting reconvened that week should go to the whips' office and tell them. Someone else asked if Clem Coughlan's family needed any assistance.

Colley's proposal about going to the whips and asking for another meeting was turned into a firm decision to put together a signed petition calling for a meeting on Friday of that week. Pro-Haughey people tried to circulate a counter petition asking that a meeting be postponed until the Tunney committee had completed its work. It was withdrawn because of the lack of support it received.

The original petition, on the other hand, was gaining significant support. Five sheets of Dáil Éireann notepaper were prepared with a paragraph typed at the top: "We, the undersigned members, of the Fianna Fáil parliamentary party, hereby demand that a special meeting of the parliamentary party be held at 11.30 a.m. on Friday the 4th of February,

1983". Ben Briscoe, Ray Burke and Ber Cowan were among those who took it around Leinster House seeking signatures. In all, forty-one deputies and seven senators signed it.

Five members of Haughey's 1982 cabinet signed: Gerry Collins, John Wilson, Ray Burke and Des O'Malley. The fourth potential candidate to succeed Haughey, Michael O'Kennedy, also signed. Two people, Denis Lyons and Michael Ahern from Cork East, wrote in modifications, substituting the word "request" for the word "demand". Among the last to sign was Hugh Byrne, the Wexford deputy who had been prominent among Haughey's opponents the previous October.

With forty-one signatories and the evening wearing on, the organisers called a halt in order to get the petition submitted to the whips' office and the parliamentary party chairman. They were happy that they had a clear majority of the deputies behind their demand. Most of Haughey's opponents also believed that they now had a majority of the party behind their demand that he should resign. If some of those who signed the petition would not vote against Haughey in a contest, there were others who had not signed it for personal reasons who, they believed, would vote against Haughey. But Jim Tunney, the parliamentary party chairman, refused to accept the petition's demand.

As practically all of the parliamentary party travelled to Donegal next morning for the funeral of Clem Coughlan, there were hints of a full-scale split in Fianna Fáil. It was conceivable that the forty-one who had signed the petition would hold their own meeting on Friday and that the pro-Haughey faction would hold a separate meeting later. But most of Haughey's opponents were determined to avoid a split now that it appeared likely that they had a majority.

After the funeral, many deputies gathered in a local hotel. Others travelled back towards Dublin, stopping in hotels and restaurants en route. Wherever they gathered the conversation was about the one subject and in the hotel in Donegal copies were already circulating of a three page-statement from Haughey addressd to "all members of the Fianna Fáil organisation throughout the country". Haughey was throwing down the gauntlet in no uncertain terms.

It was his duty, he said, to stay and lead Fianna Fáil out of its present difficulties. Therefore he called on all members of the party to rally behind him as their democratically-elected leader and to give him total support. He needed that support, he explained, to restore unity in the party and to make it clear that those who caused dissent and did not accept decisions democratically arrived at could no longer remain in the party.

He defined the central issue which went to the heart of Fianna Fáil's existence: "Are its policies and its leader in future to be decided for it by the media, by alien influences, by political opponents or, worst of all, by business interests pursuing their own ends"? He concluded with a clear hint that he would take his cause to the árd fheis which, he said, would lay down standards of loyalty and behaviour and a code of discipline.

The statement shocked and outraged his opponents within the parliamentary party. Until now, all of Haughey's counter-attacks had been carried out behind the scenes, like the attempt to get supporters to put pressure on TDs. He could deny a personal involvement in dragging the entire organisation into something which had been the preserve of the parliamentary party alone. But he was now publicly appealing over the heads of the parliamentary party to the wider organisation with a statement addressed to all members.

He was hinting as well that he would not accept an adverse decision by the parliamentary party — that having been "democratically elected leader" on one occasion, the people who had elected him could not remove him by another democratic vote. The implication, supported explicitly by party spokesmen like Ken Ryan, was that as party rules did not say anything about the election of a leader, they did not give that right solely to the parliamentary party. If the parliamentary party voted him out the implication remained that he might refuse to go, and argue his case at the árd fheis at which he would still be the party president. Total mayhem within Fianna Fáil was the likely result.

The reaction was immediate. O'Malley described the statement as "incredible and amazing". It had serious implications for the party and for parliamentary democracy in general: he was concerned, he added, at the suggestions of extra-parliamentary activity implicit in the statement. The next morning, Ben Briscoe telephoned Jim Tunney and requested a meeting of the party. Tunney eventually conceded a meeting and announced it would be held on Monday, February 7th.

Meanwhile Briscoe went on radio on Friday, February 4th, to back up his complaint that Haughey's statement smacked of dictatorship. The majority of the parliamentary party could now be regarded as dissidents because they dissented from Haughey's continued leadership and from his attempt to undermine parliamentary democracy. He said his message to his fellow TDs was: "stand up and be counted, you are now defending democracy within the Fianna Fáil party". He added that "there's something rotten, something stinks" when one saw parliamentary party politics taking to the streets.

Later in the day, Briscoe decided to table a motion for the Monday meeting demanding that Haughey resign the leadership. He telephoned Colley in Leinster House to seek his advice on the wording of the motion. They rejected motions that "called" for his resignation in favour of a stronger and more explicit formula: "That the Fianna Fáil members of Dáil Éireann request the resignation of Mr. Charles J. Haughey as party leader now". Colley took the motion to the whips' office and gave it to Bertie Ahern. It was in Briscoe's name and Ahern later told him by phone that he had to come into Leinster House to sign it. For Haughey, two weeks after the government had revealed the tapping and bugging scandals, the die was cast.

The tensions and pressures within the parliamentary party were enormous by now. Three members of the party had collapsed and two had been taken to hospital during the previous two weeks suffering from the effects of strain and endless rounds of meetings and discussions. Several were reluctant to go home for the weekend in the expectation that they would face severe and probably conflicting pressures from local organisations.

In addition, several people were now getting garda protection. It had begun with Geraldine Kennedy, who was given round-the-clock protection by armed detectives immediately after the telephone taps were exposed. The decision to protect her was taken by the gardaí, probably in the light of her experiences the previous October. Now, as the crisis headed at last towards a climax, extra garda patrols were assigned to leading party figures like O'Malley and Colley and to the latest opponent to reach public prominence, Ben Briscoe. Nerves were set on edge by mysterious events such as the apparent breakdown of the telephones of several leading dissidents at precisely the same time.

In the heightened atmosphere that prevailed, comparisions with the rise of Adolf Hitler in Germany were on some people's minds. Public perceptions of the Hitler analogy were increased by the fact that the week· marked the fiftieth anniversary of Hitler's assumption of power, remembered in numerous television docmentaries and in one drama based on the experiences of a Jewish family. The fact that Briscoe, the parliamentary party's only Jewish member, had proposed the motion that Haughey should go was seen as somehow symbolic to those who opposed Haughey. It also had some significance for Haughey supporters: among the anti-semitic messages that Briscoe subsequently received were several comments along the lines of one telephone caller who declared that: "Hitler should have finished the job".

The parallels were also pointed up by Charles McCreevy in an interview with the *Sunday Press* on February 6th. McCreevy had kept very quiet throughout the latest crisis within the party. Before it broke, he had been under pressure because of motions tabled for the árd fheis demanding his expulsion. He and Haughey had had several discussions about the motions. McCreevy assured Haughey that he had done all he was going to do to remove the leadership from Haughey when he had tabled his motion the previous October.

McCreevy came back now with a vengeance. Fianna Fáil had been reduced in the eyes of the world to a "self-centred, advance-seeking cabal of opportunists" who had no interest at all in the Irish nation. Haughey was a "disgrace to the democratic tradition of Fianna Fáil and of the Irish nation". Haughey's statements during the week had been "totally fascist in content and tenor", McCreevy added. And, he went on: "In the light of what has come to be public knowledge in the last couple of months regarding telephone tapping, bugging and the subversion of the police force, the Irish people made a wise decision on November 24th last".

Charles Haughey went on RTE radio on Sunday, February 6th, to speak publicly about his future. He claimed to have the overwhelming support of the majority of the party and said that he was not contemplating defeat. He complained of a concerted and unprecedented campaign against him in the media. When asked why he thought that was so, he said that it was one of the great questions and issues in Irish public life. There must be some other motivation behind it than himself personally, he suggested.

He defused one of the principal issues that had been exercising his parliamentary colleagues by declaring that the leadership was a matter for the parliamentary party alone and that he would abide by its decisions. If defeated as leader, he would resign the party presidency as well. "I'm a democrat at all times and despite what has been said, I'm never anything else".

Behind the scenes the lobbying by both sides was intense. Haughey supporters were using every argument they could find, including threats that they would never vote for any other leader in the Dáil. His opponents were at a major disadvantage because of the divisions among them over the succession. The O'Malley camp had made an attempt to get a joint statement from the four contenders — O'Malley, O'Kennedy, Collins and Wilson — in response to Haughey's Thursday statement. Collins had agreed but on condition that he would do it only if all four did it; he was not prepared to issue a joint statement with O'Malley alone. O'Kennedy and Wilson could not be contacted: they did not respond to messages.

Meanwhile, the Tunney committee was coming to the end of its enquiry. It met during the weekend to draw up its report. Discussion was, at times, heated and involved. The committee had no real status; it could not demand "evidence" from party members, nor could it pursue the inconsistencies that had emerged over some of the issues. The limitations of the enquiry were spelt out in the preamble to the report.

"The committee of enquiry was bound by the most serious limitations in that it was confined solely to members of the parliamentary party and the party press office. It could not call for persons or papers outside the party and was of an unsworn kind. The legal advice sought by the committee, and which was available on request to any member, indicated that the members of the enquiry and the persons offering to give evidence before them were not covered by privilege (privilege in this context meaning no immunity from having to give evidence before a Judicial Tribunal, if subpoenaed). Our legal advice is that the parliamentary party has no protection in that regard either. Accordingly, any opinion or view expressed is based on submissions made individually", said the preamble.

"At the outset, the chairman requested that our eventual report should be such as to accommodate the views of all our members expressed collectively, if possible, but also by way of individual minority report or addendum if required".

The agreement that individual members could submit minority reports had a bearing on the eventual outcome of the enquiry when one of the members, David Andrews, made such a report. He dissented from the main findings of the section on the tapping of the telephones of Arnold and Kennedy. The section exonerated Haughey.

The minority report by Andrews was just two paragraphs long. The first said that when Doherty initiated the telephone tapping, he had been motivated by "internal party considerations, rather than by considerations of national security". Doherty claimed precisely the opposite.

The second paragraph condemned Haughey.

"On the basis of the information available to me, Mr Haughey while in office was not aware of the telephone tappings of the journalists. It seems to me, however, that on the principle of ultimate responsibility, he should have been so aware".

Haughey had conceded this point during an RTE radio interview on January 20th, the day the government made known the findings of its investigation. At that time Haughey said "any head of government must take responsibility for anything that happens during his administration . . ." but he consistently refused to accept the logical consequence of his own words.

The section of the report dealing with the bugging of the conversation between MacSharry and O'Donoghue began by stating that both had read the transcript of the bugged conversation and that the committee had read extracts.

"It was reaffirmed that during these discussions Martin O'Donoghue referred, inter alia, to his own concern and that of other undisclosed parties regarding C.J. Haughey's leadership of Fianna Fáil", said the report. It then referred to Haughey's proposed resignation and the immediate aftermath.

"In that event, sums of money would be available to cover any financial embarrassment to the party following the resignation of the Taoiseach. These substantial sums of money would also be available to the party generally and to individual members of the government who might have been financially compromised by membership of the government under C.J. Haughey.

"Dr. O'Donoghue made a distinction in his mind between this latter suggestion and a suggestion of money being available in the first instance to support a party leader. He (Dr. O'Donoghue) did not wish to identify the source of the financial resources; he did however exclude members of the parliamentary party from subscribers to the fund".

The report mentioned that Doherty had spoken to Pádraig Flynn about O'Donoghue wanting to meet MacSharry and that as a consequence of what was being said, MacSharry bugged the meeting.

"Ray MacSharry's action in taping his conversation with Martin O'Donoghue is contrary to the normally accepted standards of behaviour between colleagues. It must be recorded however, that Ray MacSharry found himself in an unenviable position.

"More serious, however, is the fact that any of the discussions or proposals in question should ever have been raised or pursued by Martin O'Donoghue albeit his 'honest broker' position in the affair.

"While Séan Doherty was unaware of the purpose for which the tape recorder was required it was imprudent of him to arrange for its provision by a garda officer; more serious, however, is the fact that the tape recorder was transcribed by the Garda Siochána when the understanding was that it would be done privately.

"Mr. MacSharry could be faulted for the fact that while to his surprise the recorder was delivered by a garda officer he did not ensure that the gardaí would have no further involvement. It is difficult in the absence of any specific evidence by Martin O'Donoghue or anybody else to give a conclusive opinion. It must be stated, however, that especially in respect of the availability of finances for any members of Fianna Fáil or the party conditional on political considerations, it is in our opinion a proposition which should never have been entertained by anybody and is most damaging to the Fianna Fáil party and to politicians in general".

The remaining section of the report dealt with the events in the Burlington Hotel on Saturday, January 22nd, when, according to people in the Fianna Fáil press office, Doherty was going to make a statement detailing the activities of the coalition government in the mid 1970s which allegedly included tapping the telephones of journalists, the Workers' Party and the British embassy in Dublin.

The committee chairman, Jim Tunney, referred to the affair as "the media cock-up' but he was prevailed upon to title the particular section of the report: "Press problems of 22nd January 1983".

The section described how Tony Fitzpatrick heard on the RTE 6.30 p.m. news that Doherty was going to make a statement that the telephone lines to the British embassy were tapped. It said that Fitzpatrick immediately called RTE to deny the report and that an RTE reporter with whom Fitzpatrick had earlier been speaking told him that he had given "the impression" that this was what Doherty was about to say. "Tony Fitzpatrick denied this assertion", said the Tunney report.

"In our opinion, any apparent press office shortcomings derives from the non-availability of adequate resources to cope, not alone with the anticipated activity but with emergency or contingency matters".

The report of the enquiry was finished.

Haughey, when Taoiseach, had not been aware of the telephone tapping.

Ray MacSharry had found himself in an "unenviable position".

Sean Doherty's conduct had been "imprudent".

Martin O'Donoghue had raised matters which damaged

Fianna Fáil and politicians in general.

Blame was apportioned and Haughey had been cleared.

When the meeting of the parliamentary party convened in Leinster House on the morning of Monday, February 7th, the Tunney report was the first item to be raised. After lengthy discussions a majority agreed that it should be taken first. Bertie Ahern read out the report but members asked for copies. It was decided eventually that photocopies would be made of the separate sections of it and would be available to deputies to read in another room. After they had been read by all those who wanted to see them, the copies were collected. The intention was that the report would never be made public.

Haughey announced that he was going to seek agreement for the removal of the party whip from Doherty and O'Donoghue. There was no discussion about his plans there and then: they would come up again if he survived as leader but if he was defeated, his plans were irrelevant.

As the meeting progressed, Haughey supporters tried to keep attention focused on O'Donoghue and the issue of money being available to dictate the direction of the party. Seamus Brennan retorted that Fianna Fáil had never lived off the shillings and pence of church door collections. It had always received and relied upon money from the business community. There were several references to McCreevy's *Sunday Press* interview which was disowned and criticised by all sides of the party, not because of its reference to fascism but because of its suggestion that the electorate had been right to put the Fianna Fáil party out of government in the November election. Nobody else in the party could publicly stand by *that* statement.

Briscoe's motion, seconded by McCreevy, was not reached until 7.45 p.m. Haughey and his defenders relied on the arguments they had honed over the previous fortnight. The party leader had not had any personal involvement in the tapping or bugging; there was a media campaign to oust him to which the party could not give in or no Fianna Fáil leader would be safe; the internal enquiry completely cleared him of any suspicion; the real issue was the unknown people outside the party who were offering money to influence its members and their decisions.

Haughey's opponents broadened their attack to include the fact that he had failed to lead Fianna Fáil into government with a clear majority in all three elections that he had fought. The tapping and bugging were the latest and most serious scandals in a succession of scandals that appeared to surface regularly under his leadership.

The mood of the meeting was low key and the vote came more than three hours later. A polling booth was set up behind a partition at the back of the hall and each deputy received a voting paper from a party official as his or her name was called out. There was a brief flurry of discussion when it was noted that the ballot papers were numbered but a promise was given that they would be destroyed immediately after the vote. Those who supported the motion (and opposed Haughey) had to write "For" on the ballot paper: those who opposed the motion (and supported Haughey) had to write "Against".

While the votes were counted in another room, deputies and senators chatted. The opponents of Haughey were more apprehensive than they had been going into the meeting. Haughey and his friends had fought back very well and very skilfully during the day: his opponents were no longer so sure that there would be an overwhelming majority against him. Briscoe talked to Haughey and told him he had to talk to him before the result in case he (Haughey) won and everybody believed he (Briscoe) was afraid to talk to him afterwards. Haughey asked how it would go. Briscoe said he did not know.

Tunney returned to the room and announced the results — for the motion 33 votes, against the motion 40. Haughey had survived by 7 votes. Word was passed immediately to his supporters outside the meeting. There were no shouts or cheers inside the room. People rushed through the corridors of Leinster House spreading the word of Haughey's victory. Inside the room, TDs gathered around Haughey to shake his hand. As they did so quietly, word reached the crowd of Haughey's supporters in the street outside the gates into Leinster House. There was a wild cheer which echoed through the night air and into the room.

Haughey had won against all the predictions. He had survived the biggest political scandal in a decade and he was practically walking on air as he was swept out of Leinster House and across the car park. "Take me to my people", he said, indicating the cheering crowd outside the gates. A reporter asked if he thought he now led a united party: "I know what you think", Haughey snapped. His opponents were routed, dismayed and incredulous. But the main threat to the unity of the party was yet to come.

George Colley and Des O'Malley tabled a motion for a meeting of the parliamentary party on Wednesday, February 16th. They felt that Haughey's victory could be taken as condoning and approving the actions of his ministers in initiating telephone taps and the bugging of conversations. Their motion "condemned and repudiated" the tapping of the telephones of people not involved in subversion or serious crime and the secret tape recording of conversations between parliamentary colleages.

Haughey was not happy about the motion but Ray MacSharry was even less happy. Sean Doherty and Martin O'Donoghue had resigned the party whip the previous week in the wake of Haughey's announcement that he would ask for their expulsion from the parliamentary party. MacSharry, however, had not been censured by the party for his action in bugging his conversation with O'Donoghue. It appeared now that Colley and O'Malley were preparing to seek his expulsion as well through their condemnation of his actions.

As members gathered for the meeting in the party rooms in Leinster House, MacSharry approached Colley and asked to have a word with him. The two of them stepped into a room and MacSharry began talking about his conversation with Colley during the leadership election in 1979. MacSharry accused Colley of having told O'Donoghue about that conversation and that this was the basis for O'Donoghue's claims that MacSharry might have been compromised financially. Colley denied that he had told anybody about the conversation.

Anyway, MacSharry said, the reason he had needed money in the mid-1970s was that Colley was threatening to sue him on behalf of a client. He denied that he had told Colley in 1979 that Haughey had lent him money and had never asked for it back.

In fact, he said, Haughey had arranged a loan for him in a bank. MacSharry warned Colley that if he said anything about this in public, he, MacSharry would report him to the Incorporated Law Society for breaching the rules governing solicitors. Colley got angry and threatened to sue MacSharry if he impugned his professional integrity as a solicitor.

Colley walked out of the room and went into the meeting. MacSharry followed; neither raised the issue in public.

At the meeting, Haughey complained that the motion was divisive and made it clear that he would prefer if it was withdrawn. Several other speakers argued that it should be withdrawn. It would only re-open the wounds within the party, they said, and they complained that a report about the motion had been published in one newspaper. Pat "Cope" Gallagher, a backbencher from Donegal South West, suggested that an addendum be added to condemn and repudiate any proposition to compromise with funds any member or members of the party.

O'Malley and Colley agreed to the addition, which was clearly intended to be a criticism of O'Donoghue. A few speakers still maintained their opposition to the motion as a whole but it was clear that it would probably have majority support. Haughey did not press his objections and the motion was carried unanimously.

After the meeting, the party released a statement which watered down significantly the terms of the motion. It said the party had condemned the tapping of people not involved in subversion or serious crime, the recording of a private conversation and any attempt to compromise with funds any member of the party. It did not say that the motion had repudiated such actions and it tried to gloss over the MacSharry bugging.

The acceptance of the motion without a vote avoided a formal split within the party. The survival of Haughey as leader carried an implication, if anyone wanted to see it that way, that Fianna Fáil did not reject the use of the gardaí for party and political purposes. Rejection of the Colley-O'Malley motion would have made that interpretation unavoidable. In that event Colley had decided that he, for one, would resign the party whip. Several others had considered the possibility of taking a similar step but there was no agreement among them to act in concert.

The formal split, which had seemed inevitable during the crisis and for some time before, was avoided when Fianna Fáil officially disowned what some of its leaders had done during their spell in government in 1982.

Epilogue

Haughey was backstage, hiding behind the drapes at the back of the platform that was packed with most, but not quite all, of Fianna Fáil's TDs. In front of them, filling the great hall of the Royal Dublin Society, were the thousands of delegates and party supporters in town for the opening of the ard fheis on Friday, February 25th, 1983. The platform was dominated by a huge photograph of Haughey's face. It looked down at the crowd, smiling benignly. "We want Charlie, we want Charlie", roared the crowd. Haughey paced up and down, out of sight of the crowd. He seemed nervous and agitated but was anxious to race up onto the platform and accept their cheers. He was like a boxer — warming up in the dressing-room, shadow-boxing and working himself up to just the right pitch.

At precisely the right psychological moment, Charles J. Haughey, president and leader of Fianna Fáil (The Republican Party) rushed onto the centre of the platform and stood there, both hands clasped above his head, while his audience gave him a thunderous, almost hysterical ovation.

Speaking above the cheering at first, he appealed for no recrimination and no personal confrontation and he eased the tension between himself, his supporters and the media by extending a "special, warm welcome" to reporters. The crowd roared their approval. There was no need for Haughey to drive home the message. Everyone knew who had won the war.

The ard fheis was a potentially explosive occasion. Many of Haughey's supporters wanted to turn it into a victory rally for their hero. His opponents, bruised and battered, feared Haughey would orchestrate the occasion into a triumphant display in the spirit of Nuremburg. In the event, Haughey had his moment but he skilfully steered a course midway between both extremes.

At the front of the platform, sitting behind a table stretched along the full length of the stage, sat Haughey's new, and as he called it, "totally integrated" front bench. Brian Lenihan was the new deputy leader, and two dissidents were given places —Des O'Malley (Energy) and Bobby Molloy (Environment). Gerry Collins survived the indiscretion of letting his name go forward for consideration for the leadership; he was made spokesman on Foreign Affairs. Sylvester Barrett was back in from the cold as spokesman on Defence. Haughey could afford to have the four of them — he was, after all, in opposition and not giving out positions in government. The remaining members of the front bench were all pro-Haughey men, for the moment at least: Jim Tunney (chairman); Michael O'Kennedy (Finance); Michael J. Noonan (Agriculture); Gene Fitzgerald (Labour); John Wilson (Transport); Brendan Daly (Forestry and Fisheries); Denis Gallagher (Gaeltacht); Albert Reynolds (Industry); Michael Woods (Justice); Pádraig Flynn (Trade); Rory O'Hanlon (Health); Terry Leyden (Posts and Telegraphs); Mary O'Rourke (Education) and Bertie Ahern (Chief Whip).

Behind them was the rest of the parliamentary party. Some of Haughey's opponents applauded louder and more furiously than even his most loyal supporters. Other dissidents looked awkward and very nervous. It was not pleasant being roasted on a slowly-turning spit. Charlie McCreevy simply didn't turn up. Sean Doherty didn't either. Motions to expel McCreevy and re-admit Neil Blaney to the party were dropped from the agenda after backstage discussions with their sponsors.

Hundreds of delegates opposed to Haughey and disillusioned by the conduct of his last government decided to stay away. But Fianna Fáil headquarters ensured that the hall would be packed. Several thousand extra "observer" tickets were printed. Normally, TDs were given about a dozen observer tickets to distribute among hard-working constituency activists. It was a kind of reward for services rendered and most only wanted to witness the presidential address on the

Saturday evening. Others wanted to attend the árd fheis because it was also a great social occasion. In February 1983, anti-Haughey TDs found they were given their allotted ration of observer tickets but pro-Haughey TDs were able to get several dozen and some got up to one hundred.

Brian Lenihan whipped up the crowd just before Haughey once again stepped onto the platform to make his presidential address. It was timed to last slightly less than the normal one and a half hours. The bit over was to allow time for the extra cheering and applause.

The crowd went wild when Haughey appeared and it was several minutes before he could begin his address. He told them he would do everything in his power to prove worthy of the trust they placed in him.

"The difficulties we have had are now behind us. We are again on the high road as a great unified party; there will be no turning back; we face the future eager and determined", he declared. The bulk of the speech was unremarkable. There were obligatory references to agriculture, the economy, law and order, the Irish language, international affairs and the constitutional amendment on abortion. The predictable call on Britain to make a "final withdrawal . . . from Ireland" drew an equally predictable response from the crowd.

Haughey finished up with a word for his opponents. "Looking around me here tonight", he said, "I know one thing for sure. Those who sought to weaken or confuse us have failed".

On a balcony, Haughey's brother Jock screamed: "Name them, name them". His words were drowned in the general tumult of applause. With him were most of Haughey's close friends. As Haughey's voice rose and fell during the speech some of them paced up and down the balcony, identifying several of his enemies in the crowd below.

On the same balcony, raised on a pedestal a few inches, there was a line of chairs for Haughey's wife and daughter and some of their friends.

Haughey was given an eight-minute standing ovation by the 7,000 delegates and observers in the hall. Ray MacSharry embraced the leader; the crowd went wild. Haughey raised his arms to receive their cheers and included his friends on the balcony in the acclamation with a gesture towards them. The public address system played over and over again Fianna Fáil's song from three elections ago: "Arise and Follow Charlie".

"It was", Haughey said later, "the greatest, the best, the most wonderful árd fheis of all time".

Appendix A

Chronology of Events

1982

January 27th: Coalition government defeated on its budget and Dáil dissolved.

February 18th: General election.

February 25th: Fianna Fáil's new parliamentary party met to choose a nominee for Taoiseach.

March 9th: Charles J. Haughey elected Taoiseach by 86 votes to 79 when the new Dáil met.

March 17th: Haughey met President Ronald Reagan in Washington.

March 25th: Fianna Fáil Government introduced its budget.

March 30th: Fine Gael's Dick Burke accepted the post of EEC Commissioner from Haughey and resigned his Dáil seat representing Dublin West.

April 2nd: Argentina invaded the Falklands Islands.

April 10th: EEC, including Ireland, condemned Argentine invasion.

April 20th: Charles Haughey's election agent, Pat O'Connor, acquitted by Swords district court of the charge of voting twice in the February general election.

May 4th: Government announced that it was opting out of EEC sanctions against Argentina after a British submarine torpedoed the cruiser *General Belgrano*.

May 10th: Tapping of Bruce Arnold's telephone began.

May 17th: Publicity campaign against crime and vandalism

launched by the Minister for Justice, Sean Doherty.

May 25th: Dublin West by-election won by Fine Gael candidate, Liam Skelly.

June 15th: Fianna Fáil backbencher John Callanan died.

June 24th: Government saved by the Ceann Comhairle in the Dáil in three tied votes on the bill implementing its budget.

July 1st: Charles Haughey won a vote of confidence in the Dáil by 84 votes to 77.

July 12th: Tapping of Bruce Arnold's telephone ended.

July 20th: By-election in Galway East to replace John Callanan won by Fianna Fáil candidate Noel Treacy.

July 28th: Tapping of Geraldine Kennedy's telephone began.

July 29th: Top secret meeting called by Haughey to consider security and policy towards Britain.

July 30th: Government announced cuts in public spending.

August 13th: Malcolm Macarthur arrested in the home of Attorney General Patrick Connolly and questioned about two murders and an attempted robbery.

August 16th/17th: Patrick Connolly recalled from holiday in the United States by Haughey. He resigned as Attorney General.

September 22nd: Garda car on protection detail with the Minister for Justice crashed in County Kerry.

September 27th: Garda Thomas Nangle, brother-in-law of the Minister for Justice, acquitted in Dowra district court on charge of assaulting a man.

October 5th: Desmond O'Malley and Martin O'Donoghue resigned from the cabinet because of the Taoiseach's demand that all members profess their loyalty to him.

October 6th: Charles Haughey defeated, by 58 to 22, a motion of no confidence in his leadership tabled at a Fianna Fáil parliamentary meeting by Charles McCreevy.

October 18th: Fianna Fáil backbencher from Clare, Bill Loughnane, died.

October 21st: Cabinet launched a new economic plan entitled "The Way Forward". Ray MacSharry secretly tape-recorded his conversation with Martin O'Donoghue.

October 27th: Tapping of Geraldine Kennedy's telephone continued.

November 4th: Government defeated in Dáil confidence

motion by 82 votes to 80.

November 16th: Tapping of Geraldine Kennedy's telephone ended.

November 24th: General election.

December 3rd: Garda assistant commissioner Joe Ainsworth promoted to deputy commissioner.

December 14th: Garret FitzGerald elected Taoiseach at head of Fine Gael and Labour coalition.

1983

January 20th: Justice Minister Michael Noonan confirmed that the previous Government tapped the telephones of two political journalists and revealed that Ray MacSharry, the former Tánaiste, had bugged a conversation with Martin O'Donoghue. Garda commissioner Patrick McLaughlin and deputy commissioner Joe Ainsworth announced that they were retiring.

January 23rd: Fianna Fáil parliamentary party met to discuss the disclosures.

February 1st: Fianna Fáil backbencher Clem Coughlan killed in road accident.

February 7th: Charles Haughey survived motion demanding his resignation by a vote of 40 to 33 of Fianna Fáil members of the Dáil.

Appendix B

Who Was Who

The following were the members of the government formed by Charles J. Haughey after he was elected Taoiseach by the Dáil on March 9th, 1982:

Ray MacSharry (Tánaiste and Minister for Finance)
Brian Lenihan (Minister for Agriculture)
Des O'Malley (Trade, Commerce and Tourism)
Gerry Collins (Minister for Foreign Affairs)
Gene Fitzgerald (Labour and the Public Service)
John Wilson (Transport and Posts and Telegraphs)
Martin O'Donoghue (Minister for Education)
Michael Woods (Health and Social Welfare)
Paddy Power (Minister for Defence)
Albert Reynolds (Minister for Industry and Energy)
Ray Burke (Minister for the Environment)
Brendan Daly (Minister for Fisheries and Forestry)
Pádraig Flynn (Minister for the Gaeltacht)
Seán Doherty (Minister for Justice)
Patrick Connolly (Attorney General).

O'Malley and O'Donoghue resigned from the cabinet on October 5th and were replaced on October 27th by Gerard Brady and Denis Gallagher who were given Education and the Gaeltacht respectively. Pádraig Flynn became Minister for Trade, Commerce and Tourism in the re-shuffle. Patrick Connolly resigned as Attorney General on August 17th and was succeeded by John Murray.

The following deputies were appointed Ministers of State or Junior Ministers by the government and allocated to the following Departments:

Bertie Ahern (Taoiseach and Defence)
Sylvester Barrett (Finance)
Lorcan Allen (Agriculture)
Ber Cowen (Agriculture)
Terry Leyden (Transport and Posts and Telegraphs)
Maire Geoghegan-Quinn (Education)
Denis Gallagher (Social Welfare)
Ger Connolly (Environment)
Gerard Brady (Environment)
Tom McEllistrim (Fisheries and Forestry)

In October 1982, the following Junior Ministers were appointed:

Jim Fitzsimons (Industry and Energy)
Niall Andrews (Environment)
Rory O'Hanlon (Social Welfare)
Seán Calleary (Trade, Commerce and Tourism).

In the general election of February 18th, the following Fianna Fáil members were elected to the Dáil:

Bertie Ahern	Dublin Central
Michael Ahern	Cork East
Lorcan Allen	Wexford
David Andrews	Dun Laoghaire
Niall Andrews	Dublin South
Liam Aylward	Carlow-Kilkenny
Michael Barrett	Dublin North West
Sylvester Barrett	Clare
Tom Bellew	Louth
Gerard Brady	Dublin South East
Gerry Brady	Kildare
Vincent Brady	Dublin North Central
Matty Brennan	Sligo-Leitrim
Ned Brennan	Dublin North East
Séamus Brennan	Dublin South
Ben Briscoe	Dublin South Central

Sean Browne	Wexford
Ray Burke	Dublin North
Hugh Byrne	Wexford
Seán Byrne	Tipperary South
John Callanan	Galway East
Seán Calleary	Mayo East
George Colley	Dublin Central
Gerry Collins	Limerick West
Hugh Conaghan	Donegal North-East
Ger Connolly	Laois-Offaly
Clem Coughlan	Donegal South-West
Ber Cowen	Laois-Offaly
Brendan Daly	Clare
Seán Doherty	Roscommon
John Ellis	Sligo-Leitrim
Frank Fahey	Galway West
Jackie Fahey	Waterford
Pádraig Faulkner	Louth
Eddie Filgate	Louth
Gene Fitzgerald	Cork South-Central
Tom Fitzpatrick	Dublin South Central
Jim Fitzsimons	Meath
Pádraig Flynn	Mayo West
Denis Foley	Kerry North
Seán French	Cork North-Central
Denis Gallagher	Mayo West
Pat Cope Gallagher	Donegal South-West
Maire Geoghegan-Quinn	Galway West
Jim Gibbons	Carlow-Kilkenny
Mary Harney	Dublin South-West
Charles J. Haughey	Dublin North-Central
Colm Hilliard	Meath
Liam Hyland	Laois-Offaly
Seán Keegan	Longford-Westmeath
Michael Kitt	Galway East
Liam Lawlor	Dublin West
Brian Lenihan	Dublin West
Jimmy Leonard	Cavan-Monaghan
Terry Leyden	Roscommon
Bill Loughnane	Clare
Michael Lynch	Meath
Denis Lyons	Cork North-Central
Seán McCarthy	Tipperary South
Charlie McCreevy	Kildare
Tom McEllistrim	Kerry North
Ray MacSharry	Sligo-Leitrim
Tom Meaney	Cork North West
Bobby Molloy	Galway West

P.J. Morley	Mayo East
Ciaran Murphy	Wicklow
Michael J. Noonan	Limerick West
Willy O'Dea	Limerick East
Martin O'Donoghue	Dun Laoghaire
Rory O'Hanlon	Cavan-Monaghan
Michael O'Kennedy	Tipperary North
John O'Leary	Kerry South
Des O'Malley	Limerick East
Paddy Power	Kildare
Albert Reynolds	Longford-Westmeath
Jim Tunney	Dublin North-West
Joe Walsh	Cork South-West
Seán Walsh	Dublin South-West
John Wilson	Cavan-Monaghan
Pearse Wyse	Cork South-Central

Two members of the parliamentary party died during the term of that Dáil, John Callanan in June and Bill Loughnane in October 1982. Noel Treacy was elected to the vacancy from Callanan's death in Galway East.

There were two challenges in 1982 to Charles Haughey's leadership of Fianna Fáil. The first was immediately after the February general election when Desmond O'Malley publicly challenged Haughey for the party's nomination as candidate for Taoiseach when the Dáil met on March 9th. At a meeting of the new parliamentary party on February 25th to decide the issue, O'Malley withdrew at the last moment. The second challenge was on October 6th when the parliamentary party voted on a motion of no confidence in Haughey put forward by Charles McCreevy. Haughey won the vote by 58 to 22. The following are the 22 TDs who voted against Haughey:

David Andrews	Dun Laoghaire
Sylvester Barrett	Clare
Tom Bellew	Louth
Séamus Brennan	Dublin South
Hugh Byrne	Wexford
Seán Byrne	Tipperary South
George Colley	Dublin Central
Hugh Conaghan	Donegal North East
Pádraig Faulkner	Louth

Tom Fitzpatrick	Dublin South Central
Seán French	Cork North Central
Jim Gibbons	Carlow-Kilkenny
Mary Harney	Dublin South West
Tom Meaney	Cork North West
Charles McCreevy	Kildare
Robert Molloy	Galway West
Ciaran Murphy	Wicklow
William O'Dea	Limerick East
Martin O'Donoghue	Dun Laoghaire
Desmond O'Malley	Limerick East
Joe Walsh	Cork South West
Pearse Wyse	Cork South Central

In the general election on November 24, 1982 the following members of Fianna Fáil were elected to the Dáil:

Bertie Ahern	Dublin Central
Michael Ahern	Cork East
David Andrews	Dun Laoghaire
Niall Andrews	Dublin South
Liam Aylward	Carlow-Kilkenny
Michael Barrett	Dublin North West
Sylvester Barrett	Clare
Gerard Brady	Dublin South East
Vincent Brady	Dublin North-Central
Paudge Brennan	Wicklow
Mattie Brennan	Sligo-Leitrim
Séamus Brennan	Dublin South
Ben Briscoe	Dublin South-Central
John Browne	Wexford
Ray Burke	Dublin North
Hugh Byrne	Wexford
Seán Byrne	Tipperary South
Seán Calleary	Mayo East
George Colley	Dublin Central
Gerry Collins	Limerick West
Hugh Conaghan	Donegal North-East
Ger Connolly	Laois-Offaly
Clem Coughlan	Donegal South-West
Ber Cowen	Laois-Offaly
Brendan Daly	Clare
Seán Doherty	Roscommon
Frank Fahey	Galway West
Jackie Fahey	Waterford
Pádraig Faulkner	Louth
Gene Fitzgerald	Cork South-Central
Liam Fitzgerald	Dublin North-East

Jim Fitzsimons	Meath
Pádraig Flynn	Mayo West
Denis Foley	Kerry North
Denis Gallagher	Mayo West
Pat Cope Gallagher	Donegal South-West
Maire Geoghegan-Quinn	Galway West
Mary Harney	Dublin South-West
Charles J. Haughey	Dublin North-Central
Colm Hilliard	Meath
Liam Hyland	Laois-Offaly
Seamus Kirk	Louth
Michael Kitt	Galway East
Eileen Lemass	Dublin West
Brian Lenihan	Dublin West
Jimmy Leonard	Cavan-Monaghan
Terry Leyden	Roscommon
Denis Lyons	Cork North-Central
Seán McCarthy	Tipperary South
Charlie McCreevy	Kildare
Tom McEllistrim	Kerry North
Ray MacSharry	Sligo-Leitrim
Bobby Molloy	Galway West
P.J. Morley	Mayo East
Donal Moynihan	Cork North-West
M.J. Nolan	Carlow-Kilkenny
Michael J. Noonan	Limerick West
Willie O'Dea	Limerick East
Rory O'Hanlon	Cavan-Monaghan
Ned O'Keeffe	Cork East
Michael O'Kennedy	Tipperary North
John O'Leary	Kerry South
Des O'Malley	Limerick East
Donal Ormonde	Waterford
Mary O'Rourke	Longford-Westmeath
Paddy Power	Kildare
Albert Reynolds	Longford-Westmeath
Noel Treacy	Galway East
Jim Tunney	Dublin North-West
Dan Wallace	Cork North-Central
Joe Walsh	Cork South-West
Seán Walsh	Dublin South-West
John Wilson	Cavan-Monaghan
Michael Woods	Dublin North-East
Pearse Wyse	Cork South-Central

During the crisis within Fianna Fáil after the telephone tapping and bugging revelations in January 1983, 41 members of the party's recently elected 75 deputies signed a petition demanding a meeting about the leadership. The petition was circulated after the death of a colleague, Clem Coughlan, had caused the postponement of a meeting at which Haughey's leadership was expected to be resolved.

The petition said: "We the undersigned members of the Fianna Fáil Parliamentary Party hereby demand that a special meeting of the Parliamentary Party be held at 11.30 a.m. on Friday the 4th of February 1983".

It was signed by the following deputies:
David Andrews (Dun Laoghaire)
Michael Ahern (Cork East)
Sylvester Barrett (Clare)
Gerard Brady (Dublin South East)
Séamus Brennan (Dublin South)
Ben Briscoe (Dublin South Central)
Ray Burke (Dublin North)
Hugh Byrne (Wexford)
Seán Byrne (Tipperary South)
George Colley (Dublin Central)
Gerry Collins (Limerick West)
Hugh Conaghan (Donegal North East)
Ger Connolly (Laois-Offaly)
Ber Cowen (Laois-Offaly)
Frank Fahey (Galway West)
Jackie Fahy (Waterford)
Pádraig Faulkner (Louth)
Gene Fitzgerald (Cork South Central)
Liam Fitzgerald (Dublin North East)
Denis Foley (Kerry North)
Maire Geoghegan-Quinn (Galway West)
Mary Harney (Dublin South West)
Colm Hilliard (Meath)
Jim Leonard (Cavan-Monaghan)
Denis Lyons (Cork North Central)
Séan McCarthy (Tipperary South)
Charles McCreevy (Kildare)
Bobby Molloy (Galway West)
Donal Moynihan (Cork North West)
Michael J. Noonan (Limerick West)

Willie O'Dea (Limerick East)
Rory O'Hanlon (Cavan-Monaghan)
Michael O'Kennedy (Tipperary North)
John O'Leary (Kerry South)
Des O'Malley (Limerick East)
Donal Ormonde (Waterford)
Mary O'Rourke (Longford-Westmeath)
Dan Wallace (Cork North Central)
Joe Walsh (Cork South West)
John Wilson (Cavan-Monaghan)
Pearse Wyse (Cork South Central)

Seven Fianna Fáil senators also signed the petition. They were:

SÉAMUS DE BRÚN   BRIAN HILLERY
SEÁN FALLON   TOM HUSSEY
DES HANAFIN   EOIN RYAN
MICHAEL SMITH

On Monday, February 7th 1983, the Fianna Fáil parliamentary party decided in a secret ballot by 40 votes to 33 to reject a motion demanding Haughey's immediate resignation.

Appendix C

Malcolm Macarthur

At the end of July 1982, garda resources were stretched to the limit by four murder hunts. The killing of two people — Bridie Gargan and Donal Dunne — was not linked for some time and detectives thought at first that they were hunting two separate killers. The fact that Malcolm Macarthur killed both people was not known for certain until after his arrest on Friday, August 13th, at the home of the Attorney General, Patrick Connolly. On July 24th, gardaí everywhere were given a description of the man wanted for the attack on Bridie Gargan in the Phoenix Park in Dublin and on August 6th they were given a detailed description of the man who met Donal Dunne in Edenderry, Co Offaly, shortly before Dunne was killed with his own shotgun.

The following are the two separate descriptions of the same man, Malcolm Macarthur.

Bridie Gargan's attacker was described as:

"20/25 yrs., 5ft 10 ins., good strong build, athletic looking, dark/dark brown hair — brushed back, wavy at front, slight parting in centre and well groomed, well trimmed beard, pale complexion, good white even teeth, brown eyes, well spoken; wore white open necked shirt, dark coloured trousers, dark leather shoes and FISHERMANS TWEED HAT".

The man believed to have met Donal Dunne was described as:

DESCRIPTION

(1) 30 to 35 yrs.,

(2) 5 ft 8 ins., to 5 ft. 9 ins.,

(3) Medium to light build

(4) Dark hair neatly groomed but appears bushy or long at the back

(5) Clean shaven but may now have a light growth of beard

(6) May wear dark horn rimmed square type glasses. N.B. He has a habit of wearing the glasses on the tip of his nose and looking out over them.

(7) His hands and finger nails are well kept —they would give the impression that he is a professional type person.

(8) Speaks with what is described as a soft cultured educated accent. The accent has been described as upper class Dublin to English — it is possible that the accent is English.

(9) The man's complexion has been described as sallow to pale and sickly looking.

(10) The man has a peculiar gait i.e. he walks with a slight slouch with his head held forward. He gives the impression that he is walking against the wind. He has the habit of walking with his left hand in his pocket.

DRESS:

(1) Normally wears some type of head dress N.B. usually a peaked cap which he wears towards the front of his head with the peak down over his eyes.

(2) Dark coloured brownish/green tweed jacket. The jacket may give the impression that it is a poor fit, i.e. short in the sleeves.

(3) Dark coloured open neck shirt.

(4) Dark pants.

(5) Black leather laced boots, nicely polished.

(6) May be possession of a dark coloured mackintosh coat, which he may wear or carry over his arm.

PECULIARITIES:

(1) Normally carries a bag, which has been variously described as —

(a) black polythene refuse sack

(b) blue hold all

(c) white plastic shopping bag or indeed any type of carrying bag.

367

(2) The man has a habit of carrying some type of implement wrapped in brown paper or black plastic.

(3) He appears to have a craze for the sport of clay pigeon shooting.

(4) He likes water i.e. rivers, canals, and boats.

(5) Usually travels on foot or on bus.

GENERAL: The first impression this man gives is that he is an "odd ball" of some type. However, when he speaks he gives the impression that he is cultured and educated. He is quiet and will not speak unless spoken to. He has been described as "The French Artist Type", a Geologist and an Engineer.

The Commissioner directs that each Divisional Officer ensures that the description of this man is brought to the notice of each member within his division.

In particular he directs that enquiries be made at the following premises in a determined effort to locate this man.

(1) Hotels, Lodging Houses and Licensed Premises

(2) Shops & Cafes (urban and rural)

(3) Firearms Dealers

(4) Mental Institutions, Homes, Rehabilitation Units, Drug Units, Hostels etc.

(5) Hospitals

(6) Clay pigeon shoots (both official and flapper meetings). It is possible that this man may turn up at a clay pigeon shoot. With this in mind particulars of all clay pigeon shoots in each Division should be obtained and particular attention paid to any such meetings.

(7) Each sergeant-in-charge will report if any such person has been refused firearms certificates.

Appendix D

The MacSharry-O'Donoghue Transcript

The conversation between Ray MacSharry and Martin O'Donoghue which was recorded by MacSharry unknown to O'Donoghue took place in MacSharry's office in the context of the heightened atmosphere within Fianna Fáil just after Charlie McCreevy's motion of no confidence in Haughey split the parliamentary party 58/22. McCreevy's motion was dealt with on October 6th and the bugged conversation took place on October 21st. The transcript made by members of the Intelligence and Security Branch at Garda Headquarters in Dublin identifies MacSharry as No. 1 and O'Donoghue as No. 2. There are many grammatical errors and mistakes of punctuation in the transcript. The transcribers appear to have had a difficult task judging by the number of missing words, presumably because they were inaudible. The full text of the transcript reproduced here is exactly as it was when given by Joe Ainsworth to Sean Doherty. The errors remain but in order to assist the reader, a brief guide compiled by the authors appears at the end of the transcript. Entries in the guide are denoted by numbers in the transcript.

SECRET

Restricted to Government

Special Correspondence

21st October, 1982

No 1 : How are Martin.

No 2 : Well thanks, how did it go this afternoon.[1]

No 1 : Not so bad, I have just got the estimates now on the trial figures for the estimates for 1983.

No 2 : Well are the figures holding or are there changes.

No 1 : More or less compared to targets about 23 up not so bad.

No 2 : 23 million, we have to live with that.

No 1 : It is very good actually. Anyway what is on your mind.

No 2 : I have to meet a fello, some journalist from Business Week who is here in town so I am meeting him at 6.30 pm. Okay we will drink to it. I suppose we all have our views as to where we go from here but I must say that it seems to me so long as the present leadership holds people are going to be very jittery because some will not like going into the next general election with him.

No 1 : It is not more or less sorted out. Okay there was the aftermath of it[2] and that was mainly because there was argument about intimidation and the deadly stupid scene that took place in the rear of Leinster House that night.[3]

No 2 : I would not worry about that.

No 1 : ...... personality difference 58 22 does not matter.[4]

No 2 : Yes but there is still the question of what does it look like for the party over the next couple of years and I think most people reckon that we won't be able go go on much before the very outside next Summer and then into an election and then what. Whereas there is an alternative possibility, it is to change leaders.

No 1 : Well you know my view on that. I don't know what the alternative would be. One thing about it ever since 1970 when the ex-Taoiseach[5] was under threat and I was supposedly one of those myself...... which was untrue because I defy anybody keeping one thing in a statement...... went against the leadership of the party and until such time and you know questionably from that night and had the discussion in Brussels long before it was announced that I am supposed to be part of the group that pushed Jack Lynch and you were in that discussion in Brussels and Gene Fitzgerald and Jim Tunney were there and you knew about it before I did.[6]

No 2 :   But that is why I am talking because I like to think that one of the things I have discovered over the years, I remember the Loughnane affair too.[7] I remember that day the party and during the lunch recess the two of us managed to have a sensible chat so I have been gradually trying to learn not to get carried away by what the gossips said or by what the papers say but always try to look at what the realities are. But as I see it quite honestly the realities are while he[8] has many excellent qualities and one thing and another

No 1 :   He had a very...... press conference today we were all there and we did not have to say a word it is not an easy thing to do with Vincent Browne[9] etc packed out with political and financial correspondents they went down great. I don't know like I mean I am prepared I am not going to say that I will not listen to you after you coming over but I just don't know what sort of alternatives there could be

TELEPHONE CONVERSATION

No 2 :   Well let me give you the bones of it quickly. It seems to be that you are limping now and you are depending on Gregory and Blaney and you are always vulnerable as we could be at the moment now say one or two short bye-election time. The other option is the Labour Party and now I know that they appear to be in rags and so on but there are about 3 or 4 different factions we all know in the party and let's just say that I am satisfied from each faction that they guarantee at least one year and some of them would be interested in up to four years.

No 1 :   Why would they not guarantee it to Haughey.

No 2 :   That is the point, there is no way they can deliver it to...... because there is too much history in the party with them.[10]

No 1 :   But who can they deliver to, are they now saying that they are going to deliver it and that we must go and select their supporter.

No 2 :   No, no no they say that it is obviously our business, that certainly if their point would be if there was any change in the Fianna Fáil leadership that would put them in the position where they could say that this is a new situation give the new man a chance, let's see what policies they are going to put forward. As regards the alternative in the party well that is over to you, a large part.

No 1 :   That is over estimated too I think.

No 2 :   Well when I say over to you, let's be realistic there are about 2 or 3 ways you can fight that out. One is you create a vacancy, incidentally the way it should be done you see is I think that yourself and a number of the other senior people in the Cabinet would go in effect and say look in the best interest of everybody he[11] just announces his resignation rather than have any form of contest and when you have the vacancy then there are 2 or 3 ways of doing it. You can just have candidates again as before. You can have a right in ballot. Just go to the party and say let everyone write down 3 names and see what it looks like and then adjourn and we will have consultations or realistically there are about, you know my views since February,[12] there are about 4 or 5 people who matter and if they got into a room and came out and said that we have a Pope that would be it.

No 1 : You wouldn't see that happening, I could not see it happening. In the situation you have with George[13] and Dessie[14] you have Seamus Browne[15] and yourself

No 2 : Seamus Browne, forget it

No 1 : You are talking of coming out of a room with a Pope, he is the Pope in his mind you see this is the trouble

No 2 : I just want to say quickly if Charlie goes, George goes and I think that is the price of it within the party.

No 1 : Sure George won' go...... not now with the problems we are facing with the main bulk of people that are left, all of them that are left George in 66[16] against the Taoiseach Jack Lynch...... the bulk of what was there in 22

No 2 : That is if you are going to do a job for the party prepare him not to go and there is an awful lot of people in the middle of the party, they were not in the 22 and they do not like being pulled one way or another.

No 1 : I was always againsl personality issues and cuts in the party myself and I have always said I would be a Fianna Fail man, one true way that I know of being a Fianna Fail man is supporting the leader. It does not matter even if the party leader was Jim Gibbons he would have my support. Because that is the strength of the party over the last 50 years.

No 2 : I would agree with you except I honestly believe there may be different breed in the country we are going to be hammered in Dublin if your man[17] is still there that is the long and short of it.

No 1 : I'd don't know the details of each you know but just the abiding principles I just don't see how that can be upset, if there is the possibility in any time in the next 18 months of a general election and you have to change leader you are gone anyway, especially after what happened two weeks ago.

No 2 : You would have a better chance with anybody.

No 1 : I don't know, you talk about his standing now and at the last...... survey. Where there was 20% preferential between G. Fitzgerald and Charles Haughey. There was 30% in the general election.[18]

No 2 : I am not talking about different surveys.

No 1 : It did not really make any difference but there was one thing, I don't know like, one has to go with the majority decisions and a majority decision was taken two weeks ago[19] and I was part of that majority but there was one thing, in fact it was only briefly Albert Reynolds was talking to me about some conversation, in fact just before I met you on the way out and he was going to America, I did not have time to talk about it, but he wastalking about money and I really hit the roof when I heard my name mentioned in connection with money

No 2 : I'm supposed to have been bought for £50,000 in February[20]

No 1 : Well I mean...... in my 14 years around this an overdraft of 8,000 and 35,000, and documents to show it I am not too concerned but I mean I do not know whether it is true or not but what he was talking about was arising from a conversation with yourself was only that we would move in a direction that should save...... but as I said there was a very brief conversation, a conversation I hate having hearing bits and pieces and not being able to ask and...... and £100,000 being offered

No 2 : I certainly did not say that.

No 1 : I do not know where the story came from but that is what he was talking about, I don't give a damn what was happening in Fianna Fail and I could not care less if I was not there tomorrow myself or whenever the decision was made, if I was to go around with the arse out of my trousers I would not take a brown penny from anyone ...... I wrote and cheque and it cost me 7p or 10p to sent it back[21] but I would and I might need money and many a time I needed it before but I borrowed it. I paid it back at the expense of other things that I needed ...... with the family I have is not an overdraft but I was a bit surprised to hear that there was some talk of money and where such money would be coming from.

No 2 : I think in fairness what was said there was that I don't think what anyone was implying that there was any substance in it. After all I am supposed to have been paid £50,000 for behaving the way I did in February, but I know how true that is. What was being said was if there was any suggestion of somebody being compromised financially that it would be sorted out. But the money thing that I heard about around town was that the boss was in financial trouble and certainly again if that was one of the problems it would be better to organise some way of financing it.

No 1 : For Haughey to be in trouble, I mean he has such ...... he could not be in trouble.

No 2 : Is there not that persistent story around town, you know that there is pressure on him to get ...... development from Baldoyle up[22] because it is worth all that much.

No 1 : You know yourself that the story goes on about every Fianna Fail politician I am a long time around and I have seen in fact at the time that they were accusing Fianna Fail politicians including

James Gallagher,[23] Blaney[24] and Boland[25] in late 69 and 70 of selling their pocket Justin Keating[26] was selling his pocket but there was not a word about that, they did not manipulate any situation. In the papers yesterday, David Andrews, Fianna Fail TD, his son was appeared in court why not a F. Gael T.D's son in some paper. Anything that hits Fianna Fail.

No 2 : I have noticed that. However, I think those aspects are co-incidental as they say.

No 1 : They may be incidental but I was a bit concerned in any way that my name should be mentioned in a compromise fashion as regards finance from any source behind my back. Whatever I am involved in is straight up forward to the face that is is and there will be no change on it but money is one of those things that myself and my entire family have been very very careful about because I see myself in the media in general about 5 or 6 years ago one week broke and whatever bit of property I had left and the next week I was a millionaire.

But as regards an old pensioner who is in fact a regular contributor to Deputies through the post ...... if money came I would write a cheque and sent it back.

No 2 : It is too easy to set you up then.

No 1 : Next thing it will be in the paper that such a person was bought and then anyway who would put up such money, where would they get such money, we read in the paper I am the Joint Honourary Treasurer of the party, where is the money going to come from for the next general election how much we owe and yet if there is a compromise situation in relation to CJ or myself or others where is that money going to come from, where are we going to get it.

No 2 : There is a lot of money around allright but not

for CJ not for him to stay.

No 1 : That kind of money, you could never have a situation develop where there would be money around to move a political party in any kind of situation.

No 2 : That is why I am not going after that aspect, I am concentrating on what is the ...... for and against and how you would read the situation and that is why I came to talk to you.

No 1 : I am interested in talking to anybody and interested in listening to any story, but I just do not know how a situation like that if such a situation was to be brought about possibly if it ever had a chance of succeeding, possibly some chance of succeeding in circumstances prior to the situation of two weeks ago[27] but I could not ask any hope of even being a starter at the present time.

No 2 : Why not.

No 1 : Because the thing is openly and publicly shattered and we would look right idiots.

No 2 : It was not settled.[28]

No 1 : It was never settled, it is never going to be settled not for the next ten years, it is never settled to the fullest that you would get. And that is one of the things that I was saying to yourself and Dessie[29] the other day. I could not see the necessity for a resignation prior to ...... it is a totally different thing. And even as it turned out that is the way it is being shown. It is very difficult to justify a resignation.

No 2 : I will tell you one thing in confidence although I want to say it before I even mention it that I had already decided but I am still weighing up the pro's and con's by the Monday night[30] I had decided feck it if I'm going to oppose him[31] I will give my reasons openly in Cabinet and if he has already gone and publicly and said stand up and be counted well I don't want to seem to be seen to be trying to have my cake and eat it so I suppose the best thing to do is to resign because you are putting him in an uncompromising position does he have somebody in the Cabinet then that apparantly he ought to fire but what clinched it then anything on the Tuesday morning before the Cabinet he[32] sent for Dessie and the line that he gave to Dessie was that in fact he knew Dessie had not been involved because Dessie had been in Spain. HE[33] was convinced that I was in it up to my neck and he wanted to flush out that bastard O'Donoghue and he wanted Dessie to back him and they would deal with me so when I hear that I said well if that is what he really feels.

No 1 : Like a lot of things.

No 2 : True

No 2 : I did not think that you knew that, that is why I am telling you. That is what the man feally feels, fair enough let him run his own show. There is no point in me sitting there but I am not going to say that to anyone.

No 1 : If there is a group that will not support the leader that is not part of Irish politics. I don't know what you are putting forward, you have clearly thought an opinion or a view about assisting the party in the next general election but how many people will support that view.

No 2 : Do you mean TDs now in the party.

No 1 : Yes.

No 2 : Well supposing as I would see the easiest way of doing it is that yourself and a 4 or 5 other senior cabinet people went to CJ and said time to resign.

No 1 : You that man better that I do

No 2 : Then allright you have to face him and say of you will not go peacefully do you want to be humiliated because there is a way of doing that too. I agree once you agree to make the decisions there is no turning back.

No 1 : That is just raising ......

No 2 : It is not raising it, it is finishing it. It is a very different proposition, if leaked out as it would have to in those circumstances. If it transpired that 5 or 6 senior people had gone to him to resign and he refused and if there was then to be a ballot with a named candidate honestly you would have to agree on the name would not all the parliamentary party know what the score was, don't forget he probably would have been beaten in a secret ballot.

No 1 : Not a chance. The situation from 43 or whatever it was a few years ago to 78 [34] there is no way that it would be less than 43, none under any circumstances.

No 2 : Well it all depends.

No 1 : Whether a secret ballot or not the names were nearly right to one or two either way 58 22 on the papers before the ballot took place, and the argument that was made for secret ballot on that day was consistently made by those who had already said what they were going to do. It does not make sense.

No 2 : It is allright for some of us to stand up and say what way we will vote but I certainly know people, they vote one way in an open roll call they vote another was in secret ballot because foolishly in my opinion but nevertheless it is their entitlement they feel they cannot affor to say openly what they think themselves.

No 1 : There could be others then, you never know ...... for years and years it was known who the leader would be it was decided from the time of Lemass[35] ...... then you had the 66[36] situation and ever since that you had the situation you have now and don't tell my that my changing the leader tomorrow you are not going to have a ...... you are going to have it all the time.

No 2 : One difference the next time you have to ...... an understanding of least will 2 or 3 people.

No 1 : But you cannot do that that certain amount of understanding was there between George and Charlie how long did it last, it did not last ten minutes. Even working together after 79.[37]

No 2 : We all know now that a sort of working deal would not be on.

No 1 : One thing that had made Fianna Fail the strength that it has is the protection of its leader. You go into any constituency, half of the constituency would be for O'Donoghue and the other half would be for Andrews and they would fucking knife each other, lets face facts, knife each other for and against. But that is the way it is and you bring that right up to the leader it is going to be there but if it was never broached openly and they try and make a big play about changing rules in Jack Lynch's time. I mean Jack Lynch got rid of the middle of the ground of the party, the best known Ministers in the 25 counties outside Dublin or in the 31 counties in the country if you want to put it that way. I do not know how one could assist in that kind of situation. I was glad when you rang this morning because that was still on about what Brennan ahd said about and you may not be in as good a financial state as rest of us and that there would be £100,000 to put that right, that was said. When I saw you yesterday I said it is on my mind still, I mentioned it to Elaine, my wife at home, she was going to ring you.

No 2 : I would not blame her.

No 1 : I said no, I only heard that he said it, I will give him the benefit of the doubt until I see him face to face. If anybody wants to know what I have to say, ask me. It does not always work but that is the way I am and that is the way I intend to stay. But there are so many difficulties around and we all know them, the difficult situation in the economy, what is being done in the estimates B. Loughnane and Jim Gibbons, I hope that he is allright he is gone off the news today. [38] All of those situations lead to ...... so I don't know who you have been discussing this with in the Labour Party but as I said earlier I could not because of their current structure they could not become involved with Fianna Fail.

No 2 : Who would replace him [39] if there were a change and they say that it is entirely a matter for yourselves. Talk about four of them seperately the four different factions, one or two of them did say that naturally they would have a preference but that would not enter into it, it might affect the length of time that is all. It would be easier to contemplate.

No 1 : There conference is on this weekend. [40]

No 2 : What they do for ifuyou want to read the signs ......

End of 1 hour

GUIDE

1. The launching of the government's economic plan, The Way Forward.
2. The October 6th meeting of the parliamentary party to debate Charles McCreevy's motion of no confidence in Haughey.
3. The incident when Jim Gibbons was punched by Haughey supporters after the defeat of McCreevey's motion.
4. 58/22 — the result of the McCreevy motion: 58 for Haughey, 22 against.
5. Jack Lynch.
6. A reference to a meeting in Brussels in late 1979 at which, MacSharry maintained, other Fianna Fáil ministers were canvassing support for George Colley — before Lynch resigned.
7. Late in 1979, Bill Loughnane publicly called Lynch a liar. Lynch was in America but George Colley and others tried to have Loughnane expelled from the parliamentary party. Their efforts failed.
8. Haughey.
9. Editor of *Magill* magazine at the time.
10. An apparent reference to the antipathy between some Labour leaders and Haughey.
11. Haughey.
12. The abortive challenge to Haughey in February 1982 by Desmond O'Malley.
13. George Colley.
14. Desmond O'Malley.
15. Typographical error — transcript should read "Seamus Brennan."
16. 1966 — the leadership contest between Jack Lynch and George Colley following the resignation of Sean Lemass.
17. Haughey.
18. Opinion polls which consistently show Garret FitzGerald far ahead of Haughey in voters' preference for Taoiseach.
19. The decision on McCreevy's motion.
20. O'Donoghue worked with the conspirators during the O'Malley challenge to Haughey in February 1982. O'Donoghue's appeal to O'Malley at the meeting of the parliamentary party not to stand against Haughey came as a surprise to O'Malley and others. Some people claimed afterwards that O'Donoghue had been "bought" by Haughey.
21. Garbled version, apparently of an incident recounted by MacSharry to demonstrate his refusal to accept money from anyone. On one occasion, he returned a contribution sent to him by an old age pensioner even though sending it back cost him money.
22. A company called Endcamp was seeking planning permission for a massive housing development in north County Dublin on land between Baldoyle and Portmarnock which was not zoned for building. Haughey was alleged to have connections with the company and to be pressurising Fianna Fáil county councillors to re-zone the area and push through the planning permission. It was alleged he was doing this because of his own alleged financial difficulties and consequent need for a very quick and

large profit on the deal. No firm link between Haughey and Endcamp was ever established, however.

23. James Gallagher — former Fianna Fáil TD and uncle of Patrick Gallagher, a property speculator with whom Haughey had done business. James was a leading figure in Taca, the Fianna Fáil fund-raising group disbanded by Jack Lynch and replaced by a fund-raising committee run by Senator Des Hanafin. Patrick's business empire collapsed in 1982 with debts of some £50 million. James was refused entry to Leinster House for one of the Fianna Fáil meetings in the wake of the bugging and telephone tapping crisis in 1983. He died a few weeks later.

24. Neil Blaney.

25. Kevin Boland — former Minister for Local Government who resigned from Fianna Fáil in the aftermath of the arms crisis. An extreme republican who later formed Aontacht Eireann, a political party which disappeared without trace shortly after he founded it.

26. Justin Keating — former Labour Party TD and Minister for Industry and Commerce in the coalition government of 1973-77. Lost his Dáil seat in the 1977 general election and made little impression on national politics thereafter, despite a spell in the Senate.

27. The split over the McCreevy motion.

28. The leadership crisis in Fianna Fáil.

29. Desmond O'Malley.

30. Monday, October 4th 1982 — the day after Haughey's demand during a radio interview that cabinet members declare their loyalty to him as Fianna Fáil leader.

31, 32 and 33. Haughey.

34. A typographical error. Probably should be "58", as in the 58/22 split over McCreevy's motion.

35. Sean Lemass — succeeded Éamon de Valera as leader of Fianna Fáil. As Taoiseach, Lemass presided over an era of industrial expansion seen by some as a "golden age" of modern Ireland.

36. The leadership contest between Jack Lynch and George Colley following Lemass's resignation in 1966.

37. The leadership contest between Colley and Haughey after Lynch's resignation in 1979.

38. Jim Gibbons had two heart attacks around the time of Bill Loughnane's death. The newspapers on the morning of October 21st (the day of the bugging) said his condition was deteriorating. In fact, he made a full recovery.

39. Haughey.

40. The Labour Party annual conference in Galway.

Appendix E

Government Statements issued on Thursday 20th January 1983

1.

The Commissioner, Garda Síochána, Mr. Patrick McLaughlin, and the Deputy Commissioner in charge of the Security Section, Mr. Joseph Ainsworth, have, separately, notified the Minister for Justice of their intention to retire from the Force with effect from 1st February, and this has been accepted by the Government.

Each of them separately has made it clear to the Minister that he has felt that this is the right course to take in the aftermath of certain recent controversies, especially in relation to telephone tapping.

The Government, for their part, while recognising the seriousness of certain matters that have come to light and that are being dealt with in other statements, think it necessary to say publicly that they greatly regret that two officers who have given long and dedicated service to the State should have been caught up in these matters.

2.

According to information supplied by Mr. T.J. Ainsworth, Deputy Commissioner in charge of the Security Section in the

Garda Síochána, he, Mr. Ainsworth, received , towards the end of October, 1982, a telephone call from Mr. Sean Doherty, then Minister for Justice. Mr. Doherty asked that a tape recorder be taken by Mr. Ainsworth to the then Minister for Finance, Mr. Ray MacSharry, at his office in Upper Merrion Street. After some discussion about the type of recorder required, Mr. Ainsworth went to Mr. MacSharry's office and handed over to him a small recorder, together with a sensitive microphone which is an accessory supplied with the recorder in question, and a cassette tape and batteries were handed to Mr. MacSharry there. Mr. Ainsworth showed him how to use it. The cassette was capable of running for one hour on each side.

On the following day or the day after that, Mr. Sean Doherty again telephoned Mr. Ainsworth and asked him to have a tape transcribed quickly as he wanted it at Government. A cassette tape was sent by Mr. Doherty to Mr. Ainsworth's office and was similar to the one given to Mr. MacSharry. (This tape cassette is not one of a kind in general use). The tape was transcribed in Garda Headquarters by a member of the Garda Síochána.

When the transcript was completed Mr. Ainsworth telephoned Mr. Doherty's office in St. Stephen's Green to say that he had a dispatch ready for the Minister. He was telephoned back later and asked to take the transcript to Mr. Doherty at Government Buildings. Mr. Ainsworth brought two copies of the transcript to Government Buildings. The two copies of the transcript were handed by Mr. Ainsworth to Mr. Doherty, who returned the recorder, the microphone and the batteries which had previously been given to Mr. MacSharry.

The transcript, a copy of which had been retained by Mr. Ainsworth and is now in the possession of the Minister for Justice, has today been identified by Dr. Martin O'Donoghue as being one made of a conversation between him and the then Minister for Finance, Mr. MacSharry, and that he had not authorised the taping nor been aware that the conversation was being recorded. The conversation transcribed related solely to party political issues concerning Fianna Fáil and included nothing which could be thought to relate to matters of concern to the Garda Síochána.

The transcript of the tape has been read only by the

Minister for Justice, the Attorney General and officials of their Departments as a necessary part of the enquiry. The Taoiseach has directed that the contents of the tape be neither shown to nor disclosed to himself or any other person (other than Dr. O'Donoghue in the circumstances outlined above) but that it be retained in safe custody by the Department of Justice.

3.

Introduction

Except where otherwise indicated, references in this statement to the "tapping" of telephones are intended to refer to such "tapping" pursuant to a warrant issued by the Minister for Justice.

The statement includes references to two different Deputy Commissioners of the Garda Síochána but mainly to one of them, viz, the Deputy Commissioner in charge of the Security Section who, through most of the relevant period, was Assistant Commissioner in charge of that Section. Except where otherwise indicated, all references to "the Deputy Commissioner" are intended to refer to him.

Allegations have been widely publicised in recent weeks that the telephones of two journalists, Mr. Bruce Arnold and Miss Geraldine Kennedy, have been "tapped". There is nothing new in allegations that the telephones of journalists, whether named or not, have been "tapped" and , while there have been indications in one form or another at various times by Ministers for Justice that such "tapping" did not occur on any significant scale, there has not to my knowledge been any suggestion by any Minister for Justice that either journalists or any other group in the community were or could be guaranteed immunity from the possibility of some of their members having a "tap" put on their telephones for sufficient reason.

What distinguishes the recent allegations from most others is the fact that neither of the two journalists concerned could be thought likely either to be engaged in serious criminal activity or activities affecting security or to be in touch with persons who might be so engaged, and that this has given rise to suggestions that those two telephones were tapped for improper reasons (unconnected with serious crime or subversive activity). That was the context in which I undertook to have an investigation carried out.

Result of investigation
Because of the exceptional circumstances of this case I propose to disclose the material facts relating to it and I am doing so at this stage because it would be manifestly unfair to prolong the impact on the two journalists concerned of the publicity already given to the matter, a prolongation which could be very extended indeed if the whole matter were to be left over for the proposed Judicial Enquiry. I am doing so despite the fact that it has not been the practice in the past either to confirm or deny allegations that the telephones of identifiable people were "tapped". I am satisfied that there are very cogent reasons for that general practice and I intend to maintain it as a norm to be departed from only in the most exceptional circumstances. In fact the practice has, in the past, been departed from in at least one particular context for what were deemed to be sufficiently exceptional reasons and I am satisfied that sufficiently exceptional reasons also obtain now.

My general conclusions may be summed up as follows:

First, I confirm that both telephones were in fact "tapped".

Secondly, the facts show that the system of safeguards which successive Ministers for Justice had publicly declared in Dáil Eireann to be an integral part of the system was either disregarded in the two cases in question or, what amounts to the same thing, was operated in such a way as to be rendered meaningless.

Thirdly, the facts show that there was no justification for the "tapping" of either of the two telephones and that what occurred went beyond what could be explained as just an error of judgement.

For an understanding of the facts some background information must first be given.

System of controls on "tapping"
Details about the system have been given at various times in the Dáil and persons interested in the details will, on request, be given the references to the various Official Debates. Briefly, the

system, in so far as Garda matters are concerned, is that an application for a warrant in respect of a particular telephone is made by the Commissioner (or, in the Commissioner's absence, by the Deputy Commissioner appointed to act on his behalf). Since the early Seventies, when the formalities governing the matter were tightened up, each application has been made in a format that incorporates a formal certificate that the warrant is required for the detection of serious crime or for security purposes information as to which can be got in no other way. The written application (with its certificate) is forwarded to the Department of Justice and it includes the name and address of the subscriber but not any details in support of the application. Details sufficient to show at least the general purpose and need for the application are then given orally to a nominated officer of the Department and, in turn, are given by him to the Minister. If the warrant is granted it is sent to the Department of Posts and Telegraphs. When the need to maintain the warrant ceases, the approved procedure is that an application for its withdrawal is made but, in order to guard against any oversights in this respect, an additional requirement is that a positive review must be carried out at quarterly intervals and, if the warrant is to remain in force after such review, a certificate has to be furnished by the Commissioner that it is in fact yielding results.

Details of the methods of operating the "tap" are confidential but they involve the use of a recorder and the taking of excerpts of such (if any) of the recorded material as might be thought relevant by persons experienced in recognising what would be likely to be relevant. Except where there is a special reason — an example would be a need to make a voice identification — the recording itself is then erased and only the excerpts (if there are any) would be retained by the Garda Síochána.

Tapping of telephones of Mr. Bruce Arnold and Miss Geraldine Kennedy

An application for a warrant in respect of Mr. Arnold's telephone was made on 10 May, 1982 it being stated both in relation to this and other warrants sought in this application that "the warrants are required for security purposes and it is hoped through their operation to secure useful information concerning subversive activity which could not be obtained in any other way". The warrant was granted. An application to have the warrant withdrawn was made on 12 July and as is the invariable practice on receipt of such an application, the warrant was in fact withdrawn.

An application for a warrant in respect of Miss Kennedy's telephone was made on 28 July, 1982 and was granted. The certificate in support of the application departed in certain respects from standard — a point to which I shall return later. On 27 October, arising from the usual quarterly review, a certificate was received that the "tap" on her telephone was yielding results. On 16 November, an application was received to have the warrant withdrawn and that was done.

One point of difference arose in relation to Miss Kennedy's telephone. At the time when the initial application was being prepared, an officer in the Department of Posts and Telegraphs, who in the normal way was asked by one of the Gardaí concerned in such matters for the name of the registered subscriber in respect of the particular number, apparently consulted a record that was not fully up to date. The result was that, although Miss Kennedy was in fact already at that time the registered subscriber, the name supplied as the registered subscriber was the person who had been the subscriber before her. I should make it clear that I accept that this was a *bona fide* mistake and also that it made no practical difference to the operation of the "tap" since the "tap" relates to the particular telephone as identified by its number. It is not in dispute that the "tap" was intended to relate to Miss Kennedy, who was named in the documentation within the Security Section in Garda Headquarters. The mistake did, however, have the result that Miss Kennedy's name did not appear on the application forwarded to my Department or in the subsequent certificate forwarded in October and my Department did not know that the application for the warrant in fact related to her.

The investigation

My initial enquiries were made within my own Department which I found had some, but only limited, information. I shall deal later with my Department's role. Then, having made those initial enquiries and having confirmed from the Department of Posts and Telegraphs that the telephone number to which I have already referred was in fact that of Miss Geraldine Kennedy, I had preliminary enquiries made of the Commissioner, Garda Síochána, personally. From those preliminary enquiries, it emerged that the Commissioner was wholly unaware that a telephone in respect of which he had applied for a warrant was that of Miss Kennedy. I have already explained how her name did not appear on the documentation and the Commissioner has stated that he is satisfied that he would recall it if he had been told that a journalist as well known as she is was in fact the person whose telephone was the subject of the application.

I then asked for an investigation to be carried out within the relevant section of the Garda Síochána by the senior Deputy Commissioner, who was the most senior officer who had no involvement with the matter. As a result, that officer sought formal reports or statements from all members who had any involvement — as might be expected, the number was quite small.

The most significant report was from the Deputy Commissioner in charge of the Security Section (to whom all further references to "the Deputy Commissioner" refers). According to his report — what is said here is a summary of the relevant part — he had a discussion in April, 1982, with my predecessor, Deputy Doherty, about security matters in general and Deputy Doherty spoke, apparently at some length, about what he regarded as a serious problem of "leaks" to the media from Government Departments and possibly from the Cabinet. Some time later, the then Minister had a further discussion with him on the same general theme of "leaks" to the media. Deputy Doherty is said by the Deputy Commissioner to have referred to political correspondents in general but in particular to Mr. Bruce Arnold and to have enquired if Mr. Arnold was known to have any links with the foreign press or foreign press organisations. He is said to have spoken further about the problem of "leaks" to newspapers and to have indicated that they should be investigated and stopped and that he considered that a "tap" should be put on Mr. Arnold's telephone. Subsequent to that conversation, the

Deputy Commissioner discussed the matter with the Commissioner and an application was made for a warrant, with the result I have already indicated.

The explanation offered in the Garda report in respect of the tap on Miss Kennedy's telephone is in all material respects similar, i.e. the application followed a discussion between the then Minister and the Deputy Commissioner and there appears to have been even more emphasis on "leaks" from within the Cabinet itself and on the need to have them stopped.

As will have been seen, what this amounts to is that the "taps" were put on at the behest of my predecessor on the basis that he wanted to detect and put an end to "leaks" to the media from "Government" sources including in particular "leaks" suspected of having come from members of the Cabinet. Although it would seem reasonable to assume that in those circumstances the Garda authorities would have been told what particular "leaks" the Garda Security Section was supposed to investigate and put a stop to, how many of those "leaks" had in fact been published by Mr. Arnold or Miss Kennedy and whether they were the only, or principal, journalists involved in publishing the alleged "leaks", the Deputy Commissioner has indicated that the Minister had mentioned no particular "leaks" and had given no indication that either of the two journalists mentioned had actually published any "leaks".

The role of the Department of Justice

As explained earlier, applications for warrants are channelled through the Department to the Minister. I am informed however that, unless the reasons given for an application appear "unreasonable" on their face, the Department does not seek to question the professional evaluation of Garda officers in relation to the need for "security" surveillance or in relation to the detection of serious crime. Nevertheless, despite the general practice or policy I have mentioned, the records show that the Department did in fact enter "caveats" in relation to the two warrants in question.

Department of Justice records indicate that, in relation to the application concerning Mr. Arnold's telephone, the appropriate officer in the Department made the usual enquiry from Garda Headquarters as to the reasons for the application. I understand that he probably first spoke to a more junior officer who was unable to assist him but it is not in dispute that he eventually discussed the matter with the Deputy Commissioner.

The Departmental record indicates that the reason given was that Mr. Arnold was anti-national in his outlook and that he might be obtaining information from sources of a similar disposition. (On being informed of this record, the Deputy Commissioner states that, while he cannot recall the incident, he would wish it to be known, in fairness to Mr. Arnold and to himself, that any comment on those lines would have been intended as a reference to a view that some might hold about some of Mr. Arnold's published opinions and intended also as confirmation that there was no suggestion of any kind that Mr. Arnold had any association or contacts with para-military organisations).

The officer wrote a note to the Minister setting out the reason for the application as conveyed to him by the Deputy Commissioner and expressing the view that the warrant should not be granted.

In relation to Miss Kennedy, the application, for reasons already stated, did not have her name on it. The relevant officer of my Department made the usual enquiry as to the reasons for the application and, as on the previous occasion, spoke to the Deputy Commissioner. The officer of my Department states that the Deputy Commissioner did not indicate that the warrant related to Miss Kennedy and I should make it clear that the Gardaí have not suggested otherwise. The Deputy Commissioner stated to the officer in my Department that the Minister was aware of the detailed reasons for the application. The Departmental record shows that the officer indicated in a note to the Minister that, as he had no details, he was not in a position to make any recommendation regarding the signing of the warrant but that he understood the Minister had the details. In the context, this reference to his not making a recommendation related to the sufficiency or insufficiency of the reasons for the application but a separate (negative) recommendation was made about the format of the supporting certificate, as explained below.

Change in format of the certificate in the application affecting Miss Kennedy's telephone

As briefly indicated already, the certificate in this case departed in certain respects from the established format. In particular, the standard reference to "security" purposes had been changed to a reference to "national security". My Department was not satisfied that departures from the approved format should be accepted and, in the note already mentioned, recommended to the Minister that the particular certificate should not be accepted. It was, however, accepted.

The Commissioner states that he was unaware of the fact that the document presented for his signature involved any change. The Deputy Commissioner states that he had not appreciated that there was an "approved" (as distinct from a "usual") format for an application and that he used the words "national security" on this occasion because he had reflected on the position in relation to Mr. Arnold and Miss Kennedy and because, to his mind, the word "security" alone tended to be interpreted — in this context — as having subversive connotations and he thought that "national security" would be more appropriate to the matter of Cabinet "leaks".

Material obtained from the "tap"

I am informed that no instructions or guidance was issued to those examining the recordings from the two telephones as to what they should look out for, and that this is normal. On this occasion, however, the result was that the people assigned to the task of listening to the tapes took it for granted from the identity of the two journalists concerned that what they in the Garda Síochána were expected to look out for was material of party-political interest. Apart from the fact that some of them have said so explicitly, the proof is in the fact that the excerpts that were transcribed by them were for all practical purposes exclusively concerned with party-political matters. One or two of the excerpts did contain some references to matters of marginal Garda interest, such as actual or possible transfers, but even they were only in the context of suggested links with party-political issues.

All the excerpts were submitted as a matter of course to the Deputy Commissioner and additional copies of some of the material were given to him at his request on more than one occasion. In addition a complete new set of photostats of the material was sought by and given to him on 5 October. The Deputy Commissioner states that he cannot remember why on that particular date he should seek a copy of the full set of excerpts but that his recollection is that he wished to assemble evidence to assist him in convincing my predecessor that the warrants were producing no evidence related to "leaks".

The Deputy Commissioner states that, towards the end of October, at a further meeting with my predecesor, the latter again referred to media "leaks" and raised the question of a restoration of a "tap" on Mr. Arnold's telephone and also referred to Miss Kennedy. He — the Deputy Commissioner — states that he indicated to the Minister that such "taps" were of no value in this context and, in support of that view, offered him the entire set of transcripts to date relating to the two journalists, which the Minister took and returned at some later date. (The "tap" was still on Miss Kennedy's telephone at that stage).

Before leaving this aspect of the matter, I think it necessary to mention one further incident. At the beginning of July, the Deputy Commissioner, who had been given a transcript of a conversation on political matters between Mr. Arnold and a well-known Deputy — not then a Minister — in the Party then in Government, asked for and was given the tape (as distinct from the transcript) containing the conversation. He states that he did so to confirm his belief that the "tap" on Mr. Arnold's telephone was producing nothing worthwhile and that he erased the tape. (From the context, this would have been within a week or so).

Further Action

On the most benign possible interpretation of the facts, what has now occurred is such that is is impossible to expect the public to continue to have any confidence in a system which must depend for its acceptable operation on a respect for commitments solemnly given to Dáil Éireann by successive Ministers for Justice.

In speaking on this matter in the Dáil both of the last two Fianna Fáil Ministers for Justice before my immediate predecessor, namely Deputy Gerry Collins and Deputy Desmond O'Malley, when dealing with the safeguards that existed in relation to possible abuses, put some emphasis on the fact that it was the Commissioner — and not the Minister — who initiated the applications. In this case, the procedure was effectively reversed. Action was taken at the behest of the Minister and it is clear from the re-action now of the two senior officers (the Commissioner and Deputy Commissioner) that they felt that in circumstances of this kind they had no real option but to comply with the Minister's wishes.

In the short-term — and by that I mean the shortest time within which, consistent with other pressures on my Department, I can introduce formal changes — I give a public pledge, firstly, that I will not operate the system except fully in accord with the commitments given to Dáil Éireann and, secondly, that I have now ordered a special positive review of all warrants in existence by reference to the principle that, in applying the well-recognised criteria, the inherent seriousness of eavesdropping on what is supposed to be a private conversation is to be fully taken into account.

This, however, can only be a stop-gap arrangement. New and substantial safeguards — safeguards that are proof against the kind of occurrence described above — must be introduced.

Michael Noonan
Minister for Justice
20th January, 1983

McLaughlin, Hugh 198-9, 324
McLaughlin, Patrick 74, 116, 126,
  133-6, 140, 142, 188-9, 193-5,
  201, 222, 237, 250, 270, 272,
  301, 307ff.
McMahon, John Paul 134, 193,
  270
McNally, Laurence 203-4
MacSharry, Ray 35-44 *passim,* 64,
  70-1, 76-7, 93, 103, 171, 176ff.,
  184, 254, 276ff., 291-6 *passim,*
  314, 317ff., 333, 336, 343ff., 354
Maguire, Joe 241-2
Mansergh, Martin 36, 50, 155,
  201, 267
Mara, P.J. 38, 262, 328-9, 335
Marrinan, Jack 132, 135, 188
Matthews, Kevin 116-18, 121, 123
Mitchell, Jim 80, 110, 115, 130,
  170, 188, 196-7, 249, 274, 295,
  299
Molloy, Bobby 28, 32, 40, 42, 253,
  264, 352
Morgan, Michael 106-9, 112-14,
  119-26 *passim*
Mulcahy, Noel 31, 36, 49-50
Mullen, Michael 61, 62, 65
Mulroy, Pat 109-15 *passim,* 118-22
  passim,
Murphy, Ciaran 28, 34
Murray, John 270, 300
Murtagh, Peter 271, 306
Nally, Derek 131-5 *passim*
Nangle, Tom 240, 241-2, 247-50
Nealon, Ted 76-7, 81
Noonan, Michael 304ff., 326
Norfolk, Duke of 208, 297-300
O hAnnrachain, Padraig 78-9, 98,
  201, 232
O'Brien, Conor Cruise 84, 102,
  234, 251
O'Connell, John 27, 46, 47, 63-4,
  66-8, 76, 180-1, 293
O'Connor, Cormac 107-9, 110-17
  passim
O'Connor, Kevin 268-71, 301
O'Connor, Niamh 104, 106-7,
  110-23 *passim*
O'Connor, Patrick 25, 103ff., 272,
  274, 313
O'Donnell, Brendan 98, 140

O'Donoghue, Martin 17-19, 23-4,
  32ff., 69, 83, 172, 177, 254-6,
  258ff., 276, 279ff., 291, 301,
  313, 317, 320ff., 333, 335-6,
  343ff.
O'Kennedy, Michael 70, 73, 76-7,
  81, 93, 150, 214, 264-5, 319,
  331, 334, 342, 352
O'Leary, Michael 23-4, 38, 58, 64,
  75, 176, 276, 290
O'Leary, Olivia 270, 276
O'Malley, Desmond 18, 23, 32ff.,
  68, 72-7 *passim,* 82, 97, 177,
  252-4, 258ff., 276, 291, 296,
  327, 331, 338-42 *passim,* 348,
  352
O'Meara, Des 136-7, 139
O Moráin, Michael 142
O'Reilly, Tony 271
Paisley, Ian 151
Power, Paddy 69, 73, 162-3
Prendergast, Peter 94, 197, 288
Prior, James 75, 153-4, 206, 297-9
Rafferty, Mick 47-8, 49
Reynolds, Albert 16, 22-3, 35-44
  passim, 71-2, 77, 177, 243, 252,
  276-9 *passim,* 282, 336, 352
Ryan, Eoin 258, 335
Ryan, Ken 231, 233, 321-2, 336,
  339
Ryan, Richie 131, 137
Sands, Bobby 152
Sherlock, Joe 51, 64, 66-7, 180,
  181, 291
Skelly, Liam 170, 174
Smith, Hugh 107, 109
Smyth, Owen McCartan 205
Sorahan, Seamus 96, 205
Spring, Dick 249, 274, 290,
  291
Stapleton, John 114, 118-19
Sutherland, Peter 116, 205, 270,
  312, 315
Thatcher, Margaret 75, 144,
  146ff., 208, 209
Tuite, Gerard 206-7
Tully, Tom 129, 187-8, 268, 271ff.,
  303, 313
Tunney, Jim 42, 62, 319, 329,
  336-47 *passim,* 352
Wall, Frank 16, 136, 137

Index compiled by Helen Litton